D1376509

Nietzsche's Anthropic Circle

Rochester Studies in Philosophy
Senior Editor: Wade L. Robison
Rochester Institute of Technology
ISSN: 1529-188X

The Scottish Enlightenment: Essays in Reinterpretation
Edited by Paul Wood

Kant's Legacy: Essays in Honor of Lewis White Beck
Edited by Predrag Cicovacki

Plato's Erotic Thought: The Tree of the Unknown
Alfred Geier

Leibniz on Purely Extrinsic Denominations
Dennis Plaisted

Rationality and Happiness: From the Ancients to the Early Medievals
Edited by Jiyuan Yu and Jorge J. E. Gracia

History of Reasonableness: A Testimony and Authority in the Art of Thinking
Rick Kennedy

State of Nature or Eden? Thomas Hobbes and His Contemporaries on the Natural Condition of Human Beings
Helen Thornton

Fire in the Dark: Essays on Pascal's Pensées and Provinciales
Charles Natoli

Destined for Evil? The Twentieth-Century Responses
Edited by Predrag Cicovacki

David Hume and Eighteenth-Century America
Mark G. Spencer

Nietzsche's Anthropic Circle: Man, Science, and Myth
George J. Stack

Nietzsche's Anthropic Circle

Man, Science, and Myth

George J. Stack

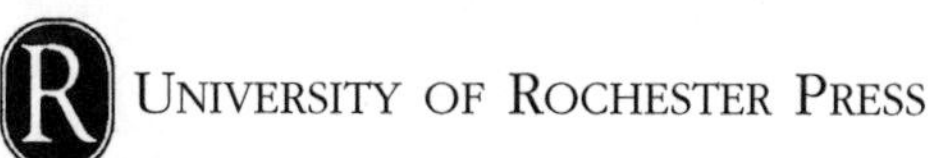

First published 2005

University of Rochester Press
668 Mt. Hope Avenue, Rochester, NY 14620, USA
www.urpress.com
and of Boydell & Brewer Limited
PO Box 9, Woodbridge, Suffolk IP12 3DF, UK
www.boydellandbrewer.com

ISBN: 1-58046-191-3

Library of Congress Cataloging-in-Publication Data

Stack, George J.
Nietzsche's anthropic circle : man, science, and myth / George J. Stack.
p. cm. – (Rochester studies in philosophy, ISSN 1529-188X)
Includes bibliographical references and index.
ISBN 1-58046-191-3 (hardcover : alk. paper)
1. Nietzsche, Friedrich Wilhelm, 1844-1900. 2. Knowledge, Theory of. 3. Science–Philosophy. 4. Anthropomorphism. I. Title. II. Series.
B3318.K7S73 2005
193–dc22
2005007616

A catalogue record for this title is available from the British Library.

This publication is printed on acid-free paper.
Printed in the United States of America.

For Christian

—a child who lives in "the innocence of becoming" with energy and joy

Contents

PREFACE

The richness and diversity of what Nietzsche called his "philosophies" make his writings a complex, intriguing philosophical puzzle. He not only defends a perspectival approach to knowledge, but his own multifaceted thought is, in fact, an illustration of this approach to knowledge. It is perhaps for this reason that his evocative works have been subject to so many differing interpretations. The once-popular and distorted understandings of "what Nietzsche said" has long since been surpassed by the restoration of Nietzsche as philosopher. A "new" Nietzsche is discovered. But this assumes that the "old" Nietzsche is thoroughly known and understood. In point of fact, what is often discerned as a new Nietzschean philosophy is but an aspect of, a dimension of, the thought of a many-sided philosopher who eschewed a systematic presentation of his reflections.

In this approach to the thought of Nietzsche, my intention is not to offer a liberal interpretation of his "text" in order to fit him into a predetermined pattern but to attempt to understand his philosophical project, as far as possible, from within. My primary stress is his lifelong preoccupation with the problem of anthropomorphism, his persistent wrestling with the question of knowledge and his reformation of its meaning, his response to a rising scientific culture, and the dynamic theory of the natural world he found intriguing and suggestive of a world-model. I place particular emphasis upon perspectivalism and Nietzsche's modified appropriation of, and critique of, Kant's analysis of knowledge. Finally, I will explore the rationale for his putative reversion to "metaphysics" in the theory of the will to power. All of these themes are interwoven in most of Nietzsche's kaleidoscopic writings. They fuel his skepticism about certainty and objective knowledge even as they stimulate his attempts to create meaning in a world in which the religious interpretation of existence is waning and a powerful culture of science is emerging. They reflect the consequences of the enormous scientific advances since Copernicus that have decentered, demythologized, and diminished the value of the human world.

I emphasize Nietzsche's critique of knowledge because his epistemological attacks on traditional conceptions of knowledge, the idea of transcendental truth, absolute truth, or "truth-in-itself" are essential ingredients of his ambitious philosophical task. He was not satisfied with simply saying that we have no access—in philosophy, in art, or in science—to a unifying holistic truth. He endeavors to *show* that there is no pathway to such "truth." Here is where his critical analysis of anthropomorphism plays a crucial role. In *The Gay Science* (sect. 374) Nietzsche once put our condition succinctly: we cannot "see around our own corner." Hence, we are ineluctably enclosed within the circle of "humanization," anthropomorphism. The access road to a trans-human "truth" is closed. As much as he criticizes epistemology, he consistently practices it and offers ingenious analyses of value-charged sacrosanct terms: certainty, objectivity, knowledge, truth.

The ironic disclosure of the anthropomorphism of our metaphorical language and of the projective human element in all knowledge eventually leads, after consideration of many knowledge-perspectives, to the conception of the creative, constructive, and transformative nature of our knowledge. Knowing, for Nietzsche, is a transformational process and an evolutionary one. Truths are contextual and the context in which they are viable is a perspectival one: that of an individual (the "truths" of individual life-experience), a culture, a historical period, a discipline, a species, or, more mystically, life itself. Nietzsche saw that truths are profoundly influenced by culture and historicity, by dominant values, by imbedded prejudgments. He was sharply aware that the disclosure of new (usually minute) truths and the multiplication of (contextual) truths undermines rather than enhances our belief in pristine objective knowledge. It is precisely because, as he says, "there are many eyes," that there are "many truths" and, consequently, there is no universal, all-encompassing, final "Truth." The replacement of theories in the sciences, as a number of early philosophers of science and scientists showed him, the caution of precise scientific methodological analyses, conveyed to Nietzsche a greater sensitivity to skepticism than did the relativity of conflicting cultural "tables of values." He is not, as some believe, anti-scientific (even though he does insist that the deepest meaning in life is an affective-aesthetic one). Rather, his thinking (especially in regard to perspectivalism and skepticism about knowledge) is informed by his response to science. For this reason, I've concentrated on his treatment of scientific theories and concepts and indicated his affinity with instrumental fictionalism in the philosophy of science. Despite his poetic and artistic temperament and style of thinking, Nietzsche was deeply affected by the scientific interpretation of nature and scientific approaches to knowledge—so much so that his probabilistic orientation towards knowledge and his experimental approach to philosophy are modeled on his understanding of the scientific mode of thinking.

Nietzsche's skeptical analysis of, and reformation of, knowledge is not an anomalous part of his overall philosophical aims. What he indirectly communicates to us is that the amplification of the "knowledge drive" is, paradoxically, a generator of metastasizing skepticism. What may justly be called his evolutionary epistemology is a case in point. The emergence of the Darwinian theory of evolution by natural selection strongly influenced his approach to the problem of knowledge. If our way of perceiving and thinking about the world has evolved over long periods of time, then it is reasonable to assume that there was a selective elimination of those who perceived and thought differently. Nietzsche exploits the implications of a biological theory of evolution in order to emphasize what is later incorporated into a pragmatic theory of knowledge. In this way he defends a version of a functionalist conception of knowledge, while opening the door to the promulgation of values that he believes will enhance life, that will be life-affirming.

In his studies of early philosophies of science and philosophical scientists Nietzsche absorbed the phenomenon of the theoretical displacements of orientations in the history of science. Although he does not formulate anything precisely like Kuhn's theory of paradigm shifts, he certainly was moving in that direction. In numerous ways, Nietzsche offers his imaginative philosophical response to various domains of scientific theory and knowledge. His chaos interpretation of nature, for example, is not merely a subjective intuitive insight: it is largely derived from his understanding of what he discerned in scientific discourse as the "indescribable complexity" of the world. Many of the perspectives on man and nature that he exploits in his critical approach to knowledge were extracted from scientific theories. Even his perspectival interpretation of actuality borrows heavily from his understanding of the implications of dynamic physical theories of the natural world, as well as biological theories of organic beings, a world that eventually included all entities whatsoever, including the microphysical domain.

Nietzsche's stress upon the perspectival nature of knowledge also serves the function of disclosing a realm of uncertainty and producing an antidogmatic approach to truth that is intended for the "new philosophers" and the "experimenters" in thought that he envisions. He urges the abandonment of what John Dewey called the "quest for certainty." Nietzsche fully realizes how difficult and unsettling his cognitive demands are. And, from what he has said in a number of places, he believes that it will require restrained and disciplined individuals who are able to look upon the human passion for convictions with a jaundiced eye, who are able to accept the reduced situation of man in relation to absolutes without despairing.

In *On the Genealogy of Morals* he acknowledges that a nondogmatic, exploratory orientation towards knowledge does not mean that man's transcendental desires, the "need for transcendence," have been eliminated. Although it is not a theme in my discussion of Nietzsche's critical epistemology, it could be said that his reformulation of what knowledge means is intrinsic to his "transvaluation of values." This aspect of his project encourages an experimental, tentative, probabilistic orientation towards claims to knowledge and truth. And it calls for an openness to experience and different modes of conceptualization that many find unsettling. On the other hand, a number of contemporary conceptions of the nature of philosophy are closer to Nietzsche's standpoint than those who have not passed through the labyrinth of his "philosophies," his perspectives, may realize.

My concluding discussion of the mythical and exoteric nature of the will to power is an extension of some of my earlier explorations of this question—one which seeks to show that Nietzsche does not end with a return to the grand metaphysics he spent so much energy attacking. I argue that the idea of a universal will to power is an artfully constructed fable that completes an anthropomorphic picture of "reality" that is essentially metaphorical. Having criticized the reliance on anthropomorphic projections in ordinary language and in philosophical and scientific discourse, in the final analysis he deliberately employs "human analogy" in order to present his perspectival vision of actuality. Furthermore, it is a vision that itself depends upon a perspectival interpretation of human nature! In this respect, as well as in his use of conceptions (such as a "causality of the will") that he strenuously repudiates, his metaphorical vision of reality is far removed from any metaphysical claim to positive *knowledge* of the secret nature of "reality-in-itself." But the vision is not metaphorical because, as Sarah Kofman argued some time ago, metaphorical language is for the "noble" or the select. Metaphors pervade *all* levels of discourse; the "metaphoric drive" is universal. As Nietzsche pointedly put it in an early formula: "there is no "genuine" expression and *no real knowing apart from metaphor.*" But this linguistic skepticism was only the beginning of his philosophical search for meaning, a critique of language arising out of philological, not yet philosophical, impulses. There was much more to be confronted, incorporated, and (hopefully) overcome in his voyage of discovery.

Kant's agnosticism about what lies behind, beneath, or beyond the phenomena we do know (primarily because we have constituted what is there out of raw materials) had to be confronted. In addition there were the scientists and proto-philosophers of science who announced that even the sciences cannot know "the true essence of things," that we perhaps know "effects," "appearances," or phenomena, but not a seemingly elusive actuality. The German philosophical physiologist Emil du Bois-Reymond argued in a then-well-known speech and later essay ("On the Limits of Natural Scientific Knowledge," 1872), that we cannot go beyond the limits of mechanist principles and, therefore, do not have and will not have reliable knowledge about the underlying features of the world. Not only do we not now know, but "we shall never know" the nature of force and matter or, on the other hand, the origin and nature of consciousness. This agnosticism about the natural world combined with the enormous complexity of the world according to physics dovetailed with questions about the nature and function of language (which is one dimension of Nietzsche's philosophy) and kindled a consuming and sometimes a self-consuming skepticism.

In a sense, Nietzsche was stimulated by the pursuit of the overcoming of skepticism. He knew far more about the sciences than has been acknowledged by most of his biographers and most philosophers. And he sought the knowledge derived from the exact sciences because he respected the care, the methods, the precision, and the "little unpretentious truths" that scientists valued. Compared to the grandiose claims of metaphysicians and what he called their "conceptual poetry," the exact sciences were like a bracing cold shower. To be sure, positivism repulsed him not only in its French form, but even more so in the dogmatic scientific realist form espoused by some of his German contemporaries. Nietzsche is often attacking German *Positivismus* in many of his critical forays against dogmatic materialism and crude metaphysical realism. The scientifically oriented thinkers in this movement were not easy targets (except when they strayed from the domain of science) because they were quite knowledgeable in the areas of biology, physiology, and physics. This is one reason why Nietzsche spent so much energy, mostly in his voluminous notes, trying to grapple with the rising, powerful, almost overwhelming scientific culture of his time, as well as trying to find a way to encompass it in a visionary philosophical counter-ideal which would be presented as a perspectival interpretation, as a synthesis of art and science metaphorically expressed.

Although my exploration of central themes in Nietzsche's philosophy, including an often neglected topic—his structuralist perspective—focuses on his published works as much possible, I've also delved into the vast resource of his unpublished notations (*Nachlass*). In doing so, I'm quite aware of Bernd Magnus's discouragement of the practice of using notes for a work Nietzsche never wrote, "The Will to Power." To put my position on what might be called the Magnus sanction simply, it seems strange not to use remarkable and often enlightening notations that display Nietzsche's experiments in thought in action, as well as his occasional explosiveness and rhetorical excesses. If only for his extensive, fascinating, and trenchant analysis of nihilism, it is extremely fortunate that his voluminous notes were preserved. What is interesting about Nietzsche's *Nachlass* is his intense, passionate, and serious engagement with philosophical questions. If, once in awhile, an enigma is recorded (say, Derrida's favorite, "I have forgotten my umbrella") it is neither surprising, given the more than one thousand pages of notes he wrote, nor consequential. To then use that sentence or any other to suggest that *all* of Nietzsche's assertions are equally ambiguous or enigmatic is either a simple fallacy of composition or a tropic excess. Although I see no problem with a judicious reliance on the notations or, for that matter, on letters to and from Nietzsche, I strongly disagree with Heidegger's assertion that the authentic philosophy of Nietzsche is contained in his notes. Nor do I think that it is plausible that the notebooks contain not just notes, but his philosophy as such, his philosophical conclusions. On the contrary, they *reveal* his remythologizing and exoteric intentions, especially in the later 1880s, as I attempt to show.

What is undeniable and important, I believe, is that Nietzsche's allusions to physiology, chemistry, biology, and physics are not merely rhetorical devices, but are related to substantive questions raised by his engagement with the natural sciences of his day. His interpretation of mankind in terms of nature (as represented in the natural sciences) and his interpretation of the natural world in terms of man is only one instance of the fruitfulness of transgressing disciplinary boundaries.

My argument that the universal will to power is a myth is an extension of and an elaboration on the late Sarah Kofman's suggestion of the mythical nature of the will-to-power "metaphor." It goes beyond her fertile suggestion by relating the will-to-power idea to scientific theories and models of the constituents of the natural world and endeavoring to show how the myth was constructed and why. One of my purposes in this exploration of the labyrinth of Nietzsche's philosophies is to show, as I've tried to do previously, how important is his involvement with the natural sciences—their language, symbolic forms, and methodological principles—for an understanding of his development and his provocative analyses of human beings, as well as of his aesthetic-scientific depiction of "the world seen from within."

What follows, then, are exploratory examinations of only some aspects of Nietzsche's philosophy. For the most part, my interpretations are sympathetic and as "faithful" to his texts as anyone enlightened by Nietzsche's conception of interpretation can dare proclaim. As much as possible, I've tried to avoid putting his thought through a logical shredder that would cut his language, as well as that of any innovative or experimental thinker, into bits and pieces. There are many technically proficient *externalist* studies of Nietzsche that display his doctrines and call attention to his contradictions, but do not dig deeply enough into the internal dialectic of his thinking. At the other end of the scale, one can interrogate Nietzsche while steering clear of the ludic arbitrariness of those hermetic, highly imaginative studies that exploit limited aspects of Nietzsche's writings and create subjective constructions remote from the core of his thinking and thus effectively dephilosophize him.

It is a canard to believe that we shall never know what Nietzsche meant. As if fulfilling his conception of the value of a "plurality of interpretations" (as questionable as some may be), the various perspectives on a very complex multiform philosophical *corpus* have actually yielded a closer approximation to what he was trying to do. What he thought, what he seems to have meant, is not only intelligible and meaningful, but is particularly relevant to many current philosophical debates and concerns. The recrudescence of many (though certainly not all) of Nietzsche's themes in recent thought is not an oddity because these themes, both in their positive and negative aspects, are, beneath the "noise" of popular culture and the whir of multifarious media, a subliminal presence.

Editions and Abbreviations

SB	*Sämtliche Briefe*. (Complete Letters). Edited by G. Colli and M. Montinari. 8 vols. Berlin and New York: Walter de Gruyter, 1986. Cited by volume and page(s).
SW	*Sämtliche Werke* (Complete Works). Edited by G. Colli and M. Montinari. 15 vols. Berlin and New York: Walter de Gruyter, 1980. Cited by volume, section and pages for volumes 1 through 6. References to the *Nachlass* (notes) are cited by volume and page(s) for volumes 7 through 13.
WDB	*Werke in Drei Bänden*. Edited by Karl Schlechta. 3 vols. Munich: Carl Hanser Verlag, 1966. Cited by volume and page(s).
Werke (GOA)	*Werke. Grssoktavausgabe*. 2nd ed. 19 vols. Leipzig: Naumann Verlag, 1901–13. Cited by volume and page(s).

Translations are my own except as indicated. All italics are in the originals.

Chapter One

Anthropomorphic Projection

> It is impossible to see any limit to the distance anthropomorphism can extend. . . . This transference of our feelings is . . . found everywhere, and in such manifold forms it is not always easy to identify it.
>
> Georg Lichtenberg, *Aphorisms*

One of the central themes that runs through Nietzsche's polymorphic writings is the influence of anthropomorphism upon our conceptions of truth and reality. The "humanization" of the world for the sake of life and its enhancement and the "humanization" of nature for the sake of mastery of it are core ideas in his thought. In some of his earliest writings Nietzsche examined under a skeptical microscope the language and concepts that we take for granted. He detected traces of an ineluctable tendency to describe and understand the nonhuman in terms of human sentiments, attitudes, and feelings. He raises serious doubts about our capacity to comprehend anything that is not filtered through notions derived from our social relations, our psychology, or the metaphorical language we use to describe ourselves and our experience. His attitude towards this tendency of anthropomorphic transformation is not, however, unambiguous. Though Nietzsche often presents anthropomorphism as a naïve mode of thinking, it also evolves in his thought to the point at which it is self-consciously employed in his numerous metaphorical images of actuality, nature, and the multiple dimensions of the self and human experience.

In his later philosophical appropriation of a dynamic world-interpretation in physical theory Nietzsche occasionally seeks to transcend the "anthropomorphic idiosyncrasy"—that is, the tendency to conceive of the cosmos in terms of a purely anthropic perspective. Especially in notes from the late 1880s he seems to delete man from his conceptual landscape and to conceive of actuality as a dynamic system of interacting "force-centers" or "power-quanta." This de-anthropomorphic perspective characterizes reality as the particular action and reaction of each "center of force" in relation to others and man is reduced to "a multiplicity of forces." But Nietzsche does not settle in this depersonalized, dehumanized vision. He seeks to create a human meaning for this radical physical-theoretical reductionism. A reconstituted anthropomorphism is then introduced in order to picture reality as a dynamically striving, waxing and waning, struggling field of forces analogous to human experience.

A skepticism concerning man's ability to discover "the true essence of things" is revealed in an unpublished essay of 1873, "On Truth and Lying in an Extra-Moral Sense." There we are depicted as "clever animals" whose existence is not the center of reality, but a fleeting moment in cosmic history. The age-old, but "arrogant," claim that man possesses vast sums of knowledge is reduced to the view that knowledge is constructed by the "human intellect" for the purpose of preserving and conserving "the life of man." The intellect is compared to the defensive and aggressive weapons of animals and is said to function as an "art of dissimulation." The "enigmatic urge for truth" is said to have begun when human beings banded together in social groupings. Even though mankind, for the sake of survival, desires "the agreeable life-preserving truth," the expression of "truth" depends upon "conventions of language" that shape the form of such "truth."

Truthfulness in ordinary discourse is a socially determined convention that requires that we use "customary metaphors." After arguing that language does not describe the truth of things, Nietzsche offers his own version of "truth": "A moving army of metaphors, metonymies and anthropomorphism." It is a "sum of human relations . . . enhanced, transposed, and embellished poetically and rhetorically." Over time such linguistic habits solidify, become "canonical, obligatory for a people." We are unable to express the "essence of things" largely because of the anthropomorphic coloration of our assertions.[1] Our language is infiltrated by tropes that we are typically unaware of using. If language universalizes what it seeks to refer to, employs arbitrary abstractions, metaphors and anthropomorphisms, then it cannot be said to represent what we experience. If language perpetuates a conceptual schema that abstracts, simplifies and incorporates idealized "identities," then it cannot be said to correspond to the phenomena encountered in lived experience.

Nietzsche offers three reasons why language is inadequate to represent actuality: (1) it expresses abstract and simplifying assumptions of identity and deletes the diversity and complexity of immediate experience; (2) it employs metaphor and anthropomorphisms that yield a humanized picture of actuality that transforms what is experienced; (3) it is used to describe "appearances" or constructs that are constituted by our psychophysical "organization" and, hence, cannot describe things-in-themselves.

In his unpublished essay Nietzsche was concerned to expose the anthropomorphic nature of both ordinary language and the language of metaphysics. For what he says about ordinary uses of natural languages is also often said about the linguistic expression of metaphysical "truths." In the course of discussing the concept of Being in ancient Greek philosophy, he remarks that "man imagines the existence of other things by analogy with his own existence, in other words, anthropomorphically and, in any case, with unlogical projection."[2]

In *The Birth of Tragedy* this critique of language is suppressed, as Nietzsche seems uncritically to embrace poetic-metaphysical language and tries to penetrate the ineffable reality of the "primal will" (*Urwille*). He conceives of the existence of the world and our phenomenal being as "a continuously manifested representation of [*die Ur-Eine*] the primal unity."[3] In this regard, he appears to have sought to discern the true essence of things, characterizing it in terms of Schopenhauer's metaphysical conception of a primordial "Will" as the ground of all things.

However, once the romantic "artists' metaphysics" of *The Birth of Tragedy* was presented and surpassed, Nietzsche's skepticism goes into high gear. Shortly after the publication of this aesthetically conceived work, he attacks, as shown, conventional assumptions about truth in "On Truth and Lying in an Extra-Moral Sense" (1873) and adopts an agnosticism about the metaphysical claims to truth he examines in *Philosophy in the Tragic Age of the Greeks* (1873).

Throughout his philosophical life Nietzsche grapples with the tension between restricting knowledge to the phenomenal world conditioned by our psychophysical organization and the desire to push his reflections beyond "appearances" to an ostensible "metaphysical" completion. Both of these poles of his thinking, however, are, directly or indirectly, affected by the very anthropomorphism that he uncovered in ordinary and philosophical language. When he attacks "knowledge" or "truth" he is concerned not only with denying transcendent knowledge, but also with questioning empirical knowledge as traditionally conceived. Such a standpoint derived, in part, from Kant's critical analyses as well as Nietzsche's own germinating critique of the scientific interpretation of "the world."[4]

During his so-called "positivistic" period, Nietzsche turned his attention away from metaphysics and held that such questions should be put "on ice." Especially in *Human, All-Too-Human*, he praised the precision of the methods of the sciences and valued the search for "little, unapparent truths." The "scientific spirit" is also lauded for its tenacity in pursuing "truths" that are often inexpedient or unpleasant. In a field close to his heart (philology), he respected the precise, accurate, and relatively unprejudiced interpretations of texts. He was especially impressed by the discipline of science that refrains from grandiose metaphysical leaps of thought and is able to function with provisional assumptions, working hypotheses, and regulative principles.

Despite his admiration for science and its "strict methods," Nietzsche was repulsed by the dogmatic "positivists" of the nineteenth century and their optimistic belief that they had attained objective truth and a clear explanation of the world.[5] Having dissociated himself from his own "temporary attack" of "romanticism," he was not anxious to embrace a scientific metaphysics. Rather, he focused on the value of scientific methodologies, the piecemeal approach to knowledge, and the healthy respect for the senses in scientific inquiry. As his recurring skepticism examines the concepts and principles of the sciences, however, he begins to see signs of the same anthropomorphism he had previously found in the attempt to describe ultimate reality in metaphysical terms. He sees that even the strict empirical sciences do not yield a purely objective, unprejudiced picture of reality.

The scientific understanding of the natural world is an "interpretation" or, more accurately, a variety of interpretations. It is a process analogous to the hermeneutic method of the philologist: the scientist interprets the "text" of nature in a manner resembling the philological interpretation of a written text. Such an interpretation is guided by basic assumptions, by perspectives, by categorical schemata that, like Kant's categories of the understanding, are construed by Nietzsche as useful, "conventional fictions." The basic conceptual posits in the sciences are characterized as "regulative fictions" that are pragmatically and heuristically useful, but are not "true." There are no uninterpreted facts discovered in the sciences. To a considerable extent the sensory-cognitive "organization" of the observer conditions the data examined.

Nietzsche maintains that the "assumptions of mechanics" are based upon ideal conceptual inventions such as the idea of "force residing in mathematical points and mathematical lines."[6] Causality does not represent actual processes occurring in the world. Rather, it is "an hypothesis by means of which we humanize the world."[7] Similarly, he cites Kant's view that the understanding does not derive its laws from nature, but prescribes them to nature—adding that this means that "nature" is equivalent to the "world as representation" or as "error."[8]

Despite his typically harsh criticisms of Kant, Nietzsche adopts a conventionalist interpretation of scientific conceptions and principles derived from his understanding of the implications of Kant's critical analysis of knowledge and his own epistemic commitment to the notion that our "conditions of existence" and our psychological make-up shape the objects of our "knowledge."[9] Nietzsche extends this assumption into the domain of science by arguing that the scientist employs constructs in order to "describe" (not explain) appearances. The strand of phenomenalism that runs through his thought encompasses scientific claims to knowledge and is understood as entailing anthropomorphism. Every claim to discover the nature of things is affected by "human optics."[10] Despite the fact that the sciences appear to transcend this standpoint, scientific "world interpretation" is also affected by "the anthropomorphic element in all knowledge."[11]

Knowing is construed as a schematization, a way of "arranging" the phenomena encountered in experience in such a way as to depict a world "for us." The scientific representation of the world is a cognitive system of symbolization, a "semiotics" that is ultimately derived from our selective sensory experience, our concepts, and our psychic nature. It is for purposes of "calculation" that we use notions such as "force," "number," "unit," "atom," and "object." What is true of ordinary language is true of scientific discourse. "The inventive power that creates categories is working in the service of our needs, namely of security and rapid intelligibility on the basis of conventions and signs."[12] That theories are considered as "interpretations" is a sign of intellectual strength. But precisely because of the hypothetical, provisional, not to say "fictional," nature of the concepts and principles employed in science, they cannot be said to provide a purely objective "picture" of reality or to reflect nature in their sophisticated mirrors.

Nietzsche's form of instrumentalism entails the belief that virtually all of the terms used in scientific claims to knowledge are, in the broadest sense, anthropomorphic. Neither Kant's categories of the understanding nor the categories employed in scientific thought reflect the ways things are. They serve to coordinate the manifold of our sensory experiences or observations. Both general conceptions and scientific categories of thought perform the same function: the transmutation of our experience.[13]

We accept the formulation of categories of the understanding because of its practical, functional value for the preservation of the species. Science, too, ultimately has a practical purpose: "to humanize the world,"[14] to construct an intelligible, familiar world of phenomena that we can master. Nietzsche conceives of the pursuit of scientific knowledge as the pursuit of power over nature, as an instrument for the technological transformation of the world. The aim of *all* knowledge is to serve life and the enhancement of life.

The world that is shaped, simplified, arranged, and organized by our sensory-cognitive "organization," by our categories, is necessarily a "humanized world." In this sense, Heidegger is correct in saying that Nietzsche's philosophy ends in "anthropomorphy—the shaping and viewing of the world in accordance with man's image."[15] But the further claim that this anthropomorphy is a "metaphysics" and not a critical *exposé* of the powerful role of anthropomorphism in human thought is contestable. What Nietzsche presents is a probing analysis of philosophical and scientific knowledge-claims, of ordinary and technical language, and of the influence of our "drives" and "affects" on our thinking that led him to admit our inability to entirely transcend "anthropomorphy."[16]

This assumption of the inevitability of anthropomorphic interpretation is central to the presentation of a will to power as an ostensible principle of explanation. The road to the postulation of the will to power was a long one which can be traced on the map of Nietzsche's variegated writings. The transference of this "force" to all beings was a consequence of his view that it is a basic psychic drive inherited from our natural history. To anticipate my later discussion, I will just note here that Nietzsche found in the ancient Greeks an unbridled "lust for power." In an unpublished essay, "Homer's Contest," he introduces what is recognizable as a psychological theory of the will to power in man. He thinks of the early Greeks as viewing life in general as an *agon*, a "contest," a passionate struggle for "more and more." Greek mythology depicts a people committed to the belief that "combat is salvation," a people who would seek to rival the power of the gods in their overweening pride (*hubris*). This striving for dominance, as well as for fame, often leads to the destruction of those who engage in it.

In comparison to "modern humanity," Nietzsche contends, the figures represented in Greek myth and described in ancient history are bold, daring, and heroic. On the other hand, they have a shocking capacity for revenge, violence, and cruelty.[17] Even though Nietzsche does not explicitly raise the specter of a will to power in this essay, it is implied throughout, and his response is ambivalent. Despite his admiration of the heroes of ancient Greece, the "tigerish lust to annihilate" he finds in someone like Alexander the Great gives him pause.

The converse of Nietzsche's admiration of the heroic qualities of the ancient Greeks is the belief that the "worship of success" and victory in the world is a sign of "meanness." To find always in world history the "realization" of the good and the just is a "blasphemy against the good and the just." Often the "universal law" is that the strong win in the world. But, Nietzsche laments, "if only it were not so often precisely what is stupid and evil."[18]

Returning to my central concern here, it should be noted that Nietzsche's preoccupation with anthropomorphism did not spontaneously generate in his mind. As we have seen, he understood Kant's account of knowledge to be based upon an implicit conception of human nature and its constituting functions. He was encouraged in this by his familiarity with Schopenhauer's emphasis upon the subjectivist slant of the first edition of the *Critique of Pure Reason*. By synthesizing Kant's attempt to correct the idealist impression he first conveyed by introducing a critical realism with Schopenhauer's stress on the intellect as in the service of the will, Nietzsche began to form the beginnings of a practical, if not a pragmatic, account of human knowledge.

Nietzsche was also influenced by Ralph Waldo Emerson's radical anthropomorphism, especially as presented in "Nature."[19] It is especially striking that Emerson called attention to the metaphorical nature of language and to the tendency for man to transfer his "spiritual" traits to the natural world. There is no doubt that such an anthropomorphic interpretation of nature played, as indicated, a significant role in the development of Nietzsche's thought.

Nietzsche found a similar, but more scientifically informed, disclosure of the prevalence of anthropomorphic projection in his careful study of F. A. Lange's *History of Materialism*.[20] In this major work Lange repeatedly uncovers personification in philosophical and scientific language. He emphasizes the role of transference in scientific discourse and highlights the use of figurative language in the theories of various scientists. Ironically, Lange reinforced and gave theoretical sanction to Emerson's impressionist version of anthropomorphic projection. Moreover, Carl Bernoulli was not exaggerating when he said that Lange's work is "the best path-finder through the labyrinth of Nietzsche's philosophical presuppositions."[21] If the hidden presence of Lange is cited now and then, this is because his influence extends beyond Nietzsche's presuppositions and is particularly strong in regard to critical epistemological issues.

SENSATION AND ANTHROPOMORPHISM

One of the primary reasons why Nietzsche often refers to our "falsification" of the world is that he took seriously the agnostic implications of Kant's theory of knowledge, as well as the factual data on the physiology of sensation that he acquired when he first began to philosophize in earnest. In *Schopenhauer as Educator* he expressed sympathy with the reaction of the dramatist von Kleist to the implications of the Kantian philosophy. He remarks that if Kant's thought suffuses popular thought, it will be in the form of a "corroding skepticism and relativism." He empathizes with von Kleist's lament that if we take Kant seriously, then "[w]e cannot decide whether what we call truth is really truth, or whether it merely appears as such to us."[22] For a time, the philosophy of Schopenhauer was a bulwark against such skepticism and a support for a tragic interpretation of existence. However, Nietzsche's study of scientific theories of sensation and perception exacerbated his skepticism.

The brief comments on sensation in "On Truth and Lying in an Extra-Moral Sense" show the influence of then-current theories of the physiology of the senses. Nietzsche argues that when we sense, say, the color red, we undergo a stimulation of the nervous system. This sensation has no specific relation to what we would now call the brain-state that occasions it. We have, then, no reason to assume that this sensation resembles the stimulus that causes it. We designate this sensation to ourselves and to others by means of a specific sound. Again, what is the resemblance of this word ("red") to the actual entity itself or to the experience of the color? The word "red" is said to be a symbol or sign or a metaphorical signification of the color experience in sensation. Our sensory experience and our judgment about it belong to an entirely different sphere than does the "object" that we assume gave rise to our sensation.[23]

Concepts, too, are said to be residual metaphors that we use to represent the original sensory experience. But they, in fact, transfigure the qualitative uniqueness of preconceptual perceptual experience. Therefore, the words we use to express concepts that are intended to describe, "picture," or "mirror" what we experience cannot be said to resemble the complex immediacy of lived-experience.

That the above interpretation of sensory experience is indebted to then-current theories is clear when we compare Helmholtz's very similar analysis:

> So far as the characteristic quality of our sensation informs us of the peculiar nature of the outer influence that excites it, it may pass as a sign of it, but not as a copy. . . . A sign need have no sort of resemblance to that of which it is the sign. The relation between the two consists simply in the fact that the same object under the same conditions elicits the same sign.[24]

Helmholtz lends a Kantian interpretation to his account of sensation, arguing that our sensations are presumed to be "caused" by processes or objects about which we know nothing at all. Attempts to account for the original cause of sensory experience can only be couched in the form of hypotheses or postulations. Lange reinforces this Kantian interpretation of Helmholtz's theory by maintaining that "colors, sounds, smells . . . do not belong to things-in-themselves, but . . . are peculiar forms of excitation of our sensibility, which are called forth by corresponding but qualitatively very different phenomena of the outer world."[25]

Because he insists upon the unconscious selectivity and value-laden interests active in sensory experiences, Nietzsche does not entirely accept the Kantian understanding of sensibility as passively receptive to "impressions." He does accept, however, the implications of Lange's conclusion that "the sense-world is the product of our organization."[26] If the sense-world is the "product" of our sensory-cognitive "organization," then the world we experience is a world *for us*, a world constituted by our senses, as well as by the "conventional language" that mankind, collectively, uses in order to describe the phenomena experienced. Nietzsche concludes that "our senses have wrapped us up in a tissue" of falsifying sensations that, in turn, "lie at the basis of our judgments and our 'knowledge'." In this sense, we have no veridical access to "reality." "We are like spiders in our own webs, and, whatever we may catch in them, it will only be something that our web is capable of catching."[27]

Although Nietzsche does not deny the receptive aspect of sensory experience, he contends that it also is an activity that involves proto-inference, that it is affected by synthesizing processes that come to fruition in conceptual thought. The sensory process is active because we do not simply passively receive "sense-impressions." Rather, there is a form-giving activity (*Formen-Aufzwingen*) in sense-experience that is selective, simplifying, conditioned by interest, feelings, drives, and impulses. It is for this reason that the world upon which our "eye" and our "psychology" have acted is a world *for us*, a world that has been shaped by our senses. Perception is a process involving simplification for the sake of the satisfaction of pragmatic needs.

Now, if "all the categories of reason are of sensual origin," if they are derived from "the empirical world" we experience,[28] then the external world that we "know" is an elaborate construction, a constituted world structured in accordance with the limitations of our senses. The "coarseness" of our sensory organs determines the limits of the sensory apprehension of "reality" and the range of our senses is limited because we are acquainted with phenomena (magnetic fields, electromagnetic waves, ultra-violet waves, etc.) that are not directly perceived. In sum, then, the qualitative world we experience through our sensory modalities is a perspectival world that we plausibly assume is quite different from the perceptual world of other creatures.[29]

If we approach Nietzsche's idea of the "falsification" of the world in terms of his analysis of sensation, we can see that he is maintaining that the world we are acquainted with through sensation and perception is a unique world of qualities, one that is "true" for us as a transmuted humanized world of experience. Despite the dramatic language in which he presents his views, Nietzsche's point is that our sensory perspective cannot be transcended. The *naiveté* of some thinkers, he remarks, was their failure to see that our senses and our "categories of reason" involved "the adjustment of the world for utilitarian ends." They mistakenly believed that they possessed a "criterion" of "truth" and "reality." That is, they tended to "make absolute something conditioned." In effect, an "anthropocentric idiosyncrasy" was taken as the measure of all things.[30]

When he turns his attention to the "mechanistic theory of nature," Nietzsche argues that it is "a regulative principle of method." The mathematical physicists (whose theory of the dynamics of nature he will rely upon) "construct for themselves a force-point world with which they can calculate." The time has come, he urges, for physicists, and philosophers as well, to "grasp an hypothesis as an hypothesis and, at the same time, to take it as a guide" for further discovery.[31] In the same spirit, we may explore the nature of the world by consciously adopting an inevitable human perspective (entailing selectivity, simplification, and synthesis) without making truth-claims of an apodictic nature. Philosophy, like the sciences, should work with provisional assumptions, regulative hypotheses, "conventional fictions" and theoretical posits without assuming that it has access to "pure truth" or "pure knowledge."

This orientation can best be understood against the background of Nietzsche's attempt to develop a philosophical interpretation of the implications of the explosion of knowledge in the scientific world of his time.

THE DYNAMIC WORLD-INTERPRETATION

Before he had made any serious effort to understand the elements of then-viable physical theories, Nietzsche had an intuitive sense of the dynamic multiplicity of forces and "free powers" immanent in the natural world. This intuitive feeling for the active forces in nature was reinforced by his reading of the physical scientists of his day. An agnosticism about the ultimate nature of matter was very much in the air during the period in which he developed his thought. Hermann Helmholtz, the nineteenth-century physiologist and physicist, stressed the postulatory nature of the physicists' speculations about the interior dynamics of the natural world. The physicist and aphorist Georg Christoph Lichtenberg, waxing philosophical, declared that "we can, properly speaking, know nothing of anything in the world except ourselves and the changes that take place in us."[32] The attempt to probe the ultimate constituents of the physical world led many nineteenth-century physicists away from dogmatic materialism and towards agnosticism or forms of idealism. Thus, skepticism concerning the physicist's interpretation of the "text" of nature was not the free invention of Nietzsche, but was suggested to him by contemporary physical scientists and other thinkers. He was only following the suggestions of Helmholtz, Lichtenberg, Emil du Bois-Reymond and others when he remarked that

> This world-picture that they sketch differs in no essential way from the subjective world picture. It is only construed with more extended senses, but with our senses nonetheless.[33]

Despite this orientation towards physical scientific theories, Nietzsche sometimes suggests that, because of its "strict methods" and its conscientious avoidance of teleology, the scientific interpretation of the world is a closer approximation to the way things are. But even given his surprising knowledge of science and, in particular, his general grasp of physical theories, it is excessive to attribute a "physics" to him. During what has come to be called his "positivistic" period he praises the "exact science" for their caution, methodology, and perspicuity. What is often identified as "Nietzsche's physics" is not *his* physics after all. Rather, it is a conglomeration of concepts that emerged out of nineteenth-century physics. The "regulative hypotheses" of the dynamic theory of nature impressed him because they avoided both teleology and mechanistic causation. And it is in a dynamic interpretation of the natural world that the concept of "force" (*Kraft*) or energy is central.

Although they were written between 1883 and 1888, the notes pertaining to physical theory and some of its basic concepts and principles in the *Nachlass* do not comprise "later" thoughts simply because we know that Nietzsche was already familiar with quite a number of physical theories as early as 1866. From his earliest exposure to physical theory, he was alert to the subtle and not-so-subtle anthropomorphic aspects of theories of nature. In *The Gay Science* he frequently chides physicists for ascribing human qualities to the natural world. He charges that the scientific "realists" have not by any means purged their thought of "the human element." Again, he remarks that we must be on our guard against interpreting nature in terms of our "aesthetic humanities."[34] And, as he does so often in his notes, he points to the fictional nature of basic scientific concepts. Against the prevailing view that science "explains" phenomena and their law-like "behavior," he insists that it, at best, *describes* phenomena and sequences of phenomenal appearances. The sciences do not explain because they operate with

> things which do not exist, with lines, surfaces, bodies, atoms, divisible times, divisible spaces—how can explanation ever be possible when we first make everything an *idea*! It is sufficient to regard science as the exactest humanizing of things that is possible.[35]

The belief that science is able to attain insight into the objective "truth" of things is a "metaphysical belief." In spite of this understanding of science, Nietzsche is very much taken by the emerging dynamic theory of the natural world. Even though this theory of nature is not uncritically accepted, and even though Nietzsche is aware of the anthropomorphic character of some of its central notions, he works with it as a kind of provisional "picture" of nature. By describing natural phenomena in terms of interacting dynamic "forces," such a theory is seen as a provisional hypothesis, a viable "world-interpretation" expressed in metaphorical terms.[36]

Nietzsche believed that the dynamic concept of "force" was going to be "victorious." The central ideas of the "new" physics were that atoms were not static, encapsulated entities, but dynamic centers of force that interacted with other force-centers in a process of "attraction" and "repulsion." These postulated "point-centers" that lie at the heart of matter are construed as the origin of the macroscopic "effects" that we are able to observe. Although Fechner, a leading philosophical psychologist, argued that the physical concept of force is an expression by which we may represent "the laws of equilibrium and motion," he denied that the explanation of action is found in "laws of force" and maintained "the totality of the relations amongst a group of phenomena."[37] Nietzsche agrees with Lange's account of the notion that the physical sciences are on firm ground only in regard to "relations" even though bearers of such relations may be introduced "hypothetically."

Nietzsche criticizes the dynamic theory of the natural world because it has not entirely transcended anthropomorphic interpretations. In the first place, the key conceptions of attraction and repulsion are derived from human experience and human relations. The mechanistic notion of dynamic motion is considered as "a translation of the original process into the sign language of sight and touch."[38] The assumption that forces obey a "law" is a supposition, a "formula" put forward as a means of facilitating the description of the entire phenomenon. This formula, as expressed, "corresponds to a complex of initially unknown forces and discharges of forces" and does not, in a strict sense, indicate that "forces" act in accordance with it.[39]

The conception of dynamic atoms construed as "unities" is a fiction put forward for the purpose of calculation and is derived from an analogy to a putative "ego" that is capable of producing "effects." Even a dynamic mechanics that is expressed in sophisticated terms cannot, in Nietzsche's view, do without "prejudices." For, in order to support such a theory,

> we always have to stipulate to what extent we are employing two fictions: the concept of *motion* (taken from our sense language) and the concept of the *atom* (= unity, deriving from our psychical "experience"): the mechanistic theory presupposes a sense prejudice and a psychological prejudice.[40]

In effect, then, a dynamic mechanics, despite its heroic attempt to present a theory of the natural world in de-anthropomorphic terms, ultimately relies upon psychistic fictions and anthropomorphic terminology. Finally, because the principle of causality is applied to phenomena, even the most sophisticated physics relies upon a fundamental "fiction" derived from our own "inner phenomenology." The idea of cause-effect relations (e.g., forces producing effects) is based upon our fallacious belief that in our actions a "feeling of force" is the cause of our actions. We have no experience, Nietzsche argues, of our "forces" compelling something. But we have a propensity to project into this process a "compulsion" that is the psychic origin of our conception of "causality."[41]

Nietzsche argues that an "inner phenomenology" is conditioned by the same cognitive processes of simplification that he believes are operative in our understanding of external events. The acts or processes that we believe take place in our psychic life are also dominated by a process of selectivity. For, "everything of which we become conscious is arranged, simplified, schematized, interpreted through and through."[42] In sum, then, when we think of dynamic force as causing effects we are projecting onto natural processes the outcome of a misleading phenomenology of our intentional psychic processes. If this is truly the case, then even a dynamic interpretation of the natural world is contaminated by an anthropomorphism that we have projected onto the realm of nonhuman processes. This is *a fortiori* the case for mechanistic physical theories.

Nietzsche is the first to admit, of course, that in spite of the psychological origin of central concepts in the physical sciences, such primitive assumptions are useful, pragmatic fictions that we probably cannot do without in our calculations and interpretations. Basic concepts in physical theory make up the heuristic tools of inquiry.[43] In the development of relativity theory and under the influence of Ernst Mach's philosophy of science, Einstein adopted psychistic theoretical conventions. For this reason, as well as for more complex reasons, Einstein avoided any apodictic claim to "truth," but argued for "the heuristic value of the theory of relativity."[44]

Nietzsche's later deliberate anthropomorphic interpretation of the dynamic theory of forces and point-centers was a conception that developed over the entire period of his productive life and is derived from his reflections on the philosophical implications of physical theory. The theory of "perspectivalism" is linked, in later thought-experiments, to the dynamic interpretation of natural processes that is provisionally adopted as a model of a physical "world-interpretation." It is clear that when Nietzsche claims in his notes that each center of force "interprets" the world from its individual perspective, he is relying upon the postulation that the interior structure of "matter" is characterized by energy-quanta, "point-centers," or "forces." Each center of force (or, for larger bodies, "constellation of forces") is said to "picture" or express the world from its own point of reference. There would be no "world" if we deducted such perspectives precisely because we would have thereby deducted "relativity." "Reality," Nietzsche avers, "consists precisely in this particular action and reaction of every individual part toward the whole."[45] Here a dialectical interaction of forces comprises his abstract world-picture. The "whole" referred to is in perpetual flux and is more imagined than known because of its "indescribable complexity."

In his notes on physical theory Nietzsche was concerned with drawing out all of the implications of what is a sketch or model of a *relativistic dynamics*. Even though the theory at this point is rudimentary, it is clear that he is provisionally adopting it in order to spell out the philosophical implications of a consistent dynamic theory of force-centers.

According to Marshall Spector, the concept of force is "primitive" in twentieth-century relativity theory in the sense that it has no "deeper explanation." It can only be clarified by indicating "what sorts of entities have masses or exert forces," which cannot be reduced to "anything more physically basic."[46] Without a technical knowledge of the rich theoretical foundation of a rudimentary theory of relativity, Nietzsche, nonetheless, accepts the notion that "forces" are irreducible physical processes and endeavors to formulate a philosophical response to this assumption. This attempt to formulate a philosophical response to a general physical theory takes place in a universe of discourse that anticipates features of later relativistic dynamics.

From his study of a major work in mathematical physics when he taught at the University of Basel, Nietzsche was already familiar with Roger J. Boscovich's relativistic theory of "point-centers."[47] In addition, he was familiar with Ernst Mach's speculations concerning the possibility of a space with more than three dimensions, as well as with the astronomer and physicist Johann Zöllner's claim that physical space is non-Euclidean. And there is no doubt that he was impressed by the observation that if such conceptual tendencies continued to develop in the physical sciences, then "the whole theory of knowledge must be subjected to revision."[48]

Many of the arguments that Nietzsche directs against naïve realists or those who espouse various forms of objectivism depend upon data culled from the natural sciences circa 1866–72 or various then-current scientific theories. He tried to formulate a counter-theory to the prevalent forms of mechanistic materialism gaining ground in nineteenth-century German scientific theory (despite the pressure of skepticism about the ultimate constituents of nature).

Provisionally adopting a physical world-interpretation that postulated a multiplicity of force-centers or "power-centers," he is led to proclaim that the constant action and reaction of such centers of force is "reality."[49] Despite his long struggle against metaphysical speculation, he seems satisfied with the advancement of his version of a process model of actuality.[50]

However, Nietzsche sought to extend his thought beyond the limits of a philosophical interpretation of the implications of a dynamic physics because he saw that mechanics gives us only "quantities" or, more accurately, mathematical and symbolic representations of quantities or quantitative processes. He saw that a "mechanistic interpretation" actually

> desires nothing but quantities; but force is to be found in quality. Mechanistic theory can only *describe processes*, but not explain them.[51]

By means of weighing, calculating and reckoning, our "knowledge" is expressed in quantitative terms. But our typical perspective is clearly qualitative in nature. Therefore, the world that we are familiar with through sensory experience and cognitive organization is a "falsified" world, is not, strictly speaking, "reality," but a humanized world that preserves the qualitative diversity of our experiences. At this point, Nietzsche raises the following question: "Might not all quantities be signs of qualities?"[52] Denying that all qualities can be reduced to quantities (except for purposes of calculation, conceptual efficiency, etc.), he avers that the qualitative world accompanies the quantitative one as "an analogy." In order to understand truly the quantitative, dynamic world-interpretation of physics, we must translate it into human, qualitative terms.

The conception of a "denatured" force, a force we cannot even imagine, is unsatisfactory. We have a natural propensity to want to go beyond the mathematical formulae that symbolize forces, to seek an answer to the more basic question: what is force? We want, that is, a "deeper explanation" of force. But this cannot be provided by physical theory itself. Such an explanation cannot be found either in classical or relativistic dynamics.

Nietzsche is concerned with creating and projecting a human meaning of a dynamic world-interpretation because he holds, as he says in *The Gay Science,* that a purely mechanistic conception of the natural world is senseless. While he conceives of a dynamic theory of centers of force as compatible with our experience of flux and interaction, the world and man are thereby reduced to depersonalized, dehumanized forces that endlessly generate effects. He was seeking to express a philosophical interpretation of the dynamic world-picture found in the physical sciences. Or, to put it another way, he was seeking to incorporate the physical theoretical conception of actuality into his general philosophy of power. Given his constructive aesthetic interpretation of the world, Nietzsche wanted to preserve the meaning and value of appearances, to protect the phenomenological diversity of man's qualitative experience from what he considered the "destructive" consequences of a purely quantitative analysis of man and nature. Whereas someone like Kierkegaard wanted to shield the spiritual, subjective domain of human existence from the incursions of the rising scientific analysis of all phenomena, Nietzsche sought to co-opt the scientific world-interpretation by negating it as objective truth and preserving it as a provisional interpretation of actuality subjected to a philosophical meaning.

Nietzsche was convinced, with good reason, that a scientific mechanistic world-interpretation proffers a "meaningless world."[53] The reduction of all reality to quantitative terms would be similar to reducing music to what can be counted, calculated, measured, or formulated abstractly. Music is a complex, qualitative phenomenon that can only be appreciated or valued as a totality, as a whole. A full and rich appreciation of music requires the "how" of human experience, a sensitivity to the nuances of sound and rhythm, an emotional response, an openness to aesthetic qualities. The reduction of music to its quantitative elements is a distortion of its meaning and value for us.

By searching out the humanistic and aesthetic aspects of scientific theory and thinking, Nietzsche indicated that even in the ostensibly impersonal process of scientific thought our "aesthetic humanities" continue to play a role. And what he called attention to has long since become a commonplace both in the philosophy of science and in the writings of scientists who reflect upon their own mode of thinking. The creative, inventive, and imaginative aspects of scientific discovery and theory confirm Nietzsche's view that the exact sciences cannot entirely transcend the domain of anthropomorphic and aesthetic projection. Thus, astronomers tell us that the elliptical orbit of the planets around the sun is not a literal depiction of this process, but a statistically informed, averaged representation of the actual orbit of the planets.

Ironically, it was early philosophers of science, as well as some scientists, who provided Nietzsche with the conventionalist interpretation of scientific concepts and theories that he frequently adopted. In fact, much of his skepticism was cultivated by the various forms of agnosticism that were expressed by scientists of the nineteenth-century.

His interrogation of knowledge typically proceeds from two standpoints: from the perspective of science he undermines common-sense beliefs (retained in natural languages) and from the perspective of the analysis of perception and cognitive-linguistic metaphors he undermines claims to truth in ordinary language and in philosophies propounding various forms of objectivism. Ironically, without the evidence garnered from the independent sciences his critique of truth and knowledge would be depleted. For example, he repeatedly refers to our senses as "coarse" because of the refinements of scientific observations and the theoretical notion that the effects of entities we perceive are different from the dynamic, "sub-atomic," or molecular changes that are theoretically assumed to be operative in the interior dynamics of such entities.

Having been informed by physiological theorists that the range of human perception is limited, that there are phenomena that cannot be perceived by us, that different organisms have different perceptual systems, he asserts that our perception yields a "humanized" field of phenomena and is like an island in the midst of a vast ocean.

Unlike some contemporary scientific realists, Nietzsche either suspended judgment on the reality of the posited entities or processes promulgated by scientists or adopted what could be called a phenomenalistic approach to the entities postulated in the sciences. Although sympathetic, up to a point, with the "small, unapparent truths" of the sciences and with the precision of scientific methodologies, Nietzsche hesitated to adopt a position such as that affirmed by Wilfrid Sellars:

> [T]he assertion that the micro-entities of physical theory really exist goes hand in hand with the assertion that the macro-entities of the perceptible world do not really exist. This position can be ruled out of court only by showing that the framework of perceptible physical objects in space and time has an authenticity which guarantees a parasitical status for the subtle and sophisticated framework of physical theory. I argue . . . that the very conception of such absolute authenticity is a mistake.[54]

Although Nietzsche would certainly agree with Sellars that beliefs about objects based on ordinary perception have no "absolute authenticity," he would (and did) argue that the unidimensional perspective of physical theory has no absolute authenticity either. We get an insight into the nature of his skeptical analysis of knowledge when we realize that Nietzsche held that beliefs or judgments based upon perception are not absolutely valid not only because of physical theoretical conceptions of "micro-entities," but because of the metaphorical and anthropomorphic nature of the language of nonscientific perception. This compounds his skepticism, as he proclaims that natural languages, long before the rise of science, incorporated an anthropomorphic transformation of perceptual experience that became "canonical." Given this twofold skepticism, we can see that the claim that our knowledge of the external world involves a "falsification" of actuality is not as implausible as it at first seems.

The overall movement of Nietzsche's thought goes from the uncovering of a naïve anthropomorphism in ordinary and philosophical language, to a consideration of the nature of reality as described in the sciences, to the final restoration of a self-consciously anthropomorphic perspective that would yield an aesthetic dimension of human experience and thought.

One of the interesting consequences of Nietzsche's critical approach to knowledge is that he consistently argues that the same simplifying, organizing, schematizing process operative in our attempts to acquire knowledge of the external world is at work in our attempts to interpret our own nature. There is nothing, he contends, as deceptive as our fabled "inner sense." Our "inner experiences" enter consciousness after they have been simplified and schematized in such a way that a "language" is found that the individual understands. This understanding is the expression of something "new" in the language of that with which we are already "familiar."[55]

Our understanding of the nonhuman is influenced by our own "internal phenomenology" and, to this extent, anthropomorphism cannot be entirely transcended. We project "psychic fictions" onto the entities and processes we observe in the natural world, and even the exact sciences retain traces of our humanizing tendencies of thought. As we shall see, what Nietzsche calls the humanization of nature or the transubstantiation of our experience of the world in terms of our falsifying internal phenomenology plays a significant role in the transference of the discovery of a fundamental will to power in ourselves to all reality. Retrieving the anthropomorphism he relentlessly exposes in the discourses of others, Nietzsche eventually negates it in its naïve form and preserves it in his metaphorical perspectival "interpretation" of the nature of reality.

Chapter Two

Agnosticism

Today every trace of dogmatism is fading away.

Nietzsche, *Nachlass*

Although Nietzsche often expresses unjust criticisms of Kant's thought, and did not have a detailed understanding of Kant's critique of knowledge, he was profoundly influenced by his epistemic analyses. The only work of Kant's that he seems to have studied with care was the *Critique of Judgment*. He read it in preparation for a brief, unpublished, and none-too-original essay entitled "On Teleology." That Nietzsche wrote this essay when he was twenty-three, and made notes on Kant in 1888 indicates the longevity of his struggle with and against a formidable philosophical foe.

Interestingly, in this early study of Kant's *Critique of Judgment* Nietzsche hesitates to adopt Kant's notion of the relation between teleology and life, but is sympathetic to the emphasis upon the applicability of a mechanistic explanation to the natural world and its inapplicability to organic life. We can already see the emergence of Nietzsche's philosophy of life, his conception of the unique nature of living beings, his preoccupation with "forms of life," and with the belief that we can comprehend life only via human analogy.[1]

Nietzsche was familiar with Kant's philosophy primarily through critical commentaries such as F. A. Lange's discussion of Kant in *The History of Materialism*, Schopenhauer's treatment of Kant in *The World as Will and Representation*, and Kuno Fischer's volume on Kant in his *Geschichte der neureren Philosophie*. Although Nietzsche's approach to Kant's analysis of knowledge is typically critical, he absorbs much of the subjectivistic slant of the first edition of the *Critique* and some of Kant's terminology.

Nietzsche's early formulation of a pragmatic account of knowledge[2] owes a great deal to his understanding of Kant's conception of practical reason. In addition, the emphasis upon the questionable nature of transcendental metaphysics, as well as the stress on agnosticism concerning actuality, which one finds throughout his writings, was indebted to Kant's general orientation. Nietzsche's focus upon "conditional knowledge" and his conception of the fictive nature of basic categories of thought were suggested, in an indirect way, by Kant's critical philosophy and its skeptical implications.

In his notes from the early 1870s, Nietzsche struggled with the problem of knowledge and critically examined the implications of the metastasizing "knowledge drive." He was at first sympathetic to the problem of inaccessible "things-in-themselves" and tried to present a contrast between the "world" that man constructs out of his *a priori* intuitions of space and time, sensory experience, categories, and the transcendental being of *Dinge-an-sich*. Although he later criticized the idea of things-in-themselves, in "Truth and Lying in an Extra-Moral Sense," he retained the notion and exploited it in his analysis of the restricted mode of "anthropomorphic knowledge."

The Birth of Tragedy reveals the dual influence of Kant and Schopenhauer. The "primal One" that lies beyond the realm of space, time, and causality is, more or less, Schopenhauer's primordial "Will." The empirical world is described in terms of Kant's epistemic conclusions. In his poetic and metaphysical representation of the essence of ancient Greek civilization Nietzsche refers to space, time, and causality as the conditions of phenomenal being. The irrational Dionysian ground of the world and existence that cannot be grasped conceptually is a substitute for the thing-in-itself. Kant's agnosticism about the realm of things-in-themselves was only circumvented by means of music, Dionysian passion, artistic creativity, and insight.

No sooner had his "romantic" and aesthetic metaphysical work appeared than Nietzsche undertook what appears to be a *volte face*. In "Truth and Lying in an Extra-Moral Sense," a strong skepticism emerges. But it is still informed by Kant's distinction between things-in-themselves and known (or knowable) phenomena. What seems to be a sudden "turn" towards skepticism in his unpublished essay is not so. By virtue of his study of Lange's *History of Materialism* from 1866 to 1872, he fully accepted the view that "the essence of things" is unknowable. He adopts Lange's emphasis upon our "psycho-physical organization" as the basis of experience and knowledge in lieu of Kant's "transcendental unity of apperception." Borrowing a suggestion from Kant himself, Nietzsche claims that the ground of our psychophysical organization, like the ground of sensibility and understanding, is unknown.

In what Nietzsche called the "artists' metaphysics" in *The Birth of Tragedy* he had already abandoned the metaphysical standpoint presented there prior to having written it. As early as 1868, Nietzsche reported his newly acquired skeptical phenomenalism to his friend Paul Deussen.

Commenting on the physiological studies undertaken "since Kant," he says that one

> cannot doubt . . . that limits are so surely and unmistakably established that, aside from theologians, some philosophy professors, and the vulgar, no one here has any illusions. The realm of metaphysics, like the province of "absolute" reality, has unquestionably been shifted into the ranks with poetry and religion. Whoever wants to know something contents himself now with a conscious relativity of knowledge—as, for example, all noteworthy scientific investigators. Thus, for some people, metaphysics belongs in the domain of psychic needs, is essentially edification; in other words, it is art, namely the art of conceptual poetry.[3]

Anyone familiar with Lange's *History of Materialism* would recognize three of his basic themes in Nietzsche's compact statement. Lange held that the studies in the physiology of the senses in the nineteenth-century gave support to Kant's stress upon the limits of sensibility and its "subjective constitution." The questioning of the capacity of metaphysical speculation to obtain knowledge of absolute reality is a constant theme of Lange's. So, too, is the reliance on knowledge acquired in the "exact sciences." Finally, the construal of metaphysics as a kind of "conceptual poetry" is a disguised expression of Lange's view that edifying, aesthetically colored conceptions of "the All" can be put forward from "the standpoint of the ideal."[4]

Since my concern here is with Nietzsche's reactions to Kant's critical philosophy rather than the accuracy of his comprehension of it, I will focus on what he made of Kant's thought. It is clear that he did not have a scholarly understanding of the details and subtleties of Kant's *Critique of Pure Reason*. Nietzsche quite often refers to "categories of reason" when he means categories of the understanding, questions the "truth" of categories such as "unity" when he is actually concerned with the validity of their ontological reference to natural entities, and sometimes misleadingly refers to the "phenomenal" flux that lies *behind* the conditioned phenomena which, in Kant's sense, are all we know.

Even though Nietzsche is cavalier in his treatment of Kant, he understood the negative implications of his restriction of knowledge to phenomena and raised some good, if briefly stated, questions about various aspects of his thought. Like Kierkegaard before him, he zeroed in on Kant's admission that "I have found it necessary to deny *knowledge* in order to make room for *faith*."[5] And he raised a simple, but relevant, question about the epistemological status of Kant's "knowledge about knowledge." He attacks the idea of "pure reason" and seeks to undermine the belief that the "knowledge-drive" is impersonal and disinterested.

Without an in-depth understanding of Hume, Nietzsche uses Hume-like arguments against Kant, calls attention to "belief" as the basis of judgment, and continually refers to the "psychistic" elements that enter into our claims to knowledge. There are no indications that he had more than a second-hand acquaintance with Hume's *Treatise* and the *Inquiry Concerning Human Understanding*. Despite the similarities of some of Nietzsche's arguments and those of Hume, his psychologistic orientation, which is the basis for many of his criticisms of Kant, was primarily derived from naturalistic and scientifically informed emphases upon the psychic and physiological basis of knowing.

Just as some contemporary philosophers employ data derived from the independent sciences in their analyses of perception or their theories concerning the mind-body problem, so, too, did Nietzsche discern the relevance of discoveries in the physiology of the senses to conceptions of our knowledge of the external world. Just as our specific sensory modalities and their functioning delimit the field of our perceptual experience, so do our historically developed conceptual frameworks condition what counts as knowledge.

In his *Prolegomena to any Future Metaphysics*, Kant claimed that the physical sciences can never discover the "internal constitution of things" or any ultimate ground of explanation that transcends our "sensibility." Scientific understanding must be based upon the objects of sense that "belong to experience" and are comprehended in accordance with "the laws of experience."[6] Whatever is known is conditioned by our sensibility and understanding, and any claims to truth that seek to go beyond these capacities are either "regulative principles of reason" or unjustified speculations. Lange quotes with approval Kant's observation that "[a]ll cognition of things based upon pure understanding or pure reason is nothing but appearance, and truth is in experience only."[7]

After discussing the question of the synthetic nature of mathematical propositions, Lange turns his attention to a "dark point in the Kantian system" that arises because of the assumption that in every act of knowing *a priori* elements are deduced from a valid *a priori* principle or they are searched out in an empirical manner. The principle from which the *a priori* is deduced is not produced and an empirical process cannot generate any necessary results. Lange maintains that the disguised method used in order to "discover" the *a priori* or the origin of the *a priori* is none other than "the method of induction."[8] The "necessity" of *a priori* knowledge is shaped in advance of experience by "the physio-psychological organization of man." Lange makes this point in order to avoid introducing any transcendental posits to account for *a priori* knowledge and law-like experiences. Here he reinterprets Kant for his own ends in order to ground knowledge in physiological determinations of the field of perception and psychistic aspects of categorical thinking. It is not so much that he misunderstands Kant as that he is engaged in a neo-Kantian revision of the knowing process, one that is presented against the background of the Darwinian theory of evolution.

Lange gives special attention to a problem that is later raised by Nietzsche and subsequent commentators on Kant's thought. He questions Kant's occasional appeals to the causal power of things-in-themselves. The thing-in-itself, he says, can have no relation to causality (the category of causality) by Kant's own restrictions since it cannot be applied to that which transcends our experience and knowledge.[9] He is not denying that there is something (matter?) that causes our sensations or appearances to our sensory modalities. Rather, he is criticizing Kant for violating his own restriction of cause and effect to "phenomena" constituted by our sensibility and our categories. Moreover, he wonders how one can think of things-in-themselves that are outside space and time and to which none of Kant's categories can apply. Kant cannot legitimately refer to the existence of things-in-themselves on the basis of his own principles because this would be to claim a transcendental, negative "knowledge" that is prohibited by his general theory.[10] Even as a "limit-concept" or *Grenzbegriff* the thing-in-itself is refined away into a vanishing unreality. Lange believes that the conceptual dissolution of the idea of things-in-themselves leads to the granting of a gain in reality to phenomena, since a phenomenon "embraces everything that we can call 'real'."[11]

The world that is constituted by our *a priori* intuitions of space and time, our sensibility, and our categories of the understanding is, for Lange, a realm of phenomenal appearances that is not only all we can know, but is all we should concern ourselves with in any account of human knowledge. This synthesis of phenomenalism (without transcendental consciousness and things-in-themselves) and agnosticism is virtually absorbed by, and reiterated by, Nietzsche. In a letter dating from 1866, Nietzsche accurately summarizes one of the conclusions of Lange's skepticism.

> The true essence of things, the last cause of all phenomena, is . . . not only unknown to us, but even the idea of it is nothing more and nothing less than the last outcome of the antithesis determined by our organization, and of which we do not know whether, beyond our experience, it has any meaning at all.[12]

Lange stresses agnosticism concerning what may be imagined to transcend phenomenal knowledge in order to support his radical phenomenalism. And he believes that Kant postulates things-in-themselves, in part, in order to avoid materialism. All "things" or "objects" are grasped by us as phenomena. What constitutes the "internal in matter" is unknown except in terms of new phenomena that are disclosed by further advances in the natural sciences. What appears to us as matter is, for Kant, "a mere chimera."[13]

By claiming that the internal dynamics of matter are ultimately inaccessible to us, Kant seems concerned to block the possibility that the appearances constituted by our sensibility and categorizing understanding might be caused by matter. By affirming that the phenomena disclosed by advances in the natural sciences do not give us access to the internal dynamics of matter, and by insisting that such phenomena are constituted by the activity of the mind, Kant has preserved the centrality of the "transcendental unity of apperception" and has avoided materialism.

By tracing the origin of sensibility and categorical thought to our physiology and our psychic functions, Lange proposed a form of materio-idealism that had considerable impact on Nietzsche's thinking. The strong strand of phenomenalism that runs through the philosophy of Nietzsche is indebted to Lange, and it is certainly true that he often wears the guise of a phenomenalist.[14]

There is an additional feature of Lange's account of the limits and nature of knowledge that had a long-range effect on Nietzsche's epistemic standpoint. In various places in his *History of Materialism* Lange refers to Kant's *Anthropology from a Pragmatic Standpoint.* He mentions that, in a rudimentary way, Kant anticipates in that atypical work a Darwinian position by alluding to man's possible evolution from the "orangutan." Moreover, Kant also hints at the functional development of "reason" in man in such a way as to suggest an evolutionary theory of knowledge. Although Nietzsche makes only one reference to this work in his notes, he was quite familiar with Lange's neo-Kantian emphasis on the pragmatic conception of knowledge. Since in "Truth and Lying in an Extra-Moral Sense" Nietzsche paraphrases Kant in the *Anthropology* in regard to the role of "deception" in social communication, we may legitimately assume that he was familiar with the entire work.[15] This means that when he refers to the evolution of man's basic concepts, he is not only applying Darwin's theory of evolution to the problem of knowledge, but is following leads suggested by Kant himself. So it is not surprising that he repeatedly seeks to look behind the curtain of our basic categories (which are invariably those of Kant) in order to speculate about why we have come to think in terms of them and to what extent they have been accepted for their serviceability in the struggle for existence.

Even though Lange does not explicitly put forward an evolutionary theory of knowledge, he frequently implies such a theory. By building on the suggestions of Lange and those of Kant, Nietzsche became one of the earliest proponents of the recently revived evolutionary theory of the development of human knowledge. Although he rejects Darwinism in a number of respects (especially in regard to the belief that organic beings are primarily concerned with an adaptation to an environment for survival rather than with an active expression of their energies), he clearly adopts a Darwinian notion of the evolution of certain concepts that serve survival and perpetuation of the species. And, as his notes from the late 1880s indicate, this is a position from which he did not retreat.

While Nietzsche eventually comes to mock the idea of things-in-themselves (particularly in *Human, All-Too-Human*), he never abandons the utility of, or the value of, the Kantian categories of the understanding. However, as much as he insists upon their usefulness, he continually characterizes them as "fictions" that have no meaningful ontological reference. He agrees with Kant about their "necessity," but emphasizes that they are necessary for our survival and perpetuation, for the "construction" of a world in which we can function, survive, and prosper.

The Birth of Tragedy interweaves, among other things, the thought of Schopenhauer, Kant, and Lange. The Schopenhauerian element is the "primal will" that lies behind or beneath the phenomena encountered in the domain of our "empirical existence."[16] Nietzsche distinguishes between phenomena and the thing-in-itself in this work and claims to have an intuitive grasp of a metempirical reality. The irrational Dionysian ground of the world cannot be grasped conceptually, since it is transfigured by the Apollonian power of artistic illusion. There is no doubt that Nietzsche retains a residual Kantianism in that he adheres to the distinction between phenomena and things-in-themselves. It is quite correct that

> in this earliest work he held, as Schopenhauer had, that there was a way of going beyond the Kantian agnosticism about the nature of the thing-in-itself. He held that music, art generally, and some Dionysian states of intoxication gave us insight into the ultimate reality which expresses itself in phenomena; and that the ultimate reality was of the nature of will.[17]

It is not, however, only Nietzsche's "romanticism" that encourages him to speculate about the primordial reality manifested to us in the empirical world of "space, time, and causality." Lange had given thinkers such as Nietzsche *carte blanche* to create a poetic, imaginary portrait of the "unknowable." He believed that Kant's analysis of knowledge received support from the agnosticism of nineteenth-century scientists about the ultimate nature of reality. And he insisted, with Kant and a number of neo-Kantian scientists, that knowledge is restricted to phenomena alone. He turned this to his advantage by proclaiming that "[n]o thought is so calculated to reconcile poesy and science as the thought that all our 'reality' . . . is only *appearance*."[18] The *terra incognita* of ultimate mystery, he felt, cried out for a poetic creation of a "world of values" that would give a meaning to man not found in what he called the "broken fragments" of scientific facts. This "free poetry," he thought, "may . . . make use of myth in order to lend words to the unutterable."[19] Lange calls this orientation "the standpoint of the ideal" and encourages the promulgation of "conscious illusions." In order to prevent "spiritual impoverishment," there is a need for the projection of new aesthetic conceptions that would bring "the world of existence into connection with the world of values."[20]

In *The Birth of Tragedy* Nietzsche had already adopted Lange's standpoint of the ideal by offering a mythopoetic image of reality that imbues life with an aesthetic meaning. It is for this reason that he does not exclude his own tragic vision of life from classification as a "conscious illusion." It is not the case that he is inconsistent when he refers to "the Socratic love of knowledge," "art's seductive veil of beauty," and the metaphysical belief that "beneath the whirl of phenomena eternal life flows indestructibly" as illusions.[21]

In both *The Birth of Tragedy* and "Truth and Lying in an Extra-Moral Sense" Nietzsche retains the distinction between phenomena and things-in-themselves even though he was already quite aware of criticisms of the latter. As we've seen, in his unpublished essay he argues that language, because of its metaphorical nature, cannot be said to "picture" either things-in-themselves or what we directly experience. Words are construed as metaphors that represent images. And concepts are understood as metaphors that are even more remote from our direct experience of unique, complex phenomena. The metaphorical nature of language precludes a correspondence between judgments and actuality as it is concretely experienced.[22] Here the agnosticism of Kant is compounded, because we do not know things-in-themselves and, because of the metaphorical nature of language and concepts, we transform the complexity of the phenomena we have perceived.

What concerns Nietzsche is the fact that our ordinary judgments are abstract, simplifying, de-individuating abbreviations of what we have experienced. We say, for example, "the leaf is brown." Thereby, we have deleted the specificity of *this* leaf, expunged its particular texture, contour, shape, etc. And we have identified it as "brown" when, perhaps, its brown coloration is only its dominant color quality. Thus, in another context, the French poet Rimbaud can picture eternity as the sun (*le soleil*) making love to the sea (*la mer*) and convey a poetic relation between masculine and feminine entities. Nietzsche could have used as an illustration of the simplifying function of language the assertion, "It is snowing." Here the specific type of snowfall, which the Esquimau language is able to express because of its various words for different kinds of snow, is unexpressed.

In other places, Nietzsche argues that the sense-organs are themselves "organs of abstraction" since the senses select out of a chaos of impressions what is of interest to us or what our senses are capable of responding to because of their limited range. What he says about the function of our sensory system points in the direction of the contemporary theory of the senses as transducers that transform the stimuli by which they are affected.

Kant's treatment of the idea of the thing-in-itself as a limit-concept both in the *Critique of Pure Reason* and his *Opus postumum* reduces it to an *ens rationis* or an indefinite concept. The distinction between an object for knowledge and the thing-in-itself is intended as an ideal distinction that has meaning for the subject. Kant sometimes comes close to characterizing the notion of the thing-as-itself as a fiction. If, as Vaihinger has said, Kant came to recognize the notion of the thing-in-itself as "fictive,"[23] then Nietzsche's treatment of it as a fictitious theoretical notion is not a drastic departure from Kant's thought.

The repudiation of metaphysics in *Human, All-Too-Human* is often seen as a renunciation of romantic thought on Nietzsche's part. The skepticism about things-in-themselves in his so-called positivistic stage of development is attributed to the fact that he had begun to "sober up."[24] Although this is plausible, we know that he was already impressed by a growing agnosticism concerning the ultimate nature of reality and had conceived of metaphysics as "conceptual poetry" before he wrote *The Birth of Tragedy*.

Human, All-Too-Human does not indicate a new epistemic standpoint. Rather, it is, in part, the fruition of his adoption of scientifically based skepticism. Instead of searching after "Truth," he urges us to be satisfied with "the little, unpretentious truths" that the exact sciences produce.[25] Having absorbed epitomes of scientific knowledge as of 1872, and having continued his studies of various scientific writings subsequently, Nietzsche came to appreciate the value of strict scientific method. Although he inscribed it in his notes later, he had already renounced transcendental metaphysical speculation because he realized that

> there are many kinds of eyes. Even the Sphinx has eyes—and consequently there are many kinds of "truths," and consequently there is no Truth.[26]

Nietzsche's growing respect for "the severest methods of knowledge" entailed a rejection of all forms of idealist and absolutist positions. All attempts to go beyond the limits of the empirical world of phenomena, to speculate about or decipher the identity of the thing-in-itself, were to be put "on ice." The "enigmatical thing-in-itself" is now, he tell us, "only worth a Homeric laugh." The essence of things is unknown to us not because it is hidden behind the veil of the thing-in-itself, but because of the sensory, linguistic, and conceptual transformational activity of man's "organization" and the evolved, inherited cognitive framework that serves his survival.

Indeed, Nietzsche not only criticizes the idea of things-in-themselves that escape our phenomenal knowledge, but he attacks Kant's theory of the "noumenal self" (which he sarcastically calls a "self-in-itself"). He criticizes the latter notion because it treats the self as a pure subject, provides for a defense of freedom, and denaturalizes man. He views Kant's position at the conclusion of the *Critique of Pure Reason* as an incomplete phenomenalism insofar as trans-phenomenal posits, at the objective and the subjective poles, are retained. By proclaiming that the true world is inaccessible to us, Nietzsche believes, Kant reopened the philosophical door to the Platonic-Christian belief in a transcendental "true world."

Nietzsche views Kant as continuing the tradition, albeit in a circuitous way, of a belief in a "reality-in-itself." The emerging doubts about the existence of such a realm, against the background of its previous acceptance for almost two thousand years, is a contributing factor to the generation of "radical nihilism." This is a reaction to the "untenability" of our existence when we realize "that we lack the least right to posit a beyond or an in-itself" that might be construed as "divine" or serve as the ground of morality.[27] What Nietzsche seems to mean here in his genetic account of the genesis of nihilism is that Kant perpetuated the false belief in a transcendental world (thereby undermining the *value* of this world) and fostered a morality rooted in the questionable conception of a noumenal self exempt from the natural world and "conditions of existence."

Once Kant's conceptions of a trans-phenomenal reality-in-itself and a free noumenal self are put in question, Nietzsche believes, then philosophically inclined thinkers begin to believe that this world, the temporal and spatial world in which all our knowledge is "conditioned" by our senses, our inherited categories, our intuitions of space and time, and our psychology, has lost the foundations of its value. Hence, the emergence of a philosophical mode of nihilism.

The postulation of a realm of things-in-themselves supports the metaphysical impulse to seek a true reality and denigrates this world as merely apparent. The outcome of this tendency is to think that "our apparent world, being so plainly not the expression of this ideal, cannot be 'true'."[28] Again and again, Kant's basic concepts and especially the notion of things-in-themselves are criticized for their undermining of our "humanized" world. In effect, Kant is attacked because he did not, as Zarathustra demands, "remain faithful to the earth." His restriction of knowledge to a world of phenomena plus the idea that there is an inaccessible reality-in-itself encouraged a belief in a trans-phenomenal "reality."

There is an irony in Nietzsche's attacks upon the notion of things-in-themselves in that he is haunted, in his own imaginative attempt to disclose the underlying dynamics of actuality, by the question of a reality that eludes linguistic description and conceptualization. As we shall see in subsequent discussions, Nietzsche claims that we are acquainted with process, change, and a "world of becoming" through our sensory experience and are supported in this awareness by the scientific evidence that discloses a world in constant, dynamic flux. However, when he puts forward his "interpretation" and "hypothesis" of a universal will to power, despite his efforts to suggest that this is a metaphorical image of reality and not a dogmatic metaphysical claim to knowledge of such a reality, he seems to fall prey to his own version of an unknowable reality-in-itself.

Nietzsche raises pointed questions about Kant's project in the *Critique of Pure Reason* when he calls attention to Kant's belief in "the fact of knowledge"[29] and to the paradox of claiming to possess "knowledge of knowledge" in a work that seeks to delimit the range of human knowledge. There is indeed a certain optimism expressed by Kant in his critical project. He remarks that,

> I am concerned with nothing except reason itself and its pure thinking; and to gain complete knowledge of these, there is no need to go far afield, since I come upon them in my own self.[30]

Moreover, Kant assumes that his analysis of knowledge is not merely hypothetical or provisional, but is necessary, *a priori*. After telling us that he wants to avoid mere "hypotheses," Kant contends that

> any knowledge that professes to hold *a priori* makes a claim to be regarded as absolutely necessary. This applies *a fortiori* to any determination of all pure *a priori* knowledge, since such determination has to serve as the measure and, therefore, as the example of all apodictic, philosophical certainty.[31]

Nietzsche construes Kant's confidence in his project as based upon belief insofar as he holds that judgments are expressions of belief that such-and-such is the case. In the manner of Hume, Nietzsche maintains that belief in the truth of judgments is a psychological question. The presuppositions of logic that inform meaningful judgments are not, he contends, "forms of knowledge." Rather, they are "regulative articles of belief." These are derived from psychistic fictions or from the selective simplifications that are operative in sensory experience. Judgments not only are fundamentally expressions of "belief," but they assume that "identical cases exist." And this assumption, in turn, is traceable to the putative sameness of sensory phenomena that are similar.

Nietzsche maintains that the primitive awareness of similar, familiar sensations occurs within sensation itself and, hence, even before a judgment is made, "the process of assimilation must already have taken place. . . . there is an intellectual activity that does not enter consciousness."[32] This note from the late 1880s is a reprise of a view he put forward much earlier—that is, that in all acts of cognitive judgment there is operative an unconscious activity of what he once called the primal intellect, or *Urintellekt*.

By focusing on the unconscious cognitive processes that he assumes are operative in sensation and perception, Nietzsche is seeking to undermine the Kantian conception of a "pure" knowing consciousness and what he characterizes as the doctrine of "immaculate perception." The *a priori*, he thinks, is not operative in pure reason or pure understanding, but arises out of sensory experience. This, of course, is an echo of Lange's earlier notion of the inductive origin of the *a priori*. But Nietzsche adds an additional feature to this critique of Kant's account of knowledge by insisting that there is an unconscious *a priori* that is preserved in concepts and language, one which has emerged out of man's evolutionary development. That is, the language of perceptual and conceptual knowledge already contains the sedimentations of the perceptual and conceptual distinctions that our ancestors unconsciously acquired. And we have inherited these.

In order for Nietzsche to attack Kant on these grounds, he must claim for himself a great deal of knowledge about the origins of human knowledge. He does so primarily on the basis of an evolutionary epistemology that depends, in large part, upon the Darwinian theory of evolution and secondarily on his analysis of the "family resemblance" between basic conceptions preserved in Indo-European languages. In a letter in which he mentions Paul Deussen, one of the leading Indologists of the nineteenth century, he noted how many similarities to ideas of Kant he found in Deussen's discussion of themes in Indian philosophy.[33] And in *Beyond Good and Evil* he calls attention to the dominance of certain "grammatical functions" shared by similar languages.[34] Insights such as these, in coordination with his conception of the unconscious intellection functioning in sensation and perception, are the foundation of many of his criticisms of Kant. In point of fact, as we've said, Kant himself anticipates an evolutionary theory of the origin of reason (and, hence, categorical distinctions) in his *Anthropology from a Pragmatic Standpoint*.[35]

Nietzsche argues that Kant postulated the notion of a noumenal self in order to satisfy "moral-metaphysical" motives.[36] There is nothing odd about this view, since Kant makes it quite clear that he posits a noumenal self at least in part in order to preserve the assumption of human freedom.

In a long, convoluted argument Kant contends that even though we cannot know things-in-themselves, we can "think" them. If we could not make this distinction between objects as they appear to us and things-in-themselves, then we could not say that the "soul" is free. Even though we cannot know it, we can think freedom. If we could not assume that the "will is free," then the ends of morality would be negated because the "soul" would be subject to "the mechanism of nature."[37] What is peculiar here is that the "free soul" is referred to as a "thing-in-itself." But what is this "thing" that is not subject to causality and is in relation to nothing else?

In notes from the late 1880s, Nietzsche extends his critique of "things-in-themselves" by analyzing the notion of a "thing." Here we find sound arguments that support his casual criticisms in his published writings. A thing existing in no relation to anything else, even the very concept of "thing," violates Kant's own stipulations concerning knowledge insofar as he makes of something that cannot be an object of knowledge something that is thought of as having the characteristics of an object insofar as it is designated a "thing." Nietzsche argues that there are no "things" (i.e., the idea of an independent entity that has a static mode of being is a theoretical fiction) and, consequently, no *thing*-in-itself. The notion of a "thing" apart from our "constitution" of it would be a mysterious one. Finally, the very idea of a "thing" incorporates the category of substance and suggests something subject to causality even though this "thing" (in-itself) exists outside time and space! In sum, Nietzsche holds that "the psychological derivation of the belief in things forbids us to speak of 'things-in-themselves'."[38]

In his critique of the concept of things-in-themselves, Nietzsche seeks to use Kant's restriction of knowledge to "objects" or phenomena against him and, at the same time, appeals to his thesis that the idea of "thing" is a psychistic fiction. Since he labors over this critical point, it is appropriate for us to consider his analysis of the origin of the concept of "thing."

In his criticism of the use of the concept "thing," Nietzsche seems to have in mind the fact that the German word *Ding* originally meant a meeting or assembly. Presumably, the use of this term in philosophical discourse served to designate a collection or "assembly" of qualities or properties. However, over time the term "thing" came to refer to something independent that has qualities. In effect, it came to be used to refer to something isolated and independent that was, more or less, a substantial object. As such, Nietzsche describes it as a psychistic or regulative "fiction." This analysis of the origin of the meaning of a "thing" as an independent object leads into the heart of Nietzsche's sustained analysis of conceptual fictions.

The idea of a unitary, self-identical "thing" is modeled on an equally fictional notion of a subject or an "ego" that is construed as an atomic, unitary being. We transfer this false conception of a unitary ego to entities encountered in experience and designate them as "things." If, as Nietzsche counsels, we surrender our belief in an "effective subject" or ego, then we should also renounce the idea of separate things acting upon one another in causal relations. As a consequence, the paradoxical notion of a "thing-in-itself" would be relinquished because we have deleted the concept of "subjects-in-themselves." If we hold that the conception of a unitary, independent subject is a fiction, then the notion of an objective "thing" is equally fictional. And if there are no things, then, *a fortiori*, there are no things-in-themselves either. This, in turn, would allow us to negate the deleterious notion of a distinction between appearances and things-in-themselves. We will come to see that the so-called "apparent world" (the world in which we live and have our being) is the "true world"[39] and the previously elevated transcendental "true world" that lies beyond or behind our experiences and knowledge will be erased from our thought. The world we know, insofar as we do know it, is a world "for us" that is "true for us" in the sense that we survive in it, function in it, and master it by virtue of our functional knowledge.

Unsatisfied that he has dispatched the ghost of things-in-themselves, Nietzsche mounts yet another argument against this notion. Presenting an analogy between "facts in themselves" and Kantian things-in-themselves, he contends that, against the nineteenth-century positivists, there are no pure, uninterpreted facts. Rather, there are only "interpretations" of selected phenomena that are then facts *for us*.

We do not discover any "facts-in-themselves" because we cannot even refer to such "facts" apart from our subjective constitution of them or our interpretation of them.[40] The supposition of a thing-in-itself is as unjustified as is the assumption of facts-in-themselves or, for that matter, a meaning-in-itself. The meaning of a fact lies in our interpretation of it. So, there can be no facts-in-themselves because we project meaning onto the phenomena before we designate them as facts. This imposition of meaning on selected phenomena we experience originates from a specific perspective. Before Husserl, Nietzsche emphasized the meaning-giving and intentional nature of our recognition of, and selection of, facts. The difference is, however, that it is not a transcendental consciousness that imposes meaning on its *noema*, but it is the psychistic and organic being of a complex individual who interprets phenomena from his or her perspectival "optics" of life in the context of specific "conditions of existence."

If there are no "given" facts, then it is also the case that there are no given or hidden things or things-in-themselves.[41] For purposes of simplification and rapid communication we may speak of "things" as a useful fiction which has instrumental value. However, the belief that things have a constitution "in themselves" is a false belief since they have no such constitution apart from "interpretation and subjectivity." This would falsely "presuppose that interpretation and subjectivity are not essential, that a thing freed from all relationships would still be a thing."[42]

Nietzsche further argues that the "distinction between the thing-in-itself and the thing-for-us is based upon the older, naive form of perception" that assumed that there is "force" in things. But it is now seen that "force" is projected into "things" which are construed as substances that act upon or "affect" a subject. Seemingly following Hume, but going beyond him,

Nietzsche claims that this equation of "thing" and "substance" does not pertain to any essential feature of phenomena. Neither thing nor substance refer to any genuine ontological realities. These ideas have been inherited from the past and are preserved in "language."[43] The sedimentation of past beliefs and the nature of grammar have given rise to the idea of substance. The conceptions of substance and thing are regulative fictions derived from an analogy to the self (as substance, as subject). Even though such concepts have a proper use in imprecise language and are pragmatically useful, they refer to nothing that has ontological reality.

Kant had said that our knowledge is restricted to phenomena that are constituted by our specific mode of sensibility, our categorical understanding, and our *a priori* intuitions of space and time. Taking his cue from Lange, Nietzsche accepts the general view that the phenomenal world is the "product of our organization," but adds that our psychology enters into our knowledge of the world. Even though he insists upon the important role that our senses (and our psychology) play in our knowledge, emphasizes our psychic importations into experience, and takes seriously the reality of the body, he sometimes approaches idealism.[44] For the phenomenal world is our construct and it exists *for* us.

Although he believes that we are continually responding to stimuli or effects that are external to us, Nietzsche's commitment to phenomenalism seems to preclude any claim to have access to a trans-phenomenal "reality." Since he also insists that the "inner world" is phenomenal too, insofar as the same interpretive process we apply to external phenomena is operative in our attempt to understand our own states of being, he seems to have cut himself off from any knowledge of trans-phenomenal actuality.

The world structured by our senses, our inherited basic concepts, our inherited language, and our "psychology" is a world that exists for us—is, in fact, the only world we can know. It is an elaborate constructive falsification built with categories that are characterized as "fictions" or "inventions." Despite his attack on the idea of things-in-themselves, despite his unfair criticisms of Kant, Nietzsche continues to think within the framework of Kantian categories of the understanding. He says often enough that such categories are practically useful fictions and admits that they may be *necessary* for the preservation of the species.[45] At one point, he grants that *a priori* truths are "provisional assumptions" that have practical utility. And the concept of causality, in the manner of Hume, is considered as a "habit of belief" that we, as a species, adopted in order not to perish.[46]

Concluding that Kant did not offer a satisfactory account of the origin of *a priori* categories, Nietzsche repeatedly seeks to proffer his own version of their origin. His most succinct claim is that "our categories of reason are of sensual origin: derived from the empirical world."[47] What has to be added to this is that this empirical world is itself an already-constructed world on which our instincts, our organic needs, our selective perception, our language, and our psychology have been at work. And, as his scattered remarks on knowledge, both in his notes and in his published works, indicate, the genitive plural pronoun does not only refer to ourselves, but to our ancestors who survived in their environment and reproduced.

Nietzsche seeks the "necessity" of the categorical scheme in Kant's thought not in a transcendental deduction of the categories, but in its practical utility, a utility that has evolved over time. He presents his views concerning why the Kantian categories of the understanding have come to be dominant ways of organizing our experience of the world. The phenomenal world he refers to so often is essentially the world according to Kant minus things-in-themselves. Thus, he contends that "the world with which we are concerned is false, i.e., is not a fact, but a fable and approximation on the basis of a meager sum of observations."[48] This is a world comprised of selective, limited observations that are subsumed under Kantian categorical determinations. Our knowledge of such a world extends only up to the point at which it is useful for the preservation and continuation of the species, as well as for our "mastery" of it.

It is Nietzsche's intuition of actuality as flux, as a constant process of "becoming" (in coordination with the scientific evidence for, and theoretical representation of, a dynamic, impermanent sequence of events that are unobservable in ordinary perception and elude our common-sense concepts) that is the basis of his emphasis upon the approximate, if not false, construction of the phenomenal world.

Nietzsche more or less accepts the Kantian restriction of knowledge to phenomena or objects that are constituted by our senses and our cognitive-linguistic scheme. But he denies that there is "pure" knowledge and offers an alternative interpretation of the process of coming-to-know. He agrees that when Kant says "reason does not derive its laws from nature but prescribes them to nature," he is putting forward a conception of nature that is "completely true."[49]

Since all knowledge acquired by man's "knowledge drive" is construed as ultimately a kind of practical knowledge, it is natural for Nietzsche to interpret all of Kant's categories as hypothetical notions, as conceptual fictions. His skeptical orientation leads him to view the constituent principles of Kant in light of his regulative principles of reason in what may be called his inchoate philosophy of "as-if." Having absorbed a conventionalist understanding of basic scientific conceptions, he interprets Kant's delineation of knowledge in terms of a conventionalist conception of philosophical determinations of knowledge. The categories are not pure *a priori* classifications of our experience insofar as they have a history, and insofar as they are reflections of an evolved way of thinking that has proved highly beneficial in the service of life and our interests.

Having been developed and preserved by generations of thinkers, our basic philosophical categories (that Kant, among others, has made canonical) have come to be understood as *a priori*. But what is designated as *a priori*, Nietzsche insists, has evolved out of centuries of human experience. This is what he means when he says that they have their origin in experience.

The "falsification" of actuality that has entered into our knowledge of the phenomenal world was not created by Kant, but occurred long before Kant formulated and gave philosophical sanction to it. Conceptions such as "unity," "cause," "substance," "accident," "thing," and "object" are useful fictions that have been transmitted to us precisely because of their serviceability. If we accept Nietzsche's emphasis upon the creative, constructive, and inventive nature of knowledge, and if we grant the fictional nature of our inherited philosophical categories, then we can understand why he says that our knowledge entails a falsification of actuality. He is assuming, among other things, a history of epistemology that has evolved over a long period of time but whose origination has been obscured by time and linguistic habits.

If we hold Nietzsche to the phenomenalism he often seems to adopt, then the world interpreted from the perspective of our species, the world organized in terms of fundamental categories, shaped by the limitations, "coarseness," and selective nature of our senses, suffused with beliefs derived from our psychology (as well as that of earlier human beings), is the only world we *can* know.

If, as Nietzsche says, the world of appearance is reality for us, then he is inhibited in his efforts to contrast the world constructed by us to a realm of fluctuating becoming that eludes our knowledge. Does he not fall into the Kantian stance that projects a reality-in-itself that is inaccessible to us? Even though Nietzsche accepts, at times, the phenomenalistic restriction of knowledge to an apparent world and even acknowledges that it is true for us, this is not a typical attitude. Thus, as a case in point, he maintains that appearance belongs to reality and is, in fact, a form of its being. That is, a "calculable world of identical cases" is said to be created through appearances. "Appearance," then, "is an arranged and simplified world, at which our practical instincts have been at work; it is perfectly true for us; that is to say, we live, we are able to live in it; proof of its truth for us."[50] But the problem is that he is unsatisfied with this conception of anthropomorphic truth. He seeks to penetrate the phenomenal world of appearances in order to disclose the trans-phenomenal nature of becoming.

Nietzsche insists that knowledge entails falsification for a number of reasons. Our senses select out of a panorama of possible sensations and perceptions a limited range of stimuli. Our intellect functions with symbols, metaphors, images, and rhetorical figures. Our abstract ideas are economical simplifications, "coarse metaphors."[51] The accumulated tropes of natural languages, the metaphysical distinctions preserved in language, all of the inherited and culturally reinforced habits of thought embodied in language infiltrate our conception of the world.

> Partial permanency, relative bodies, identical events—with these we falsify the true state of affairs; but it would be impossible to have knowledge of anything without having falsified it in this way.[52]

What is peculiar here is that Nietzsche has already presented plausible arguments in support of the general notion that the process of knowing is a conditioning process in which the factors previously mentioned transform what is there and, to that extent, he does not have to refer to a supposed "true state of affairs" to support his skepticism. By virtue of his very conception of knowledge he cannot consistently refer to a true state of affairs.

If Nietzsche held fast to his position that the phenomenal world is an apparent world that is "true" for us, but has no absolute, independent reality, he would at least have defended a consistent phenomenalism. By claiming that there is an authentic reality that is quite unlike our world of phenomena, he violates his own strictures on knowledge and generates a paradox.

The postulation of a dynamic, fluctuating process as a reality inaccessible to our senses, transcendent to our categorical determinations, and indescribable in language, reproduces a variation on Kant's conception of things-in-themselves. But this technical difference does not help Nietzsche's case. If we hold him to his own critical analysis of knowledge, then he has effectively prohibited any legitimate claim to *know* that there is a trans-phenomenal realm of becoming or that it is, as he sometimes says, "indescribably complex."

A reasonable consistency would prevail if Nietzsche had held that the world of phenomena that we know is a constructed world, one created out of all the factors we've indicated, a world that is not reality and not "true" in any strong sense of the term. In the interest of consistency, Nietzsche should have retained an agnosticism about any putative trans-phenomenal realm. Since such a domain is said to elude conceptualization and linguistic description, he should have adopted a Wittgensteinian stance and said that "whereof one cannot speak, one must be silent."

In *Human, All-Too-Human*, Nietzsche admitted that a "metaphysical world" is logically possible even though "nothing could be said of it."[53] Subsequently, he waged linguistic warfare against the idea of another world, a "true world," beyond this one. It is not so much that he is exclusively concerned with rejecting knowledge or claims to truth about the

Kantian thing-in-itself or any correspondence to it.[54] Although it is true that he wants to preserve "empirical knowledge," this is misleading if it is taken to mean that Nietzsche simply uncritically embraces the domain of empirical facts. Although in his *soi-disant* positivistic phase he does praise the strict methods of the exact sciences and admires the restraint of attending to "small, unapparent truths," he is skeptical about the scientific world-picture and thinks of it as a valuable, but not exclusive, perspective on knowledge. He approaches the theories and concepts of the sciences in a manner similar to his approach to the categories elucidated by Kant.

Remembering what Kant had said about our "prescription" of *a priori* laws "to nature," Nietzsche remarks that it is "our laws and our conformity to laws that we read into the world of phenomena." The presuppositions of mechanics are considered as ideal inventions or "fictions" that serve to make the natural order intelligible to us.[55] The assumption of the existence of bodies, surfaces, and lines is a reflection in scientific discourse of our belief "that there are substances and things and permanency. Just as certainly as our concepts are inventions, so certainly are the constructs of mathematics inventions."[56]

The sciences operate with "regulative hypotheses," "regulative principles of method," theoretical posits and provisional assumptions. The "ideal, regulative method" of the sciences is as much based upon "regulative fictions" as is the philosophical (i.e., Kantian) organization of the world. There is an element of anthropomorphic projection in scientific discourse just as anthropomorphism haunts philosophical principles and conceptions. We find nothing in the external world, Nietzsche maintains in the spirit of the eighteenth-century natural scientist Georg Lichtenberg, except what we have already projected there; and we call this conceptualized knowledge "science." It is not the case, despite his admiration for the exact sciences, that Nietzsche came to believe that the sciences give us access to the "true" world. Although he certainly ranked scientific knowledge far above the "conceptual poetry" of metaphysical speculation, he did not equate "empirical knowledge" with perfect, veridical knowledge.

Having anticipated Vaihinger's theory of conceptual fictions, as well as some aspects of Poincaré's conventionalist interpretation of scientific knowledge, Nietzsche could have remained ensconced in the security of a radical phenomenalism. But he was tempted to look behind the phenomenal world—under the influence of Heraclitus, Lange, the Buddhist doctrine of *anicca* (impermanence), and, ironically, the dynamic theory of nature emerging in physics—to disclose the process nature of actuality. Influenced by the emerging view that neither in experience nor scientific investigation do we encounter a "fixed and independent" reality, but only a "world of relations," Nietzsche postulated a dynamic process of becoming that eludes cognitive-linguistic description. Even our senses cannot grasp becoming as becoming because of the "synthetic, creative factor of our knowledge" that pervades our "sense-impressions." Committed to the view that "our sense organs are organs of abstractions," Nietzsche generates internal problems in his critical analysis of knowledge.

Nietzsche repeatedly assumes a knowledge of "becoming," an awareness of an actuality that eludes our "coarse" (and abstracting) senses and our understanding. Our interpretive understanding of the world is a projection of "meaning" into a domain that "is in flux, incomprehensible, elusive."[57] The world that we describe and refer to in terms of categorical schemata, the world with which we are acquainted though our selective and limited senses, is a "simplification for practical ends." "The character of the world," Nietzsche insists,

> is in a state of becoming as incapable of formulation. . . . Knowledge and becoming exclude one another. Consequently, "knowledge" must be something else: there must first of all be a will to make knowable.[58]

In a post-Kantian spirit, Nietzsche emphasizes the active, organizing, creative, and synthesizing process of knowing that imposes "being" on a fluctuating actuality. In terms of his critique of and reformulation of knowledge, he cannot consistently claim to know that there is a trans-phenomenal process of becoming. This would be a trans-phenomenal, temporal sequence of occurrences that is presumably unaffected by our senses, our psychic importations, or our conceptual fictions. Furthermore, how can this actuality be known to be a "relations-world" or something in constant dynamic motion? "A world in a state of becoming," Nietzsche writes, "could not, in a strict sense, be 'comprehended' or 'known'."[59] But that there is such a "world of becoming" he frequently asserts. Despite his criticisms of metaphysical theories of reality, Nietzsche projects a process theory of actuality and reminds himself to think of entities as processes.[60]

What is called "processes" in the *Nachlass* corresponds to the image of nature as "chaos" in *The Gay Science*. Neither logic nor language is able to express the chaos of becoming. It is "our inevitable need to preserve ourselves" that leads us "to posit a crude world of stability."[61] The repeated emphasis upon the practical function of knowledge coincides with an evolutionary theory of knowledge to which Nietzsche often appeals.

What is rarely noticed, however, is that the positive knowledge-claims that are made about the chaotic, absolute flux are not based upon metaphysical conceptions of reality such as those of Heraclitus or Buddhist thought. Rather, they typically rely upon the dynamic "world-picture" emerging in physical scientific theories. From F. A. Lange and many eighteenth- and nineteenth-century scientists, Nietzsche learned to think of the natural world as a dynamic system of interacting "forces," an "atomistic chaos," a "sub-atomic" field of attractive and repulsive forces. Although he approaches scientific theory and its theoretical posits in a conventionalist manner, Nietzsche also employs the process theory of nature implied by the sciences against common sense realism and the cognitive-linguistic schema that lend support to it. Thus, to cite one of many instances in which he tentatively adopts a physical scientific standpoint in order to undermine our faith in our senses, he claims that what we perceive through our "coarse senses" as a solid and impenetrable mountain would be seen as a dancing chaos of elements if our senses were finer.[62] What he is doing, in this instance, is provisionally assuming the "truth" of the physical theoretical interpretation of matter in order to indicate the limitations and restrictions of our inherited sensory modalities, our commonsense "knowledge."

Despite his harsh comments on Kant, Nietzsche more or less accepts Kant's general conception of knowledge as construction and accepts the known world of phenomena as functionally valid for us. What is added to the construction of a world of phenomena is the influence of our psychology on our sensory and conceptual activities, the evolution of categories of the understanding, and metaphorical tropes that are preserved in our language and thought. And despite his criticisms of the notion of things-in-themselves, Nietzsche does not manage to extricate himself from a distinction between an apparent world of phenomena that we know and what may be characterized as a becoming-in-itself that, strictly speaking, can neither be described nor known.

It is his adoption of a conventionalist interpretation of scientific theories and entities that prevents Nietzsche from seeking to resolve the problem of things-in-themselves as Peter F. Strawson tries to do. Strawson grants to Kant that to a being that is a member of "the world of science and everyday observation the spatio-temporal objects of that world can sensibly appear only by *affecting* in some way the constitution of that being." Furthermore, the way that objects appear, the characteristics they appear to have, certainly depend "in part upon the constitution of the being to which they appear."[63] At least in part, "our physiological make-up" conditions the phenomena that appear to us. However, Strawson argues that, in a sense, we do know what things are in themselves insofar as these are objects that have the properties ascribed to them "in physical theories" or "physiological theories."[64]

The problem with this attempt to obviate the notion of things-in-themselves is that it goes against the grain of Kant's analysis of experience and knowledge. The objects of scientific knowledge are constituted precisely in the way as are all other common objects of knowledge. The "properties" that scientists ascribe to objects within a theoretical framework are not exceptions to Kant's analysis of "the laws of experience."

Thus, Strawson's endeavor to avoid the problem of things-in-themselves depends upon a scientific realism that the structure of Kant's account of knowledge does not accommodate. In the *Critique of Pure Reason* Kant argues that "the order and regularity in the appearances, which we entitle nature, we ourselves introduce. We could never find them in appearance, had not we ourselves, or the nature of our mind, originally set them there."[65] Clearly this conception of our understanding of the natural world includes the scientific study of nature and thereby blocks the way, within a general Kantian framework, to any defense of the pure objectivity of the scientific account of nature, of objects, and of their properties.

Since Strawson is sympathetic to so many aspects of Kant's analysis of knowledge and grants the contribution that our sensory system makes to the phenomenal appearances we experience, it is difficult for him to eliminate the problem of things-in-themselves by appealing to a scientific realism that is ultimately incompatible with Kant's thought.

From the early 1870s to the late 1880s, Nietzsche continually showed his preoccupation with epistemological questions that issued out of the *Critique of Pure Reason*. In general, he interpreted Kant's thought in terms of the conditioning effects that our psychophysical "organization" and our categorical scheme have on what we come to know. His emphasis on the metaphorical aspects of natural languages added an additional agnostic dimension to his epistemic skepticism.

Relying on his studies of a variety of scientists and early philosophers of science, he embraced a conventionalist theory of philosophical and scientific concepts and anticipated Vaihinger's theory of fictions, emphasizing the pragmatic usefulness of such conceptual fictions. The phenomenal world of common sense, which he considers a creative, inventive "falsification" of actuality, is fundamentally the world understood in terms of Kant's categories of the understanding and his account of "sensibility" or sensory experience.

Nietzsche's initial post-Kantian agnosticism about ultimate reality (with the exception of his temporary, nondogmatic defense of an artists' metaphysics in *The Birth of Tragedy* put forward as a species of "Jesuitism") is later replaced by his own intuitions and his acceptance of the Heraclitus-Langean-Buddhist theory of "becoming"—a process theory that was buttressed by his grasp of dynamic theories of nature in then-contemporary physics. His "genesisiology" is put forward on the basis of the confluence of a number of interpretations that depicted actuality as a dynamic, unceasing flux.

Even though he characterized metaphysics as conceptual poetry, Nietzsche defends a process theory of reality that entails knowledge of immanent, exceedingly complex, dialectical, interactive relations. He has avoided transcendental metaphysics (e.g., Platonism and Hegelianism), but has embraced an immanent theory of actuality that reduces it to an "absolute flux" in which there are no "identical cases," no self-identical entities. Insofar as he precludes knowledge, in any strict sense, of this fluctuating, chaotic process, he has, as we've said, retained something analogous to Kant's things-in-themselves: a process-in-itself or a becoming-in-itself.

What complicates his critique of knowledge is that he often derives a process theory of actuality from scientific theories of the dynamic constituents of entities and the complex interaction of "forces." In such instances he appears to accept a realist interpretation of the "world-picture" of the natural sciences at least in a provisional way. He tends to adopt this perspective in order to highlight the falsity of common sense and traditional philosophical conceptions of reality. Coeval with the adoption of this perspective, he undermines it by arguing for the conventionalist nature of scientific theory and scientific posits, thereby defending a version of theoretical antirealism. Perhaps the *rationale* for this is closely related to the attempt to give a human meaning to the de-anthropomorphic world-interpretation of the natural scientists that he often discloses.[66] This is a question that will have to be explored in subsequent discussions.

Chapter Three

A Dynamic Theory of Nature

> Like geometry each scientific theory is our own, human.
>
> R. J. Boscovich, *Theory of Natural Philosophy*

Although interpretations of Nietzsche's philosophy often allude to the theory of nature propounded by the Serbo-Croatian physical theorist Roger Boscovich,[1] there have been few attempts (until recently) to see whether there is a strong relationship between Boscovich's theoretical physics and what has sometimes been called Nietzsche's "cosmology" or "physics." In addition, the close relationship between central conceptions in dynamic theories of nature and Nietzsche's conception of the will to power has not often been explored.[2] Although Nietzsche rarely refers to Boscovich by name, the enthusiasm he expresses for his theory of nature finds its way into remarks in *Beyond Good and Evil* and occasionally in his notes.

Boscovich's *Theory of Natural Philosophy* anticipated a number of themes in twentieth-century physical theory. Working against the background of the triumph of Newtonian mechanics, Boscovich challenged some of its key principles. And he developed an imaginative theory of matter that anticipated and provided the groundwork for a field theory of physical action.[3] On the basis of his study of bodies in collision, Boscovich formulated a theory of the structure of matter that postulated dimensionless, indivisible "points of force."

Boscovich focused upon themes that came to fruition only in the general theory of relativity and quantum physics. He regarded Newton's system as a generally accurate description of the universe, but held that the law of gravitation was a "classical limit" that was approximately accurate as applied to extensive distances. He maintained, however, that for phenomena of atomic size Newton's classical law was insufficient. At the atomic level forces of attraction are replaced by continuous oscillations between both attractive and repulsive physical forces.

The development of the idea of a pervasive "will to power" present in all dynamic entities can be traced, in Nietzsche's thought, from his critical insight into the psychological drive for power over others as a kind of overcompensation for feelings of inferiority or as an expression of *ressentiment* to his empirically derived assumption that there is a biophysiological drive to master an environment or strive for dominance.

Later, as a thought-experiment, he extends his principle of explanation "to the universe *simpliciter*."[4] This projection of the theory of the will to power into the world *in toto* has puzzled some commentators on Nietzsche's thought and has sometimes been understood as a strange, almost mystical, cosmic monism. Some claim that the notion of a universal, pervasive will to power was probably based upon empirical data. It has even been argued that the "extreme hypothesis that the will to power is the basic force of the entire universe" may have been derived from the view that "the constitution of the human mind might conceivably require it to interpret not only human behavior but the entire cosmos in terms of the will to power."[5]

Certainly, it was Nietzsche's proto-psychoanalytical observations on human behavior that led him to hold that a power drive is a central characteristic of our psychological make-up. And it is also the case that empirical data derived from biological studies suggested that, from the simplest organism (the amoeba) to the most complex, there is evidence of a striving for mastery, dominance, a *nisus* towards appropriation. The case for inorganic manifestations of power is not quite as clear as in the former instances. There is no need for speculation concerning the "constitution" of the human mind in order to explain why Nietzsche conceives of natural phenomena in terms of willing (since he tells us, in his unpublished writings, precisely why he does so). Since the basis of his rationale for adopting this view is directly related to his reactions to, and interpretations of, Boscovich's theory of nature, I will pause to discuss this issue here.

In the course of criticizing "materialistic atomism" in *Beyond Good and Evil,* Nietzsche argues that such a theory is retained only as "an abbreviation of the means of expression." He attributes the undermining of materialism to Boscovich. For it was he, according to Nietzsche, who taught us to renounce our belief in the last remnant of the philosophical notion of substance: "stuff," "matter," and the "particle-atom."[6] Nietzsche discerns in Boscovich's theory of nonextended force-points not only the negation of dogmatic materialism and the undermining of the concept of physical "substances," but a valuable conceptual weapon that can be used to attack mechanistic materialism as well.

If "matter" is conceived to be composed of unextended force-points, then the concept of "solid" matter is negated and, as Nietzsche saw, "we have got rid of materiality [*Stofflichkeit*]."[7] It is this aspect of a dynamic, energistic theory of natural phenomena that attracts him to Boscovich's revolutionary physical theory. Since he first discovered the rudiments of this then-novel theory of matter in his reading of Lange's *History of Materialism* in 1866, his interest in the implications of physical theory for philosophy in general, and his own philosophy in particular, antedated his earliest major philosophical works. In this regard, then, it is an understatement to say that Nietzsche "may have had some idea of a theory of energetics."[8] For he had read Lange's report that Boscovich

> found contradictions in the doctrine of the impact of atoms, which could only be solved by supposing that the effects which are usually ascribed to the resilience of material particles are due to repulsive forces acting from a point situated in space, but without extension. These points are regarded as the elementary constituents of matter.[9]

In his earliest reflections, Nietzsche was impressed by the new conception of the physical world emerging in nineteenth-century physical theory. He was stimulated by neo-Kantian interpretations of the scientific picture of the cosmos, as well as by the unique conception of the sub-macroscopic structure of the material world found in Boscovich's eighteenth-century work. The specific aspects of this complex physical theory that impressed Nietzsche are fairly numerous and serve to elucidate much that remains somewhat obscure in his *Nachlass* and in his abbreviated references to "physics" in his major works. The most general claim made by Boscovich is that his theory reduces all of the principles of Newtonian mechanics to a single principle: the law of forces. In addition, his interpretation of the structure of matter sought to vindicate Leibniz's principle of continuity.

As a result of his study of the distortion and recovery of shape that occurs in the impact of bodies of macroscopic size, Boscovich concluded that there must have been *continuous* retarding of the relative velocity throughout the period of impact and that this retardation process was a finite one. This phenomenon confirmed Leibniz's theory of a universal continuity in physical processes. And it was Leibniz's metaphysics of nature that originally suggested the idea of force-points to Boscovich. Certainly, his concept of force-points resembles Leibniz's monads in many respects. For both are construed as entities without parts, extension, or figure. In regard to the recognition of what has been called "Nietzsche's *Monadology*,"[10] it is probable that the assertions that suggest a monadic conception of "reality" are intimately related to the Leibnizean elements preserved in Boscovich's theory of the interior dynamics of matter. Perhaps, by focusing upon Boscovich's theory of oscillating centers of force so scrupulously, Nietzsche unconsciously or inadvertently incorporated Leibnizean themes into his conception of perspectival "interpretations."

The theory that natural processes can best be understood in terms of a law of forces is closely related to the basic assumption in Boscovich's thought: that matter is composed of indivisible, nonextended, discrete points.[11] Between each elementary dyadic set of points there is a constant force that is expressed as attraction or repulsion. The postulated propensity towards recession or approach in these points is, in large-scale bodies, manifested as force or *vis matrix*. This *vis matrix* is considered as the real equivalent of "force" since it varies directly with mass. The mutual forces ascribed by Boscovich to pairs of points are actually accelerations or propensities for mutual approach or recession of two points that depend upon the distance between specific points at a given time. The "mass" of a body is the number of force-points that are combined to form a body, and force is construed as the "product" of mass and acceleration.

Boscovich argues that there are a finite number of physical points that are in dynamic relation to other such primitive elements and that are subject to finite processes of attraction and repulsion. Although the postulated dyads of points may be understood as comprising a "material" system, they are described in such a way as to suggest a dynamic *system of relations*. Boscovich's kinematic theory of the ultimate constituents of "matter" precludes, in the final analysis, anything like absolute rest.

It was the phenomenon produced by the exertion of force of one molecule upon another in direct collisions that suggested to Boscovich the elasticity of molecular structures. This, in turn, led to the presupposition of minute, elastic physical particles. By virtue of imaginative speculation, he further postulated that there must be infinitely "small" particles, elements or points that compose the interior structure of matter. Because each point acts upon, or is acted upon, similar points, or because such points influence other elementary points, point-centers were conceived of as "centers of force."[12]

Included in Boscovich's dynamics are the following central notions: that there is action at a distance; that entities differ one from the other in shape and force-potential in terms of the number of, and disposition of, the points composing them; that entities are temporal and local modes of existence; that all of the phenomena of nature are ultimately reducible to fundamental forces and the "compositions of the forces with which the particles of matter act upon one another";[13] and, finally, that the general theory of forces can be represented in a purely geometric pattern. As a corollary to the above, Boscovich contended that there cannot be any abrupt changes in velocity without a passage through intermediate velocities. This supported the assumption that there is no possibility of a change of magnitude or velocity without a transition through intermediate stages. In effect, it provided justification for Leibniz's law of continuity.[14]

Given Boscovich's theoretical description of an indefinite process of forces of attraction and repulsion, we are presented with a model of the material world as a dynamic system of forces whose external "expression" takes the form of macroscopic "bodies" or phenomena. At a sub-macroscopic level point-centers are conceived of as perpetually interacting in terms of action and reaction or an oscillation between attractive and repulsive forces.

As if his dynamic, kinematic theory of natural processes were not original enough, Boscovich suggested that there is no absolute space. He contends that each material point exists in two real modes of existence, one pertaining to space and the other to time. These modes of existence are "produced" and eventually perish. And they are the basis for all actual relations of distance. Distance is characterized as *either* a spatial or "local" relation between two points or as a "temporal relation between two events."[15]

Having insisted upon the "analogy" of space and time, as well as upon the relative determination of distances of actual or hypothetical material points, Boscovich concludes that his theory of forces excludes both "rest" and absolute spatial location. Because the forces that connect points of matter are constantly changing, we are not able to have a direct knowledge of "absolute distances." Therefore, we are unable to "compare them with one another by a common standard."[16] The rationale for denying both "rest" and absolute spatial location involves an assumption that Nietzsche could not accept—that is, that the forces which emanate from material points are continually changing because no single material point ever returns "to the same point of position in which that point of matter once was situated."[17] This claim runs counter to Nietzsche's conception of the eternal recurrence of the same. For it entails the notion that—expressed in the language of Boscovich's physics—each particular material point or constellation of points can return to its original position or state.[18]

Although *A Theory of Natural Philosophy* is rich in original insights, it is not necessary, for our purposes, to deal with every specific aspect of Boscovich's theory. Before turning to a discussion of the influence that this theory of dynamically interacting force-centers had on Nietzsche's "later" philosophy, it may be mentioned that there is no reason to assume that the notes comprising the *Nachlass* "represent hypotheses which Nietzsche abandoned" or that the unpublished notes (written between 1882 and 1888) do not contain ideas that Nietzsche espoused.[19] For, as we've seen, he was fascinated by physical theories and their philosophical implications as early as 1866, six years before the publication of his first major work, *The Birth of Tragedy*. In the 1870s and into the 1880s Nietzsche continued to read a variety of scientific thinkers: Robert Mayer, one of the formulators of the theory of the conservation of energy; Johann Zoellner, the astronomer and physicist; Emil Du-Bois Reymond, the philosophical physiologist; Ernst Mach, the physicist and early philosopher of science; Boscovich once more; and others who were proto-philosophers of science. He invariably searched out the implications of science and their meaning for philosophy. Nietzsche's thought in his "later" unpublished writings marked a *return* to scientific issues. Naturally, he criticizes theories or modifies them from different philosophical perspectives, utilizes them, entertains or rejects various hypothetical notions, and engages in a free-wheeling mode of philosophy of science *avant le nom.*

In *Beyond Good and Evil* Nietzsche praises the work of Boscovich and Copernicus. Both are described as successful enemies of "what meets the eye."

> Whereas Copernicus had to persuade us to believe, contrary to all our senses, that the earth *did not* stand still, Boscovich taught us to disavow the final "fixed" thing in regard to the earth—the belief in material "stuff," in "matter," in the little residual earthly clump atom. This was the greatest triumph over the senses that was ever achieved on earth.[20]

Boscovich's theory of the structure of "matter" not only transcends the picture of the world based upon sensory experience, but it also undermines mechanism and previous forms of materialistic atomism. Nietzsche criticizes central claims of Boscovich but, at the same time, reinterprets and incorporates the dynamic notion of force-points into his "hypothesis" of *der Wille zur Macht.* In doing so, he applies his theory of perspectivalism to the central postulations of Boscovich's physical theory. Nietzsche argues that the "physicists" left something out of their "world picture." What was left out was

> precisely this necessary perspectivalism by virtue of which every center of force—and not only man—construes all the rest of the world from its own viewpoint, i.e., measures, feels, forms, according to its own force.[21]

Appealing to Boscovich's conception of centers of force, Nietzsche argues that physicists—including Boscovich—did not see that (1) man is not an exception to their general theory and that (2) their interpretation of the "internal" structure of "reality" suggested a mode of perspectivalism. As always, it is the *philosophical implications* of physical theory that fascinate Nietzsche, not the "truth" of the theory. Both metaphysics and physical theory are shaped by our language, our sensory experience, our psychological propensities, and our conceptual schema. And, to this extent, anthropomorphism is an ineluctable feature of thought in any universe of discourse.

The complex interaction between the thought of Boscovich and Nietzsche's transformation of it is apparent in Nietzsche's criticisms of "mechanism." He argues that mechanism no longer claims to explain events, but seeks only to describe sequences of phenomena. Newtonian mechanics is gradually being replaced by "the dynamic interpretation of the world" that conceives of "matter" primarily in terms of *dynamis*, potentiality, power or energy.[22] Nietzsche champions these tendencies in physical theory and is especially impressed by the conception of elementary "force-centers" or what he characterizes as *Machtquanten* or "power-quanta."

Universalizing Boscovich's insights into the structure of "matter," Nietzsche claims that it is the multiplicity of dynamic centers of force interacting through "cooperation" or conflict that makes up the universal, fluctuating process of "becoming." In the language of Boscovich, he describes "all events, all motion, all becoming, as a determination of degrees and relations of force."[23] He obviously appropriates, from Boscovich's original mathematical theory, his conception of nonperceptible, nonextended power units or force-centers that manifest their "power" in and through their effects. In addition, each power-center is conceived of as the sum of its effects and its relationships with other power-centers.

Each relation of force is construed as manifesting through its effects or actions varying amounts of power, as a dynamic unity or oscillating center of activity. The "external world," then, is pictured as a dynamic, energistic system of power-relations. It is not, Nietzsche insists, to be understood as a system of "objects," "things," or "substances" (insofar as these are construed as conceptual or psychological "fictions") in causal relationship.[24] It is quite correct that this "dynamic theory of matter" that conceives of matter as "consisting of point-centres" that interact with other centers and that "consists exclusively of the actions of these forces" is a theory that "had a very strong attraction for philosophic minds." However, it had far more attraction for Nietzsche than it did for other thinkers who have sometimes been associated with it.[25]

If Nietzsche were a less self-consciously critical thinker, he might have been satisfied that he had arrived at a "monistic metaphysics" and had characterized the ultimate nature of reality as an infinitely complex, continually changing dynamic process that is comprised of force or energy manifested in action and reaction, attraction and repulsion. Like other process philosophers whom he so closely resembles, he could have derived from an energistic theory of nature a metaphysics that claimed to have discovered the ultimate nature of reality or "the ultimate explanatory principle for entities constituting the world."[26]

Why does Nietzsche turn the screw of his philosophical reflections one more notch? Why, in other words, does he proclaim that it is not a "denatured" force, power, or energy that is ultimate reality, but a pervasive "will to power"? Is it, as Kaufmann suggested, that this "extreme hypothesis" is derived from the notion that the human mind is constituted in such a way as to "require" that it interpret not only the comportment of man, but the entire cosmos in terms of a universal will to power? Since I have already suggested that this is not the rationale for the assumption of the "hypothesis" of the will to power, I will offer a possible answer to the question posed. It will involve a dialectical interrelationship among three fundamental themes: a critical analysis of the central conceptions of Boscovich's theory of nature; the principle of the inevitability of anthropomorphism in philosophic and scientific thought; and, finally, the critical analysis of the concept of "will."

Without recapping the details of Nietzsche's elaborate, critical analyses of truth and knowledge, the background against which we may understand his appropriation of, and transformation of, Boscovich's theory of the structure of nature may be briefly sketched. In "On Truth and Lying" Nietzsche maintained, as we've seen, that language cannot tell us anything about the way things are—cannot, we might say, "picture" the world. For, language rests upon a subtle translation of sensory impressions into images that are themselves "metaphors." Words are, in turn, "metaphors" for images. General notions or concepts are metaphors that are remote from our immediate experience because they have been purified of the uniqueness and felt immediacy of our actual experience.[27]

Any assertion that purports to describe "reality" is necessarily a distortion of what is immediately encountered in experience. The "truths" expressed in language are not known to "correspond" to any extralinguistic "reality." Rather, they express a relationship among a variety of metaphors or the customary mode in which these metaphors are used by speakers of a natural language. Nietzsche warns us not to let our freely created metaphors become petrified into conventional linguistic forms. The outcome of this preliminary analysis of language is that language cannot express or preserve "truths" about reality because it proffers simplifications and anthropomorphically colored metaphors and does not truly represent any independent actuality. Summarizing his position, Nietzsche asks: *Was ist . . . Wahrheit?* And answers that "truth" is

> a mobile army of metaphors, metonyms, and anthropomorphisms—in short, a sum of human relations, that have been enhanced, transposed, and embellished poetically and rhetorically, and which, after long use, appear to be formal, canonical, and obligatory to a people—truths are illusions of which one has forgotten that this is what they are. . . .[28]

In the *Nachlass* the Kantian "categories of the understanding" are characterized as "logical fictions" that are not "true" of anything. They are fictions that have proven useful for the preservation of the species. In *Beyond Good and Evil* Nietzsche says that the time has come to ask not how synthetic *a priori* judgments are possible, but a more basic question: why is belief in such judgments necessary? Perhaps such judgments must be believed to be true because they serve to preserve our species in existence. Perhaps we must believe that such judgments are "true" even if they are "false."[29]

Arguing that there are no separate "things" in the world (since everything is in relation to something else), Nietzsche avers that the idea of causality that assumes separate entities in a force-product relationship is not true—does not represent states of affairs in the actual world. The error we make is to reify cause and effect. We should construe them as "pure concepts" that are *konventioneller Fiktionen* ("conventional fictions") that enable us to communicate and designate sequences of phenomena.[30] Throughout his remarks Nietzsche provides pragmatic analyses of the Kantian categories, as well as of a number of primitive concepts used in philosophical discourse. He expresses his understanding of the role of logical distinctions and categorical determination in the following way:

> The aberration of philosophy is that, instead of seeing logic and the categories of reason as means toward the adjustment of the world for utilitarian ends (principally, toward an expedient falsification), one believed that one possessed in them the criterion of truth and reality. The "criterion of truth" was in fact merely the biological utility of such a system of fundamental falsification; and since a species of animals knows of nothing more important than its own preservation, one might indeed be permitted to speak here of "truth."[31]

Throughout most of his creative life, Nietzsche was fascinated by the interpretations of man and the world that he found in the natural sciences. By the time he was passing through his "positivistic" phase he toyed with the idea that science, as opposed to metaphysics and theology, might lead to an apprehension of precise, fragmentary truths that are disclosed by the "strict method" of scientific inquiry. Although adamantly opposed to the notions of "absolute truth" or "eternal truths," Nietzsche thought, for a time, that we may be able to approach actuality by means of the empirical truths of the independent sciences. It is precisely because there are so many minute, specific truths and so many different "kinds of eyes" to see them that he proclaims that "there is no Truth."[32]

Intrigued by the experimental, tentative, piecemeal approach to knowledge that he found in the sciences, Nietzsche was impressed by the apparent absence of prejudices, by the objectivity of scientific inquiry, by its apparent avoidance of "anthropomorphism." Soon, however, he began to see the metaphorical, interpretative, constructive character of the language of the sciences. Metaphysical presuppositions embedded in natural languages tend to reappear in the language of the scientist. However, the scientists who are philosophical are aware of the provisional, hypothetical, conventional nature of the language they use. Unperturbed by the increasing multiplicity of scientific theories, Nietzsche sees in the "plurality of interpretations a sign of strength."[33]

Perhaps if it were not for the dogmatic tendencies of nineteenth-century positivism, Nietzsche might have been satisfied with the application of the hypothetical, experimental style of scientific inquiry to philosophical questions. For he modeled his approach to philosophical issues upon sympathetic understanding of the techniques and methods of the scientist. "In place of fundamental truths," he said, "I put fundamental probabilities—provisionally assumed guides by which one lives and thinks."[34] As long as science retained a skeptical "conscious relativity of knowledge," he was quite sympathetic with its aims, its theoretical orientations, and its methodological variations. However, the claims to truth and "objectivity" on the part of the positivists, as well as his own recurring skepticism, led him to look upon the conceptions of the scientists—even those of favored thinkers such as Boscovich—with a jaundiced eye.

Nietzsche's critical understanding of scientific claims to truth is found in his critique of the positivists' reliance upon objective facts. Against a positivism that stops at objective phenomena, Nietzsche argues that there are no facts, "only interpretations. We cannot establish any fact 'in itself'."[35]

Granting the interpretive nature of all scientific inquiry, the mechanistic understanding of natural phenomena has an appropriate and convincing impersonal quality to it. "Mechanistic procedures" endeavor to leave out of account "reason" and "purpose" and, therefore, avoid the teleological explanations that Nietzsche repudiated. And yet, at the same time, even the mechanistic interpretation of the world retains "psychistic fictions" such as the notion of "cause" and seems, in the final analysis, to give us only designation, not comprehension.[36]

In Nietzsche's view, then, the scientific interpretations of the world are not free of metaphors, mythical notions, hypostatizations, "regulative fictions" or, in effect, the same "humanizing" propensity that he had found in the language of philosophy. Language, even the "abstract," sophisticated language of the sciences, simplifies, organizes, classifies, abbreviates, separates and orders the phenomena that it is used to describe. It is, in a sense, a powerful Apollonian instrument that man uses in order to form and express a "world" in which he can function and live effectively. In *Twilight of the Gods* Nietzsche says that

> In its origin language belongs in the age of the most rudimentary form of psychology. We enter a realm of crude

> fetishism when we summon before consciousness the basic presuppositions of the metaphysics of languagee . . . the presuppositions of reason.[37]

The "reason" that is expressed, preserved and conserved, in language—including the language of science—retains the diachronic accretion of psychistic and metaphysical assumptions that are used in order to attain an ostensible objective "truth." In a strict sense, Nietzsche believes, actuality as a dynamic process of becoming eludes linguistic description or elucidation. Our "means of expression" cannot express the complexity of change and it is our need for preservation that leads us to postulate "a world of stability."[38] Nietzsche persistently defends his conception of "reality" as a complex multiplicity in a constant process of becoming and proceeds to borrow from the language of physical theory in order to characterize the dynamics of "becoming."

An important question has been raised concerning Nietzsche's attempt to validate his doctrine of the "will to power" in that he repeatedly "contested the claim that science tells us anything about reality."[39] Although it is risky to try to trace the internal development of an individual's thought, I believe that Nietzsche seized upon the dynamic picture of actuality presented in Boscovich's thought (despite his criticisms of scientific claims to objective certainty) for two basic reasons. In the first place, he consistently argued that man is inseparable from nature. Because inquiries into the structure of the natural world have direct bearing upon the question of the nature of man, they have, at the very least, heuristic value. He saw the separation of man and nature as humorous: "we now laugh when we find 'Man and World' placed beside one another separated by the sublime presumption of the little word 'and'!"[40] Again, in *Human, All-Too-Human* he remarks that "we speak of Nature and, in doing so, forget ourselves: we ourselves are Nature. . . ."[41] In one of his earliest essays, *Homers Wettkampf*, he states a basic theme that is recurrent in his writings.

> When one speaks of humanity, the idea is fundamental that this is something which separates and distinguishes man from nature. In reality, however, there is no such separation: "natural" qualities and those called truly "human" are inseparably grown together. Man, in his highest and noblest capacities, is wholly nature and embodies its uncanny dual character.[42]

It would be expected, then, that a thinker committed to such an understanding of man would look to the physical sciences for indications of the nature of man or for models that may illuminate our understanding of mankind.

The second reason why Nietzsche appropriates so much of Boscovich's kinematic theory is more speculative than the first. But I believe that it has some plausibility in regard to his philosophical tendency to seek, wherever possible, analogies that stress the intimate relationship between man and nature. Boscovich's dynamic theory of "matter" seems to approximate Nietzsche's understanding of the dynamic, expressive, energistic character of man himself. In general, we are conceived of as, in the manner of Leibniz, *un être capable d'action*, a complex multiplicity of drives, propensities, and intentions.

In his psychological observations Nietzsche discerned numerous signs of power motives underlying human behavior—tendencies towards mastery, dominance, and appropriation. Given his psychologistic interpretation of thought,[43] of language, and of logic, he was attracted to a theory of nature compatible with his conception of man as a "plurality," as an oscillating center of "drives." In addition, Boscovich's conception of "matter" as composed of centers of force coincided with Nietzsche's growing conviction that *Kraft* ("Force") or *Macht* ("Power") was the pervasive characteristic of all "entities." Boscovich's theory of nature, then, provided him with an interpretation of "reality" that coincided with his psychology and his rudimentary philosophy of biology.

Aside from such reasons for the appropriation of central themes in Boscovich's thought, there is a more general factor that should be considered. Perhaps Nietzsche embraces this dynamics because it reinforces his conception of a dynamic realm of becoming that has no place for "rest." The fluctuating, kinematic image of nature in Boscovich's physical theory seems a confirmation of Nietzsche's emphases upon processes, dynamic interactions, and flux. In effect, his theory of natural processes coincides with what he had first found in Heraclitus, then in Lange and Buddhism:[44] a model of "reality" as a perpetual, impermanent, fluid process.

In *Thus Spoke Zarathustra*, Nietzsche proclaims that "it is of time and becoming that the best parables should speak: let them be a praise and a justification of all impermanence." And in *Twilight of the Gods* he condemns the "Egypticism" of philosophers who hate the idea of becoming. Praising Heraclitus's vision of universal flux, he is but reiterating his early enthusiasm for his thought: In *Philosophy in the Tragic Age of the Greeks* he had praised Heraclitus's idea of "becoming."

> The everlasting and exclusive coming-to-be, the impermanence of everything actual, which constantly acts and comes-to-be but never is . . . is a terrible, paralyzing thought. Its impact on men can . . . be compared to the feeling during an earthquake when one loses one's familiar confidence in a firmly grounded earth. It takes astonishing strength to

> transform this reaction into its opposite, into sublimity and the feeling of blessed astonishment.[45]

In Lange's study of materialism, Nietzsche found a recrudescence of Heraclitus's thought buttressed by empirical evidence and physical theories emerging in nineteenth-century thought. Lange follows the evolution of post-Kantian scientific interpretations of nature to the point at which he concludes that the physical scientists who probe the submacroscopic structure of nature uniformly disclose dynamic relations, constantly moving processes, an evanescent stream of becoming. A fixed, permanent, substantial "reality" is an illusion, an imaginary construction. "An existence absolutely fixed and independent of us while it is yet known by us—such a reality does not exist and cannot exist."[46] By way of his prodromal "philosophy of science," Lange provided additional justification for Heraclitus's vision of actuality.

Despite the critical eye and word that Nietzsche casts upon the religion of Buddhism, he did not fail to notice that there is a consistency in the denial of the "absolute reality" of the world in Buddhism. This consistency is seen as "an insight into the erroneous procedures by means of which" the concept of a "world-in-itself" is arrived at.[47] In this regard, there is a resemblance between Nietzsche's concept of the "eternal ring of becoming" and the Buddhist conception of the "impermanence" (*anicca*) of actuality.

Despite the thread of continuity he traced from Heraclitus to Boscovich, and despite the fact that he applauded the emergence of a "dynamic interpretation of the world," Nietzsche also believed that even this interpretation cannot really "explain" stress or pressure. Nor can it dispense with the idea of *action in distans*, an idea modeled upon human perception. The "denatured force" in the dynamic theory of nature is a strange, very "abstract" notion that is difficult to understand. The concept of force must be complemented by the concept of an "inner will" as a "creative drive," as a "desire to manifest power."

Even a sophisticated mathematical physicist such as Boscovich cannot avoid anthropomorphic notions in his novel postulates: "action at a distance," repellent or attractive forces. That such notions are anthropomorphic "fictions" is seen, Nietzsche believes, by the fact that we cannot conceive of "an attraction divorced from our intention."[48] Attraction and repulsion are terms derived from our psychic reactions. Warming to his subject, Nietzsche attacks Boscovich's central notion that "forces . . . obey a law." This is not the case, because "the unalterable sequence of certain phenomena demonstrates no "law," but a power relationship between two or more forces."[49]

Following out the consequences of his criticisms of a dynamic theory of *Kraft*, Nietzsche is led to a startling conclusion. "There is nothing for it," he writes, "one is obliged to understand all motion, all 'appearances,' all 'laws,' only as symptoms of an inner event and employ man as an analogy to this end."[50] It is startling because he has repeatedly criticized philosophical and scientific claims to knowledge or "truth" by searching out even the slightest hint of anthropomorphic importation or "anthropocentric idiosyncrasy" (*anthropozentrische Idiosynkrasie*). And now he is arguing that we cannot "understand" basic scientific conceptions except in the most anthropomorphic fashion imaginable!

Throughout his discussion of the fictive nature of Kant's categories of the understanding and the useful fictions employed in the physical sciences, Nietzsche insists that it is our sensory modalities, as well as our "psychology," that shape and give rise to "phenomenal" notions such as the projection of geometric forms or numbers into the natural world, the idea of "thing," the concept of causal activity (modeled on our own subjective impression of causal efficacy in "willing"), or the ideas of "motion," "substance," "unity," etc. If, he argues, we subtract these very useful, but phenomenal, conditional conceptions from our model of actuality, "no things remain but only dynamic quanta, in a relation of tension to all other dynamic quanta; their essence lies in their relation to all other quanta, in their 'effects' upon the same."[51]

Nietzsche here strips Boscovich's theory of the structure of natural entities of every anthropomorphically colored notion. He retains his ideas of "combination of forces," "centers of force" and "quanta of force" that exist only in relationship to other such "forces" or "point-centers" and, at the same time, proffers his own explicitly anthropomorphic interpretation of the dynamic *nisus* expressed *via* such forces. Having pared Boscovich's physical theory to its essential elements, he then appears to seek a "metaphysical" principle that focuses upon the inner dynamics of the force-centers postulated in this theory.

Nietzsche develops a complex, hypothetical argument in defense of his standpoint that proceeds in the following way: if language is a metaphorical transformation of the "language of the senses," and if what is real is an ultimately "unknowable" flux of becoming, then language is used to formulate a system of "fictions" that enable us to function effectively in a "world" that is shaped and formed in terms of words and concepts that we have freely created. Perhaps, we may come to believe, the language of the sciences affords a closer approximation to the nature of actuality and is more precise and relatively devoid of anthropomorphic terms or metaphorical expressions. Upon careful examination of the central terms used in scientific discourse or in the presentation of scientific theories or interpretations, it becomes clear that the sciences are also riddled with "logical fictions" and hypothetical constructs that retain a subtle, but very real anthropomorphism.

Having adopted a particular physical theory (that of Boscovich) and deleted its anthropomorphic terminology, Nietzsche leaves us with a viable model of the dynamics of actuality. However, if we analyze the concept of "force," we seem unable to grasp its meaning except by analogy with man or in terms of an "inner event" or "inner world" that may be understood in human terms. If the humanization of nature (and natural processes) is ineluctable, then we may put forward a provisional, experimental conception of "reality" in self-consciously anthropomorphic terms.

If we are seeking that qualitative factor that better describes (to us) "force" or "energy" (*Energie*),[52] then we may ask whether we believe in a "causality of will." Provisionally adopting the notion of the causal efficacy of will (which is itself assumed to be the origin of our belief in causality *per se*), then we may assume that a causality of will is the sole mode of causality. Furthermore, if there is a "basic form of will" that pervades all dynamic units (or constellation of units) of force or energy, "then one would have obtained the right to define all efficacious force univocally as: *will to power*."[53] This would be "the world seen from within" (*die Welt von innen gesehen*). This is Nietzsche's creative and imaginative "interpretation." In a reprise of his philological training, he characterizes the physicists' notion of "nature's conformity to law" as an interpretation of the ambiguous "text" of nature.[54]

The thinker whom Heidegger calls "the last metaphysician" synthesizes central elements of Boscovich's theory of nature (transmuting them in the crucible of his imagination) and his own hypothesis of the cosmic *nisus* underlying natural processes. Having pondered the philosophical implications of the discoveries of the physical sciences, and having appropriated, transformed, and reduced Boscovich's theory of the elementary structure of nature, Nietzsche incorporates them into what appears to be a holistic "metaphysical" interpretation of the fundamental nature of reality.

By projecting *Wille zur Macht* as "the primitive affect" that is expressed through a multiplicity of "force-centers," Nietzsche has superimposed an anthropomorphic "interpretation" upon Boscovich's dynamic conception of the elementary structure of "matter." Even though it is possible that the idea of interpreting the physical world in terms of "spirit" *may* have been suggested to Nietzsche by Goethe,[55] it may also be the case, as he himself hints, that he sought to provide a *qualitative* interpretation of Boscovich's kinematic, quantitative interpretation of nature. For he remarks that an interpretation such as Boscovich's "desires nothing but quantities; but force is to be found in quality."[56]

The question that haunted Nietzsche in his attempt to appropriate central insights in Boscovich's thought was: How can we truly understand "forces" that are capable of "attraction" and "repulsion" without translating them into human nature? If we assume a universal "striving for power" in all entities, can we truly understand this notion "divorced from the feeling of enhanced or diminished power?"[57] By answering these questions in terms of a reductive principle (the will to power) that is itself based upon an analogy with man, he has not simply yielded to the "pathetic fallacy." Rather, he has reaffirmed a fundamental position that he never truly abandoned. In his early essay, *Philosophy in the Tragic Age of the Greeks*, he had said that we imagine the existence of other things or nonhuman beings in terms of our existence or analogically—that is, "anthropomorphically and, in any case, with nonlogical transference."[58]

Because of Nietzsche's typical analytical mode of thinking, the anthropomorphic transformation of a dynamic interpretation of natural processes is not the last word. There are many instances in which the *nature of man* is interpreted in terms of a dynamic synthesis of "forces." The individual is conceived of as a "relative unity" that is actually a plurality of "urges," "instincts," "drives," "passions," or *powers*. Reason is intermingled with passions and desires, as part of a relational interacting complex. And each passion itself is said to include a "quantum of reason." Willing is understood as an intentional directionality, a "movement" towards something or away from it.[59]

All of the above seem like transfers of Boscovich's conception of the attraction and repulsion between point-centers or "force-centers" to the domain of human psychology. Furthermore, Nietzsche maintains that just as a "thing" is a "fiction" (since each entity is ostensibly a conglomeration of centers of force), so, too, is the "subject" a "logical fiction." Each individual is a constellation of quanta of energy or force that waxes and wanes in terms of the enhancement and diminution of "power." Therefore, the various dimensions of, or aspects of, human activity are construed as differentiations of "will to power."

When Nietzsche ventures to characterize the apparent unity of all dynamic entities (including man), he uses a term that is, I believe, modeled upon Boscovich's conception of indivisible "force-points." For he remarks that, in a relative sense, we may refer to "atoms" or "monads." Each dynamic individual may be conceived of in terms of a conglomeration or constellation of "will-points" (*Willens-Punktationen*) that are continually "increasing or losing their power."[60] What we find in Nietzsche's thought-experiments in his later notes is a hypothetical, anthropomorphic interpretation of Boscovich's theory of the interior structure of nature and a dynamic, "naturalistic" interpretation of man that is clearly analogous to Boscovich's general theory of the structure of "matter" or, more precisely, "force-centers."

Having traced the influence of Boscovich's theory of nature on various aspects of Nietzsche's thought, and having indicated that he offers an explicitly anthropomorphic interpretation of the "text" of nature in terms of his hypothesis of the "will to power," we are still left with a final twist in his philosophy that has rarely been noticed. In order to "explain" or "understand" the meaning of "force," Nietzsche averred, we must rely upon a human analogy. Force accounted for in terms of an "inner event" is explicable in terms of a *qualitative factor*. The qualitative factor that we are familiar with, he argues, is a belief in a "causality of will." If there is a causal efficacy of will, then we may say that a causality of will is the only mode of causality. Therefore, let us postulate a "basic form of will": *Wille zur Macht*.

What is positively strange in this hypothetical argument, which leads to the (hypothetical) conclusion that there is a universal will to power pervading all "entities" (or, more accurately, processes), is that what is taken to be the central doctrine in Nietzsche's thought is based upon the assumption of a causality of will that he repudiates. For he argues in *Twilight of the Idols*, in the *Nachlass*, and elsewhere that the belief in the causality of will is entirely *fallacious*.

The "belief" in causality in nature is derived from the "belief" that we are causally efficacious in willing. However, this is a false causality. For,

> we believed ourselves to be causal in the act of willing; we thought that here at least we caught causality in the act. Nor did we doubt that all the antecedents of an act, its causes, were to be sought in consciousness and would be found there once sought as "motives."[61]

On the basis of "facts of consciousness" it was assumed that we had a guarantee of causality. The primary "fact" that supported this guarantee was "the will as cause." But, Nietzsche argues, we now reject a putative "empirical" basis for a causality of the will. In addition, the very notion of a "will" is questionable. If the concept of the "will" is questionable, then the whole notion of "mental causes" is undermined. According to Nietzsche's analyses of "will," "inward facts," and "mental causation," then, the analogical argument for a "will to power" is without support. The human will is neither a "capacity" nor "something that is effective."[62]

By means of an "internal phenomenology" Nietzsche tries to uncover the basis for our belief in "cause." He argues that this belief in causality is founded upon a "belief in force and its effect." When we act there arises a "feeling of force" that we associate with the subjective feeling of force and the action is not experienced, but is created by thinking compulsion into the entire process. In this way, we achieve a kind of "comprehension" of the process in that we have made it "more human," "more familiar."[63] Nietzsche is consistent in his treatment of the "knowledge" acquired by virtue of an "inner phenomenology." It involves simplification, schematization, arrangement, and interpretation: there are no more pure "facts" in the "inner world" than there are in the "outer world."

Even though Nietzsche attacks the idea of a "will" or a "will in general," he does not deny that there is *willing*.[64] Since willing is always intentional in the sense that it entails directedness, it is the most plausible analogue for an understanding of "striving" in inorganic entities. If "all events that result from intention are reducible to the intention to increase power,"[65] then the attempt to understand natural processes "from within" requires that we postulate "directedness" in nonliving (as well as in living) processes. We interpret manifestations of "force" or "power," then, in terms of willing. Hence, the hypothesis of the "will to power."

The outcome of Nietzsche's complex "phenomenology" of the inner world and its relation to the postulation of the will to power is that, despite the fact that our "internal phenomenology" necessarily involves a simplification of the actual process of "willing," we are unable to comprehend "force" or constellations of "centers of force" except as analogous to our subjective experience of force. Just as causality is a "falsification" of the relationship among events in external actuality, so, too, is the interpretation of the causality of willing in the "inner world." However, both ways of interpreting phenomena are *necessary* and inevitable; they involve the humanization of nature and the subjective interpretation of our experience of "inner" processes.

Nietzsche retains the de-anthropomorphic elements in Boscovich's physical theory and applies them to an interpretation of the dynamics of human existence and, at the same time, provides an anthropomorphic interpretation of "force," "power," or "energy" based upon an "internal phenomenology" characterized as misleading or fallacious. This is the paradoxical *dénouement* of his appropriation of Boscovich's theory of nature and his interpretation of its philosophical meaning.

Chapter four

Perspectivalism: Knowledge/ Interpretation

> . . . that every elevation of man brings with it the overcoming of narrower interpretations; that every strengthening and augmentation of power opens up new perspectives and enjoins believing in new horizons—this runs through my writings.
>
> Nietzsche, *Nachlass*

Among many paradoxical conceptions in Nietzsche's writings, one of the most consistently defended in his theory of perspectivalism. It is central to his epistemic reflections and lies at the heart of many of his fundamental ideas. But although perspectivalism has been analyzed quite often, some aspects of it have not received sufficient attention. What complicates matters is that Nietzsche introduces various levels of perspectival analyses. Moreover, he intermixes perspectivalism as an epistemological method with his own imaginative perspectival interpretation of actuality, a source of a great deal of confusion and of questionable renditions of his thought.

Although Nietzsche's views on various moral or valuational perspectives tend to attract the most attention, they are not the only or the most basic modes of perspectival analysis. Even though he refers often to the variety of values that have been elevated in different cultures and in different periods of history, his own "table of values" is not relativistic. He consistently values what affirms and enhances life, whatever elevates the type "man." Where we find an ingenious use of relative points of view is in Nietzsche's employment of a variety of conceptual perspectives. These are the foundation for the construction of a global interpretation of the nature of actuality.

The first suggestion of the importance of perspective for understanding, the one that was the model for many subsequent uses of this method, was derived from the hermeneutic problem of deciphering the meaning of texts in philological studies. A text has to be interpreted against a background of general cultural knowledge and in terms of a literary, historical, and valuational context. Thus, to cite one of Nietzsche's insightful exercises, he discerned in Socrates' attitude toward life a "pessimism" that had only previously been noted by Kierkegaard (though in a somewhat different way).[1] Commenting on Socrates' words in the *Phaedo* as he was dying, "Crito, we owe a cock to Asklepios, pray do not forget to pay the debt," he points out that it was the custom in ancient Greece to offer a rooster to the god of health, Asklepios, after one had recovered from an illness. Hence, Nietzsche interprets this seemingly innocent remark to mean that, in dying, Socrates wants to give an offering to the god because he is recovering from the illness of life. Viewing life in this way suggests a nihilistic attitude of mind.[2] Nietzsche offers an illuminating interpretation of a text (by placing it in a cultural-valuational context) that has often been seen as an indication of Socrates' noble considerateness in the face of death.

Sensitivity to the problems of textual interpretation spread to a variety of aspects of existence, to questions of truth in philosophy and science, to the general issue of our knowledge of the world. After philological interpretation, Nietzsche learned from his early sympathetic reading of Ralph Waldo Emerson that our subjective way of experiencing and thinking about the world is a powerful force virtually impossible to shake off. In his essay "Experience," in particular, Emerson taught an eighteen-year-old Nietzsche to see that we ineluctably view the world through subjective "lenses," that our moods, our age, our situation in life, and many other factors influence how we experience the world and how we think about it.[3] Later Nietzsche finds a place for many of Emerson's observations on the powerful effect of subjectivity on our experience and thought. And he virtually paraphrases the American poet and essayist when he insists, in *Beyond Good and Evil*, that our categorical thinking and our belief in synthetic *a priori* "truths" are determined by "the perspectival optics of life." Our organic being and our inherited "organic values" profoundly condition our perceptions and our thought. What is true of man is true of the entire organic kingdom. That is,

> The entire organic world consists of an assemblage of beings each surrounded by a little universe which they have created by projecting their strength, their desires, their habitual experiences outside themselves, thereby contriving their external world. The aptitude for creation (for modeling, discovering, inventing) is their primary aptitude. . . . Vast masses of such customs have ended up by congealing to a point at which an entire species live by them. They are probably propitious to the conditions of existence of such beings.[4]

Our organic "interests," needs, and "values" are not separate from the diachronic development of our perceptual and conceptual habits. Added to inherited modes of perceiving and thinking is the individual perspective of a unique organic being. Each individual not only interprets the world from his or her own perspective, but from perspectives that have evolved in the "human species" and even those that "make life itself possible."[5] Committed to this understanding of perception and thought, Nietzsche is led to deny that we have access to apodictic truth or absolute truth. Or, put another way, since there are so many perspective "truths," "there is no Truth." He prides himself on having renounced a belief in such "Truth," saying:

> what distinguishes our philosophical position is a conviction unknown to all previous ages: that of not being in possession of the truth. All our predecessors were in possession of the truth, even the skeptics.[6]

Unlike C. S. Peirce,[7] Nietzsche avers that there never will be a convergence on truth, a future state in which man, through philosophy or science, will arrive at a set of fundamental truths. Aware how unsettling this is, he admits that it takes a strong individual, a genuine "free spirit," to accept such an unpalatable standpoint. Sarah Kofman accurately reports Nietzsche's position when she says that a person with a "noble will" is one who is able to discard a particular perspective that has been adopted for a long time and is able "to see the world with 'other eyes'."[8] And, even though Nietzsche doesn't explicitly say it, I believe that the ability to live and think without dogmatic truth is one of the many requirements for entry into the school of *Übermenschlichkeit*. For, much of what he demands of his "new philosophers," his "free spirits," and those with "noble will" is demanded of his "beyond-men."

Nietzsche not only absorbed the agnosticism of people like Emil du Bois-Reymond and other nineteenth-century scientists who said, in unison, "we shall be ignorant" of the ultimate constituents of actuality, but he appropriated the perspectivalism displayed in the various philosophers and scientists he read.[9] Perusing reports on then-recent studies on the physiology of sensation and perception, he was particularly impressed by the way certain phenomena such as ultraviolet rays exert their influence on material objects and processes, even though they are imperceptible.

The investigations of nineteenth-century scientists suggested that sensory processes are involved in a kind of "abstraction" since percipients are only aware of selected effects that apparently result from imperceptible "motions." Our perceptual experience provides a limited, selective awareness of conglomerations of appearances that are relative to each perceiver. Moreover, Nietzsche's acquaintance with detailed studies of physiological theory led him to assert that "the sense-organs are organs of abstraction."

A critical approach to the scientific interpretation of the world suggested that the sciences do not give us an unvarnished picture of the objective structure of the external world. Rather, they disclose an immense complexity of phenomena simplified by our senses and cognitively organized in terms of hypothetical notions such as "substance," "things," or "forces."

From his studies of the works of scientists like Mayer, Nietzsche jotted down observations that contributed to the growth of his idea of perspectival knowledge. Thus, he remarks that

> even in chemistry we ought to speak of "similar" qualities and not of "the same" . . . Nothing repeats itself; in truth every atom of oxygen is nonpareil.[10]

Even the concept of similarity, the cornerstone of scientific knowledge, came to be considered as a convenient fiction. With Lange, Mach, and others, Nietzsche agreed that the concept of the atom was purely hypothetical. In effect, his exposure to the methods and results of the sciences up to the 1870s and 1880s instructed him in various forms of conventionalism in scientific theories and concepts. Because of this he was one of the earliest philosophers to rely on a conventionalist orientation and to exploit it for his own philosophical ends. If the scientists, by their own admission, do not provide apodictic truth, despite the discipline of their methodologies, then the search for pure, objective truth must be abandoned.

One by one, Nietzsche saw all the avenues to objective knowledge and truth blocked. Religion generates a kind of metaphysically colored image of reality that alleviates man's fears and satisfies some of his psychic needs, his need for transcendence, his psychological need for security. Metaphysics is sophisticated "conceptual poetry." It yields interesting world-views, but discovers no objective truth. Ordinary language is saturated with metaphors, anthropomorphisms, and remnants of the metaphysical beliefs of our ancestors. Kant's analysis of knowledge leads to an agnosticism about the true nature of things and obscures a knowledge of truth-in-itself. And, finally, the impressive exact sciences report an agnosticism about the ultimate constituents of reality. Moreover, the independent sciences operate with "personification" and anthropomorphic projections. Responding to these factors, Nietzsche came to see that the ultimate truth that previous thinkers believed they possessed or might some day possess simply does not exist.

Nietzsche's perspectival account of knowledge was not a free creation of his imagination: it was taught to him by Emerson (in an impressionistic and poetic way) and, more importantly, by the eighteenth- and nineteenth-century scientists whose strict methodologies and "small, unapparent truths" he had come to respect. It is against this background that he confidently proclaimed that "the perspective nature of the world is as deep as our understanding can reach today."[11]

It has been pointed out that Nietzsche relies upon the metaphorical notion that the world is a text subject to a plurality of interpretations.[12] This is both understandable and, up to a point, appropriate. However, before raising questions about this view, it may be pointed out that there is insufficient emphasis upon the fact that Nietzsche understands the sciences as themselves offering diverse interpretations of this "text." This neglect leads to placing too much emphasis on a literary interpretation of the "text" of the world to the exclusion of Nietzsche's stress on the variety of the interpretations of the "text" of nature that have been proffered by the independent sciences.

Minimizing the profound influence of the sciences on Nietzsche's critique of previous conceptions of objective knowledge, Nehamas, on occasion, misconstrues some of his key notions. Thus, for example, he cites the remark made in *The Gay Science* pertaining to the way the world has become "infinite" to us once again in the sense that "it may contain infinite interpretations."[13] Nehamas assumes that Nietzsche's denial that the world has a determinate character is equivalent to such an assertion. But the reference to the "infinite" nature of the world is a paraphrase of Lange's observation that the scientific theories concerning the multiple perceptual systems of different species of organic beings, as well as the specificity of the sensory system of each individual, leads us to think that "a whole infinity of different interpretations is possible."[14] Thus, Nietzsche uses this observation to argue for the indeterminate nature of the "text" of the world in terms of scientific, not literary, interpretations. Because of the specificity and differentiation of sensory systems and functions, each percipient organic being (as well as species and sub-species) is aware of a different "world" or ineluctably perceives it from its own unique perspective.

But Nietzsche not only relies on differentiation among perceptual perspectives (even though, as Nehamas points out, he does fall back on visual metaphors). Rather, he suggests that knowledge frameworks condition our interpretation of a variety of phenomena. And this position was adopted primarily because of the influence of skeptical scientific thinkers who were already doing what would later be called philosophy of science.

Nehamas is mistaken when he avers that, in arguing that science is an interpretation of the natural world or a class of phenomena, Nietzsche "does not seem . . . to be claiming that no particular theory can ever be true."[15] This is precisely what he is claiming. Nietzsche saw that the sciences advance by the replacement of theories, by proposing new world-interpretations that undermine the knowledge claims of previously regnant theories. If this sounds a bit like Kuhn's conception of "paradigm shifts" in the development of science, this is because it is a rudimentary expression of the same conception of the historical development of the sciences. On the basis of his readings of a variety of scientific works Nietzsche encountered numerous conventionalist theories of science, as well as the suggestion of an instrumental, fictionalist conception of scientific theory and concepts that were brought to fruition. To be sure, he recognized the great value of the "fragments of truth" that the exact sciences ferret out. Nonetheless, he was instructed in the hypothetical, provisional, model-creating nature of scientific theory formation. In fact, he even modeled his idea of how philosophy should be done on the experimental and hypothetical methods of the sciences. And he understood that "science" is not a unified totality of symmetrical theories and facts, that the adoption of different methods, different working hypotheses, and different theoretical frameworks by the exact sciences precludes the assertion of a unified scientific truth. Truths—yes; Truth—no.

The conceptions of a pure, timeless knower, of pure reason, of pure knowledge are philosophical myths. The "disinterested" pursuit of knowledge or a "disinterested" knowledge-drive are contradictions in terms. Just as all perceiving is perspectival, so, too, is all knowing. Objectivity, Nietzsche implies, is an approximation-process. The greater the number of "affects we allow to speak about one thing, the more eyes, different eyes, we can use to view one thing, the more complete will our 'concept' of this thing, our 'objectivity', be."[16] The reference to "affects" in this context coincides with Nietzsche's frequent claims that the pursuit of knowledge is motivated by nonlogical factors. In the next breath he mentions the role of "the will," or, more accurately, willing in the striving for knowledge. He believes, with good reason, that, in the absence of affects and willing, we would not seek knowledge, perspectival or otherwise. And this notion coheres with his general view that our interpretations of phenomena are ineluctably value-laden interpretations. And the valuations that infiltrate our perception and thought are rooted in our organic being and, hence, given his co-optation of the principle of evolution, the inherited perceptual and conceptual orientations that have been transmitted via man's natural history.

The role that Nietzsche's evolutionary epistemology plays in his arguments in defense of perspectival knowing cannot be ignored if we would understand his considered position. The sensory impressions we have of common phenomena, our feelings about what we perceive, have been inherited. Before our way of perceiving and experiencing the external world was "settled by heredity," "long periods of time must have elapsed."

> Countless numbers of those of our species whose perceptions of distance, of light, of colors, etc., were essentially different

> were elbowed aside and could only with difficulty perpetuate their species. For thousands of years the different way of feeling must have been suspect and shunned as "madness."[17]

From the beginning of organic life, Nietzsche speculates, a harsh process of selection was operative. The "exceptions" who "felt otherwise" than their cohorts, who experienced their environments in ways that differed from those whose perceptual and conceptual habits we inherited, perished. Here we can see why, among other reasons, Nietzsche argues so vociferously in defense of his "exceptions" and why he wants to create a cultural environment in which they can survive and flourish. That is, he sees the cultural evolutionary process as more and more favorable to "the average of the species" and fears the "destruction" of exceptional individuals in a rising and powerful mass society. Hence, his attempt at a reversal of values, his concern to find a place for his exceptions (the "beyond-men") in a "higher culture." What is missing in this general conception of human evolution is the important distinction between biological development (even though, of course, it continues to be operative), and psychocultural evolution. This is a weakness in his thought, since he slides casually from one to the other and does not always make clear that his central concern is focused on what he believes are the deleterious tendencies of modern cultural (valuational) evolution. For it is this that fuels his attempt to create an "antithetical ideal."

Out of our inherited perceptual and conceptual orientations have emerged two general perspectives: the aesthetic and the scientific. A third perspective offered by Nietzsche involves a tragic philosophical vision of existence that synthesizes art and science in association with a Dionysian affirmation of life in the face of its contradictions, antitheses, and suffering. This is his global valuational perspective, one he proposes in lieu of the Judeo-Christian table of values and opposes to all forms of world- and life-denial, to the dominance of a culture of science, to the emerging mass culture. Since our concern here is with his concept of perspectival knowledge, we will bracket consideration of the various phases and stages of what he called his "philosophies" that led him to embrace a "Dionysian pessimism" or a Dionysian religion of life.

Whereas in *The Birth of Tragedy* Nietzsche presented his aesthetic, tragic interpretation of existence in opposition to the growing "scientific" (in the broad sense of *Wissenschaftlich*) or Alexandrine culture, as well as to the closely related Socratism, he then sought to find a place for science in his centaur-like philosophy. This was his response to Lange's insistence that no serious philosopher could any longer afford to neglect the important theoretical work and discoveries in the "exact sciences."[18] Even his "artists' metaphysics" in his first work was, as we've seen, presented in the mode of "Jesuitism." Before the appearance of *The Birth of Tragedy* Nietzsche had already moved beyond the theoretical standpoint he defended there. His so-called "positivistic" period was presented as a dialectical phase of his development in order to display, in a favorable light, the perspective of the "exact sciences." Moreover, he shows that the methods and results of the exact sciences disclosed a "conscious relativity of knowledge" within the sciences, as well as a welter of diverse, scientific perspectives.

What Nietzsche discovered in his study of the findings of the sciences was that the independent sciences, in terms of their variegated perspectives, give us a fragmentation of "the world" and knowledge. Theoretical physicists disclose a grey, meaningless, "atomistic chaos." Mechanistic materialists present a world-picture of a strictly determined sequence of physical events which is, as he says in *The Gay Science*, "senseless." Physiologists showed that the phenomena we perceive are limited, that our senses selectively respond to a restricted range of stimuli, and that our sensory system transforms the stimuli that act upon it. Our sensory field gives us a world that exists only for our brain, our nervous system, our selectively responsive senses. And, bearing in mind the presumed inherited ways of perceiving we possess, our sensory world is one out of a number of other previously eliminated modes of perception that mankind is capable of having. The chemists uncover the extraordinarily complex processes of interaction that are continually occurring in physical objects and describe the body chemistry that is necessary to our life, our thought, our action, all of our functions. In science after science the extraordinary complexity of nature and the nature of man is revealed from a bewildering variety of perspectives.

Nietzsche tries sporadically to make sense, in a philosophical way, of the metastasizing scientific conceptions of reality. He came to the conclusion that each of these competing perspectives has some value and validity. And he came to see that, despite man's hope that it would be possible, the sciences do not yield a unified truth about reality. Since, as he learned, theory replaces theory, experiments confirm or disconfirm hypotheses, facts are called into question and are replaced by new facts, science is a multilinear, multidimensional, continually changing, dynamic enterprise. The truths of science are theory-laden perspectival truths.[19] If, as an imaginative thought-experiment, we accepted the "truth" of each viable, extant, scientific conceptions of "reality," we would have a disparate, often incongruent, kaleidoscope of "truths."

Some readers have raised questions about the self-refuting nature of Nietzsche's perspectival theory of truth. If this orientation is "true," then something escapes the network of mere perspectives. That is, perspectivalism is treated as an exception to its basic principle that all theories are solely perspectival. To obviate such a criticism, it has been said that Nietzsche is proposing a second-order theory about theory.[20] Although a plausible treatment of this issue, it should be emphasized that Nietzsche puts forward the perspectival theory of knowledge in a tentative way, as a response to the growing number of competing theoretical stances in modern thought. Moreover, he suggests that his account of knowledge is adopted for heuristic purposes. His theory only encounters the kind of paradox that every theory of knowledge faces—that is, the problem of defending the epistemic premise of a theory of knowledge in terms of the restrictions placed on knowledge by the theory itself. Thus, the claim—"A proposition is a picture of reality"—in Wittgenstein's statements in the *Tractatus Logico-Philosophicus* is questionable in terms of the implied reduction of knowledge to logical truths and the empirical propositions in the natural sciences. A perspectival theory of knowledge is a recommendation for an epistemic procedure: let us seek to understand any given phenomenon in terms of as many relevant perspectives as can be applied to that understanding. In that way, Nietzsche seems to say, we will approach a reasonable "objectivity." What he proposed is close to contemporary practice both in the sciences and in some domains of philosophy. The maximization of perspectives exposes the multidimensional nature of many fundamental issues and questions.

If it is charged that Nietzsche's proposal for a method of inquiry is itself an interpretation, he would acknowledge the point and nonetheless defend the value of a perspectival approach to knowledge. All interpretations, including interpretations of how knowledge can be acquired, are, for Nietzsche, value-interpretations. In regard to foundational issues, his general stance is to accept the defeasibility of his prescriptions. In fact, the position he adopts clearly anticipates anti-foundationalism.

In addition, like every account of the means of acquiring knowledge, perspectivalism is confronted by the problem of epistemic regress. Epistemic positions or orientations ultimately rely upon beliefs that are accepted for good reasons. Since the justification of a basic belief cannot depend upon other beliefs, there must be a "terminal belief" in order to avoid a regress of justificatory beliefs. Such a terminal belief cannot, however, depend for its justification on other beliefs.[21]

Perspectivalism is by no means groundless, even though, like any other epistemic presupposition or stipulation, it does not rest upon an absolute, apodictic justificative foundation. No one can see everything from a God's-eye view or from Spinoza's *sub species aeternitatis*. A transperspectival, ubiquitous, and absolute vantage-point is a fictional abstraction. Nietzsche, moreover, precludes the possibility that the accumulation of perspectival knowledge will yield a total panorama of universal and absolutely valid truth. Presumably, a plurality of fragmentary contextual truths would provide us with a more accurate understanding of any phenomenon or event in what is construed as an approximation-process. Perspectivalism has the function of a working hypothesis that serves a heuristic purpose. It is designed to overcome narrow perspectives that seek to delimit the range of human knowledge, to undermine dogmatic, one-dimensional ways of knowing.

The so-called paradox of perspectivalism is not, as Danto once said, that it itself is a specific "perspective" and, hence, its truth entails that it is false.[22] Rather, each narrow perspective falsifies the range of what can be known and the multiplication of perspectives reveals the incongruities and paradoxes of actuality.[23] There is no one "true" way of understanding the world, but there are fruitful as well as restrictive interpretations of knowledge and its acquisition. Perspectivalism is both a fertile method of discovery and itself a novel perspective on knowledge.

Nietzsche learned from the sciences that presuppositions, provisional hypotheses, and guiding principles are used for the purpose of discovery in the absence of apodictic claims to truth. In the manner of Ernst Mach, he proposes a method of perspectival knowing as a philosophical *Gedankenexperiment* or "thought-experiment."[24] As a methodological procedure that is apparently open-ended, the concept of perspectival knowledge, like some thought-experiments in the sciences that cannot be put to empirical, experimental tests, is neither true nor false. Hence, here there is no real "paradox" of perspectivalism. On the other hand, alternative perspectives may elicit previously obscured "truths" or may provide evidence supporting the conceivability of a truth-claim that may imperfectly relate to its possibility.[25]

Perspectival knowing is a method of discovery and a plausible description of the knowing process. The attributions of perspective to organic beings are based upon biological and physiological studies that disclose the species-specific and local orientations toward particular environments. Given the continuously changing conditions of existence of all organic beings, as well as the enormous variety of forms of life, there is a virtual infinity of perspectives possible and a tremendous number actual at any given moment. The human perspective is construed as an island in the midst of an ocean of numerous other orientations toward the surrounding world. Various species, at various times and in various environments, survive on the basis of highly specific perceptual modes, styles, or "sets." Only we, as far as we know, have access through history, comparative religious and cultural studies, linguistics, anthropology, sociology, ethnology, literature, and other studies to the variety of collective perspectives mankind has had and currently has. And within small groups, social organizations, whole societies, and civilizations—within these externally conceived "unities"—there are multitudes of individual perspectives that are value-laden and driven by a "will to knowledge" directly or indirectly in the service of life. Each organic entity uses its perceptual and "cognitive" capacities (or, in the case of nonhuman organic beings, presumed "cognitive" capabilities) in order to preserve itself in existence. Every living being in this sense is ineluctably "egoistic," as Nietzsche insists often enough, or, as Emerson once said, is imbued with a "natural egoism."

It is central to my approach to Nietzsche's perspectival concept of knowledge that it be distinguished from his global *perspectival interpretation* of actuality. For Nietzsche creates difficulties for himself when—primarily in his notes from the late 1880s—he extends his concept of perspectivalism by projecting it, as an elaborate thought-experiment, into the domain of the nonorganic (in the traditional sense of the "organic" that he rejects in his depiction of a dynamic, panpsychistic interactive field of "force-centers"). In doing so, he transgresses his own restrictions on knowledge and presents a questionable version of actuality if, as many have believed, he is engaged in a regression to metaphysics.

There is a secondary, virtually ignored, aspect of his proposal for an antidogmatic multiplication of perspectives. If, as he says in *On the Genealogy of Morals*, the aim of perspectival knowing is to attain a "more complete 'concept'" of something, a more complete "objectivity,"[26] even, a "future objectivity," then why does he (apparently) open up the range of possible perspectives so expansively that the "objectivity" he posits would, *de facto*, be impossible to attain? Moreover, the knowledge to be attained by means of many "affect-interpretations" (*Affekt-Interpretationen*) and "perspectives" would certainly be deferred until a presumably numerous diversity of them had been considered.

By virtue of his desire to escape the limitations of narrow, one-dimensional perspectives, Nietzsche has, in the absence of any stated restrictions, parameters, or conditions of contextual relevance, undermined the goal of attaining even approximate knowledge or approximate objectivity. If we must wait for *all* perspectives to be considered, then there would be no terminus to the process he describes. Of course, if we are considering purely theoretical, abstract, or metaphysical possibilities, then there would be no question about reaching an end-point since this would pertain to the entire history of such speculation up to the present and beyond. But, despite the open-endedness of his appeal to a plurality of perspectives, Nietzsche is concerned with augmenting our knowledge, as imperfect as it may be, and approaching "objectivity" in order to open up "new-horizons," to augment the sphere of knowledge, to "overcome narrower interpretations," in order to bring about an "elevation of mankind."[27]

Because of the openness (or vagueness) of his advocation of a "*variety* of perspectives," Nietzsche provided the open sesame for the "play of interpretations" that has been espoused by postmodernists who, with the notable exception of internally inexplicable political and moralistic stances, defer conceptual or cognitive closure indefinitely. As his writings indicate again and again, Nietzsche valued knowledge, as limited or as incomplete as it is, very highly. He practiced perspectival knowing by seeking to understand, as far as possible, a diversity of valuational and knowledge perspectives, even those he strenuously opposed, in order to attain liberation from unidimensional points of view, from inherited perspectives he believed were detrimental to the enhancement of the life and ascent of the type "mankind."[28] The goal of the accumulation of perspectives, consonant or dissonant, was the attainment of a secular form of *gnosis*.

Though previously unnoticed, there are internal tensions and seemingly unconscious ironies in the entire section in which the idea is introduced of applying a diversity of "perspectives and affect-interpretations" to a given event, phenomenon, or state of affairs in order to approximate "objectivity." Nietzsche illustrates what the champions of the ascetic ideal would say when they "philosophize" by pointing to the Vedanta-philosophy in the Hindu tradition. He asserts that this philosophy demotes the value of physical being to illusion, denies pain, manyness, and the antithesis of subject-object. All of these are "errors" that deny "what is felt as true, real and actual" and controvert what "the authentic instinct of life most unconditionally establishes as truth."[29] The Vedantists even deny their own "reality," "deny belief in one's ego." Furthermore, this philosophy negates the senses, appearance, even reason itself. It propounds "a violation of and cruelty against *reason*." Finally, with "voluptuous delight" this "ascetic" self-contempt and self-mockery of reason decrees: "there *is* a realm of truth and being, but reason is *excluded* from it." Nietzsche then compares this way of thinking to Kant's exclusion of the noumenal realm from our comprehension, calling it "a remnant of this prurient ascetic conflict that loves to turn reason against reason."[30]

In a passage devoted to urging the use of many "eyes" and many perspectives he launches a preemptive strike against the *perspective* of Vedanta philosophy, as well as that of Kant's "Intelligible character of things"! Without defending either, on what basis does Nietzsche call them "errors"? He characterizes them as "reversals of accustomed perspectives and valuations" by which, he claims, the "spirit" has waged war against itself! On this basis, much of Nietzsche's thought, especially in its negative, not to say nihilistic, phases could be characterized in the same way. Even some of the specific "errors" he finds in Vedantism are not absent from his own thought. Does he not criticize the "subject-object" dichotomy, deny the reality of the "*Ich-Subjekt*" (=the "ego," the "subject"), describe the commonsense "world" as false, as an "illusion," and does he not exemplify a thinker who "loves to turn reason against reason"? Moreover, the precise notion in Kant's thought—the postulated *"intelligibler Charakter"* of things—is adopted in a positive way in the only argument supporting his theory of the will to power that he published. Thus, he avers, that "The world seen from within, the world described and determined in terms of its 'intelligible character' . . . would be 'will to power'."[31] If this is the conclusion to a genuine argument for the will to power as the ultimate reality (a claim I will dispute in my concluding chapter), then Nietzsche adopts a perspective in *Beyond Good and Evil* that he describes in *On the Genealogy of Morals* as a residue of the "lubricious ascetic schism that loves to turn reason against reason."

Perhaps Nietzsche could escape inconsistency here because he argues for the value of the Vedantist perspective he repudiates (by appealing to the validity of commonsense realist beliefs!) as part of the "preparation of the intellect for its future 'objectivity'." Considering perspectives that may seem to be comprised of "errors, nothing but errors" is a useful "discipline" in order to learn "how to employ a *diversity* of perspectives and affect-interpretations in the service of knowledge."[32] So, whoever seeks knowledge ought to examine "perspectives and valuations" that one completely opposes and rejects. What is clear in this frequently cited passage is that Nietzsche is *not* talking about any individual or collective perspective whatsoever and thus is not, in this context, opening the door to any and every conceivable or imaginable perspective. He is referring to metaphysical theories or world-views and, *paradoxically*, appealing to commonsense realism[33] *against* the monistic absolute idealism of the philosophy of the *Vedas*. Moreover, the use of perspective in the passage under scrutiny is *not* one that "refuses to restrict its proliferative play"[34] since the "antinaturalness" of the thinking of "the ascetics of the Vedanta philosophy" is condemned as full of errors, a violation and mockery of reason, as an illustration of spirit raging against itself. Presumably, the future "objectivity" that Nietzsche refers to will *exclude* some, perhaps many, perspectives and will, therefore, not be quite as catholic as advocates of the postmodern temper seem to believe.

As if there were not enough thorny issues raised in this single segment of *On the Genealogy of Morals* (a work very appropriately subtitled, "A Polemic"), there is at least one more to examine. Nietzsche tells us that objectivity in this context is understood as "the ability to be master of one's for and against and to employ them or not." However, in a reference to this theme in the "Preface" to *Human, All-Too-Human* (1886) he insists that there is a "*necessary* injustice in each for and against, injustice as inseparable from life, life itself as *determined* through perspective and its injustice."[35] After expressing this generalization (which makes all perspectives, all pros and cons, equally *Ungerechtig* and presumably equally contentious), Nietzsche then shifts conceptual gears, as he often does, from *description* to judgment (usually *contra*) and on to prescription (usually *pro*).

The value-perspectives of some are narrow, needy, small, secretly self-preserving, mean, resentful of the "richer, the higher, and greater. . . ." Again, what such people are *Wider* or "against" is very valuable and supposedly less "unjust." Once again, Nietzsche wants to exclude or efface a perspective he rejects in terms of *his* pros and cons, his perspective. A gloss on this passage explains that the "future objectivity" (mentioned in *On the Genealogy of Morals*) is a call to fight the previous injustices "perpetuated in the name of Truth that permeate objectivity's checkered past."[36] This linking of two passages in different texts is certainly perceptive. But does it alleviate the circularity of Nietzsche's ardent defense of his new, spacious, and expansive perspective? As long as he is engaged in *describing* the *de facto* situation—namely, that mankind has embraced, does embrace, and probably will continue to embrace a variety of perspectives and affective interpretations—he is on secure ground. And his proposal to discern, consider, and even "try on" many of these perspectival orientations in order to attain a more accurate picture of the "indescribable complexity" of actuality *and* the human world (thereby transcending narrow dogmatic standpoints) is a sound one. However, his *prescriptions* often seem to work against the presumed ideal of a "plurality of interpretations" and are buttressed by other perspectives he obviously and perhaps for good reason privileges! While there certainly is a positive value in exposing and critically appraising narrow and rigid singular perspectives, Nietzsche's method of perspectivalism makes it difficult to avoid circularity and requires an abundant armamentarium of rhetorical strategies.

In the preface that we've been examining, Nietzsche anticipates a point made a year later in the *Genealogy* where he asserts that "the ever freer spirit begins to unveil the riddle of . . . great liberation" by becoming master of himself and his virtues, telling himself that:

> You shall gain control over your for and against and learn to understand how to display the one and the other in accordance with your higher aim. You shall learn to comprehend the perspectival in every valuation. . . .[37]

The higher goal or aim includes recognizing the problem of a "rank-order" of values and seeing "how power and right and extensiveness of perspective grow with each other up into the heights."[38] This remark is entirely consonant with valuations expressed elsewhere, particularly in the *Genealogy* in the previously mentioned note at the end of the first essay in which it is proclaimed that *the* problem for future philosophy is "the *problem of value*, the determination of the *rank-order of values*." Finally, in *Ecce Homo* Nietzsche tells us that in the *Genealogy* he attacked the powerful and "*harmful*" ascetic ideal and offered his own "*Gegen-Ideal*" or "counter-ideal" via *Zarathustra*.[39]

Having gone through many difficult stages of evolution as a thinker and as a person, having experimented with numerous value-perspectives both intellectually and psychologically, he had overcome narrow, cramped, and fixated perspectives and had arrived at a reductive criterion of judgment. Those global perspectives that are natural, affirmative, and life-enhancing are creative and elevating and those that are anti-natural, negative, resentful, or life-denying or that undermine the value of life in this world are ultimately destructive of individual and cultural life—are, in effect, a "will to nothingness." The means by which he had arrived at *his* table of values are found in his writings themselves and are the consequence *of the application of his method of perspectival knowing*. The transvaluation of values he proposed as his culminating work already pervades his extant writings, published and unpublished.

Since Nietzsche accepts that there can be no rational or logical demonstrations of what ought to be valued, there is an inevitable circularity in the persuasive arguments for or against a given value or system of values, particularly because virtually all of them serve the preservation of life or, in general, seem to "work," whether highly effectively or marginally. Nevertheless, the exposure of values underlying perspectives, insofar as this is possible, as well as the display of the narrowness of a given perspective, has a powerful impact on those open to such questions. Since most value-perspectives are inherited or accepted passively within a given society or culture, the effort to show the negative and oppressive nature of such perspectives can itself have the liberating effect Nietzsche so passionately desired to bring about. It could with justice be said that liberation through knowledge or *gnosis*—absent absolutes and certainty[40]—is a paramount value for Nietzsche.

In his reflection on the history of knowledge and the history of *Weltanschauungen* (a term that already suggests perspective, a *schauen*—a looking at, gazing upon, viewing—the world), Nietzsche saw plainly the contingency of dominant knowledge-frameworks and world-interpretations, as well as their longevity once they harden into dogmas. Various philosophers pointed to the obvious relativity of perception, and Emerson impressed upon Nietzsche the host of psychic factors that shape our "subjective" ways of experiencing people, events, and phenomena. In his *Essays* Emerson also described how our feelings or affects are projected into the world, how our "subject-lenses" color what we experience.[41] In addition, his surveying of scientific theories conveyed to Nietzsche the contingency of many scientific theories and an insight into the internal theoretical disputes in the exact sciences. Biological theories had an especially important influence on a thinker who very early on was determined to develop a philosophy of life both in an existential sense and in terms of a conception of the nature of life. Repeatedly, he speculates about the emergence of the "knowledge-drive" out of the most elemental forms of life and out of what appears to be nonorganic. In fact, his considered view was that, in a strict sense, "there is no inorganic world."[42]

The method of perspectival knowledge developed virtually throughout Nietzsche's creative life and was as much shaped by his understanding of science as it was by historical understanding and his own observations of the natural world, of others, and of himself. Without at all ignoring the strong poetic and aesthetic dimension of Nietzsche's thought, we also should not neglect his experiential, if not strictly empirical, explorations and their intimate relation to his global, metaphorical portrait of actuality. Nietzsche sought to understand the relation of perspective to the historical horizon. One of his central projects, as we've seen, was to employ experimental perspectives in order, by indirection, to lead others out of narrowly circumscribed perspectives[43] to a more encompassing perspective. Since he believed that life itself is determined through perspective, the expansion of our horizon of perspectives would contribute to the enhancement of our lives.

It is crucial to my account of Nietzsche's perspectivalism to separate his exploratory and speculative *descriptions* of the pervasiveness and relativity of perspectival valuations (which are often not reflexively recognized as such) and his own valuational *prescriptions*. On a descriptive level he continually unveils the linguistic, cultural, historical, political, collective, and individual relatively of perspectives. While some diverse perspectives are compatible on some general levels, invariably there are conflicts among varying perspectives. In this regard, it is, descriptively, a considerable understatement to say that the "adoption" of (or, more specifically, the existence of) "multiple perspectives" might produce chaos.[44] It has; it does; and, no doubt, it will.

There are not only contradictory or conflicting perspectives operant in the world, but, having forgotten that "valuations are given only in a perspective," each individual contains within himself or herself "a profusion of contradictory valuations and *consequently contradictory drives*."[45] Here Nietzsche is working with an assumption that runs through his writings—that the evolution of, and history of, mankind has engendered many more complex individuals by virtue of the accumulation of a variety of internalized perspectival valuations. Presumably, the more knowledgeable an individual is, the more acute his or her observations and reflections are, the more complex will be the nature of and interaction of these accumulated perspectival valuations. Such a person will feel "many pros and cons" and will possess "a great method of knowledge,"[46] no doubt precisely because of the heightened awareness of competing multiple perspectives.

Again, Nietzsche is engaging in a kind of speculative-interpretive descriptive psychology, a thought-experiment grounded in plausible, approximate knowledge.

Nietzsche's critiques of Christian doctrines and culture, Buddhism, Vedantism, ascetic "priests," Platonism, utilitarianism, socialism, communism, mechanistic materialism, and so forth, obviously shows the actuality of objective relativism. And he often displays, in an ironic or sarcastic way, his disapprobation of valuations held by many historical peoples past and present. Very often Nietzsche is a biased reporter of beliefs and values held by others, particularly in the realms of moral and, on occasion, aesthetic values. He is rarely neutral in his description of the value-systems of those he opposes. In the judgments he injects into his representation of valuations he is often critical of some of the described sets of values that are objectively relative to a time and place, a culture and a people. Nietzsche is strongest in his polemics against what he considers debilitating, illusory, delusional, self-destructive, antinatural, and life-denying or life-undermining valuations.

When Nietzsche *prescribes* values or value-orientations his relativistic mode of analysis evaporates. Apologists for his views claim that he simply defends his point of view because he holds that some values are better than others. He openly privileges his perspective while, at the same time, suppressing others. It has been said that we then have to "supplement the idea of . . . perspectivism with some notion of him as a diagnostician of culture who privileges those specific perspectives he thinks are good for us at this time."[47] Except for the specificity of "this time" (which erases the futurity Nietzsche invariably emphasizes), this is an accurate statement. But it is one that elicits common reactions. Isn't Nietzsche's cultural diagnosis itself merely another perspective? For what reason does he privilege this particular perspective? Does he do so because it's true? If he does, is he "really a perspectivist"?[48]

Based upon a consideration of a variety of perspectival evaluations, a living in them and going beyond them, Nietzsche begins to *prescribe* his experimental, perspectival values. What is prescribed is not known to be apodictically certain, is not an absolute perspective, and, therefore, not a "truth" in the traditional sense of the term. The search for knowledge, the striving for "self-overcoming," the acceptance of objective nihilism (that there is no given, objectively discernible meaning in the cosmos), the *creation* of meaning, the faithfulness to *this* world, the valuation of the most transitory moments of life, the instinctive willing towards freedom (which is equated with the psychological striving for power in the *Genealogy*),[49] the Dionysian affirmation of life in the face of its injustices, contradictions, and sufferings—all of these and many more make up a valuational prescription that Nietzsche proffers to us as a possible perspective, one which is not dogmatically imposed on anyone and not proposed as valid for everyone. The philosophical "attempters" who were projected into the future (even though Nietzsche was *already* doing what he prescribed for his "philosophers of the future") "will certainly not be dogmatists." But, like all philosophers, they will probably privately be friends of their own "truths."[50] In regard to the valuations he worked so hard to clarify and express in many ways, Nietzsche was *not* a relativist. His *prescriptive* valuations are those that represent his competitive "counter-ideal," his rank ordering of values, his "transvaluation" of previous values. Nonetheless, he was a careful, probing, and incisive analyst of a "variety of perspectives" and of their (putative) origins. And he evaluated them in terms of a more general valuational criterion that prized life, the enhancement of life, the affirmation of existence, health, strength, naturalness, power as energy and power as a state (a "feeling of power"), and self-overcoming. But, a critic may ask, aren't these value-interpretations also perspectives? "Yes," Nietzsche would have to respond, "of course . . . but have I not tried to show you or anyone *why* I have defended and promulgated an entire set of interrelated valuations? Have I not shown my readers my pros and cons, put my cards face up on the table, and displayed reasons for believing that the value-perspective I've presented is *better* than those I criticize? Do not misunderstand me—I am the reverse of a value relativist!"[51]

POLYPERSPECTIVALISM

If anything is an obstacle to grasping the sense of Nietzsche's method of perspectivalism, it is the metastasization of perspectives in his writings, what has accurately been called "*polyperspektivalismus*."[52] The range of the attribution of perspective extends from the *soi-disant* "inorganic" world through simple and complex living organisms to man. A multiplicity of perspectives is found in historical periods, literature, cultures, languages, philosophy, science, societies, social and political groups, classes, etc. All of these various perspectives are central to Nietzsche's endeavor to attain a global, philosophical, multiperspectival understanding of as much of the extreme complexity of actuality as is possible. Ineluctably, his speculations about the specific perspectives of nonhuman organisms rely heavily on human analogy, if not on anthropomorphic projection.

One of the chief perspectives that Nietzsche concerned himself with from his earliest writings to his last series of notes was what could be called a philosophy of biology. In his earliest attempts at the essay form he speculated about the inheritance of genetic traits, the physiological roots of temperament, the emergence of individuality as it evolved over long experience and the relation of man to the "development" of all living forms.

Both "Fate and History" and "Freedom of Will and Fate"[53] reveal an orientation towards science in an eighteen-year-old student that runs through much of his writings. However, it is not science in itself that attracts him, but what it reveals about life and the condition of human existence, its philosophical meaning. The dialectical relation between the scientific depiction of life and the cosmos and the poetic-aesthetic, imaginative vision of life, the world, and the nature of mankind produces the dynamics, the tensions, the intensities of Nietzsche's coruscating thinking. He once told his friend Erwin Rohde that "Science, art, and philosophy are now growing into one another so much in me that I shall one day . . . give birth to a Centaur."[54] He did precisely that by creating a truly centaurian philosophy.

The "biologism" in Nietzsche's philosophy that Heidegger resisted in his *Nietzsche* and criticized in his lectures on Hölderlin during 1934–35[55] is essential for an understanding of the development of the concept of perspectival interpretation or the process of "assimilation" of objects of interest, concern, and value for an individual or a species for the sake of survival and "growth" (*Wachstum*). Again, it was Lange who first suggested to the twenty-one-year-old philology student that *our* world is not necessarily *the* world because many other species that have a different "organization" than ours live in different worlds. Therefore, "a complete infinity of different interpretations (*Auffassungen*) is possible [for] all these different modalities of apprehension of differently organized beings."[56] Nietzsche builds on this observation and often speculates about the internal processes of nonhuman organisms.

In the search for nutrition organic beings are engaged in an error-prone and dangerous activity. Those that survive are endowed with the "primary need of the organic," or "simplification." Nietzsche imagines that the "organs for *seeking* [nourishment, incorporation] *grow stronger*." Though many "errors" will be made in this "trial and error" activity, there will be contingent successes and these will increase. Through "error" organic beings occasionally hit upon "lucky accidents," successful trials that reinforce learning. Nietzsche does not hesitate to characterize such trial-and-error learning in organisms a mode of "thinking."[57]

It is such speculations that lead Nietzsche to make claims about nonhuman life-forms that he later applies to our knowledge-process. "Error," he writes, "begins in the organic world . . . specific errors by virtue of which organisms live."[58] In effect, through error "knowledge" is acquired that itself is creative error because it involves radical "*Simplifikation*," narrow perspectives, and recognizing other entities on the basis of a generous (hence, erroneous) perception of similarity. The linkage of adaptive behavior of simpler organic beings to human cognition is a familiar one in Nietzsche's repertoire of analogies. "Making the same [in human judgment] is equivalent to what incorporation of approaching matter is to an amoeba."[59]

In a seemingly odd way, Nietzsche understands preorganic beings as achieving a form of concentrated perfection, as complete, integrated, resistant, and enduring. They are construed as simple holistic powers that are incapable of error, disguise, deception, or dissimulation! Once again, he freely extends anthropomorphic interpretation to preorganic entities in his pattern of analogical thinking. Reminding us of his uncanny, imaginatively fueled desire to seek to penetrate the inner nature of everything, Nietzsche maintains that "Thought in a primitive state (preorganic) is producing one's own forms, as with crystal."[60]

The earliest expression of anthropic transference to the natural world is found in a letter in which Nietzsche spontaneously reports his elation in the midst of an intense storm. "The storm broke with immense force, with wind and hail." At that moment, he tells his friend, the turbulent will of mankind, as well as its "eternal 'Thou shalt,' 'Thou shalt not,' " was a matter of indifference. "How different," he continues, "the lightening, the wind, and the hail, free powers, without ethics! How fortunate, how strong they are, pure will, without the obscurities of the intellect."[61] Although his admiration of Emerson and Schopenhauer at this time is a relevant factor in this impression of natural powers (since both stress the immanence of will in nature), it is a sentiment that Nietzsche deeply felt and, as his later interpretations of nature show, it is one he never abandoned.

The idealization of the preorganic world, as strange as it may seem, is relevant to an understanding of perspectival knowing and its transformational function in all organic beings. In a note from 1885 Nietzsche says that perception is also furnished for the preorganic world and that it is "certainly absolutely precise." "It is there that 'truth' reigns." Presumably, the purity of this "perception" is without distortion or "error." By way of contrast it is in the organic domain that "*determinateness* and *semblance* begin."[62] This distinction between the preorganic and the organic is a fundamental notion for Nietzsche that shapes his reformulations of truth and knowledge. With living beings semblance, deception (as in mimicry), and life-preserving falsification emerges and is then transmitted to future individuals and species by means of evolution. Reversing common sense and traditional philosophical conceptions, Nietzsche maintains that "error," "illusion," and "untruth" are the basis for the functioning of, and preservation of, all organic beings. Moreover, they are the roots of what we call truth and knowledge. This is one of the reasons why he typically refers to "truth" and "knowledge" in an ironic tone.

Heidegger has said that "the 'perspective' is never the mere angle of vision from which something is seen; rather, this perspectival vista looks towards conditions of preservation and enhancement (for life)."[63] Though it is correct that perspective is *not only* a point of view or angle of vision, it includes it. The "perspectival vista" is not one-dimensional, as Nietzsche describes multiple levels of perspective operative in human experience and thought. Again, Heidegger's disdain for Nietzsche's "biologism" hobbles his interpretation of perspectivalism. Nietzsche places emphasis on *perception* as the most pervasive mode of perspective in all beings. Asking himself a "fundamental question," he wonders

> whether the perspectival is proper to the being, and is not only a form of observation, a relation between different beings? Do the various forces stand in relation, so that the relation is tied to perceptual optics? That would be possible if *all Being were essentially something which perceives.*[64]

Since Nietzsche grants that perception may be attributed to all beings, there is some degree of interaction among different "perceiving" entities. If such a bewildering variety of beings survive (which they do) by means of significantly different modes of perception, there is no privileged perceptual function or orientation. Each organic entity is said to "create" its local environment by means of an "experimental" encounter with it in which mistaken or inappropriate actions and responses are gradually eliminated and functional, productive ones are repeated. Since Nietzsche does not deny that all beings are acted upon by a chaotic series of multiple stimuli in different ways, these shape their *immediate* environment by a process of transformation. This is the activation of a perspective. In all perception there is an imposition of form on what may be characterized as a primitive "thatness"—a fluctuating field of stimuli experienced differently by different beings. Thus, the "fundamental capacity" of all organic individuals is "The capacity to create (forming, inventing, fabricating)."[65]

This presumably instinctive and spontaneous activity is considered necessary to life. It entails selectivity of response, simplification, and the projection of unity and sameness onto other beings in the environment. These are the fundamental "errors" (unlike the erroneous trials that involved wasted energy and potentially dangerous encounters with predators or harmful situations) that comprise the falsifying perspectives necessary for life. Selectivity is determined by basic drives, interests, feelings, or "affects," a process that already reveals a relatively narrow perspective, especially among lower organisms. Simplification involves imposition of form and reduction of a manifold into separate segments or parts. It is primarily an imaginative act since, Nietzsche proclaims, "Everything that is [designated as] . . . simple is imaginary, is not 'true'."[66] This same process of active simplification, as we've seen, is manifested in a sophisticated way in language.

Experiencing themselves and other beings as unities is a form of simplification that life-forms employ in organizing a field of stimuli. What is experienced as a unitary being is actually a complex multiplicity. It is perceived as an "as-if" unity. Perceptual recognition and appropriate responses to certain stimuli are facilitated by this transformative projection of unity. Finally, the active preservation of durational processes "presuppose perspectival *illusion*."[67] This is the case because we perceive relative duration presumably as an experienced, relatively slower tempo of change. Analogically we then assume different senses of duration in other organisms. Nietzsche speculates that our subjective time-sense may be exclusive to our species and may bear no relation to "actual time" or temporality as such. He then imagines that if we could "perceive more rapidly, we would sense the illusion of permanence much more strongly."[68]

Invariably, the perspectival activity of organic beings is characterized as "false" and "illusory." However, the construction of a "world" through perspectival transformation is a creative, powerful, and practically functional "error" that has enabled extant species to remain in existence. These "errors," seen from a non-Nietzschean standpoint, are "truths" or those perceptual modalities and interpretations that have proven serviceable for life and have been transmitted to us. This is the point of the often cited assertion: "*Truth is the kind of error* without which a specific kind of organic being could not live."[69] In the context of the development of Nietzsche's thought, this is not as odd as it may sound. The sedimentation of the accumulated constructive errors of mankind that have proven most useful for the purpose of survival and perpetuation are christened "truths." And Nietzsche admits that we certainly possess "truths *for us*" or, as many contemporary philosophers, particularly philosophers of science, express it, we have "our (putative) truths" or our "putative knowledge."[70]

What has been called Nietzsche's falsification thesis is specifically linked to the conditions for the possibility of life in all its forms and not only to language. The rejection of the "metaphysical correspondence theory" of truth is not by any means the sole basis for Nietzsche's critical analysis of truth. Nor is it accurate to saddle him with a "metaphorical" concept of perspectivism because he uses "visual" metaphors to illustrate his claims about knowledge.[71] Perspective is rooted in the nature of and conditions of existence of particular forms of life and is already active in sensory awareness before it is modified by concepts and linguistic expression.

A question raised by some recent commentators concerning how Nietzsche can claim that the truths of common sense and science do not agree with underlying reality unless he knows the nature of that reality is a replication of a question raised a century ago by a perceptive German commentator. In order to speak of falsity or error does not Nietzsche presume knowledge of what actuality is? He "must know what truth is and consequently that there is truth." Moreover, how can Nietzsche "know that something is an error, as, generally the concept of *error* is constitutive?"[72]

Invariably, Nietzsche tends to understand the complex and elaborately developed phenomenon in terms of the more primitive expression of it.

Thinking and knowing, for example, are analogous to the "assimilation" and "incorporation" of nutrients. Logic emerges out of simplification, abstraction, and the nonrational habits of seeing "sameness" where it is not present. All knowing, then, entails form-projection and thereby *transformation* of whatever is "there." Specific basic perspectives for all forms of life are "errors" precisely because, considered in isolation, they are limited perspectives. In human thought there is a continuation of the instinctive activity in lower organisms that is a reduction to simplicity of a complex field of stimuli and generalizing "sameness." "In *our* thinking what is *essential* is arranging new materials in an old schemata (=Procrustes' bed), *making* the new the same."[73]

It has been said that the method of perspectivism "purports to offer a positive account of perspectival knowing."[74] On the contrary, it is a general method of accumulating partial, imperfect knowledge that points to the way in which narrow, restricted, and one-dimensional modes of knowing have generated interpretations of life, the world, and existence that tended to harden into dogmas over time. Nietzsche's thought itself illustrates how the adoption of various perspectival ways of knowing reveals the complexity, ambiguity, and uncertainty of actuality. Perspectivism is a retrospective critique of the interests, drives, needs, and subjective projections operative in the philosophies of significant thinkers. Prospectively, it is a method designed to undermine absolute claims to truth-in-itself, to put in question any future attempts to promote *one* truth, *one* perspective, *one* conclusive answer to the riddle of existence. Nietzsche saw clearly how often absolute claims to "Truth" in religion, metaphysics, and politics have led and will continue to lead to tyrannical and violent fanaticism.

Like others who have considered (hypothetically) and psychically accepted (for a time) a variety of knowledge-perspectives, Nietzsche internalizes and brings them affectively to experiences and to questions concerning what a given event or phenomenon is. He is a conceptual, epistemic, and theoretical pluralist who believes that those who would follow his paths of thinking and attend to his texts will probably never regress to a single, central, exclusive, or absolute way of knowing even though they can consider, entertain, and follow the implications of such conceptual possibilities. His own "philosophies" have been constructed out of a number of knowledge-perspectives and he does not want to settle in the comfort of a dogmatic certainty that requires a narrowing of focus, an exclusion of paradoxes, contradictions, and ambiguities, a fixation on a single paradigm of "truth" and "knowledge."[75]

In his various descriptive accounts of perspectival experiencing and knowing Nietzsche does not make clear the context in which what has been called "affective investment" is operative.[76] When he opens the door to an indefinite number of perspectives, he presents us with a method of knowing that would defeat his own emphasis on the *practical* use of knowledge and would not serve as a functional replacement of theory of knowledge, the role for which it was designed. As a concrete case in point, one close to Nietzsche's heart when he looks upon scientific perspectives favorably, we may wonder if perspectival seeing alone suffices for genuine scientific observation. Meaningful observation requires prior *knowledge*, not only an affective perspectival cathexis. As a chorus of scientists and philosophers of science have said, scientific observation is theory-laden. "Brainless, photosensitive computers—infants and squirrels too—do not make scientific observations, however remarkable their signal-reception and storage may be."[77]

It may be the case that Nietzsche does not indicate the context in which multiple perspectives are applied to any object, phenomenon, or event because he is quite aware that he has, in fact, already illustrated perspectival knowledge-frameworks in his own writings. His own "philosophies" comprise multiple perspectives. His endeavor to uncover *homo natura* is accomplished in terms of the juxtaposition of various knowledge-perspectives: the aesthetic interpretation of existence, the positivistic perspective, the mechanistic and dynamic perspective of physical science, the psychological, artistic, sociological, edifying, and nihilistic perspective, etc. Unfortunately, it is not uncommon for such descriptively represented knowledge-perspectives to be taken as prescriptions. Particularly since, for the most part, they are artistic and sympathetically persuasive examples of descriptive "phenomenology" or the "methodology" Nietzsche prizes.[78]

Returning to the question pertaining to how, given his interpretation of the knowing process as involving "error" (as in "trial and error" or "error" in the sense of creative falsification), Nietzsche *knows* that our construction of actuality is erroneous, the simplest answer is that he doesn't directly know this. Though he insists that what we construe as reality is manifested to us solely by way of our active participation in the construction of it, as well as our projection into it of our (psychic) "primal poetry,"[79] at times he reverses himself.

> The question is whether there could still be many other modes of creating such an *apparent* world—and if this creating, logicizing, adapting, falsifying is not itself the best guaranteed *reality*.[80]

Here the experimental nature of Nietzsche's thinking is transparent. After pushing his skepticism as far as he can, he then puts in question the very consequences of his skeptical analyses. In a note from 1872 he raises an objection against Kant that resembles his comments in the above passage: "If we grant all of [Kant's] propositions, it still remains completely *possible* that the world is as it appears to us to be."[81] We are fairly secure, then, in saying that Nietzsche has no certainty that our senses, concepts, language, and our psychology distort or falsify our world-representations. But he continually alludes to a multiplicity of factors strongly suggesting this: to a mass of indirect or intuited data, to subjective experience and reflexivity, and to plausible, if imaginative and anthropomorphic, interpretations of primal, instinctive actions, responses, and perceptions, and to various levels, forms, and patterns of "knowing." Nietzsche's reformulation of knowledge, which owes so much to accounts of theories, observations, and experiential data in the sciences, is a consequence of the clash of incongruent, rather than incommensurable, perspectival interpretations.

Incommensurability, as formulated by Feyeraband and Kuhn, denies meaning invariance in regard to principles, theorems, and terms in different paradigms. Some principles involved in the determinations of the meanings of prior theories are inconsistent with those of the new theory. The meanings in the replaced theory are either eliminated or changed in the new theory. There is no theory-neutral language related to nature in nonproblematic ways. Feyeraband and Kuhn claim that there is no theory-independent vocabulary to which one could appeal. Kuhn argued that

> In the transition from one theory to the next words change their meanings or conditions of applicability in subtle ways. Though most of the same signs are used before and after a [scientific] revolution . . . the ways in which some of them attach to nature has somehow changed. Successive theories are thus, we say, incommensurable.[82]

Although Nietzsche deals with what could be called the incommensurability of metaphysical and scientific theories, his notion of an extensive perspectival knowing is much more encompassing than this Kuhnian conception and more radical. If we examine perspectivalism from the standpoint of the "knowing" being, it is not necessary to leap outside of his account of knowledge and claim, as many have, that it is based upon an "interpretation" of actuality as a dynamic system of constantly changing "wills to power" or his "power ontology." There is such a global, metaphorical depiction of actuality in Nietzsche's interpretation of "reality" in terms of a set of knowledge-perspectives. But it is, as I'll try to show, a mythical construction.

The active transmutation (*Verwandlung*) of "what is there" pervades knowing and we are described as "form and rhythm-constructing beings." In the absence of the transformation of the world in terms of rhythms and forms nothing would be given to us as "the same." Nothing would be experienced as repeated and there would be "no possibility of experience and appropriation, of *subsistence*." In what Nietzsche calls the original act of appropriation—perception—there is already "form-imposition." Starting in perception, continuing through metaphors that are denuded as concepts, the process of knowing transmutes the manifold of impressions or "stimuli" not into a "picture" of an "authentic actuality," but into "our own actuality"[83] or the world *for us*.

It is not the case that Nietzsche's "power ontology" generates perspectivism; nor is this postulation of a vast multiplicity of "wills to power" an "objective precondition" of perspectivism.[84] While it is true that from very early on Nietzsche was attracted to a pluralistic ontology, his perspectival method developed coeval with the view that organic beings appear to be unities, but are composed of a virtual "infinity of individuals." This reference is associated with an observation in Goethe's *Morphologie* which Nietzsche later cites.[85] This idea of a plurality of "living beings" within the organic individual preceded the later construct of a constantly interacting conglomeration of "forces" in the development of a world-interpretation that fuses biologism and aspects of dynamic physical theories.

It is questionable to portray Nietzsche's perspectivalism as "metaphorical" in a pejorative sense or to hold that it surpasses what has been called the "falsification thesis." The fact that he adopts a "visual metaphor" in regard to knowing is hardly unique to Nietzsche since in most languages basic terms for knowing are visual or sensory metaphors. The Sanskrit word for "knowledge" (*vidya*) is derived from *vid*, "to see" and Descartes referred to "seeing" truth by means of "the natural light of reason." The Greek *theorein* meant "to behold," "to look at." The word for "see" in a number of languages is often used as equivalent to "understand."

Perspectivalism is not in conflict with the notion of the "falsification" of actuality since knowledge implies transformation, abstraction, simplification, and "assimilation." The latter process is analogous, for Nietzsche, to the physiological process of assimilating nutrients and is synonymous with "humanizing" or anthropomorphically transforming what is assimilated. And humanization is the most powerful, fruitful, extensive, and useful process that we unconsciously and, sometimes, consciously employ. But it is, for this reason, a falsification of actuality, an extremely creative one. Given the creative, constructive, form-giving nature of knowing, perceptual/cognitive assimilation entails a mode of "falsification" of what is experienced and known. Contrary to some interpretations of perspectivalism,[86] there is no inconsistency between this notion and the acquisition of perspectival knowledge since it admits a plurality of "truths" . . . "*for us*." We cannot know the way the world (or any of its dimensions) is apart from our "schematization" of it because the "world" or, more accurately, "worlds" mankind has known, knows, and will know are elaborate constructs formed by perceptions, cognitions, psychic processes, culture, history, language, evolutionary change, metaphysical beliefs, etc.

For Nietzsche, there is no nonperspectival knowledge at all and the only "better" or more insightful perspective is one that has considered, thought through, and tentatively adopted a variety of general perspectives and has been liberated from restrictive, one-dimensional cognitive-affective standpoints. Most perspectives are not only incommensurable, but, as we've said, incongruous. Every individual, group, social, cultural, historical, and institutional cognitive-affective perspective is ineluctably restricted, relatively narrow. Consequently, they are "false" by virtue of what they include and exclude. Interpretations function from "a determinate perspective," that of "individuals, a community, an ethnic-group, a state, a church, a belief, a culture."[87]

Perspectives function in a dynamic, relational, dialectically interactive field in which there are weak or strong interactions (as ironically replicated in recent particle physics). Although, in terms of his concept of knowledge, Nietzsche cannot *know* actuality from a transperspectival or meta-level perspective, he can (and does) point to signs of its enormous complexity. There are "worlds" only insofar as there are perspectives and each of these relative "worlds" is concurrent with innumerable incongruent worlds or horizons of experience. Nietzsche claims that "Nichts ist *congruent* in der Wirklichkeit" [Nothing is *congruent* in actuality].[88] He does not suggest an "omniperspectival" possibility of complete knowledge. This would defeat his belief that there will probably never be a convergence on such a holistic "truth," and would negate fundamental assumptions in his thought.

To hold that entities differently constituted, in different "conditions of existence," and necessarily actively engaged in different interpretive-perspectival activities would not contribute to the dissolution of holistic truth, but rather point to "truth" positively conceived,[89] is questionable. That is, an indefinite number of incongruent perspectival "truths" (if they could be known) would, in fact, undermine any unified concept of truth. As a description of how we know and as a method for the accumulation of knowledge by means of different modes of knowing, perspectivalism is pluralistic.

What Nietzsche desired to subvert is the belief that there is a single, particular or global perspective that is the only valid or significant one. This is *a fortiori* the case when thinkers (such as Nietzsche's nemesis, Dühring, as well as others) claim to have unproblematic knowledge of what actuality-in-itself is; who erase uncertainty, ambiguity, and every other perspective on actuality; who are blithely unaware that their depiction of *Wirklichkeit* is a restricted perspectival interpretation. Nonetheless it is one that *does* provide us with knowledge in Nietzsche's sense: "Knowledge is the falsifying of the multifarious and incalculable into the identical, similar, and calculable."[90]

Knowing entails the transformation and transmutation of the chaos, the complex process, and the rhythmic interactions that sensory experience and intuition, as well as the theories of biologists, physiologists, physicists, and philosophers of science disclose. These strongly suggest the character of actuality. If it were not, Nietzsche avers, for "the coarseness of our senses," we would be able to perceive the dancing chaos in which we exist.

Consistently stressing the absolute flux of becoming, Nietzsche accepts the notion that the act of representing (*Vorstellen*) is subject to change and instability. Conceiving of representation as if it were characterized by sameness and stability may be "a *condition of existence*" for us. Our mode of thinking must comprehend actuality in the way it does in its representation of our world. For "thinking would be impossible if it did not *misconstrue* the nature of being (*esse*) from the beginning: it must *affirm* substance and sameness because knowledge of what is completely fluctuating is impossible." He concludes that how we comprehend our experiences, our environment and our world is contrary to the fluctuating dynamism of actuality. This is necessary in order for our species to survive, function, and master its environment effectively.[91]

Nietzsche sometimes erases the line between subjective and objective, sometimes emphasizes subjectivity, points to their interaction or characterizes the "subject" and the "object" as necessary fictions. By vacillating on this question he often sows confusion. But one thing is certain: he intends to subvert traditional foundationalist philosophical standpoints.[92]

The will-to-knowledge has been and remains a preconscious activity closer to an instinct than to a self-conscious intentional process. At one time, Nietzsche used the term *Urintellekt* or "primal intellect" to refer to such instinctive modes of "knowing." In its most basic mode knowing is compared to alimentary functions of incorporation and assimilation. In addition, it involves an imposition of form, organization, and meaning (or their equivalent in nonhuman forms of life). The focus of these processes in a field of experience is a phenomenon or event of interest or concern, attraction or aversion, desire or fear. The range of this "assimilation" is extensive and whatever is "incorporated" has been subjected to a process of transubstantiation, has already "been anthropomorphically organized."[93]

There is an ineliminable "subjective" dimension to the "knowing-process" (*Erkenntnissprozess*) that encompasses not only emotive or nonrational factors, but all of our "value-interpretations." However, the "subject" that Nietzsche and his postmodern followers decenter, displace, or erase is the "metaphysical subject," the isolated, disembodied, untouched, timeless, nonnatural, transcendental subject, or what Nietzsche sarcastically calls "the subject-in-itself." He does not repudiate the psychophysical organic individual or deny bodily subjectivity. In *Zarathustra* he reinstates the body to its rightful place and praises its (philosophically) neglected wisdom. The bodily self is not the substantial unity it appears to be, but a dynamic unity comprised of what are variously described as drives, forces, atoms, power-quanta, or will quanta [*Willens-Quanta*]. In the psychic aspect of our being "every drive is a type of thirst for power, every one has its perspective, which it wants to force on the other drives as a norm."[94] Relying on the functions of the body, we may conceive of "man as a multiplicity of living beings, partly struggling with one another, partly adjusted and subordinated to one another."[95]

The central point here is that, despite occasional tendencies toward idealist subjectivism, Nietzsche never effaces *organic subjectivity*. To be sure, he continues to idealize preorganic being because there is supposedly no error there, and in fact, this domain is ranked above that of living beings. In "the inorganic domain . . . there is a nonindividual spirituality [*Geistigkeit*]. The organic being has its own angle of vision of egoism, repeatedly preserving itself in order to continue [in existence]."[96]

Subjectivity, individuality, interest, and "value-interpretation" enter into our orientation toward and comprehension of anything whatsoever.

> The question "what is that" is an assignment of meaning, as seen from something else. The "essence," the "entity," is something perspectival and already presupposes a plurality. At bottom there always lies "What is that *for me*?"[97]

The constructive nature of knowing is amplified in Nietzsche's approach to the knowledge-process. More or less, he relies upon basic physiological theses: that our senses are limited, selective in their responses to a multiplicity of stimuli, and are engaged in a primitive form of "abstraction." As we've seen, he often refers to the simplifying activity of our senses, to their "coarseness," to their selective shaping of the perceived world. Since our senses are organically individuated, and since our psychic orientations and interests vary over time, the "world" we experience is necessarily *our* world. Many of Nietzsche's observations on the sensory dimension of perspectival "knowing" have long since been incorporated into the psychology of perception. Some of his insights would be included under the notions of "perceptual set" or perceptual styles.

Not only the perspectival optics of *our* life influence the way we perceive our environment. The world we encounter through perception not only exists "for us" as individuals, but it exists "for us" as a species because Nietzsche is committed to a version of the evolution of our sensory system. The way that we now perceive the surrounding world is the consequence of a long process of natural selection. And as we've seen, this assumption about the development of a way of perceiving the world plays a key role in the analyses of concept-formation, as well as in repeated claims that coming-to-know involves "falsification" in the sense of transformation.

Relying in part on his intuition of the dynamic becoming of actuality and, in part, on the disclosure of the extraordinary complexity of actuality in the sciences, Nietzsche conceives of sensory experience and cognition as modifying what is experienced and known. As he puts it, "thought consists in falsifying by transforming, sensation consists in falsifying by transforming."[98] Here, as in many other places, an acquaintance with the nature of a dynamic actuality is assumed in order to argue that what we normally take to be presented to us is already transformed by our evolved modes of perceiving and thinking. This is not an arbitrary assumption because Nietzsche relies on the emerging conception of actuality in the scientific world-interpretation. Despite his conventionalist understanding of scientific principles and concepts, despite his strong tendencies towards antirealism, Nietzsche quite often adopts the scientific approach to actuality and uses it for dialectical purposes. That is, he uses it to put in question our previous ways of thinking about the external world, as well as commonsense realism.

In an extended note, Nietzsche clearly indicates that much of his skepticism about objective knowledge is derived from his response to the evolution of the scientific temperament. He maintains that, little by little, "thanks to the sharpening of the senses" and an attention to detail, "cases of identity or likeness are admitted ever more rarely." The external world is more and more "differentiated." Speculating on mankind's prescientific conception of entities, Nietzsche contends that "for incalculable periods of time on earth a thing was thought of as identical and consubstantial with a single one of its properties." Gradually, "many distinct qualities pertaining to a single thing" have been granted. Obviously thinking of the emergence of a scientific culture and mentality, he asserts:

> The more refined the sense, the stricter the attention, the more numerous the demands of life, the harder . . . it became to admit that our "knowledge" of a thing, in fact, amounts to a definitive knowledge, to a "truth." Finally, when our methodological caution brings us to the point we have reached at the present day, we no longer claim the right to speak of truths at all, in an absolute sense.[99]

As scientists and proto-philosophers of science had shown him, the improved methodologies of the exact sciences reveal that we have only relative knowledge, knowledge of "effects." At best, we are left with fragments of truth. Moreover, a number of nineteenth-century scientists argued that the ultimate constituents of the natural world elude us, emphasized the limits of natural scientific knowledge, and embraced agnosticism. In the note cited above, Nietzsche reflects this atmosphere by asserting that "we have abjured out faith in the knowability of things, likewise our faith in knowledge."[100]

The conception of an isolated, distinct "thing" is a fiction, and the notion of a thing-in-itself is "a contradictory fiction." Knowledge in the sense of a holistic and unitary understanding of actuality is found nowhere, "is . . . only a fiction."[101] So, Nietzsche's skepticism about objective knowledge, as well as his perspectival treatment of knowledge, is strongly fueled by his understanding of the philosophical implications of the growth of scientific knowledge and the emergence of agnosticism in the sciences about the fundamental nature of actuality. Whereas someone with the temperament of C. S. Peirce could accept with confidence the self-corrective nature of science, accept the provisional nature of its propositions, and embrace fallibilism while hoping for the eventual convergence of scientific knowledge about reality in a remote future, Nietzsche is plunged into a metastasizing skepticism in response to his understanding of the implications of scientific theories, strict methodologies, disclosures of a senseless "atomistic chaos," the emergence of a dehumanized world-picture.

Whether agnosticism has a Kantian form (i.e., we cannot know things-in-themselves) or a nineteenth-century scientific form (i.e., the essence of things is unknown to us), Nietzsche argues that even in such instances there is a false claim to knowledge. That is, knowledge of the *distinction* between the essence of things and the phenomenal world. In order to justify this distinction, he insists, we would have to think of our intellect as having a "contradictory character." To think of it

> on the one hand, designed to see from a perspective (after the manner required of creatures of our species, if they are to maintain themselves in existence), and on the other hand, endowed simultaneously with a faculty for conceiving this seeing *as* a seeing from a perspective . . . as capable, in other words, both of believing in "reality" as though it alone existed, and also of judging this belief a perspective-limitation with respect to true reality. But a belief judged in this way is no longer a belief, as a belief, is it dissolved.[102]

Once we accept that there are an indefinite number of perspectival "truths," once we have admitted the perspective-limitation of every perceptual-cognitive standpoint, Nietzsche maintains, we can no longer retain the metaphysical realist notion of an independent reality that transcends all perspectives. Here he leaves the model of the literary text (which informs Nehamas's study of Nietzsche so deeply) behind. For the indefinite number of more or less interesting, more or less fruitful interpretations of a text never denies the existence of a text. But what Nietzsche is suggesting in the above notation (and elsewhere) is that reality is not a "text," that the perspectival disclosure of appearances, of apparent worlds, is what we mean by "reality." Reality is comprised of appearances that exist for a plurality of beings. Whereas a literary text would remain even if all interpretations of it were deleted, there would be no world, no "reality," if all perspectival interpretations were erased.

Nietzsche maintains that the belief "that things have a *constitution in themselves* quite apart from interpretation and subjectivity, is *an entirely idle hypothesis*, it assumes that *interpretation and subjectivity* are not essential, that a thing outside all relationships would be a thing."[103] This inevitable degree of subjectivity also enters into the physicist's world-interpretation. Every sensory, cognitive-affective individual interprets actuality from a specific perspective that is in part inherited and in part shaped by conditions of existence or, in the sciences, by prevailing paradigms. Nietzsche is committed to the view that as there are changes in conditions in life, changes in "affects," changes in theoretical orientations and methodologies, so, too, are perspectives changed.

A *perspectus* is what is ascertained or "known" from a particular point of view. There is a "plurality of interpretations" and, hence, a multiplicity of meanings because there is a plurality of interpreters. Nothing we know has a completely independent constitution-in-itself. By implication, Nietzsche is extending a Kantian approach to knowledge in an extreme way since anything we claim to know has already been constituted by interpretative simplification, perceptual form-imposition, selective arrangement, and every other sensory, cognitive, and affective contribution to the knowing process.

Despite what is said in thought-experiments about "*the* world" and *the* "phenomenal world," an unavoidable implication of perspectivalism is that, at any given moment, there are as many "worlds" as there are centers of interpretation. To be sure, some of these worlds are more or less perduring as a consequence of a temporarily shared collective cultural perspective. Thus, references can be made to regnant "world interpretations" in physics or, for that matter, any interpretation of a world that is shared by any social group. Any such phenomenal world is created and sustained by those who share a given set of perspectives. There are, then, a multiplicity of "apparent" worlds that are incongruous, related to one another, or overlap each other. What we come to know is a set of apparent worlds that comprise reality-for-us at a specific stage of development, individual or collective. All other worlds that exist simultaneously for other interpreters, because of constant change (perceptible or imperceptible), are subject to momentariness, though not, of course, typically experienced as such.

Again, we can see why the metaphor of a text subject to a indefinite variety of interpretations breaks down as Nietzsche generates a complex conception of multiple concurrent perspectives. If reality were construed as a text, and if we held Nietzsche to his idea of a series of multidimensional perspectives, then he would find himself in the Kantian position he energetically attacks. That is, he would have to admit that, since perspectival interpretation conditions whatever we can claim to know, there must be a text-in-itself (analogous to a thing-in-itself) which eludes our knowledge. Actuality cannot be consistently conceived of in terms of the metaphor of a text because Nietzsche insists often enough that there is no "reality-in-itself."

The perspectival conception of knowledge denies neither the utility nor the existence of human knowledge. What it does is radically to reinterpret the meaning of "knowledge." The valuation of knowledge emerged out of man's tortuous natural history and was perpetuated essentially because of its practical usefulness. In the final analysis, for Nietzsche, all knowledge is practical knowledge. Knowledge is also valued because it can be a source of joy (insofar as this is a consequence of a "feeling of power"). Thinking of his own idea of "joyful science," Nietzsche writes (in notes for *Thus Spoke Zarathustra*), "To know: that is a joy to the lion-willed." This may seem odd considering how much energy he expends in seeking to undermine our faith in knowledge. But it is not truly odd because I believe that he has in mind his own conception of endeavoring to accumulate as many perspectives on man, life, world, nature, and existence as possible, to see with a hundred eyes.

Having abandoned the belief that knowledge leads us to pure forms of objective truth, Nietzsche embraces a perspectival interpretation of the meaning of knowledge. Returning to the passage in *On the Genealogy of Morals* in which it is said that the more "affects" we bring to bear on a given phenomenon, the more closely we approximate "objectivity," we may consider it in a different light. Since Nietzsche has already said that a great deal of discipline and development of the intellect is necessary in the search for "objectivity," and since he is alluding to his own notion of perspectival knowledge, he is using the term "objectivity" in a new, almost ironic, way.

Since any given phenomenon has different senses in different perspectival frameworks (or knowledge-domains), the phenomenon about which we seek knowledge is not the same. Moreover, Nietzsche has stressed the incongruity of various interpretations of man, nature, life, etc., and has referred to the incongruity of multiple, specific perspectives. An implication of this is that the accumulation of perspectival interpretations does not, in any traditional sense of the word, bring us closer to any integrated "objectivity." So it would seem that Nietzsche is recasting "objectivity" in such a way as to say that the multiplication of perspectives, even if they are actually or apparently "incongruent," is the only form of knowledge we can possess. Probably thinking of the "new philosophers" he envisions (or perhaps the "beyond-men" he hopes for), Nietzsche remarks that it is very important to put to use in the intellect "the most diverse perspectives and psychological interpretations." It is important, that is, to have one's "pros and cons" under one's power.[104] By referring to how one appropriates intellectually and employs the knowledge acquired by considering multiperspectival interpretations, he suggests a link, once again, between critical analyses of truth and knowledge and a certain mode of *Existenz*. There is, in fact, a self-reflexive element in this remark since we have in Nietzsche's writings themselves many illustrations of perspectival knowledge.

PERSPECTIVAL INTERPRETATION

It is when Nietzsche, mostly in his notes, seeks to transcend the barriers he himself has erected in order to make apparent ontological claims meant to support his polyperspectivalism that he runs into trouble. As Danto pointed out, Nietzsche "sometimes wants to be saying what the world is like." He particularly refers to the view that "the world" is comprised of "points of origin for perspectives," and that these points are conceived of as "active-powers" or "wills."[105] He was right to call Nietzsche on this even though the context in which these experimental remarks are made is not given consideration. And the claim is even more questionable because of the suggestion that the centers of power or force Nietzsche postulates is a "metaphysics" that expresses what the structure and composition of reality "ultimately must be."[106]

One of Nietzsche's unfortunate habits is to argue for a plausible critical position (e.g., an analysis of knowledge as perspectival) and then to shift abruptly to a positive conception of the nature of reality in defense of an epistemic point. Thus, his discourse, at times, shifts from a self-standing critical restructuring of "knowledge" to ontological assertions that his critical standpoint abjures. This occurs so often precisely at crucial points in his argument that what he says seems at least puzzling, if not simply contradictory. Although this way of presenting his thought cannot be defended, it should be said that the entire construction of his theory of a plurality of "wills to power" has to be placed in a context that highlights its tentative, experimental nature and form.

Given his conventionalist understanding of scientific theories and posits, Nietzsche is fully aware of the provisional, imaginative, and metaphorical nature of his philosophical, global "interpretation" of actuality. His interpretation of the nature of actuality is more closely related to a mythical or aesthetic construction than to an assertion about the ultimate nature of reality one finds in traditional metaphysical discourse. The anthropomorphic (and, hence, metaphorical) conception of reality as comprised of "wills to power" is constructed out of a series of interconnected knowledge-perspectives that have been selectively adopted out of a collection of competing knowledge-perspectives.

It is possible that C. S. Peirce put forward his "metaphysical speculations" in a spirit of fallibilism and that they represented his guess at the riddle of the Sphinx. Under the inspiration of Ralph Waldo Emerson's poem "The Sphinx," Peirce offered his guess at the riddle in terms of provisional speculations that did not pretend to resolve ultimate questions and that were subject to revision in light of new experience or new knowledge. With allowances for a dramatic and aesthetically colored presentation of his thought, much of this could be said, with equal justice, of Nietzsche's philosophic project, even in regard to the similar influence of Emerson on his attempt to offer a guess at the riddle of the Sphinx. In *Beyond Good and Evil* he alludes to Emerson's metaphor for metaphysical pursuits, which he derived from his reading and rereading of his *Essays* over a twenty-six-year period. In this case, it was Emerson's *Nature* that suggested to him that all metaphysical theories are, more or less, guesses at the riddle of existence. If Peirce approaches these "guesses" in the spirit of fallibilism, then Nietzsche approaches them in a spirit of skeptical experimentation. His aim is to complete the anthropomorphic interpretation of actuality in order to give the cosmos a human meaning.

Even if this understanding of his forays into speculative, experimental interpretation were granted, we still have to deal with Nietzsche's transference of perspectival interpretation to the domain of the nonhuman. We have already seen that he embraces the plausible view that all forms of life, both individually and collectively, have diverse perspectival "interpretations" of the world. By defending such a position, he seems to imply two things: (1) that there is an analogy between the perspectival interpretation of phenomena, which is a complex process in man, and the orientation to a world of preconscious animals and plants, and (2) that the perspectival interpretations of nonhuman entities are unconscious. The first implication is a continuation of a pervasive feature of his thinking. Since we are part of nature and have evolved within the natural world, we may be considered as a microcosm. As such, it is reasonable to assume that the process of perspectival interpretation found in our psychic, perceptual, and conceptual functioning also occurs, in some form, in nonhuman organisms. If Nietzsche were reminded that this transference of a human activity to the nonhuman is an anthropomorphic understanding of other beings, he probably would reply that this is inevitable since mankind comprehends the nonhuman by making it familiar, by virtue of anthropomorphic projection. Interpretative understanding is not possible without metaphorical transformation and nothing in nature can be understood unless it is translated into human symbols or signs. This is why one of his basic propositions (previously discussed) expresses a de-anthropomorphic concept of nature that he comes to realize cannot be consistently sustained. First

> the dehumanization of nature and then the naturalization of man; afterwards, the pure concept "Nature" has been attained.[107]

The second implication—that if there is a mode of perspectival interpretation in nonhuman organic beings, then it must be an unconscious process—is related to the assumption that mankind's perspectival interpretations of phenomena have been and, for the most part, still are unconscious processes.

The theory of perspectival interpretive experience and knowing is an uncovering of something that has been generally unrecognized or unconscious in man's development. What came to be considered as objective knowledge was, in fact, a form of knowledge that has evolved and that is conditioned by language, by "our psychology," by our sensory system, by our cognitive acts of organization and simplification, and by the categorical modes of thinking we have inherited from our ancestors because of their serviceability for our conditions of life. And what later was valued as a scientifically attained knowledge of the objective world was also conditioned by all of the above factors and by the diverse theoretical perspectives and diverse "strict scientific methods" applied to "the world." In addition, as the American linguist Benjamin Whorf argued independently of Nietzsche, natural languages, as well as cultures at different historical periods and within historical epochs, profoundly condition our world-conceptions and determine what counts as "knowledge."[108]

The problem with distinguishing between Nietzsche's perspectival analysis of the knowledge-process and his own perspectival interpretations of actuality is that he slides from one to the other (especially in his notes from 1885 to 1888) without signaling the differentiation between the two. In his published works, for the most part, he makes clear that when he refers to actuality he is presenting his guess at the riddle of existence, his "hypothesis," his "interpretation." In such instances, he stresses that he is offering an experimental perspectival interpretation of the ultimate nature of actuality. This does not violate his perspectival approach to knowledge. Rather, it exemplifies it. Thus, the extension of "interpretation" from a specific perspective to all entities is part of his experimental interpretation of actuality and is distinct from his perspectival treatment of knowledge, despite his tendency, in his notes, to fuse the two.

To claim that "perspectivalism is only a complex form of specificity" is consistent with Nietzsche's notion of the irremovable individual element that enters into knowledge-claims. However, the context in which this is said shifts to a speculative-imaginative depiction of the dynamics of actuality.

> My idea is that each specific body strives to become master over all space and to extend its force . . . and to thrust back all that resists its expansion. But it continually encounters similar efforts on the part of other bodies and ends by coming to an arrangement ("union") with those which are related to it, thus they conspire together for power. And the process goes on.[109]

In this curious passage all physical bodies are construed as active centers of force (in the manner of Boscovich's physical theory) which, in terms of a metaphor derived from man's social existence and social relations, seek to extend and increase their power by means of cooperation. Each body confronts a similar nisus on the part of other bodies. Here Nietzsche employs two modes of metaphorical transference: physical bodies (like man) are related to other entities in terms of the perspectival specificity of their being and bodies (like social man) form unions to increase their power. By thinking of all bodies as having specific perspectives, he is clearly using the concept of "perspective" in an anthropomorphically derived way. Hence, the way in which he believes human beings are oriented towards other beings is transferred to all "bodies" via anthropomorphic projection. Therefore, we know that he is here not claiming positive knowledge about the points of view of nonhuman bodies. For this reason, the reference is not to be included in his perspectival theory of knowledge.

What lends support to my segregation of the perspectival conception of knowledge from purely inventive and experimental depictions of the "perspectives" of nonhuman entities is that the "bodies" referred to are assumed to be reducible to monadic "force-centers" that are nonextended. And these are construed as interpreting their reduced "world" from their perspectives. This is a psychistic version of Boscovich's natural philosophical theory of nonextended point-centers. As we've seen, Nietzsche fully understands that such a theory of nature is a sophisticated construction out of ideal theoretical posits. Since he views physical theories as saturated with conventionalist notions and ideal fictions, he does not accept Boscovich's "interpretation" of the natural world as an objective representation of the true essence of nature. Rather, he adopts this theory because it is compatible with his antimaterialism and his "interpretation" of actuality as a fluctuating, dynamic "relations-world," a realm of interrelated, interacting processes.[110]

By adopting Boscovich's theory of the ultimate constituents of the natural world, Nietzsche celebrates the fact that in his theory "we have got rid of materiality."[111] Without being committed to the "truth" of this dynamic theory of nature, he selects it as a model for his reductive philosophical interpretation of actuality. In this regard, he accepts Boscovich's perspectival interpretation of the natural world in order to construct his own philosophical perspectival interpretation of the dynamics of the world. Nietzsche's understanding of force is a translation of this physical theoretical notion into the form of mankind's reflexive awareness of its own "force" (i.e., drives, instincts, passions, affects, etc.). Analogically, he construes Boscovich's "point-centers" (the fundamental elements of the natural world) as "will-points," "will-quanta" or what he also calls "wills-to-power."

Since these unobservable centers of force or energy are understood in terms of human analogy, Nietzsche extends psychic functions to them. Just as Leibniz conceived of monads (spiritual substances) on the model of the human mind conceived of as an immaterial substance, so, too, does Nietzsche understand his dynamic, nonsubstantial, relational "monads" in terms of an analogy with what he holds are the reductive characteristics of human beings. This interpretation of actuality is thoroughly experimental and based upon a number of interrelated "perspectives." It is a consequence of his creative use of his own perspectival account of knowledge!

Nietzsche's experimental attempts to disclose the ultimate nature of reality and to project various modes and levels of "perspectival interpretation" into the preorganic domain is not part of his perspectival theory of knowledge, but a consequence of his particular use and application of it. So, the inclusion of his hypothesis that even "will-points" are capable of some degree of presumably unconscious "perspectival interpretation" is not part of his perspectival analysis of knowledge, but an experimental result of his application of a number of knowledge-perspectives to the questions of the ultimate nature of reality. It is as far from a metaphysical theory of reality as one can get.

It is not the case that Nietzsche "intends the will-to-power hypothesis to cut beneath the fictional level of thought to give us . . . the world as it is."[112] Nor is the following defense of his putative "metaphysics" an accurate one:

> Nietzsche is committed to a definite if rather unorthodox metaphysical world-view, and he intends his statements of it to be taken, not as false, but as true—as true not merely in a relative or perspectival sense, but as true in the sense of being accurate and adequate expressions of the way the world really is.[113]

If Nietzsche intended this, then he has returned to a metaphysical standpoint that he had consistently repudiated and has leaped beyond the boundary of his perspectival account of knowledge. This is not merely counterintuitive, but it neglects consideration of the self-conscious means by which he has elaborately constructed what he himself calls his "interpretation" of reality. Consistently, he applies his perspectival conception of knowledge to the project of attaining a human meaning for the de-anthropomorphic picture of "reality" that he found in the sciences. His global understanding of mankind, nature, and actuality as totality is a consequence of his extensive use of epistemic, differential, perspectival interpretations. He is no more claiming a grasp of objective "structure" or objective truth than he believes that others, despite their conviction, have attained it.

Since any claim to truth, to knowledge, is subject to the conditions shaping knowledge that we have discussed, Nietzsche's own comprehension of *homo natura*, nature and "reality" is no exception to his characterization of knowledge. Moreover, given all that he has said about the metaphorical nature of language and our pervasive reliance on "anthropomorphism," it is strange that he repeatedly relies upon the very metaphorical, anthropomorphic transferences he believes underlie all conceptions of "the world" if he is proclaiming positive knowledge of the authentic nature of actuality.

Having committed himself to the view that the understanding of the nonhuman in terms of man is a transformation of what is so understood, his philosophical interpretation of nature is a self-conscious, if creative, "falsification" of nature in terms of his selective use of knowledge domains. Nietzsche has insisted that the sciences, insofar as they still retain anthropomorphic notions, do not thereby yield objective truth about the natural world. If physical theories are, as he contends, ingenious, creative "world-interpretations," what are we to think of his blatant anthropomorphic interpretation of the natural world?

"Nature," Nietzsche tells us, "must be represented by analogy to man, as erring, experimenting . . . as struggling and overcoming itself."[114] Putting aside the use of "must" where "may" would be more appropriate, we see in this instance that this is a specific (anthropomorphic) perspectival interpretation of nature which, in terms of its metaphorical form, cannot be put forward as "true." If Nietzsche interprets nature in general and the energies of nature in particular in terms of human analogy,[115] then he is quite aware of the transformative nature of this perspectival interpretation. Despite this, it is not a wholly outlandish notion if we assume that man is a microcosm, has evolved out of nature, and has arrived at a self-conscious understanding of his condition. Or, said differently, nature has come to self-consciousness in mankind. So, this anthropomorphic transference, though not arbitrary, is based upon other perspectival interpretations of our place in nature that are, in turn, derived from scientific theories about mankind's biological, cultural, and psychic evolution.

Nietzsche constructs his interpretation of reality by relying upon "human analogy" and a metaphoric model that sanctions transference of a putative human striving for power to a "willing-to-become-stronger emanating from each force-center outward."[116] We have at work here a twofold anthropomorphic interpretation. Nature, *in toto*, interpreted in accordance with human analogy and, by extension, the fundamental reductionist elements in a specific physical theory of the natural world (i.e., Boscovich's force-points) interpreted in terms of a specific interpretation of human nature!

The more Nietzsche relies on such anthropic images and transferences, the further his thought recedes (by virtue of his own criteria) from any previous concept of objective knowledge. However, this is not an error on his part: he is exploiting his own perspectival approach to knowledge in order to construct an interpretation of reality that itself is built out of the bricks of a number of perspectival interpretations of man-in-nature and the natural world itself.

All of the arcs of thought about nature and the "reality" seen from within or discerned beneath an "incomprehensible fluid Proteus nature"[117] pass through man. Except for a temporarily considered de-anthropic picture of "reality" as a complex of dialectically interacting, fluctuating "forces" (in which we are construed as a conglomeration of "forces"), Nietzsche's global philosophical reflections are radically anthropocentric. However, this is not the end of the story. For the conception of the nature of man, which is continually shaped and reshaped, is itself a consequence of an employment of various knowledge-perspectives. The nature of man is not a pure given either, but is a construction built out of a number of perspectives. Nietzsche's conception of the self is not an exception to his conviction that all knowing is interested, affect-charged, and, hence, perspectival. Even as he sets himself the task of interpreting "the frightful original text *homo natura*," he does not do so unaided. The very project itself reflects the influence of the rapidly advancing naturalistic interpretation of the being of human beings.

If, as he does, Nietzsche assumes that our natural history has contributed to the complexity of our being, and he repeatedly seeks to explore the disguised and repressed remnants of the supposed ferocity of our ancestors in our being, this is because he adopts (up to a point) the Emersonian and Darwinian conceptions of human evolution. Before he became familiar with Darwin's theory of evolution, he absorbed Emerson's unsentimental portrait of our natural inheritance. In "Fate" Emerson refers to the "hints of ferocity" in nature that are in us, the cruelty and the "habits" of spiders, snakes, and tigers that are in human nature as well.[118] The picture of the natural world as an arena for the struggle for existence, combined with the idea of man's evolution from more primitive forms of life, reinforced Nietzsche's way of understanding the nature of man. This perspective strongly conditioned his understanding of the *negative* dimension of human nature.

Nietzsche, a passionate student of humanity, invariably sought out images of mankind in virtually any domain of knowledge. And, as many have said, he analyzes this interesting species with lynx-eyes and in a proto-psychoanalytic way, and he seeks to disclose, unmask, and expose the unconscious motivations of our actions, as well as the deception and self-deception to which we are vulnerable.[119]

Goethe's early emphasis on the individual as a complex multiplicity that appears as a unity was a biophilosophical model of organic beings informing much of Nietzsche's analyses of the internal dynamics of all entities, as well as his conception of bodily subjectivity and the multiple drives or impulses to which it is subject.

This conception of organic beings as multiplex influences the conception of the self as a dynamic "multiplicity" of urges and functions, and is preserved in the interpretation of organic beings as comprised of irreducible "wills to power." Such a perspective on the nature of beings serves as one of a number of different ways of understanding them and *homo natura* as well.

In his absorption of the understanding of the important role that the unconscious plays in human life, Nietzsche appropriates a perspective on man suggested in an inchoate way by Emerson, in an indirect way by Schopenhauer, and in an explicit way by Hartmann in *The Philosophy of the Unconscious*. Even though he lambastes Hartmann's advocacy of a world-process that leads mankind to penetrate the folly of volition and see "the misery of existence" and long for "the peace of nonexistence," Nietzsche was deeply affected by Hartmann's conception of the variety of the influences of the unconscious on life and human behavior. He combines this pre-Freudian recognition of the importance of the unconscious in existence with the understanding of Darwinism as uncovering nature "red in tooth and claw" in an early remark about what lies beneath the surface of conscious life. Reflecting on how much about ourselves is hidden by a superficial "consciousness," Nietzsche comments on

> the fatal curiosity of the philosopher, who longs, just once, to look down through a crack in the chamber of consciousness. Then perhaps he will come to suspect the extent to which man, in the indifference of his ignorance, is sustained by what is greedy, insatiable, disgusting, pitiless, and murderous—as if he were hanging on the back of a tiger in dreams.[120]

The psychological analysis of the central features of mankind is a perspective that contributes to Nietzsche's imaginative interpretation of the supposed fundamental nature of reality. What has come to be called his "biologism" is a significant perspectival aspect of his interpretation of the nature of man. This philosophy of biology itself comprises multiple perspectives that have been selectively applied to *homo natura*. The attribution of a "striving for power" to man is a consequence of examining human behavior (religious, political, social, intellectual, etc.) from a number of diverse perspectives. All in all, the multiplication of perspectives on the concept of "the human" occupies much of Nietzsche's attention and contributes to an *approximation* of human nature. What Nietzsche offers, then, is a construct of human beings in terms of a number of selective perspectives. Since he has prescinded the attainment of unalloyed essences, his philosophical construct of our nature makes no claim to certainty or exclusivity. The conclusion that the fundamental trait of mankind is "will to power" is a consequence of a creative use of his own analogical perspectival analysis of knowledge.[121]

What Nietzsche obscures in the development of his construct of human nature is the circularity of his central philosophical enterprise (a circularity that can be disclosed in every such interpretation): the fact that the attempt to provide a perspectival knowledge of human nature is already guided by and influenced by the perspectival-interpretative orientation, the presuppositions, and selective activity of the thinker who undertakes such a task. This is not a flaw in Nietzsche's thinking since, as his method of perspectival interpretation shows, he is quite aware of this process in the thought of others and in his own. The selectivity of viable perspectives in regard to an attempt to comprehend any specific phenomenon inevitable includes a subjective dimension. The difference between Nietzsche and many previous philosophers is that he is self-consciously aware of the way a thinker anticipates the outcomes of his or her inquiry by virtue of the particular perspectives on a phenomenon he or she adopts. The value-influenced choice of viable perspectives is neither a disinterested process nor necessarily an arbitrary one.

If our analysis of Nietzsche's proposal for a method of perspectival knowing of the nature of man is plausible, then we may come to think that he is not, as Heidegger and others have maintained, proposing a "metaphysics" of a universal will to power. Nor is he claiming, in any positive metaphysical sense, that all "will-quanta" or nonextended "will-points" interpret the world, presumably in a highly specific, limited sense, from their perspectives. The ascription of perspectival interpretation to such nonextended "wills-to-power" is, as Nietzsche knows, an instance of metaphorical transference, humanization, transmutation, and, consequently, falsification. Hence, it makes no claim to ontological truth, despite Nietzsche's assertive tone and rhetorical strategies.

The metaphorical interpretation of actuality as comprising a plurality of interrelated wills to power is itself derived from a prior interpretation of the basic nature of mankind. And this, in turn, is a consequence of the application of a number of diverse perspectives to the question of the central trait of the being of man. The hermeneutic circle that Nietzsche embraces and characterizes as his "fundamental proposition" is the interpretation of man in terms of nature and of nature in terms of man. Thus, when Heidegger claims that Nietzsche argues for the "agreement" (*Einstimmigkeit*) between his theory of the will to power and reality[122] he shows that he has not grasped the persuasive metaphorical model Nietzsche created and has underestimated his analysis of the limits of our "knowledge." Moreover, he underestimates the subtlety of Nietzsche's thought and overlooks the tentative, exploratory, experimental, and probabilistic nature of his philosophical project. In terms of Nietzsche's understanding of anthropomorphic, metaphoric language and the perspectival nature of knowledge-claims, it is counterintuitive and implausible to believe that his dramatic, imaginative, and poetic vision of actuality is intended as a metaphysical claim to truth, rather than a symptomological reductive speculation.

Nietzsche's avowal of an experimental approach to philosophy must be taken seriously. For it is largely based upon his underestimated acquaintance with scientific theory formation and scientific approaches to knowledge—that is, the tentative, hypothetical, and provisional nature of even the most disciplined mode of inquiry. Not only is he alert to the role that "the presuppositions of method" play in all cognitive inquiry, but he asserts as his principle and practice a kind of probabilism that abjures apodictic knowledge and, *a fortiori*, avoids any claims to certainty. Both in regard to the thought and principles by which one attempts to live, these are only "provisional" and, hence, hypothetical guides that one can reasonable adopt.

> In lieu of fundamental truths, I put fundamental probabilities—provisionally assumed guiding principles by which one lives and thinks.[123]

And this statement of method is derived from his grasp of the theoretical orientations and practices of the sciences and one he intends to apply to the activity of philosophy.

One of Nietzsche's most interesting and fruitful provisionally assumed guides for thinking was his general conception of perspectivalism, one he frequently puts into practice and uses as a philosophical weapon against dogmatic, one-sided, uniperspectival claims to truth. And even perspectivalism is not dogmatically projected *ad infinitum*, since he admits that it may obtain only as far as our knowledge extends today. In the domain of knowledge, as in the realm of values, Nietzsche is the inveterate *Versucher*—"attempter," "experimenter," "tempter."

Chapter Five

Fictionalism in Science

> Theories are our own inventions, our own ideas; they are not forced upon us, but are our self-made instruments of thought.
>
> Karl Popper, *Conjectures and Refutations.*

> Our concepts are inventions.
>
> Nietzsche, *Nachlass*

Nietzsche's theory of the fictional nature of logic, scientific concepts and principles, and philosophical categories has rarely been discussed in detail. My concern here is to elucidate the instrumental theory of fictions in his thought and the role it plays in his critical analysis of knowledge. I will also briefly analyze some of the negative consequences of this general theory for his own thought.

One of Nietzsche's fundamental claims is that our senses, concepts, psychology, and language contribute to the simplification of phenomena and what we come to know and construct as *our* "world." The intellect is thought of as an instrument, the primary function of which is the organization and simplification of a presumed flux or an ostensible "chaos of representations." Reason and intellect are in the service of life and their functions serve to construct a "world" in which we can act effectively, in which our various "needs" and "drives" are satisfied. Our sensory modalities are selective and conditioned by interest, need, and serviceability. They exclude extraneous detail and, as a result of a long evolutionary process, have developed a precision that is adequate to the preservation needs of the species. We are able to perceive only what is useful for us, only up to the point beyond which our sensory system would be overwhelmed by stimuli. Because of the inherited, acquired, and contemporary psychic factors that enter into our sensory awareness, there is no such thing as "immaculate perception." Perception is pervaded by interest and is value-laden.

Nietzsche's conception of the threshold of our modalities of sense is compatible with recent studies on the psychology of consciousness. Our consciousness is "outward-oriented" and concerned primarily with action; the primary function of sensory awareness is "biological survival." The mass of stimuli that bombard our senses must be selectively limited by a process of "multilevel . . . filtration." This "filtered input" is, then, the basis for our "construction" of our immediate environment. The content of sensory experience is processed in relation to needs, interest, and, ultimately, survival. Furthermore, it is plausibly assumed that our mode of sensory awareness "is only one possible consciousness."[1]

Nietzsche's generalization concerning the "coarseness" of our senses and their selective response to stimuli has received support from empirical data and scientific opinion.[2] The implications of his conception of sensory experience are that we each perceive phenomena from our own perspective and perceive a "world" that is a world "for us." In the sensory process, then, is found the first indication that the "world" in which we live, respond, and act is a "humanized world." Since the world we perceive is presumably one among many, and since our needs, drives, and desires often shape such a world, the environment we experience does not literally "picture" actuality.

Nietzsche, in characteristic hyperbolic fashion, declares that the world apprehended in sensory experience is fictitious. But even though we may grant him the Kantian point that our sensibility conditions the succession of "appearances" that we perceive, it is an exaggeration to say that our sensory system literally and *in toto* "falsifies" reality. For if our sense modalities *did* falsify actuality in a significant way, then we probably would not survive at all. Since we have achieved *de facto* biological survival, our senses must select out or "construct" a world that is at least compatible with actuality or is an *approximation* to the actual entities surrounding us.[3] To be sure, Nietzsche's point is well taken if we assume that our sensory field is the only one that promotes survival, or believe that our sensory experiences enable us to arrive at a truly objective representation of "reality." In this restricted sense, we may agree with him that our sensory world is not necessarily *the* world and that it does not necessarily represent the "true" nature of things.

LOGICAL FICTIONS

The analysis of the fictional and instrumental nature of logic is more complex than the arguments concerning the restricted, selective "world" we experience through our senses. From his earliest writings Nietzsche criticized the notion of a faculty of reason and questioned the validity of a science of reasoning. Reason and logic have an instrumental value "as expedients of life." The principle of identity is said to be derived from the false notion that there are things that are "the same." Our assumption that there are "identical things" leads us to formulate a logical principle of identity that, in fact, refers to no actual being. The subjective compulsion to believe in the validity of logical principles is held to be derived from our prelogical projection of "postulates into events."[4] If the world seems logical to us, this is only because we have first made it logical.

Nietzsche claims that our postulation of "identical things" in the world is the result of a kind of unconscious logical process that is only much later formulated in principles such as that of identity. Although he doesn't elaborate on this point, there is a hint of the structuralist theory that there is a kind of unconscious *a priori* that has developed in human consciousness and later is incorporated into natural languages.

Although Nietzsche may be on the right track as far as the *origin* of the principle of identity is concerned, he obscures the fact that this principle was never intended to apply directly to empirical phenomena, but rather to the identity of concepts and propositions. In effect, he seems to overlook the formal, tautological nature of the principle of identity. By assuming that logical identity and empirical identity are symmetrical notions, he weakens his argument. In general, though, his point has validity in the sense that even though the idea of logical identity may be applied to the world of phenomena, it cannot be said to represent any actual, empirical entity that is necessarily subject to change.

Nietzsche's argument against the law of contradiction is a sophisticated one. The assumption that we cannot affirm and deny one and the same thing is derived from experience and does not express any *necessity*. If, as Aristotle maintained, the law of contradiction is the most certain logical principle, then should we not consider what is already presupposed in it? Either this principle is asserting something about "reality" (i.e., that "antithetical predicates cannot be prescribed to it") or it is an imperative that prescribes that such predicates ought not to be ascribed to reality. In the former case, one suspects that this assumes a knowledge of "reality" independent of the principle. In the latter case, the principle of contradiction would be an imperative and not a knowledge-claim. In effect, it would be a positing of a world that we might construe as "true." If logical axioms or principles are considered as adequate to "reality," then we would have to have a prior acquaintance with "being" or reality. This, naturally, is not the case. If, on the other hand, logical principles are but means by which we "create" a conception of reality, then they are tools by which we represent the real to ourselves by a kind of logical fiat. Finally, Nietzsche suggests that the principles of logic presuppose a metaphysics, a theory of the real, that is itself fallacious.[5]

Basically, it is our belief in "things" that lies at the foundation of logic. It is our positing of isolated "things" or "substances" with "properties" (predicates) that is the support for principles of logic. Since such posited entities do not exist or do not have any real referents (in Nietzsche's view), logic is composed of "regulative fictions," based as it is upon fictional entities. In effect, logic is said to apply only to "fictitious entities that we have created." It is an attempt to comprehend actuality by virtue of a schema of "being" that we have posited for the purpose of calculation and formulation.[6] There is, then, no correspondence between logical principles and actuality. Therefore, such principles are useful fictions needed for formulation, calculation, and the simplification of a dynamic reality.

If we trace Nietzsche's argument further, we find that we have posited fictitious notions such as "substance," "object," "things,"[7] and their "properties" on the basis of an analogy with our own being. The conception of the "ego" or "subject" as a being that has specifiable attributes is our model for the creation of the idea of things or substances that have predicates or attributes. But this notion of an atomic subject that is not affected by change and becoming is itself a fiction. Such fallacious metaphysical assumptions are projected into "the world" and are, in time, taken as models of external objects.

The implication of this aspect of Nietzsche's epistemology is that logical principles or axioms are fictional because they are derived from a fallacious metaphysics of the external world, which is, in turn, built upon the foundation of an equally fallacious metaphysics or psychology of the "ego." It is no wonder that he refers to the basic laws of thought as "regulative articles of belief" that correspond to no reality.[8]

Despite his critique of logic, Nietzsche never denies its value as an instrument by which we "arrange" the world for ourselves or "create a world which is calculable, simplified, comprehensible . . . for us."[9] Not only is the instrumental value of logic affirmed, but also "logical fictions" are necessary as a "condition of human life." At one point, he presents an evolutionary argument. Those who were slow to subsume entities under a "conjectured identity" had a low probability of survival, but those who falsely treated the similar as identical tended to survive and prosper.[10] Nietzsche's analysis of the origin of logic is quite similar to his interpretation of sensory experience. And both accounts serve to show the generally fictional nature of the world we have "constructed" not only for pragmatic reasons of survival, but for the sake of mastery of our environment.

By undermining our belief in the common-sense world that has come to be accepted as the "real world," Nietzsche rids us of the notion of an "apparent world." In one sense, then, his theory of instrumental fictions is meant to be a critical, epistemological description of the origin and fallacious nature of our "picture" of reality. At the same time, it is crucial to his attempt to negate the dichotomy of a "true world" and an "apparent world." If he had remained faithful to his critical epistemic standpoint and to radical phenomenalism, Nietzsche could have forcefully defended his claim that our senses and our logical axioms generate an alteration of reality. His position would then be an anticipation of the fictionalism of Hans Vaihinger. Vaihinger's theory of fictions asserts that the "falsity" of an idea is no reason to suppose that it is not useful, or that it has no "practical importance."[11] However, even apart from the "hypothesis" of the will to power, Nietzsche seems to be inconsistent in his fictionalist theory in that he makes claims about the "world of becoming" that cannot be known, given his skeptical epistemology, to be valid, not to say "true." Before turning to this issue, we will attend to the extension of instrumental fictionalism to "categories of reason" and scientific concepts and principles.

CATEGORIES AS FICTIONS

Nietzsche's arguments in defense of the notion that categories of the understanding are "fictions" are similar to those he trained on logic. He begins and ends his critique of the "truth" of the categories with an attack upon the specifically Kantian "categories of the understanding." The creative power which invented the categories was ultimately "in the service of our needs," of "our need for security," for abbreviated signification, for rapid understanding.[12] It is the practical "utility" of categories that elevated them to the status of "truths." In one sense, he admits that the categories of reason are "truths": as conditions of life for us—as, in effect, conditional truths. But it would be a mistake to assume that they represent, or correspond to, any feature of actuality.

It has rarely been pointed out that this interpretation of the meaning of the categories is really not too far removed from the agnosticism implied in Kant's theory of knowledge. For even in Kant's account, the categories of the understanding are *a priori* concepts that are necessary features of the structure of the human mind, concepts that constitute phenomena as objects of knowledge. Insofar as Kant emphasizes the spontaneous, active function of the understanding, Nietzsche only radicalizes Kant's notion by arguing that the mind constructs categories by means of which the world is interpreted. Since Kant's categories of the understanding are imposed upon our experiences, we do not know, in any apodictic sense, that they correspond to actual features of the external world. At times, Nietzsche refers to our "constitution"[13] of the world very much in the manner of Kant.

Nietzsche repeatedly questions the ontological significance and reference of the concept of causality. He argues that we do not experience any "cause," that "Hume was right" to argue that the idea of causality is rooted in habit. However, this is not a habit of the mind of an individual, but of mankind. Our belief in causality is derived from our fallacious assumption that there is a metaphysical "subject" that is capable of efficacious action. We derive the notion of cause-effect from the belief that "we are causes."[14] It is interesting, in regard to this point, that when Aristotle turns to an explication of the doctrine of the four causes he typically relies upon the model of *human action*. Relying once again on a familiar analogy, Nietzsche argues that the idea of causality has its origin in a false account of a "subject" effecting an action. Therefore, it is itself a fictional notion. Ironically, once he has exposed the fictional, though functional, nature of "causality," he asserts its necessity and admits that the principle of causality can be adopted as a provisional assumption.[15] Although the concept of causality is a deeply rooted "habit of belief," this does not mean that it is "true." In effect, what Nietzsche has done is to reinstate the concept of causality as a useful, heuristic notion that is *necessary* as a condition of life for us. If we could extract from Kant's theory of knowledge any hint concerning the truth-value of the idea of causality, we would have something very close to his view. At no point does Nietzsche ever claim that the concept of causality is *meaningless*. Causality is a meaningful and pragmatically justified category that he is not about to abandon even as he designates it a "fiction." It is, in fact, included in the categories that are "true for us."[16]

Among the other categories Nietzsche analyses, he contends that the concept of "unity" is a fictitious notion because there are no actual unities. Granted that we need "unities" in order to calculate, this does not mean that there *are* such "unities." Repeating a familiar argument, Nietzsche claims that the "concept of unity" is derived from our concept of an "ego." It is based upon our idea of ourselves as unities and derived from our psychic experiences.[17] If there is no "ego," and if the "I" is not a unity but a "plurality," then the concept of "unity" modeled upon this false interpretation of the self is also fictitious. The conception of a metaphysical "subject" is a reflection of our belief in a unity that underlies the "different impulses" and to which we ascribe a variety of states. Nietzsche's alternative "hypothesis" is that the "subject" is a complex "multiplicity" or dynamic plurality of drives, impulses, desires, and passions.[18] We may note, *en passant*, that he uses the fictional idea of a "subject" and subsumes it under the *category* of multiplicity without any suggestion that this notion might also be a conceptual fiction. It is not possible, strictly speaking, for Nietzsche to provide criteria by which to distinguish between veridical and fictional categories. Consequently, he cannot consistently grant a privileged conceptual status to central terms in his own interpretation of "reality."

For the concept of substance Nietzsche reserves his harshest criticism. In the manner of Hume, he denies the idea of the self as a substance, as well as the belief that there are material substances. The concept of substance is a consequence of a grammatical model of subject-predicate relations. The belief that there is a spiritual substance that thinks is not a substantiated fact, but a "logical-metaphysical postulate." It is because we assume the existence of such a mental "substance" that we project substance into the world of phenomena.[19]

Nietzsche is not consistent in his accounts of the origin of the idea of substance. On the one hand, he often argues that it is the grammatical structure of language that leads us to assume a "subject" as an agent or as a being having attributes. On the other hand, he also wants to say that our language retains psychological or metaphysical beliefs that, in time, become canonical sedimentations. It is clear, however, that the idea of a unified, substantial "I" (or *Ich-Subjekt*) that endures through time and change is anathema to him. The self, for Nietzsche, is a dynamic, complex multiplicity that develops, regressively or progressively, in time.

The concept of substance is a falsification of reality and of the self that has gained currency because we need to think of an unchanging "something" that gives us a sense of stability and security. Again, the root of the concept of substance is found in language, not in external things.[20] But language reflects our psychological prejudices, the simplifying tendency of our senses, as well as our (supposed) fear of change and transitoriness. The concept of substance applied to an isolated "subject" is then projected into the world as a means of creating stability, permanence, and the satisfaction of psychic needs. Again, the category of substance has pragmatic or functional value. The only "truth" it has it a utilitarian one; it is a useful, meaningful "fiction."

Nietzsche is not content to rest in a purely critical stance. He not only attacks the idea of substance, but claims insight into the nature of beings. Simply put, he claims that entities are "processes." Each being is a dynamic constellation of "forces" that interacts with other sets of forces. He assumes that each entity that we conceive of as stable or permanent is continually undergoing change and is characterized by an increase or decrease of "power." And each cluster of dynamic "forces" is construed as interacting with other such conglomerations in a process clearly described as dialectical. The very existence of entities is "relational" since each center of force is affected by or affects other centers of force. All of these assertions, of course, depend upon the use of veridical categories of thought. And, in accordance with Nietzsche's epistemic instrumentalism, they must involve a "falsification" of the real. In a sense, he is quite aware of this paradox, for he does say that "linguistic means of expression" are useless for expressing "becoming." It is our preservation demands that lead us to posit a "crude world of stability."[21] In addition, "in a world of becoming, 'reality' is always only a simplification for practical ends, or a deception through the coarseness of [our] organs, or a variation in the tempo of becoming."[22] If we grant these strongly worded claims, then it would seem that Nietzsche should have suspended judgment concerning the nature of "reality" or the constitution of entities or, more accurately, dynamic processes. Since he does not do so, we can only conclude that his own picture or representation of "reality" cannot be accurate or "true."

Concentrating on the ideas of unity, substance, and causality, Nietzsche maintains that they are not "true," that they serve only for the simplification of the world for the sake of preservation and action. The metaphysics based upon them is presumably a "falsification" of the real, the result of an "anthropocentric idiosyncrasy." The world-picture that came to fruition in the Kantian metaphysics of experience is fundamentally false; it is an interpretation of the world that is useful, but inaccurate. In sum, "the world that we have not reduced to terms of our being, our own logic, our psychological prejudices, does not exist as a world at all."[23] The corollary of this is that the world that has been so "reduced" is not entirely "real" either, since it is a thoroughly humanized "world" constituted by us.

Even though it is often said that the particular world-picture that Nietzsche seeks to undermine is that of "common sense,"[24] this is not entirely the case. For, he also seeks to undermine a philosophical one, specifically a Kantian version—that is, a world in which there are "unities" that are "substances" that act upon one another in terms of a universal system of cause-effect relations. And because Kant was determined to present a philosophical justification for the prevalent scientific (Newtonian) conception of the physical world, the world-picture that Nietzsche criticizes is also that of Newton.

To be sure, Nietzsche does also seek to undermine the commonsense conception of "reality" in the sense that he finds in ordinary language a "philosophical mythology" that presumes a "knowledge" of the truth of things. The creators of natural languages also believed that they had expressed "knowledge of the world," but what they had done was "only given designations to things." Neither ordinary language nor philosophical (Kantian) conceptions give us a genuine knowledge of "reality."[25] Again, we may wonder how Nietzsche, using a language impregnated with metaphysical presuppositions and "psychistic fictions" and relying on concepts that are presumably contaminated by fictional characteristics, could presume to describe the authentic nature of "reality." Before considering this question, I will examine his instrumentalistic interpretation of scientific terms and principles.

SCIENTIFIC FICTIONS

That Nietzsche's understanding of the meaning and use of scientific terms and theories is a form of "instrumentalistic fictionalism" is quite clear when we see that such a view holds that scientific concepts and theories are "not intended as formulations of belief or as truths," but, rather, are "employed . . . as mechanical devices for coordinating or generating *bona fide* assertions."[26] With the exception that such "*bona fide* assertions" in science do not strictly refer to objective ontological entities or events (which Nietzsche typically claims), this is a reasonable account of his position.

Despite the impressive achievements of the physical sciences, they do not, according to Nietzsche, offer us a "true" picture of the physical world. The physicist operates with nonexistent things, "with lines, surfaces, bodies, divisible times and spaces."[27] In the physical sciences we find not explanation, in the strict sense of the word, but descriptions and interpretations. The interpretation of the world in physical science is "an arrangement of it" in accordance with a specific (scientific) perspective.[28] Having shown to his satisfaction that many a metaphysical theory of reality is a "system of falsification," Nietzsche turns his attention to the scientific world-view and applies similar criticisms. In doing so, he is not merely being imaginative and inventive. For the thesis that science works with hypothetical notions, fictions, ideal phenomena, ideal laws, and a mathematical symbolization of the world was very much "in the air" when Nietzsche wrote. He is, in this regard, an early contributor to the development of the philosophy of science and, specifically, to instrumentalist and conventionalist interpretations of the scientific enterprise.

Nietzsche criticizes the concept of the "atom" as a fictional notion that is, once again, derived from an analogy to our false conception of ourselves as atomic subjects. Since there are "no subject 'atoms'," there are no physical "atoms."[29] The concept of the material atom is the last lingering sign of the substance theory. The atom is a "reconstruction" of phenomena that is modeled upon a fallacious "phenomenology" of the self as an atomic unit that is capable of producing "effects." "Effective atoms" are construed as if they were "primitive subjects."[30]

Again and again, Nietzsche attacks the idea of the atom as an anthropomorphic fiction. However, he also admits that, for the sake of simplification, calculation and picturability, the notion of the "atom" has a practical and heuristic value. One wonders if he would have held on to such an interpretation in the face of the development of atomic energy and the atomic bomb. When we consider the power for good and ill that has been generated by virtue of the atomic theory of matter, we realize that Nietzsche was writing in a period in which scientific theory was developing at a rapid pace and the technological application of theory was lagging. It is perhaps for this reason that he had so much confidence in his fictionalist interpretations of basic concepts in science. Additionally, physical scientists such as Helmholtz and Mach had already suggested conventionalist views of scientific concepts and theories.

Borrowing the conception of "regulative fictions" from Kant's regulative principles of reason, Nietzsche designates scientific concepts and principles as "regulative articles of belief." Attraction and repulsion are anthropomorphic projections. Action at a distance is a fiction constructed on analogy to our perceptual experiences. The concept of "force" suggests a "willful" discharge of energy. Many of the assumptions of mechanics are "based upon ideal inventions" or formulations useful for calculations (e.g., "force residing in mathematical points and mathematical lines").[31] Referring to Kant, he stresses that human understanding does not merely find laws in nature, but actively prescribes them to the natural world.[32]

In the spirit of the philosophical physicists of his day, Nietzsche conceives of the mechanistic interpretation of the world as a "regulative principle of method," a methodology that seeks to provide a "symbolization of the world." Ernst Mach maintained that mathematics is an "economy of counting," that "numbers are arrangement-signs which, for the sake of perspicuity and economy, are themselves arranged in a simple system."[33] He suggests that the mathematical representation of the physical world and its processes is not a "true" representation of the world or its events. Many physical scientists of the nineteenth century were neo-Kantians who emphasized the agnostic aspects of Kant's thought and stressed the active, creative, and constructive activity of the mind in scientific theory-construction. Like them, Nietzsche speaks of "provisional truth" or hypothetical conceptions. We recognize in his position the phenomenalistic interpretation of science that was earlier enunciated by Berkeley in *De motu* and that is familiar to us in its various contemporary forms.[34]

What impressed Nietzsche in the methods of the physical scientists was the ability to accept a hypothesis as a hypothesis and avoid any claims to apodictic truth. The tentative, piecemeal, hypothetical approach of the scientist is seen as a sign of intellectual strength in that the scientist sees the value of accepting a theory or a concept as if it were "true" for the sake of further discovery. This is in the spirit of his suggestions, in his notes, for philosophers of the future: "What is needed is that something must be held to be true—not that something is true."[35] Simply put, it could be said that Nietzsche wanted to make the regulative, hypothetical methods of scientific inquiry the model for philosophical inquiry. How far his own thought is consistent with this intention is, of course, a moot question.

The "regulative hypotheses" of the physical scientists do not enable us to grasp a "true" representation of the world. Science is not a literal representation of the physical world and its processes, but a symbolization, a theoretical system of signs that is useful for simplification, calculation, and comprehension. Nietzsche discerned how often scientists rely upon "models" of events or processes that are not direct pictures of what may be called first-order phenomena. In this regard, again, the views of a number of philosophers of science and recent and contemporary physical theorists are more technical versions of his insights. Earlier, Mach had argued that "theory plays a part in physics similar to that of certain auxiliary concepts in mathematics; it is a mathematical model for facilitating the mental reproduction of facts."[36] Furthermore, the mathematical representation of physical events is a schematic representation of such events.

> Although we represent vibrations by the harmonic formula, the phenomenon of cooling by exponentials, falls by squares of time, etc., no one will fancy that vibrations in themselves have anything to do with the circular functions, or the motion of falling bodies with squares.[37]

Even though Nietzsche presents his instrumentalistic fictionalism in a typical hyperbolic fashion, it was and still is a viable, if contestable, standpoint. If we stretch his conception of the intellect as virtually designed for schematic simplification to cover the idea of "simplicity" in scientific method, we can find recent analogies to his own viewpoint. Thus, it has been argued that our belief in the simplicity of nature is rooted in our "perceptual mechanism," in our "subjective selectivity that makes us tend to see the simple and miss the complex."[38] The very relativity of our selective, simplifying tendency is incompatible with "the absoluteness of truth."[39] Furthermore, this selective bias towards simplicity affects not only our perceptual experiences, but the creation of "experimental criteria," "the texture of a conceptual scheme," and theory-selection.

If we take the idea of the simplification of the world through sensory experience, logical classification, and categorical schematization in Nietzsche's thought as tantamount to the role of simplicity in science, there is an analogy between his claims and those of some contemporary philosophers of science, especially in regard to the question of truth. Simplicity in theory is considered incompatible with "high *a priori* probability," and even though it is, within limits, relevant in a favorable way to "systematicness and testability," it is not so in regard to "accuracy and truth." In addition, it has been held that, in a strict sense, all factual theories are "false" or, at best, "approximately true."[40]

In regard to his alertness to the function of "cognitive metaphors" in scientific theory, Nietzsche is not far removed from contemporary philosophy of science. Certainly, he would concur with the claim that "theoretical explanation should be viewed as metaphoric redescription of the domain of the explanandum."[41] Again, he would certainly agree that "the process of metaphoric description is such as to cast doubt on any simple identification of the metaphor's reference with the primary system" of observed phenomena or observational descriptions.[42] Nietzsche often enough refers to the metaphoric "models" employed in the sciences and to their value for convenient communication.[43] Where he is incautious or bold is in his sweeping assertion that the concepts, principles, and laws employed in the sciences are all fictional and in his reluctance to admit, except occasionally, that they are "approximations" to the structure of the physical world. He is on respectable ground when he raises the deeper question concerning the "truth" of scientific theories. Here he would find allies in contemporary philosophy of science. Inevitably, our preconceptions, our particular categorical schemata, do influence what "picture" of nature we find acceptable. In this regard, it has been said that

> though Nature must . . . be left to answer to our interrogations . . . it is always we who frame the questions. And the questions we ask inevitably depend on prior theoretical considerations. We are concerned . . . with preformed concepts. . . . [W]e must recognize that "preconceptions" of this kind are . . . inevitable.[44]

A habitual commitment to fundamental scientific concepts or frame-dependent assumptions tends to "blind us to other possibilities." Admittedly, Nietzsche's response to the hypothetical, tentative, and provisional nature of scientific theory and practice was radical. However, his conception of the instrumental and fictional nature of much of the scientific enterprise is, with some modifications, defensible and certainly remarkable for his time and place.

In point of fact, his reaction to scientific theory and his attitude towards extra-theoretical claims to strictly objective truth—his critique of scientific realism—is similar to the views of the antirealist who is critically discussed in so much contemporary discourse in epistemology and philosophy of science.

Like Mach, Nietzsche viewed language as an "instrument of communication" dominated by economy of expressions, inevitably prone to simplification. He would agree that "experiences are analyzed or broken up into simpler and more familiar experiences, and then symbolized at some sacrifice of precision."[45] Although it is true that Nietzsche "stressed the evolutionary dimension of cognitive effort" and opposed the search for comfortable certainties by attacking "all claims to theoretical adequacy or finality by an intellect evolved in the service of man's biological needs,"[46] he did far more than that. He developed a rudimentary instrumental fictionalism that anticipated later developments in the philosophy of science and saw that the nineteenth-century's faith in the scientific world-picture was not entirely justified as "truth."

In his monologue (which he hoped would become a dialogue) with the physical scientists of his day, Nietzsche tried to reflect back to them the philosophical and cultural implications of the triumph of science and the "ontological relativity" it seemed to entail. Stepping back from the numerous details composing the work of science, he believed that he discerned a vast enterprise devoted to the "humanization of nature" for the sake of mastery over it. In the intricate, complex abstractions of the scientists he perceived the hand, the psyche, and the intellect of man at work transforming the world in his own interests, manipulating "reality" for the satisfaction of his needs and for practical aims. Unfortunately, the very strength of the theory of instrumental fictions seems to preclude any "true" account of the dynamic processes that Nietzsche postulates as underlying the phenomenal world we, for the most part, construct.

ESSENCE AS PROCESSES

Despite the fact that he has vociferously argued that our sensory system presents a highly selective representation of the real, and despite the fact that "logical fictions" infiltrate our conception of the world, Nietzsche nonetheless proffers his perspectival interpretation of reality. That this is intermixed with criticisms of philosophical and scientific theories and basic concepts indicates that it is not only a calmly stated conclusion, but is one of the reasons for his attacks on other interpretations. If we grant that our senses organize and simplify the complexity of what is presented to us, if we admit that our senses are "coarse" and limited, then we know that a conception of reality cannot be built upon sensory experience alone. If we accept a fictionalist and pragmatic conception of logic, or if we admit that "sufficiency for the guidance and testing of our usual deductions, systematic simplicity and convenience, accord with our psychological limitations and mental habits [and] operate as criteria in our conscious or unconscious choice of 'good logic',"[47] then we cannot look for a purely logical symbolization of the world that is "true."

Ironically, Nietzsche eventually appeals to a philosophically modified *scientific* interpretation of actuality. The irony arises because he spills so much ink telling us that the interpretation of the world offered in the physical sciences is purely hypothetical, riddled with "conventional fictions," and certainly not a portrait of a "true world." Inevitably, he is forced to rely upon categories that his own instrumentalism must construe as theoretical "fictions."

There is no doubt that Nietzsche is one of the earliest thinkers to put forward a process theory of reality in light of scientific theories. Even in the inchoate form in which it is presented, he repeatedly describes actuality as in a constant state of "becoming," as never fixed or permanent. At one point in his *Nachlass* he reminds himself to remember that "essence is processes."[48] What he means is that, insofar as there is an "essence" of actuality, it comprises a multiplicity of processes. This view is compatible with his general conception of a "world of becoming" that is transitory and continually changing. The individual, too, is a dynamic system of "forces" or "drives" that strive equally for supremacy. We are most familiar Nietzsche avers, with our desires, our needs, our passions, our drives. These interacting and competitive "forces" are *our* reality.[49]

What is true of the "reality" of the psychic complexity of our subjectivity is also true of the body. The body is a dynamic system in which different functions or processes "strive" for dominance, in which the dynamic organic unity operates through shifting "centers of force." What takes place in the body is analogous to "commanding" and "obeying," to "feeling, willing and thinking."[50] In effect, the body is conceived of as a complex relational structure described in terms of a social hierarchy. Given that Nietzsche ascribes to the psychic and physical dimensions of the self a deep complexity, his own forays at description are obviously simplifications, schematic portraits of a living reality that, in a strict sense, cannot be precisely described. The point is that the psychophysical individual is conceived of as a dynamic process in which centers of "force" are constantly shifting, in which each physiological and psychic process is now dominant, now recessive.

Man is an organic being that strives for the discharge of its energies, that seeks appropriation and mastery, and is motivated by a striving for "power." Even though Nietzsche describes the individual in psychological terms and interprets the functioning of the body in psychistic terms, he is presenting an obviously naturalistic conception of the individual that is clearly modeled upon the dynamic theory of "nature" that he adopts for heuristic purposes and describes in his notes from the late 1880s. Just as what we call "physical objects" are reduced to "dynamic quanta" or "constellations of forces," so, too, abstractly conceived, is the self. Drives, desires, needs, and passions are conceived of as "forces" that act upon one another or seek dominance in their dialectical interplay. Here it is precisely the dynamic theory of natural entities that is applied as a "model" to the psychophysical being of man that is characterized as riddled with anthropomorphisms, constructed out of "fictional" elements and a purely "phenomenal" account of the external world.

The model employed in order to describe the postulated dynamic interactions in human beings is a construct, a hypothetical interpretation derived from a number of viable perspectives, both physical and psychological. In terms of his own criteria, it is fundamentally an anthropic appropriation of physical-theoretical concepts that are themselves interpretations of the "essence" of the natural world or, more accurately, the reduction of "essence" to exceedingly complex processes.

When we turn to the attempt to describe the nature of reality as such, we find that it is usually characterized as a "becoming" that has no aim, that is a pulsating rhythm of "quanta of forces" that presumably "strive" for "maximal power." Change is said to be brought about by "the encroachment of one power upon another power."[51] Each entity is thought of as a "combination of forces" that interact with other force-constellations. In organic beings, the life-process is said to be characterized by a "form-creating force working from within that *utilizes* and exploits 'external circumstances'."[52] The "spiritual" expression in life is conceived of as a "tool" that is itself in the service of the enhancement of life, a "higher life."[53]

Borrowing ideas from an emerging dynamic theory of nature, Nietzsche claims that each collection of "dynamic quanta" is in a relationship of tension with all other dynamic quanta. Every center of force construes the rest of the world of entities from its own "viewpoint," and it measures, forms, and feels in accordance with its own current state of force. Despite his reliance on this image of actuality, he points out, as we've seen, that the scientific interpretation of the world is constructed by means of subjective fictions.[54]

While he freely uses the dynamic theory of natural processes, Nietzsche realizes that this world-picture is provisional, inevitably relying upon "conventional fictions." If we eliminate from this interpretation the "phenomenal" notions of number, activity, motion, and the concept of "thing," we would be left only with dynamic centers of force existing in a relation of tension with other such complexes. Nietzsche denies that such processes are subject to laws of force. "The unalterable sequence of certain phenomena demonstrates no 'law,' but a power relationship between two or more forces." The "regularity" we attribute to sequences of events is a "metaphorical expression" designed to treat event-sequences "as if" they were following a "rule."[55]

We do not have knowledge, in the strict sense, of physical processes because we are able to symbolize them in mathematical formulae. Rather, we have succeeded only in designating and describing processes in an abbreviated way for convenience and purposes of calculation.[56] Although obviously impressed by the principle of attraction and repulsion as a principle of explanation, Nietzsche characterizes such a notion as a "fiction." It reflects our tendency to understand "events" as informed by an intentionality that we are familiar with in our own purposive actions. Attraction and repulsion are anthropomorphic notions that we falsely attribute to physical processes in order to seek to understand them. This, once again, is the product of our ineluctable tendency to "humanize" the natural world.[57] Despite this, however, it is argued that actuality is comprised of "relations," dynamic interactions between imperceptible force-centers, and thereby, in effect, deleting essentialism. Aside from the conception of a dynamic field of relations of force or *Energie*, other aspects of the mechanistic theory of nature are a kind of "sign language derived from our logical-psychical world."[58]

Although some have referred to the fragmentary writings on physical theory in his notes as Nietzsche's contribution to physics,[59] this is misleading. As we have seen, he does not accept wholesale the "dynamic interpretation of nature"; nor is there anything in this particular interpretation that Nietzsche himself invented or created. It is but a general summary of the key concepts and principles of eighteenth- and nineteenth-century physical theory (e.g., those of Boscovich, Mach, Mayer, and the theories discussed by Lange and by Dühring in his *Kritische Geschichte der allgemeine Principien der Mechanik*). Rather than putting forward a miniature physical theory he is presenting in provisional, experimental form an interpretation of reality in terms of selected features derived from the world-picture of the physical sciences in the latter part of the nineteenth century. He is, in effect, following his own advice to adopt a "method" of inquiry based upon a Machian "economy of principles."[60] Since he criticizes the very dynamic theory he partially adopts for its anthropomorphism, its reliance on "psychistic fictions," he is obviously not accepting it as a literal representation of "reality." Instead, he is weighing the philosophical implications of such a theory for an understanding of processes that belong to "the same order of reality."[61] His attempt to penetrate the nature of actuality is necessarily provisional, hypothetical and, in the final analysis, guided by instrumental fictions.

Even though he is skeptical about our understanding of "denatured" force, Nietzsche finds the concept of "constellations of centers of force" appealing as a physical interpretation of the world. It is not that he had no "clear idea of what he meant by 'force' or 'centers of force'." And it is equally erroneous to chide him for failing to see that "the nature of the world is something to be determined experimentally,"[62] since he is quite aware that he is dealing with a theoretical conception of the structure of nature that is, like contemporary views, based upon theoretical assumptions about "force," "mass," and "acceleration." Nietzsche, like many physical scientists, would be quite surprised to be told that the nature of the physical universe must be determined "experimentally."

Having read Boscovich's *Theory of Natural Philosophy* with care and enthusiasm, as well as the works of Zöllner, Mayer, and Mach, Nietzsche had acquired a rough working knowledge of recent and contemporary developments in the physical sciences even before he published *The Birth of Tragedy*. Nietzsche understood the concept of *Kraft* well enough to realize that it was a postulation put forward to "explain" observable "effects." He understood it well enough to see that a "force" we cannot imagine is really inconceivable, that the idea of force serves to indicate that which is the basis for the external discharge of energy. Finally, he realized that the conception of *Kraft* as a dynamic center of energies banished the conception of solid matter and effectively undermined the concept of "materiality."[63] The "centers of force" that Nietzsche refers to are hypothetical "point-centers" that were assumed to interact with other such "entities" through attraction and repulsion. In regard to such notions, he remarks that "the assumptions of mechanics" rest upon ideal constructs.[64]

Because Nietzsche has concluded that all flux is a "determination of degrees and relations of force,"[65] he is prepared to offer a philosophical interpretation of Boscovich's interpretation of the interior dynamics of the world. "The world" is nothing other than the "totality" of actions emanating from "every center of force." And "reality" "consists precisely in this particular action and reaction of every specific part toward the whole."[66] This conception of reality is clearly a philosophical interpretation of the quantitative, dynamic theory of forces in a constant process of interaction. This notion is not yet the qualitative, anthropomorphic interpretation of the physical-theoretical world-picture expressed in terms of the "will to power." (Since the "hypothesis" of the will to power is put forward in order to gain a human understanding of the "world" as seen "from within," and since it is analyzed elsewhere, we shall defer any discussion of it here.)

A question that remains is, can Nietzsche's conception of reality be treated consistently as an exception to his instrumental fictionalism? The answer, I believe, has to be no. He believes that the world-picture of then-recent physical science, despite its impressive qualities, is constructed with psychistic fictions, regulative articles of belief, and theoretical entities. Therefore, any philosophical interpretation of such a theory is equally affected by fictions posited for instrumental (specifically, theoretical) purposes. In this regard, Nietzsche's form of instrumentalism undergoes alterations and metastasizes even though his application of it to science virtually approaches contemporary versions.[67]

Nietzsche's understanding of instrumentalism passes through three basic stages. First, he offers evolutionary arguments concerning the utility of certain logical principles or categorical determinations for the preservation of the species. Second, he argues that we posit fictions and construct a "world" in which we can effectively act for the sake of the enhancement of life. Third, he sees the instrumental role of scientific principles and constructs in terms of the "practical" tools of working scientists (e.g., simplicity, calculation, symbolization, formulization and economy), as well as in relation to the practical aim of science as the mastery and control of natural "forces" for the sake of the development of the species and its "feelings of power." At each point in these stages fictions play a significant role as tools for the schematization of the "physical world."

Paradoxically, Nietzsche is unable to interpret reality even in his restricted, reductionistic terms without employing categories that, if he is internally consistent, must be fictions. The concept of "force," for example, is said to be comprehensible only as something that exists as if it were "will." That is, force can be understood as a willful "commanding of other subjects" which, as a result, "change."[68] But this is immediately recognizable as an anthropomorphic "fiction."

It is clear that a theory of actuality as a system of centers of force that act and react in a relationship of tension or "struggle" cannot do without a category that is included in Kant's table of categories, but is scrupulously avoided by Nietzsche's critical rapier—that is, the category of "relation." Certainly, it would seem that if "unity," "substance," and "causality" are construed as fictions, the category of "relation" should not be given a privileged status, despite its plausible application to the cosmos, history, society, and individuals. Again, the concept of "plurality" (*Vielheit*) is used with no hint of its fictional nature. Rather, it is central to Nietzsche's conception of actuality, as well as to his conception of the psychological "self." The concept of an interaction of "dynamic quanta" of energy certainly appeals indirectly to the category of "reciprocity" (*Wechselwirkung*) and assumes its veridical nature.

Finally, there are three central categories that Nietzsche relies upon in constructing his philosophical interpretation of the dynamic theory of nature that must be considered as theoretical fictions: "force," "action," and "passion." Insofar as he critically analyzes the category of causality and insists that it is a "conventional fiction" or a "regulative article of belief," he cannot spare these three categories from his critique. This is *a fortiori* the case if his critical analysis of the categories of "reason" is primarily directed at Kant. For Kant sees the ideas of *Kraft*, *Handlung* and *Leidenschaft* ("force," "action," and "passion") as "predictables" that are derivative concepts of the understanding and encompassed by *die Kategorie der Kausalität*.[69]

Nietzsche's attempt to give a philosophical meaning to the physicists' dynamic world-interpretation has to be considered as a hypothetical, fictional interpretation that cannot make legitimate claims to truth. Of course, anyone may follow Nietzsche and accept his interpretation of "reality" as constructed out of instrumental fictions that we may embrace as if it were "true." Unfortunately, his positive assertions about actuality suggest that he is not fully aware that his cherished interpretation cannot entirely escape the nets of his own critical epistemology. The more we are persuaded by his arguments in favor of an instrumental fictionalism that encompasses sensory experience, logical principles, categories, and scientific theories of nature, the more we must insist that Nietzsche's thought be subject to the same kind of critical analysis. This is especially the case because the theory of fictions is not merely a contingent feature of his thought, but is central to it, and is a weapon that he freely uses against his opponents.

If he had been a more cautious, less imaginative thinker, Nietzsche might have found shelter in a radical phenomenalism[70] that would have been compatible with his version of instrumental fictionalism.[71] However, the need to complete a multifaceted picture of actuality and to offer his imaginative, perspectival interpretation of the riddle of existence carried him far beyond a purely critical, cautious philosophical stance. It is characteristic of him to seek to go beyond the theoretical obstacles he created in order to present his aesthetically conceived vision of a "reality" that expresses itself in a bewildering variety of protean forms.

CHAPTER SIX

THE STRUCTURALIST PERSPECTIVE

The fact of the matter is that the "real world" is unconsciously built on the language habits of the group.

Edward Sapir, *Language*

Although Nietzsche is mentioned in the works of structuralist thinkers and is a strong presence in the writings of Foucault, the precise relationship between his analyses of consciousness, language, and structural analysis has not been delineated. This dimension of the philosophy of this many-sided thinker has been recognized, but not fully explored. Although Nietzsche is not the pure type of structuralist, he is, nonetheless, very much concerned with the uniformity in forms of thought and language that he believes have determined the cognitive-linguistic system of those who think, speak, and write in Indo-European languages. This concern is central to his critical stance in relation to sedimentations of language and thought that he believes have perpetuated a false, but pragmatically useful, conception of the world.

PROTO-STRUCTURAL ORIGINS

In all probability, Nietzsche found the first suggestion of a structural analysis of language in his study of F. A. Lange's *History of Materialism*. He discovered this work in 1866 and returned to it for inspiration from time to time, specifically incorporating some of its critical analyses into his epistemological notes of the late 1880s. Since we have sufficient evidence that he studied Lange's rich critical history of materialism with great care[1] and praised it as a "treasure-house," we are justified in looking there for a foreshadowing of his own structuralist leanings.

In the course of examining recent work in anthropology and in the "psychology of peoples," Lange refers with approval to a study of Bastian's, *Der Mensch in der Geschichte* (1830), considered an important contribution to "ethnopsychology" or "*pragmatisch Anthropologie.*" Specifically, Lange praises Bastian's sympathetic understanding of primitive peoples and his recognition of the complexity and richness of their cultures. What he has to say about the value of Bastian's study is especially interesting in light of the subsequent development of structuralism. He remarks that Bastian saw

> that the similarities in the mental condition of peoples, and especially in their mythological traditions, are to be explained, not so much by their descent from a common primitive stock, as by the same psychological disposition, which must necessarily lead to the same or similar creations of superstition and myth.[2]

Lange assumes that primitive societies share common psychological tendencies and that these proclivities are preserved and reflected in language. He sees the science of "linguistics" as an important tool by which the concepts of mind and nature may be brought closer together.[3] In general, he suggests that language reflects or expresses a culture and that a culture is an expression of psychophysical orientations at a particular stage of life and development. Without using the term, he implies that, as Wittgenstein held, language is an expression of a "form of life" (*Lebensform*). Moreover, he emphasizes that many of the basic issues in philosophy center around problems of language.

Language is a system of "signs" not meant to designate "particulars." Lange agrees with Epicurus that language evolved in practice and its signs have come to have specific meanings "by convention."[4] He views the growth of "ultra-logical formal analyses" in medieval philosophy as a reflection of the "rise of empiricism." There is a need for precision in the use of language in order to attain "accurately defined signs for the things we mean to express." A clarified analysis of linguistic signs is needed because languages contain "the prejudices of past centuries" and the beliefs of men at primitive stages of development.[5] There is also a need for a theory of the significance of words or signs in which special attention would be paid to the relation between the word and its meaning. So important a key to an understanding of the human world is the analysis of language, that "the whole problem will . . . sooner or later have to be taken up again . . . in another connection and with another purpose."[6]

The proper understanding of the nature of language is essential for a philosophical understanding of the world. If we assume, Lange says, that words provide adequate "pictures" of things, then we open ourselves to innumerable errors. Words are, at best, "arbitrary signs" (*gebrauchende Zeichen*) for certain ideas.[7] The conventional meanings of linguistic signs are not, however, insignificant; they provide a means of understanding the patterns of thought, the values, and the psychological beliefs of peoples.

Although Lange does not develop a theory of language and does not elaborate upon his *obiter dicta* concerning language, he does plant seeds of thought in Nietzsche's mind that eventually germinate. And, of course, neither Nietzsche nor Lange is interested in the analysis of language as an end in itself. The examination of language is a means of seeking to understand the psychocultural basis of human thought and to gain some insight into how we have come to have the cognitive-linguistic framework we do have.

LANGUAGE AND ACTUALITY

From his earliest reflections on language, Nietzsche was convinced of its functional, social foundation and its rhetorical nature. Words are metaphorical "signs" that refer to immediate experiences that are complex and characterized by specificity and are present to us as physiological occurrences in the brain. By means of repetition, social acceptance, and conventional agreement, these arbitrary signs (when spoken or written) come to be used to signify objects or events. Concepts, as we've seen, are considered as secondary metaphors which are further removed from immediate experience. A word is a sign that radically simplifies what it refers to or indicates and that arbitrarily assigns meaning to something. We attribute gender to commonly perceived entities and economically simplify that to which we refer. We identify a "tree" (*Baum*) as masculine, but identify a "flower" (*Blume*) as feminine. We say, "The stone is hard," and thereby attribute a quality to something that is, in fact, a subjective response to a stimulus. Words used to refer to common entities may designate only an aspect of their behavior.[8] This is a metaphorical trope or perhaps a synecdoche. By means of such arbitrary, symbolic, reductive signs a "world" is created, a linguistic-conceptual world that is then taken to be actuality. But the metaphorical representation does not correspond to an extralinguistic actuality since tropes transform what has been concretely experienced.

The simplifying nature and function of language are illustrated by the fact that we represent perceptual experience in language in a denuded way. We say, for example, "This is a leaf," and thereby ignore or delete the specific texture, shape, color, or surface appearance of what we actually perceive. By virtue of this simplification, linguistic signs serve rapid communication and a kind of stenographic transmission of basic information. All in all, Nietzsche argues, language has a practical, social function and is suffused with tropes. Adequate and functional language becomes canonical over time and a "primitive world of metaphor" is accepted as valid even though it is "the petrification and coagulation of a mass of images."[9] The gradual congealing of commonly accepted metaphors eventually comes to be appropriated as a justified and accurate representation of "the world," a world that has, in fact, been created, anthropomorphically transformed.

There is a persistence of metaphorical forms that accumulate diachronically and infiltrate later philosophical and scientific discourse. In time, Nietzsche points out, the "exact sciences," as they develop, endeavor to separate their language from these metaphorical, anthropomorphic sedimentations. For a long time, however, the web of linguistic-conceptual metaphors tends to enclose mankind in a representation of "the world" that is accepted as an expression of "truth." This imaginative, socially colored and determined "truth" is, however, actually a form of "anthropomorphic truth" (*anthropomophische Wahrheit*). In his brief, overly condensed analysis of language in "On Truth and Lying in an Extra-Moral Sense," Nietzsche replicates some of his derivative lecture notes on ancient rhetoric and, at the same time, sketches (in 1873) what was later to become the humanistic or pragmatic conception of truth.[10]

Although he doesn't call it such, Nietzsche is speaking in his early essay about "ordinary language." One of his central points is that ordinary language is composed of metaphorical signs, the origin of which has been forgotten. The rationale for the use of an inherited linguistic system is in part conventional and, in part, the practical values that it retains—values that are "life-preserving." The linguistic-conventional world constructed out of the bricks of metaphorical signs is not lived-actuality. Rather, it is a "symbol-world" in which we can function, act, and survive, a world which is, in a sense, ideal. The creative, rhetorical, aesthetic nature of language serves to construct a human world of meaning in which man feels at home.

An analysis of ordinary language will not give us an unalloyed access to the specific character of actuality; rather it manifests imagination, metaphorical construction, and a sedimentation of rudimentary beliefs that have proven valuable for the preservation of life. Not only does language not picture actuality, but it simplifies, transforms, and embellishes it. The analysis of ordinary language leads not to actuality as such, but to a world of shared attitudes, values, and beliefs, a social world that is pervaded by conventions. Insofar as ordinary language expresses "truths," these are humanized "truths," "truths" for those who share a common natural language. J. L. Austin's observed that

> our common stock of words embodies all the distinctions men have found worth drawing, and the connexions they have found worth making, in the lifetimes of many generations. . . .[11]

This is appropriate to what Nietzsche is saying, but not exactly in the way it is usually taken.[12]

The words and distinctions that have been preserved in natural language have, as Austin says, "stood up to the long test of the survival of the fittest . . . in all ordinary and reasonably practical matters." Nietzsche would be in complete agreement with this even though, as we shall see, he pushes the formation of the basic structure of existing natural languages back into the remote past and insists that precisely because languages are rooted in "practical matters," they are comprised of conventional, arbitrary signs that express "anthropomorphic truth" only.

Embodied in ordinary language is a world-view, a primitive metaphysics that, in Nietzsche's view, reflects the psychocultural world of our remote ancestors. The "world" that is disclosed in an analysis of ordinary language is not only our world, but ostensibly the inherited simplified world of earlier peoples, a world that is an expression of the average or typical human being. Nietzsche does not oppose the beliefs embodied in ordinary language to the false beliefs retained in philosophical language[13] for the simple reason that the language of philosophy gave sanction to a linguistic-conceptual framework that was inherited from the "ordinary language" of our ancestors.

One of Nietzsche's aims was to expose what he believed was the fallacious metaphysical assumptions immanent in the grammatical structure of ordinary language. He would not agree with Wittgenstein's claim that "what we do is to bring words back from their metaphysical to their everyday use."[14] This is not possible because what has come to be accepted as an ordinary, everyday use of language already entails primordial metaphysical assumptions and beliefs. No natural language is metaphysically neutral. "Every word is a [preconceived] judgment."[15]

LANGUAGE, THOUGHT, AND STRUCTURE

Nietzsche is not a Darwinian in the sense of believing that, by means of natural selection, the "fittest" have survived. Rather, he holds that "evolution" in relatively recent times has tended to favor the average of the species and has tended to eliminate "exceptions." However, he accepts mankind's evolutionary development and applies to it his analysis of language. He avers that "everything essential in human development happened in prehistoric times."[16] This belief leads him to say that contemporary languages (especially Indo-European languages) still contain the classifications, distinctions, and linguistic forms that are rooted in man's remote past. The symbols and patterns of thought that are incorporated in early Western thought are not considered original creations of philosophers. The earliest identifiably philosophical discourse already has incorporated inherited tropes and metaphysical distinctions that have evolved within the diachronic development of a natural language. Nietzsche maintains, then, that

> language belongs in its origins to the age of the most rudimentary form of psychology: we find ourselves in the midst of a rude fetishism when we call to mind the basic presuppositions of language.[17]

Nietzsche's thought here is informed by his early, extensive philological studies of Greek literature and philosophy. He saw clearly how the early Greek thinkers intermixed mythological, poetic and "scientific" language in their writings. He saw, too, that these thinkers employed words that were rooted in mythopoetic discourse. Thus, for example, when Democritus proclaimed that all natural events occur "according to necessity," he gave a "scientific" meaning to what was previously the name of the goddess of necessity, *Ananke*. And Nietzsche knew that what was true in the case of the traces of mythological language in early philosophical language was also true in regard to the preservation of the inherited distinctions and differentiations in language that are (retrospectively) identifiable as metaphysical distinctions and differentiations made in the remote past.

The metaphysical distinctions and presuppositions embodied in natural languages are subsequently projected as products of *Vernunft* or "reason." What comes to be accepted as "reason in language" (or, in recent terms, the logic of language) is an inheritance from man's historical, cultural, and psychological past. Although we may be skeptical about Nietzsche's projection of the "origins" of language into the murky prehistoric past, we may nonetheless grant his point that the long period before the formalization of language brought about sedimentations and crystallizations of usage and meaning, and these were later incorporated into the formal structure of language, into its "logical" structure. Nietzsche assumes in his reflections on language that a diachronic evolution of language-use preceded the formal study of the grammatical structure of language. If this plausible assumption is granted, we can understand why he says that

> very much later, in a world a thousand times more enlightened, the security, the subjective certainty with which the categories of reason could be employed came all of a sudden into philosophers' heads.[18]

What he suggests, then, is that when philosophers present their conceptions of man, nature, and reality, they unconsciously accept and give sanction to logico-grammatical forms that are assumed to be canonical, fixed, and incontrovertible. In this sense, philosophical thinkers formalize and give validity to beliefs and patterns of thought that are, in turn, a reflection of a *Lebensform*, a way of being, a psychic orientation towards life, man, and the world the origins of which have been forgotten. Language not only reflects a "form of life," but it reflects an ontological order. Thus, in examining the concept of "being" Nietzsche claims that it was formalized by Parmenides only insofar as "language inevitably speaks in favor of the notion of being."[19] What this means, even though Nietzsche does not express it precisely this way in the same context, is that a natural language entails an ontology, inherited from the past, the origin of which has been obscured by time. Thus, to cite one among many illustrations, when Thales says that "all things are full of gods," this may indicate a kind of polytheism, a remnant of a more primitive animism, or, perhaps, it may be a metaphoric reference (via the word *theoi*) to what we would call "powers." Nietzsche could point to this statement as embodying a prescientific conception of entities that, in turn, reflects a linguistically supported ontology.

This same process of preserving earlier beliefs about the world or man continues in modern times insofar as a certain system of word-signs or modes of discourse comes to predominate in a given culture during a historical period. Thus, for example, the designation of an entity as a *res* or "thing" becomes canonical over time and eventually gives sanction to what Heidegger (in *Being and Time*) calls a *Dingontologie* ("thing-ontology"), one he finds specifically prevalent in the philosophy of Descartes.[20]

From all that he says about the sociopsychological basis of language-use, Nietzsche would probably agree with de Saussure that "everything in language is basically psychological, including its material and mechanical manifestations," and that "linguistics provides social psychology with . . . valuable data."[21] And, he might add, it provides philosophers such as himself with even more valuable data. In different ways, Nietzsche reiterates what Wittgenstein will later say: language is an expression of a form of life. But he suggests a proviso: the "form of life" expressed in language reflects the "conditions of existence" of the language-users and the psychophysical traits of a social group or culture, of particular *types* of human beings.

In *Beyond Good and Evil* Nietzsche presents an insightful analysis of the similarities of patterns of thought among peoples who share a common "affinity of languages." Just as Lévi-Strauss will find a common pattern of thought in a variety of myths (and variations on myths) of primitive peoples, so, too, does Nietzsche see a similarity in the pattern of philosophical thinking, a "family resemblance" of modes of philosophizing among Indians, Greeks, and Germans. The shared philosophical concepts belong to a "system" circumscribed by "a definite fundamental scheme" of possible forms of thought. The forms of thought in Indian, Greek, and German philosophy are said to be rooted in an "innate systematic structure." He assumes a "primordial" origin for this systematic structure, one that has been forgotten.

What underlies this affinity of conceptual schemata is "the unconscious domination and guidance by similar grammatical functions."[22] Like the structuralists, Nietzsche traces the grammatical structures to cultural conditions of life and, further, to "*physiological* valuations and ethnic conditions."[23] What

Nietzsche is suggesting is a kind of deterministic theory that assumes that psychophysical and ethnic characteristics determine culture, which conditions linguistic forms and which, in turn, determine forms of philosophic thought.

Nietzsche extends his analysis of conceptual structure beyond the point of the French structuralists. For, in the latter, the emphasis is upon the supposed "unconscious *a priori*" in thought that is rooted in the "*unconscious* infra-structure" of linguistic phenomena.[24] Lévi-Strauss is concerned with the social-psychological origin of language use and symbolization. The individual is understood, in the context of a cultural system, as one who is directly and automatically bound to his total society and its system of beliefs and sentiments.[25] Nietzsche wants to say that the form a culture takes, the beliefs and sentiments it shares, are derived from the physiological condition of the peoples comprising a culture. This, of course, has to do with his postulation of ascending and descending expressions of "power" or energy. But in the case of Nietzsche and the French structuralists, there is a common assumption: patterns of thought are expressions of a presumed unconscious process.

It is Nietzsche's contention that the way Western man has come to represent (in concepts and language) a "world" is the result of an evolutionary process, a process that is still continuing. The phenomena we discriminate, attend to, select out of our experience and "human emotions," are focused upon our "human needs" and are part of a world-picture that mankind has constructed over a long period of time.

Nietzsche believes that the world represented by our linguistic-conceptual scheme is suffused with errors and fantasies that have been "inherited by us."[26] The words and concepts that have survived over long periods of time are the bricks of an edifice that is not an authentic representation of actuality. The scientific analysis of what he considers the "origin of thought" reveals that the dominant "world of representation" is one of many possible worlds and is infiltrated by primitive psycholinguistic beliefs. The scientific uncovering of the development of this structure of language and thought enables us to transcend, for a time, the entire process. However, it is extremely difficult, if not impossible, to escape from this inherited pattern of language and thought insofar as we are influenced by the "power of primitive habits of feeling."[27] At times, it is suggested that the power of what the structuralists call the unconscious *a priori* is such that we cannot conceive of the world in terms other than those that have become habitual and canonical. Nietzsche is led to admit that even though language is dependent upon "naive prejudices,"

> we cease to think when we refuse to do so under the constraints of language. . . . Rational thought is interpretation according to a scheme that we cannot throw off.[28]

Such a view may give comfort to the linguistic structuralist who wants to believe that the limits of language are the limits of thought. However, even though Nietzsche does realize that we cannot arbitrarily cast off an inherited, highly functional, extraordinarily useful way of thinking, he extends his analysis of psychocultural, conceptual-linguistic scheme to a point at which he equates it with an average, typical, and fallacious cognitive framework.

After a number of approaches to the analysis of, and description of, the basic terms and categories by which we interpret actuality, Nietzsche engages in a critical appraisal of this conceptual-linguistic scheme. Here he parts company with the structuralists who seem to desire only a scientific, objective analysis of the phenomena of immanent structure in thought and language independent of any value judgment concerning it. The final outcome of structuralism is anti-individualism, since the individual is significant and comprehensible only as a part of the cultural-linguistic system. Against Sartre, Lévi-Strauss argues that there are no isolated individuals, no free subjective individuals. Each individual is shaped and formed by custom, habitual patterns of behavior, conventions, social institutions and by the "unreflecting totalization" of language which operates beneath consciousness and will.[29] Up to a point, Nietzsche would agree with this in the sense that he is concerned with showing how our beliefs, our categorical schemes, and our ordinary and philosophical language are atavistic. The other side of the coin, however, is that this capacity to uncover the cultural and psychic origins of patterns of thought can liberate some individuals from the power of the practical, utilitarian, and "common" way of thinking.

> The individual is something quite new which creates new things, something absolute; all his acts are entirely his own. Ultimately, the individual derives the values of his acts from himself; because he has to interpret in a quite individual way even the words he has inherited . . . as an interpreter he is still creative.[30]

The paradox of the penetration of a linguistic or conceptual structure is that whoever achieves such a comprehensive penetration has attained a standpoint outside the cultural system that is analyzed. Lévi-Strauss tends to use the vast empirical data he has accumulated from the study of primitive societies, primitive thought patterns and myths, *against* the presumption of "civilized" nations. But anthropological structuralism must itself partake of the inherited patterns of thought, the categorical determinations, the habits of inquiry that are part of the Western scientific, cultural system. As in psychoanalytical theory, the insight into the previously unconscious feelings, needs, and thoughts that have conditioned one's behavior ought to be a liberating factor in one's experience.

At times, Nietzsche suggests that when we uncover the "fictions" or mythical notions that have shaped previous linguistic-conceptual schemes, we have, for better or worse, transcended the very structures of languages and thought that were previously operative. The weak link in the structuralist's chain is the posture of value-neutrality, the merely elucidative orientation which is adopted. Once we admit the omnipotence of cultural systems, of conventional language-use, and of unconscious *a priori* concepts, we are prohibited from positing cultural ideals, goals, or aims that are possible. Not only that, but a strict structuralist cannot criticize, morally or aesthetically, *any* actual cultural system. It is perhaps for this reason that Nietzsche, despite his agreement with what has become the structuralist standpoint, was driven to criticize the conventional, traditional, common linguistic-conceptual scheme he spent so much energy uncovering. It is interesting to contrast this attitude to the tendency of Wittgensteinian thought to preserve the *status quo*, to bow to the wisdom of conventional "rules," conventional understanding, and acceptable, expected patterns of language, thought, and behavior.

THE GENIUS OF THE SPECIES

Nietzsche's analysis of language and conceptualization pointed to the practical, life-preserving, socially binding function of inherited ways of thinking. He adopts a critical, ironic attitude towards the pragmatic use of language and thought because he felt it entailed a reduced interpretation of actuality, one that prompted one to *value* only the practical and utilitarian products of one's culture. He correctly saw that this powerful, but one-sided, development would be disastrous for the creation of a higher artistic culture, for the building of a unified cultural style, for the cultivation of creative, "exceptional" individuals.

Nietzsche saw that a predominantly pragmatic language tends to produce a practical culture, a spirit of "scientism" that would eventually undermine the enhancement of life. The positivistic, empirico-scientific interpretation of life, man, and world is seen as a substructure, as a basis for a higher culture, not as a terminal conception of knowledge and reality. In general, he is opposed to any linguistic-conceptual scheme that either devalues time, becoming, and actual existence (Platonism) or reduces actuality to quantitatively measurable "facts." In this regard, he is concerned with the introduction of what Foucault calls an *episteme*:

> the total set of relations that unite, at a given period, the discursive practices that give rise to epistemological figures, sciences, and possible formalized systems.[31]

Even though Foucault is thinking primarily of "scientific" ways of thinking, talking, or writing that achieve prominence at a particular time, his idea of *episteme* encompasses what may be called a cognitive, discursive orientation or system that attains social meaning at a given time. Nietzsche's bold generalization is that from archaic times to the philosophy of Kant, a pattern of thinking and speaking and writing has dominated Western thought. The "world as representation," which Kant presents as our knowledge of the phenomenal world, is actually the sedimentation and formalization of a linguistic-cognitive framework that has been implicit in Western thought and languages for a long period of time. This *episteme* has proven enormously useful, has survival value, and has contributed to man's capacity to master the forces of nature. It is a sketch of structuralism on a sprawling canvas. In order to defend such an elaborate claim, Nietzsche appealed to the theory of the family resemblance of Indo-European languages. In addition, he attempted to show that habitual modes of consciousness preserved in such a family of languages tend to reflect what he called "the genius of the species."

In *The Gay Science*, Nietzsche argues that consciousness is not necessary in order for us to act, think, feel, will or remember. Our life could proceed without the "mirroring" of it in what comes to consciousness. A "consciousness of" our experience is not necessary for our experience to take place as it does. Seeking the "purpose" of consciousness, Nietzsche offers an "extravagant supposition": that the power and subtlety of consciousness is proportionate to the "capacity for communication" of a man or animal. Moreover, this capacity is said to be proportionate to the "need for communication." Throughout "successions of generations," this need for communication has accumulated. Consciousness has developed, Nietzsche continues, under the pressure of the need for communication between man and man. This is a variation on an earlier theme: the valuation of knowledge, language, and truth was socially determined and retained for its life-preserving utility.

Nietzsche's orientation here has, of course, become familiar to us in the form of the premises of Anglo-American pragmatism, humanism, or instrumentalism. The argument is a familiar one: if man has evolved over a long period of time, then the emergence of consciousness, knowledge, truthfulness, communication, and language-use must serve a sociobiological function, a "life-preserving" function. In regard to the original, if not the only, function of thinking, C. S. Peirce once observed that the intellect is an effect of the struggle for survival, a power or function that serves the continuation of the species.[32]

Consciousness emerged presumably out of a necessity of communication for the sake of defense and protection. There was, Nietzsche tells us, a deep need to know what one felt, to know what one lacked, what one thought. At this point in his argument, he admits that he is not denying the reality of consciousness in man; rather, we always think, but this is primarily unconscious cognition. The thinking that enters conscious awareness is only a small part of our "consciousness" and, he says, the most superficial part. In this conscious thinking language attains dominance:

> for this conscious thinking is done in words, that is, in communication-signs, by means of which the origin of consciousness is revealed. In short, the development of speech and the development of consciousnesss . . . go hand in hand.[33]

The emergence of conscious thinking or self-conscious awareness is coeval with the development of *die Sprache* ("speech" or "language"). Communication with others by means of signs (*Zeichen*) serves to inform others of our subjective states of mind; it is a bridge between one human being and another. Those who were "sign-inventors" were the most self-conscious individuals, the most social of social beings. This extension of the need to communicate continues apace and serves the practical needs of the species.

At this point in his argument, Nietzsche takes a decidedly structuralist turn. He observes that what comes to consciousness in us is not essentially a manifestation of *individual* existence. That is, self-consciousness arises out of our social nature. This is *a fortiori* the case with the emergence of symbolic communication in language. What may be called linguistic self-consciousness develops rapidly and becomes more refined in relation to "communal and gregarious utility." As much as we all endeavor to understand ourselves individually, we continually find ourselves thinking in terms of what is "nonindividual" in ourselves, in terms of an average consciousness. If we do manage to think in individualistic ways, we tend to be overpowered by the language and hence the thought of the collectivity: imperiously, the perspective of the group, the species, guides our thinking. The "genius of the species" dominates us.[34] This is tantamount to Lévi-Strauss's emphasis upon the "individual" in primitive societies as completely dominated by a symbolic system (in large part preserved in language), the origin of which is unknown. For him, a social system is comprised of symbolic relations that are expressed through different forms of communication; the cognitive processes and linguistic signs and their meanings are the means by which members of a society produce, maintain, and elaborate conceptual models. Interpersonal relations and language-use "express" these conceptual-schematic models.[35]

Although the individual is real enough, each social relationship and sign-communication involves the "individual" in a network of signs, meanings, and conventions that make individuality irrelevant. More interesting, in regard to Nietzsche's standpoint, is that Lévi-Strauss assumes that he, the anthropological observer, can understand the symbols and signs of another cultural group because he shares its basic patterns of thinking. That there are such "collective representations" virtually coincides with what Nietzsche, with ironic psychic distance, calls "the genius of the species."

Nietzsche maintains that even though our actions are "personal, unique, and absolutely individual," as soon as we translate them into consciousness (= language) they are no longer understood as such. The world we become conscious of is a superficial "symbolic world" generalized for the sake of rapid and easy communication. The continual evolution of this collective consciousness leads to greater superficiality and greater falsification. What we typically may be said to "know" (public "knowledge," social "knowledge") is what has utilitarian value for the species. And the belief in this utility of knowledge may turn out to be a "fateful stupidity by which we shall one day be ruined."[36]

The categorical fictions of "subject," "object," "substance," "cause," "effect," "unity," etc., are, for Nietzsche, elements by which an intelligible world is constructed. What is taken as the phenomenal world is a world seen from the perspective of the species. If language was developed primarily for the sake of communication, then its signs are designed to be relatively simple, abbreviated, a kind of "code" that serves the practical interests of the majority. The structure of this symbolic world of significations presumably evolved long ago.

Nietzsche is concerned to show the social, cultural genesis of "knowledge" and the "common" values, beliefs, and attitudes preserved in ordinary language. Grammatical functions have guided thought and produced metaphysical and ontological conceptions in the hands of philosophers. Wittgenstein asserts that perplexities and errors occur in philosophical discourse when language "goes on holiday" or when ordinary language is misused. For Nietzsche, on the contrary, the dependence upon accepted grammatical functions or structures has given rise to philosophical error. Thus, formerly one believed in the "grammatical subject," an "I" (elsewhere called an *Ich-Subjekt* or "I-Subject") that is the *condition*; the predicate "think" was the *conditioned*. Kant tried to reverse this Cartesian formula by suggesting that "think" is the condition, the "I" the conditioned—that is, the "I" is construed as a synthesis created by thinking. Kant may also have entertained the possibility that the I-subject, the personal-I or the "empirical self" has only an apparent existence. This tendency of thought, Nietzsche points out, is a replication of a powerful notion in "*Vedanta-Philosophie*."[37] Here his analogical reasoning on the basis of common linguistic-conceptual structures was informed by his study of the works of his friend Paul Deussen (e.g., *Die Sutras des Vedanta* and *Das System des Vedanta*).

Even if Nietzsche is sometimes a bit cavalier in his discovery of linguistic-conceptual synonymy in different philosophical cultures, his general orientation is very close to that of the structuralists who look for similar patterns of language and thought in a variety of myths. By emphasizing that similar modes of thought emerge out of similar grammatical systems and by indicating cross-cultural relationship, Nietzsche inadvertently undermined his occasional suggestion of an ethnic determination of culture and, hence, linguistic-cognitive schemes. Apparently, a shared grammar, common "grammatical functions," generate similar patterns of philosophical thinking independent of cultural and ethnic differences.

Whereas structural anthropologists seem to accept social and linguistic meanings as integral parts of symbols in a cultural system, Nietzsche is critical precisely of inherited concepts. At one point, he argues that philosophers ignore the possibility that our shared "concepts and words are our inheritance from ages in which thinking was very modest and unclear." This inheritance from our most remote, most foolish, and most intelligent ancestors should be the object of our "absolute skepticism."[38]

Inherited patterns of thought and habits of language are said to be derived from primordial mythic beliefs, the origin of which has been obscured by time. The "primitive mythology" that Nietzsche criticized is composed primarily of the following: the belief that the I is a "subject," an I-substance that is a "doer" that performs "deeds"; the belief that there are "substances," "objects," "things," "causes," and "effects"; the idea of "being"; and the belief that there is a "will" that causes "effects," that there are "unities," etc.

For Nietzsche, the word and concept "being" is an expression of one of the oldest beliefs of man, one retained in thought and language. The concept of being is considered as the basis of logic and language, a notion that entails assumptions of unity, substance, permanence, stability, and certainty. This elementary concept is said to be derived from a transference of our belief in ourselves as a unitary substance to actuality. In his early essay on the pre-Socratic philosophers, Nietzsche held that the concept of being in Parmenides' thought was an expression of a quest for certainty, a postulate based upon the belief in man's unified being. That is, the experience of oneself as a living, breathing unity suggested the idea of being.

> Words are but symbols for the relations of things to one another and to us. . . . [T]he word "being" designates only the most general relationship which connects all things. . . . Through words or concepts we shall never reach beyond the wall of relations.[39]

The word "being" is an anthropomorphic, nonlogical projection into the world of the nonhuman. It does not signify any extra-linguistic reality.

Rather, it refers to the thought of something unified, stable, and permanent. "Being" is a thought-symbol derived from a transference of the psychistic belief in one's "unitary nature." When Nietzsche speaks of words and concepts as "metaphors," he means it in the etymological sense of "a transfer" (*metapherein* = to transfer).

Nietzsche typically traces linguistic-conceptual useful "fictions" to "psychistic fictions," beliefs that he assumes appeared relatively early in man's development. As he engages in a "structural analysis," he not only wants to expose the collective structure of human thought. He also wants to remind us of the psychic and metaphorical nature of many basic conceptions, in order to undermine what he considers the perpetuation of a fallacious metaphysics or ontology. Without saying so, he suggests that Western thought for a long time has been dominated by a kind of linguistic *a priori*, the creative, inventive and metaphorical nature of which has been forgotten.

The aim of Nietzsche's abbreviated structural analysis of the philosophical language of Kant (and others) is not purely descriptive. His intention is to liberate us from what he considers "mummified" concepts, to enable us to transcend inherited linguistic-conceptual structures. One of his central points is that language is inadequate to describe becoming.[40] A "world" that can be spoken about intelligibly is necessarily a psychic, linguistic, and conceptual construction; that is, it is a symbolic representation that is a structure that exists for us. Every understanding of actuality that can be expressed in language is an interpretive understanding by means of "signs." The scientific world-interpretations in physics, for example, are constructed out of "formulae" or "sign systems" (e.g., logico-mathematical signs). Whatever value such "conventional signs" (*Zeichen-Convention*) may have, they do not pertain to "actuality" (*Wirklichkeit*).[41] Every interpretation of any aspect of actuality is presented in terms of conventional conceptual and linguistic signs.

The paradox that Nietzsche encountered when he tried to undermine the validity of inherited conceptions is that this linguistic-conceptual structure is so deeply ingrained in Western culture that it has become a kind of cultural *a priori*. It is virtually impossible to evade its long shadow. Nietzsche admits that "we cannot change our means of expressions [= our language] at will."[42] However, he insists that we can, as he does, come to understand that our inherited conceptual-linguistic scheme is composed of "signs" that have functional value, that this fruitful and powerful "semiotics" has no genuine ontological reference. This would be a step toward philosophical liberation.

The implication of Nietzsche's critical appraisal of transmitted structures of thought and language is that a new means of expression should be developed. Even though he tried to do this, he found himself caught in the linguistic network from which he wanted to escape and found himself relying on the very linguistic forms he sought to overcome. If the symbolic system of meaningful signs that has lasted for such a long time generates a putatively false world-interpretation, and if we are prone to fall back upon ancient habits of thought and language, then we are, in Nietzsche's terms, prevented from attaining an authentic understanding of actuality precisely because of the enormously useful, practically valuable conceptual-linguistic system that has become canonical. In a sense, we would almost be in the situation of the primitive peoples that Lévi-Strauss has studied so meticulously. For we seem to be conditioned by forms of thought and linguistic forms we cannot shake off. Of course, as Nietzsche saw, we are not completely overpowered by a particular symbolic system of conventional meanings. We are able to uncover the structure that has come to dominate our thinking and thereby, to some extent, we are liberated from the coercive power of such symbolic systems.

As in the case of Foucault's structuralist theory, it seems that when a novel *episteme* emerges in a historical period there is a shift of meanings, constructs, and signs that may come to dominate for a long or a short period the language used to discuss or describe a class of phenomena. Nietzsche assumed that a transition to a new, global conceptual-linguistic scheme was not only beneficial, but needed. His positive, if often vague, philosophical program was designed to inaugurate a new world-interpretation. He fully accepted the consequences of his radical critique of alternative cognitive-linguistic structures (including feelings, attitudes, beliefs, and language-use) and of his understanding of a given interpretation of actuality as a more or less viable or useful system of significations: that every symbolic, interpretive structure is ultimately inadequate, "false" or inappropriate to a deep understanding of a protean actuality.

Language and conceptualization are the most powerful tools that man has devised to disguise the presumably chaotic, incongruent, antithetical, protean, and terrible aspect of *Wirklichkeit*. Although the scientific "conscious relativity of knowledge," the precision of method of science, and the reliance on sense-observation give us an "approximation" to the structure of actuality, the conventional fictions, suppositions, "regulative articles of belief," and logico-mathematical postulates employed in the sciences provide a "model" of actuality, not a literal picture of it.

We do not come closer and closer to "truth" in any absolute sense with the creation of novel systems of signs. What happens is that one general, totalistic linguistic-conceptual scheme replaces another. Although Nietzsche applies this notion to all interpretations of man and reality, his position is not unlike Kuhn's idea of the establishment of, and replacement of, conceptual paradigms in science.[43]

Nietzsche would not agree with the suggestion of Lévi-Strauss that the similarity among mythical patterns of thought indicates a kind of collective, necessary, unconscious *a priori*. And this for two reasons: he believes that a highly useful, practical and life-preserving means of communication and thought evolved sometime in the remote past, and he avers that symbolic systems or world-interpretations are *contingent*. They are construed as necessary only because we have forgotten the contingent origins of the symbols or signs that were "invented" by "artists in abstraction."

Over a long period of time, certain global ways of thinking (speaking and writing) come to be accepted as "the truth" and petrification sets in through a kind of cultural inertia. His thinking commits Nietzsche to the view that our species has lived in many *worlds*, still lives in different worlds and will continue to live under the sway of emergent cultural, intellectual, and linguistic systems. There is no absolutely "true" world-interpretation because of changes in global perspectives.

Each dominant world-interpretation is pervaded by postulates, values, ways of thinking, perceiving, believing, and judging that are preserved by a typically unconscious acceptance of a symbolic, cultural, cognitive-linguistic world-orientation. Most individuals in a sociocultural system more or less accept the values, meanings, and interpretations current in their cultural system. So far, Nietzsche's views are consonant with those of the structuralists. However, he holds that there is no necessity in the survival of a previously powerful and dominant system of signs, nor is there any ban on an entire culture or civilization taking a new direction. His central "task" or "mission" is precisely to offer a path to a challenging, and creative cultural, intellectual, and linguistic system. If Nietzsche had the slightest confidence in his "countermovement" against what he saw as a leveling of man and culture, then he clearly believed that there is a contingency in history, that man can follow any number of possible paths in the openness of the future.

Even though the "exact sciences" may bring us closer to the nature of the constituents of the actual world, they do not bring us closer to *the* "truth." The scientific interpretation of the world is also a conceptual-linguistic structure, the power of which lies in its acquisition and use of *praktische Erkenntnis*. The world of "ordinary language" gives sanction to ordinary beliefs, thoughts, and values; it tends to make the uncommon, as Nietzsche says, "common." Whatever is held in common, whatever is commonly believed, gains enormous power. The conventions, "rules," and accepted ways of speaking in everyday life become coercive, as in the case of "popular culture." Because ordinary language contains distinctions, differentiations, and discriminations that are generally shared by others who share a common "form of life," it impinges on all thinking. Whether we are considering a scientific understanding of the world or ordinary ways of speaking about what is, what our actions are, we find ourselves in the position of trying to disentangle ourselves in our thinking from powerful, pervasive, and functional ways of thinking, speaking, or writing.

Nietzsche certainly recognized that the understanding of the operative presence of a sociocultural, conceptual, and linguistic system does not immediately liberate us from the powerful influence of deep-rooted structural forces. His self-consciousness about language, especially the language of the sciences, led him to see that there is no single interpretation of an event or a phenomenon; rather, there is a "plurality of interpretations." An implication of this insight is that there is really not only one viable "system of signs" (or, as Wittgenstein would say, "language game"), but a number of concurrent "means of expression." The selection of one conceptual-linguistic scheme could not be made on the basis of "truth" or on the basis of functionality (for, each sign-system has its proper function), but solely on the basis of what underlies each world-interpretation or world-orientation: value. It is at this point that Nietzsche leaves his "structural analysis" behind and parts company with the structuralists.

STRUCTURE AND VALUE

Structuralism gradually evolved from a method of analysis to a general philosophy. The search for structure in *language* led to the search for structure in anthropology (especially in the study of myths) and it continued on to the analysis of the structure of the unconscious and the patterns and structures in literature. Methodological questions and orientations shape structuralism; it looks for the *eidos*—the form, the order, the interrelationship of various behaviors or modes of discourse. Because of its tendency to undermine, negate, or put aside the subjective perspective of individuals, structural analysis resembles a kind of natural history of man that selects out objectivity everywhere.

Nietzsche also attempted a kind of natural history of man, looking upon human behavior, morality, beliefs, and knowledge-claims with a cosmological eye. But he was never solely interested in uncovering patterns of belief, forms of thought, or semeiotics. Repeatedly, he insisted upon man's capacity for transformation, for "transvaluation," for reshaping culture. By understanding forms of thought and language that have dominated our past, he thought that this insight could be the basis of a kind of cultural "self-overcoming." Ultimately, he could argue persuasively only in defense of *his* system of values, *his* cultural ideal, *his* interpretation of the best symbolic system for mankind. The important thing was to have an "aim," a meaningful direction, a goal that he believed would lead to a culture that would transcend previous structural determinants, to reach beyond its "structures."

We gain insight into Nietzsche's intentions when we see that he was concerned to project a cultural ideal that would be based upon aesthetic principles and aesthetic sensitivities. Such an ideal culture would be rich in significations.

> The aesthetic state possesses a superabundance of means of communication, together with an extreme receptivity for stimuli and signs. It constitutes the high point of communication and transmission between living creatures—it is the source of languages. This is where languages originate. . . . The more complete phenomenon is always the beginning. . . . Every enhancement of life enhances man's power of communication, as well as his power of understanding.[44]

The search, then, is for a fresh beginning, a condition of existence that would generate new ways of experience, thought, feeling, and language-use. Presumably, Nietzsche's attack upon previously dominant, inherited psychic, conceptual, and linguistic forms was intended as a negation of a negation, a clearing the way for a new symbolic interpretation of actuality and *Existenz*. In this regard, his structural analyses were not purely descriptive, since he desired, as all religious, social, and political innovators do, to "transvalue" values previously preserved in a cultural, cognitive-linguistic system of significations.

The neutrality, objectivity, and value-free structural analyses of the French structuralists prohibit judgments of value or considerations of how man ought to live. As is the case with Lévi-Strauss, there is a tendency in structuralism to see all cultural, social, and conceptual-linguistic systems as having equivalent value. Lévi-Strauss explicitly denies that there is any significant difference between the supposed "prelogical" thinking of the primitive and logical thought. "The savage mind," he tells us, "is logical in the same sense and the same fashion as ours . . . as our own is when it is applied to knowledge of a universe in which it recognizes physical and semantic properties simultaneously."[45] Although he admits that primitive people view the world from a different (more concrete) perspective than that of a civilized man, he implies that a value judgment of better, more effective, more productive, more liberated "forms of life" is precluded by "structural analysis."

Nietzsche's evocative prescriptions for the transformation of the human world carry him beyond the proto-structuralist tendencies in his thought. He is opposed to theoretical, linguistic, and existential inertia. Rather than seeing man as bound by a finite number of conceptual-linguistic schemata by virtue of a putative universally shared linguistic-intellectual structure, he considers man the as-yet unfixed species, a species that must fight its natural tendency to perpetuate previously functional ways of thought and linguistic forms. In effect, he sought to do battle with a deep-seated proclivity toward cultural *stasis*. In place of a structural stasis he offered *ekstasis*: a "standing out from" the conventional world, an ecstatic *Existenz*.

His critical structural analyses seem to have been designed to serve that end. When Nietzsche says, in one place, that "men of knowledge" leave everything "as it is," he is not expressing his typical standpoint and is not referring to himself. There is no reason to assume, as Kaufmann has suggested, that he shares Wittgenstein's view that

> philosophy may in no way . . . interfere with the actual use of language; in the end it can only describe it. . . . it leaves everything as it is.[46]

Such a position is far more compatible with the scientific descriptive method of structuralism than it is with a philosopher who boasted that "we make experiment with truth."[47] Nietzsche saw the role of the genuine philosopher as a "law-giver," an innovator, a *creator of values*. There is almost nothing in him of the linguistic structuralist's tendency to preserve and conserve, to accept conventional social and cultural "rules," to see ordinary language as a repository of human wisdom. Nietzsche was by no means opposed to order; but he was opposed to an order of the "common" and the ordinary, an order that supported the judgment of the "last man": "each is the same."

Nietzsche is as much a critic of philosophical language as of "ordinary language." And he sides with the "artists" who desire to "alter and transform" our image of ourselves and the world more than he does with the "men of knowledge" who look upon the human world with (ostensibly) cool, scientific detachment. His structural analyses of language are hardly undertaken in the spirit of cool reason. Although he, too, found a "logic" in language, he also found the "illogical."

We may contrast Nietzsche's analysis of the categorical fictions that he believes have contributed to a misleading ontology and, hence, to what he considers a distortion of values, to Quine's neutrality in the face of a quite similar disclosure of the symbolic and mythic nature of basic terms employed in the language of the sciences. Quine argued that his empirical orientation led him to "think of the conceptual scheme of science as a tool, ultimately, for predicting future experience in the light of past experience." This conventionalist and instrumentalist orientation virtually parallels Nietzsche's analysis of what he takes to be the traditional philosophical cognitive-linguistic scheme (embedded in Kant's conception of the "phenomenal world") and is quite similar to his conventionalist interpretation of the language of science.

Quine regards a basic scientific concept such a "physical objects" as a "conceptually imported" "cultural posit." The rationale for retaining such an "irreducible posit" in the "structure" of scientific discourse is reminiscent of Nietzsche's understanding of the persistent use of "conventional fictions" in philosophical and (nineteenth-century) scientific discourse.

> The myth of physical objects is epistemologically superior to most in that it has proved more efficacious than other myths as a device for working a manageable structure into the flux of experience.[48]

If the precise, relatively refined, and commonly used terms in the physical sciences are "myths" or "cultural posits," it is safe to assume that many psychological terms are also in the same category. Presumably, by extrapolation, we may assume that each determinate cultural system is pervaded by numerous unconscious "cultural posits" that are elements in a total network of symbols and signs.

If, as Quine argues, "science is a continuation of common sense," and if Nietzsche is right about the commonsense understanding of the world, then the scientific interpretation of the world is a continuation of a linguistic-conceptual structure that evolved and crystallized long before the earliest glimmer of philosophy or science. Common sense, according to Nietzsche, represents a sedimentation of socially valued psychistic beliefs that come to make up practical or "anthropomorphic" knowledge. If, as Quine says, scientific understanding rests upon "myths," then the common sense from which it is derived must, *a fortiori*, rest upon more primordial beliefs. And this is precisely what Nietzsche had argued.

Continuing his analysis, Quine classifies the following as cultural posits or myths: "forces," "atomic" entities, "subatomic" entities, "classes," "classes of classes," and all "abstract entities." This "thorough pragmatism" of Quine is virtually a justification of Nietzsche's analysis of the "practical," "inventive" nature of the constructs employed both in philosophy and the scientific "symbolization of nature."

The significant difference between Nietzsche and Quine on this point is that the former is exercised by what this kind of critical analysis of basic presuppositions in science implies for the notion of truth. For Nietzsche, the scientific linguistic-conceptual scheme is obviously a powerful and exceedingly useful representation of actuality that is a "means" for the transformation of the earth. However, this powerful instrumental system of "interpretation" has the potential to undermine not only the aesthetically conceived "cultural pyramid" Nietzsche envisions, but any coherent, unified and meaningful culture at all. The domination of a single, pervasive cognitive-linguistic system of meanings tends to devalue, undermine, and exclude attitudes, values, and beliefs that are incompatible with such a cultural structure. In this regard, Nietzsche accurately predicted some of the negative consequences of a predominantly practical, pragmatic, utilitarian, quantitative, and positivistic *Weltanschauung*.

Nietzsche would not share Quine's sanguine, rationalistic optimism about the continual progress of, and extension of, the scientific perspective (especially a perspective that self-consciously analyzes the fictional and mythical bases of its conceptual and interpretive framework). He correctly saw that the dominance of technicity and the technological *hubris* of modern man would have long-range effects upon human history, social values, and the feelings and actions of individuals. He understood that very few individuals could endure a network of relativity, agnosticism, and skepticism. Put succinctly, he believed that the one-dimensional apotheosis of the scientific world-picture would eventually lead to the nihilism that he himself had lived through and gone beyond already. As always, he was primarily concerned with the *effects* on culture and human existence of a dominant cultural ideal. On the other hand, he also saw quite clearly that the scientific interpretation of actuality would clearly come to dominate Western civilization. He did not (as some of his critics believe) want to negate science or its methods as such; rather, he believed that the practical power of science could serve as a substructure for a rich, creative, and innovative cultural system.[49]

Nietzsche was concerned with uncovering various forms of "scientism." In a sense, he saw that a fallacious and pretentious scientism could come to pervade Western culture in the way in which superstitious beliefs pervade primitive societies. He did for scientism what Lévi-Strauss later did for the notion of kinship in a primitive society. While the latter showed how customs, behavior, attitudes, thoughts, and language supported conventional beliefs about "kinship,"[50] Nietzsche reminded scientists of the anthropomorphic, conventional, hypothetical, and mythical conceptions they employed in order to construct their *Welt-Auslegung* (world-interpretation). He repeatedly pointed to the ontological, metaphysical, and epistemological foundations of scientific inquiry that were shaped and formed by primitive, unexamined beliefs or "myths." He argued that science is the most thorough humanization of nature imaginable.[51] In effect, he carried out what could be called a "structural analysis" of science and a critical exposure of the fictions of scientism.

Nietzsche's optimism about the perfectibility of man, his faith in the possibility of "overmen of the future," was largely based upon his belief that the forgotten or unconscious forms of thought and language that have conditioned and dominated human culture and existence in the Western world could be surpassed, that ostensible "primitive" beliefs could be consciously repudiated. This presupposition led him to claim that if the transmitted conceptual-linguistic shackles of the past could be thrown off, mankind could be liberated, could consciously and freely will a new beginning, create an innovative cultural world in which the creative potentialities of human beings could come to fruition.

If it were possible for mankind consciously and intentionally to create a *new*, total, social, cultural, and conceptual-linguistic "structure," then one of the basic premises of structuralism could be undermined: the theory that "the human mind Is . . . determined in its myths": and, therefore, presumably "determined in all of its manifestations." Lévi-Strauss cites with approval Ricoeur's characterization of one of his central views as "Kantianism without a transcendental subject." If there is such an unconscious, Kantian (= universal) *a priori* without a subject,[52] then there can be no genuine novelty in human thought. Or, as Lévi-Strauss puts it elsewhere, "The entire process of human knowledge . . . assumes the character of a closed system."[53] The implication of these observations is that there are a finite number of "systems of truth" that are expressed by man in various cultural, conceptual, and linguistic "structures." Presumably, then, Nietzsche's optimism about the possibility of novel "experimental truths" would be considered unwarranted. Here, once again, his philosophy moved outside the orbit of structuralism. Insofar as he engages in what Foucault calls "the archaeology of knowledge," he does so not as an end in itself, not for the sake of an illuminating penetration of the various interrelated forms of discourse prevalent at a particular historical time-period. Instead he looks for the value-interpretation, the hidden values, that shape not only modes of discourse during a long period of time, but also the feelings, behavior, attitudes, and cultural forms that are expressions of value-laden "forms of life."

Whereas Foucault describes the compatible modes of discourse within a prevailing historical universe of discourse (e.g., the idea of madness from 1500 to 1800, the concept of "natural history," the theory of "political economy," etc.) presumably for the sake of a kind of "understanding" or *Verstehen* of a pervasive *episteme*, Nietzsche is interested in the psychological needs, the physiological conditions of life, the *pathos* that underlies a culture's cherished beliefs. He offers, for example, a two-dimensional phenomenology of the "ascetic personality" in which he sees the strengths and the weaknesses, the positive and negative features of this type of human being. Like the structuralists generally, he is interested in the "origins" of patterns of behavior, belief, and conceptual-linguistic schemata. But he always searches for the creation of values by individuals. He views the consolidation of habits of thought, ways of life, forms of discourse or systems of belief as expressions of the *pathos* of life. To be sure, cultural systems, inherited concepts, and language-forms do condition the lives of millions; and yet there are innovators, exceptions, paradigmatic individuals who create or alter cultural systems.

Nietzsche was profoundly concerned with the needs, drives, and passions that generate a given *episteme*. His structural analyses of Platonism, Christian culture, Kantian philosophy, and the scientific interpretation of actuality are by no means value-free. Despite his affinity with the structuralists, he would, in the final analysis, probably view their work, as impressive as it is, as a species of scientism.

In a Nietzschean spirit, one may wonder whether the growth in the twentieth century of formalism, logico-scientific methods of analysis, linguistic structuralism, anthropological structuralism, and symbolic systems may not be a converse reaction to a persistent, underlying conflict of, or chaos of, values. It is Nietzsche's consistent concern with the problem of value in relation to the quality of human life and culture that effectively separates him from the formalism of the structural analyses of the recent structuralists whose orientation he to some extent anticipated in aspects of his thought.[54] A question he once asked may be appropriate to the structuralist perspective as a philosophical standpoint: "Is scientism [*Wissenschaftlichkeit*] perhaps only a fear and an evasion of pessimism?"[55]

Chapter Seven

Evolutionary Epistemology

> Life is the condition of knowing.
>
> Nietzsche, *Nachlass*

A consistent theme in Nietzsche's thought is that all things have developed or evolved. He strongly defends the notion that our modes of perception, our concepts, and our language have developed over long periods of time and are subject to evolutionary change. In this sense, he presents a prototypical version of a naturalized epistemology and employs it as one of the weapons in his armamentarium in his critical analysis of knowledge.

Most of the elements incorporated in recent forms of evolutionary epistemology can be found in Nietzsche's multidimensional analyses and speculations concerning the development over time of ways of perceiving and thinking that eventually become sedimented and dominate historical periods. From his earliest writings to his last thought-experiments he disclosed the anthropomorphic nature of truth, the utilitarian function of perception, cognition, conceptual schemata, and language, intimately relating them to their survival value.

In the *Essays* of Emerson Nietzsche first found a general conception of evolution that linked man's "natural history" to the "ferocities of nature" and pointed to the presence in man of primal traits and tendencies.[1] Later, in the writings of Schopenhauer, he found a foreshadowing of evolutionary thought and the view that the intellect is a tool of more basic drives, an instrument comparable to the aggressive and defensive "weapons" of animals. Moreover, in Schopenhauer's "On Philosophy and Science of Nature," he would have found a surprisingly detailed evolutionary theory.[2] Shortly after his discovery of Schopenhauer, Nietzsche became familiar with Lange's *History of Materialism* and no doubt absorbed his sketch of Darwin's theory of evolution by means of natural selection. In fact, in his notes from the mid-1860s he linked Empedocles' insight that extant organic beings were the result of random, natural experiments over time and not design to "the Darwinian theory."[3]

In "On Truth and Lying in a Non-Moral Sense," Nietzsche alluded to the evolutionary basis of perception and concept-formation and adopted Schopenhauer's characterization of the intellect as a tool used in the struggle for survival. In addition, he argued that we value truth, intellect, and knowledge not as intrinsic goods, but because of their life-preserving function. Our knowledge is tantamount to "anthropomorphic truth" or the practical truth that is in the service of life. The world constructed out of perception, concepts, and language is a humanized world in which we can live and function effectively. All knowledge, that of an inherited "commonsense" as well as that of science (in the broad sense of *Wissenschaft*), is a consequence of a continual process of humanization that, directly or indirectly, serves the instinctive biological interests of mankind. Even though, in his notes from the late 1880s, Nietzsche calls the belief that the world for us is *the* world an "anthropocentric idiosyncrasy," he never retreats from his assumption that the linguistic-conceptual system of commonsense, as well as emergent scientific perspectives, are both the result of evolutionary processes.

In spite of occasional quarrels with some of Darwin's views—particularly that the aim of organic beings is preservation rather than the expression of energy and the enhancement of their "power"—Nietzsche, in general, builds his evolutionary epistemology out of Darwinian bricks. Whereas Darwin tends to stress the priority of biological evolution, Nietzsche freely moves back and forth from references to biological evolution and cultural evolution. In this respect, his remarks on our conceptual-linguistic frameworks and their diachronic transformation express a co-evolutionary orientation that encompasses inherited patterns of perception, thought, and language and the powerful influence of culture on how historical peoples experience and think about their world.

Although he grants that a long evolutionary process has been at work shaping mankind's adaptable and flexible "nature," Nietzsche rejects the Hegelian idea of a progressive development of "spirit," in that it encouraged a worship of success and the valuation of "the actual" as the best. In "On the Use and Abuse of History for Life" he tries to undermine Hegel's theory of necessity in the historical process by insisting that there is contingency in history. Here he seems, as in other instances, to transpose the notion of random selectivity in biological evolutionary thought to human history in such a way as to preserve an openness in the future. Animals, he claims, may have reached a kind of evolutionary plateau, but mankind is still an "as yet unfixed species."[4] The natural evolutionary process has no discernible progressive or positive directionality. It aims "merely at evolution, and nothing else."[5] Although this is a vague assertion, it is coincidental with recent evolutionary thought.[6] Evolution has no determinate goal and fitness does not entail the survival or perpetuation of the best types in a species.

Despite occasional remarks in *The Origin of Species* about improvement of an organic type, Darwin himself hesitated to defend progressive evolution dogmatically. Within a "kingdom" he was inclined to think that "highest" usually means that form that has undergone the most "morphological differentiation."[7] Ironically, Nietzsche also refers to a morphology in reference to the "will to power" in terms of a form of human life that would be physiologically and psychologically differentiated by virtue of its greater complexity and its willed integration of contradictory drives.

Anticipating later neo-Kantian evolutionary epistemologists, Nietzsche construed basic categories as useful because of their adaptive value. He traced what came to be christened *a priori* categories to their presumed origin in *a posteriori* beliefs of our ancestors. Not only did he claim that the (predominately) Kantian categories of the understanding have their roots in the physiology and psychology of early mankind, but he practically anticipated, as we've seen, the French structuralists' view that there seems to be an unconscious *a priori* that is shared by people of different cultures. He avers that

> the categories of reason . . . could have prevailed, after much fumbling and groping, through their relative utility. —There came a time when one collected them together, raised them to consciousness as a whole . . . commended them. . . . From then on they counted as *a priori*, as independent of experience, as ineluctable. And for all that they may only represent the usage appropriate to certain races and species—their "truth" is merely their utility.[8]

The categories that have become canonical have no legitimate ontological reference, but they have practical utility. They organize the "chaos" of impressions we experience, serve the perspectival optics of life, and contribute to our survival. Nietzsche speculatively projects the rudimentary development of such categorical formations back to the perceptual and conceptual practices of our remote ancestors. An implication of such an imaginative speculation is that philosophers have presented exceedingly sophisticated formal accounts of ways of thinking that were presumably pre-existent, but unconscious, for our ancestors.

Our way of perceiving the world has also developed over a long period of time. Those who perceived differently than our ancestors neither reproduced nor survived. Probably, Nietzsche thinks, they were described as mad. Such "exceptions" were pushed aside and eliminated because their perceptual-cognitive functions were ineffective and non-adaptive in a dangerous environment.

That the world is believed to have a logical structure is also a paradoxical evolutionary outcome since, for Nietzsche, the logical emerged out of the non-logical. Mankind has come to think that the world has a logical structure because its inherited pattern of thinking projects logic into the world. In *The Gay Science* Nietzsche argues that those who "reasoned" in a different way than we currently do perished. Whoever was unable to discover likeness in regard to dangerous animals or food, whoever was too cautious and slow in deduction, diminished his or her "probability of survival."[9] Discernment of likeness or "equality" of type and reasonably rapid deductions favored survival and reproduction. However, this disposition to comprehend the similar as the equal is an "illogical inclination." By understanding similar entities as "equal" or identical our ancestors simplified and falsified what they experienced. This became the primal foundation of logical thinking.[10] Certain strictly inaccurate ways of perceiving and thinking of entities had a high degree of survival value. Over time these habits or patterns became the primitive basis of what is later formulated first as the idea of identity and then the notion of self-identical concepts. These then became the rudiments of logic. A falsification of the relationship among certain perceived beings was at first valued for its practical utility. Much later this concept of self-identical entities was transferred from the ostensible ontological domain to the formal domain of logic.

By linking modes of perception to concept formation and attributing their form to evolutionary development Nietzsche approaches the sociobiological theory of primary and secondary epigenetic rules. Such rules are conceived of as biological constraints on development and on our capacity for learning. Presumably, they have emerged by means of a naturally selective evolutionary process and have been transmitted genetically. The information attained by means of primary epigenetic rules are then organized, structured, and evaluated by the secondary rules.[11] Given his emphasis upon the physiological basis of the "perspectival optics of life," instincts, percepts, and values, Nietzsche's position coincides with that of sociobiologists. Nonetheless, he is not committed to a strict form of genetic determinism because he insists upon the powerful impact of culture on beliefs, values, and perceptual and conceptual orientations. In this regard, his standpoint is a genetic-cultural co-evolutionary theory.

Looking backward, Nietzsche assumes a long, selective evolutionary process in which, at different stages of development, specific types of human beings have survived, reproduced, and transmitted their perceptual and cognitive capacities to us. Looking forwards, he stresses mankind's capacity to modify its nature by means of the adoption of a radical cultural ideal. He calls this *his* "principle of selection." He often calls attention to the way in which cultural systems condition the lives of millions. Cultures function in a selective way. They promote, encourage, and reward certain types of people and, in a psychological way, thereby cultivate specific types of the species. Thus, retrospectively, Nietzsche places relatively more weight on biological evolution (e.g., by emphasizing the physiological bases of cultures), but prospectively he stresses valuational, psychic, and cognitive cultural evolutionary factors. Those exemplary individuals whom he calls "lucky accidents" may be, he thinks, consciously cultivated by virtue of his own valuational, philosophical, and psychological "disciplinary" conceptions. In regard to his positive, if visionary, values, Nietzsche almost reverses the order of typical evolutionary theories by underlining cultural conditioning factors and making biological factors secondary. His form of co-evolutionary conception, then, is a cultural-biological one.

PERCEPTION/COGNITION

Thinking of the history of interpretations of nature, Heidegger observed that what is deemed nature was first historical. Nietzsche tends to reverse this view by claiming that what becomes historical is at first natural. One of the central reasons for adopting such a view, though certainly not the only one, is his respect for the discoveries of the exact sciences. What often seems like intuitive insights in his observations are, in fact, judgments derived from the sciences. In his notes he speculates that the natural world would appear "cold and lifeless" if it were not for the "errors" that we've inherited from our ancestors. Having been schooled in these perceptual-cognitive errors, we now perceive mountains as grand, impressive, and awesome. They generate feelings of majesty or produce soothing effects. Our ancestors, on the other hand, probably saw them as threatening and frightening.[12] The reference to a cold and lifeless nature is analogous to the depiction of the natural world as an "atomistic chaos" in "Schopenhauer as Educator"—a view appropriated from extant physical theories with which Nietzsche was quite familiar.

In another place, Nietzsche argues that every organic being is surrounded by a miniature world that has, in effect, been created. It is the organism's external world. Over time, however, the perspective of organic individuals has been diminished in the developmental process. Whole species share "*congealed* customs, habits, ways of seeing." All of these are no doubt "propitious to the conditions of existence of such beings."[13] Here Nietzsche relies upon what is virtually a dictum of evolutionary theory: the evolutionary process favors species survival and more or less uniform instincts, habits, and patterns of behavior if they provide adaptive advantage. It does not have as its outcome increased individuation. As one evolutionist has put it, "Only populations, not individuals, evolve."[14]

Nietzsche explains the gradual erosion of singular organic, individualized perspectives in terms of a biological model. We are particularly skillful at practicing mimicry, more so even than insects. And the mind is exemplary in this capacity, for it practices "patience, cunning, simulation, great self-control, and everything that is mimicry."[15]

In the social and moral domain the human practice of mimicry almost attains perfection. It is manifested in the ability to conform to local customs, to learn to see, speak, and think as others do. It is prevalent in the morality of custom. Mimicry is compared to an individual's ability to hide beneath the classifications of "man" and "society," to adapt to a social environment for the sake of an indirect power obtained by conforming to the customs of one's time and place.[16] The group mentality that Nietzsche attacks so vehemently is perpetuated by mimicry. A morality of custom depends upon the passive assimilation of the customary values of one's social group and is largely dependent upon the mechanism of mimicry. The fundamental values are organic perspectival values. Mankind is said to have surpassed the animal kingdom because it has, through the evolutionary process, "*forgotten*" its previous "perspective valuing" and has acquired a multiplicity of conflicting values.[17] This is a source of suffering in that we have developed a paradoxical nature in which multiple values are in conflict. However, it is also a sign of strength because it implants a capacity for further development and transformation: it is the basis for a multiplication of perspectives.

For Nietzsche, all perceptual and cognitive perspectives are essentially valuational perspectives that have their origin in our natural history. However, he qualifies this stress on biological history by calling attention to the significance of cultural systems of values or "tables of values" that percolate through entire societies and function in selective ways. Strongly defended, widely disseminated, and socially rewarded cultural values tend, over time, to undermine the intentions, projects, status, and power of "exceptions" who cannot or will not espouse or embrace them. Schemata of values, like generally shared, historically dominant cognitive paradigms, have negative effects upon many who are unable or unwilling to adopt them. The elimination of "exceptions" during man's natural history continues in a more subtle and indirect way in later psychosocial evolution.

Nietzsche reminds us in his speculative anthropology of the fate of earlier "exceptions" whose perceptions were sharper than those of their contemporaries and whose cognitive practices were more circumspect and cautious than those of others. By implication, he thinks of the coming cultural world in which other types of "exceptions" may be eliminated, one way or another, unless an existential space is carved out for them in the future. Nietzsche's projected exceptions must cultivate strong powers of resistance to the sociocultural forces that, more and more, tend to negate difference or genuine, created individuality.

The higher cultures of the modern world, Nietzsche insists, rest upon a "terrible foundation" since they have emerged out of a natural history in which harshness and ruthless cruelty were often agents of natural selection. Our perceptual functions, our conceptual patterns, have been inherited from ancestors who survived in a harsh and threatening environment. Their "epigenetic rules" were creative "errors" that have proven serviceable and adaptable in the struggle for existence. Nietzsche never denies the pragmatic value of these inherited perceptual-conceptual modalities of functioning of our predecessors. But he insists that these ways of perceiving and thinking are fallacious and have no ontological validity. This is what he seems to mean when he defines "truth" (or the inherited bases of truth-claims) as that kind of *error* without which a certain species could not have survived. Those who were unable to simplify rapidly what they experienced, those who perceived phenomena "in flux," whose sensory discrimination may have been more precise than that of others, tended to lose biologically selective advantage. Nietzsche contends that "for a long time the changing process in things had to be overlooked, and remain unperceived; the beings not seeing correctly had an advantage over those who saw everything "in flux."[18]

An adaptive, practical, life-preserving form of knowing has evolved, derived from a presumed transformation of actuality. Nietzsche sees this inherited and highly useful mode of knowing narrowing, in alliance with the sciences, to a strict utilitarian orientation that will shunt aside alternative ways of perceiving, thinking, and feeling. Although he admires and praises the "small, unapparent truths" disclosed by the exact sciences, as well as their anti-metaphysical orientation, he worries about the long-range effects of scientism on culture. In a preface to *The Birth of Tragedy* he takes pride in himself for examining "the *problem of scientism*," for analyzing the rising culture of science and seeing it "for the first time as problematic, as questionable."[19]

In *The Gay Science* he says that the belief that similar entities are "equal" is the primal origin of the concept of substance. And this concept, in turn, is the foundation of logic. This is so even though "in the strictest sense, nothing actually corresponds" to permanent substances or self-identical entities in the natural world.[20] Our ancestors, presumably unconsciously, perceived and thought about the beings in their environment in a simplifying way: perceived and thought of complex beings, processes, and events as simple. Here Nietzsche anticipates Quine's evolutionary epistemology on a number of points. For Quine maintained that we tend to believe in the uniformity of nature because we believe in the simplicity of nature. It is a bias of our inherited perceptual functions and our tendency to believe that "things similar in some respects tend to prove similar in others."[21] As previously noted, Quine's characterization of basic concepts (such as "physical objects") as "myths," is analogous to Nietzsche's view that concepts such as "substance," "thing," "object," etc., are useful fictions.

Nietzsche makes the speculative claim that specific types of human beings with particular perceptual and conceptual habits were favored in the struggle for existence in a dangerous environment. Once again ruminating about ancestral "exceptions" who perished, he claims that "every high degree of circumspection in conclusions, every skeptical inclination, is a great danger to life. No living being might have been preserved" if such a pattern of thinking were widespread. Therefore, "the contrary inclination—to affirm rather than suspend judgment, to mistake and fabricate rather than wait, to assent rather than deny, to decide rather than be in the right"—was "cultivated with extraordinary assiduity."[22] Because of the value of such modes of cognition, particular types of psychophysical individuals were selected out for perpetuation in the evolutionary process. Presumably we have inherited these highly effective patterns of thought even though they involve simplification, error, and fabrication.

COMMON SENSE/SCIENCE

William James once proclaimed, in a pragmatic spirit, that

> our *fundamental ways of thinking about things are discoveries of exceedingly remote ancestors, which have been able to preserve themselves throughout the experience of all subsequent time.*[23]

He goes on to say that this development of modes of thought is what we call "common sense." This is an observation that Nietzsche had previously made in terms of the gradual, early formation of a set of basic categories that philosophers later formulated. In addition, he claimed that what has become common sense was also the initial basis of a logical mode of thinking that became habitual.

> The course of logical thought and reasoning in our modern brain corresponds to a process and struggle of impulses, which singly and in themselves are all very illogical and injust; we usually experience only the result of the struggle, so rapidly and secretly does this primitive mechanism now operate in us.[24]

By virtue of the evolutionary success of the cognitive-linguistic framework that our predecessors built the foundation for, we have acquired the commonsense interpretation of a humanized world that has proved remarkably efficient. Since Nietzsche is a radical neo-Kantian, he almost invariably refers to Kant's categories of the understanding as the model for the ideal formalization of modes of thinking that were, in the remote past, adopted unconsciously. Ironically, the Kantian conception of the phenomenal world undermined the belief that the "world as representation" is actuality "in itself." The world conditioned and constituted by our intuitions of space and time, our senses, and our categories cannot be known to be reality-in-itself. As early as 1868, Nietzsche understood and accepted the agnostic implications of Kant's account of knowledge. As previously noted, he appropriately summarizes the implications of then-recent scientific studies since Kant in a letter to Paul Deussen. We can no longer doubt the limits of our knowledge or the illusions of transcendental speculation. The metaphysical presumption to know an "absolute" reality is a form of "conceptual poetry." All that the exact sciences grant us is a "conscious relativity of knowledge." Metaphysics can no longer be the pathway to an understanding of the "true in itself," whether as "art or religion."[25]

In a note from 1872 Nietzsche states the dilemma posed by Kant's critique of reason: in terms of Kant's account of the basis of human knowledge; the world could actually be as it is constituted by us, but we would be unable to know this! Kantian agnosticism is, as we've shown, combined with the world-interpretations of physicists and the work of physiologists and other scientists to stimulate in Nietzsche's thought the scope of this virtual assault on the commonsense world-picture. Neo-Kantian scientists supplant the commonsense conception of the world by more sophisticated theoretical interpretations and discoveries in the exact sciences. A reflective thinker, whether scientist or philosopher, cannot avoid finding himself or herself in a split world or, more precisely, in two competing conceptual worlds. Without Whitehead's mathematical and scientific prowess, Nietzsche nonetheless was one of the earliest modern philosophers to identify the emergence of the "bifurcation of nature."

If many of the elements composing the evolved commonsense conception of the world are undermined or reinterpreted from a different perspective, then a perceptual-conceptual structure that has proven serviceable for life and survival is eroded by the powerful scientific, post-Kantian interpretations of actuality. Nietzsche was sensitive to this emerging phenomenon and often views it as a crisis for Western thought and culture. Having read and absorbed accounts of physiological theories since Kant, he dramatically captures the consequences of such theories in *Daybreak*.

> The habits of our senses have wrapped us up in a tissue of lying sensations which in their turn lie at the base of all our judgments and our "knowledge"—there are no means of exit

> or escape to the real world. We are like spiders in our own webs. . . . [W]hatever we may catch in them, it will only be something that our web is capable of catching.[26]

His most extreme reaction to the metastasizing agnosticism in the writings of nineteenth-century scientists is found in *The Gay Science*. Against the background of the first explosion of scientific knowledge—the neo-Kantian physiological studies of Helmholtz, the physical theories that postulated the atomistic structure of matter, unextended centers of force, sub-atoms or *Unteratomen*, and increasing theoretical complexity—it seemed as if previous beliefs about ourselves and the natural world were being destroyed. As Nietzsche put it,

> the insight into the general untruth and falsity of things that now come to us through science—an insight into delusion and error as conditions of knowledge and sentient existence—would be unendurable. *Honesty* would have disgust and suicide in its wake.[27]

Aside from this extreme, emotive reaction to "deceptions" disclosed by science, Nietzsche's response to the immediate and long-term implications of scientific knowledge and the dominance of a scientific culture cannot be underestimated. In *On the Genealogy of Morals* he insists that mankind has belittled itself, has been given a "piercing sense of [its] emptiness," has been moving, since Copernicus, towards the void. And in his notes he focuses upon the "nihilistic consequences of present natural science." Its practices seem to generate "a certain self-annihilation, an antagonistic attitude towards itself—a kind of antiscientificality. Since Copernicus, man has been rolling away from the center towards X." All of this is like a Sartrean "counter-finality." An evolved will to knowledge, itself a consequence of an evolved "will to power," has created a "pyramid of knowledge" and a multiplication of theories that reduce us to insignificance and undermine the possibility of holistic scientific truth.

The very precision of the methods of the exact sciences, Nietzsche believed, not only confounds previously serviceable commonsense beliefs, but has cultivated a refined skepticism. "Thanks to the sharpening of the senses and the attention entailed in the conflicts and developments of exceedingly complex forms of life, cases of identity or likeness are admitted every more rarely."[28] This evolved correction of previous, more careless, generalizations about "identity" or "similarity" is specifically developed in the context of scientific inquiry. We should say that phenomena have "similar qualities" not "the same" qualities, even in chemistry. Moreover, these properties we identify as "similar" are "similar" for us."[29] Notice how Nietzsche had once criticized our ancestors for erroneously having taken the similar for the identical and used this point to argue that a falsification of experience and actuality had been transmitted to us by virtue of the utility of such habits of perception and thought. Now he relies on scientific precision to drive home the same point. There is little doubt that, despite his view of the negative consequences of the rise, spread, and influence of science, he often relies on scientific data or theories in order to undermine the previously regnant commonsense conception of the world.

By stressing the similarity we discern between entities or properties Nietzsche virtually anticipates Quine's "partial explanation"—in terms of natural selection—of why we, "as we are now," are capable, with better than random chances, of making reasonably accurate inductions. These inductions are said to be "based on our innate, scientifically unjustified similarity standard."[30] Replacing "innate" with genetically transmitted perceptual-conceptual propensities, Quine's point is virtually that of Nietzsche. He clearly shows that the evolution of scientific consciousness effectively subverts previously inherited habits of perception, thought, and observation. This questioning of prior notions of similarity is particularly relevant to the operation of secondary (conceptual) epigenetic rules because, as Quine expresses it, "there is nothing more basic to thought and language than our sense of similarity; our sorting of things into kinds."[31]

On the basis of the refinements of scientific methods and observations, our genetically transmitted apprehension of similarity, it turns out, is, as Quine puts it, "scientifically unjustified." Hence, the earlier sense of "the similar" was, as Nietzsche surmised, a practical, but false, sense and usage. Nonetheless, it is a *fundamental* sense. Hence, there is a sea-change, as Nietzsche argued, in our scientific picture of the natural world that puts in question what had served, presumably for thousands of years, as unreflective categories of thought. So, in spite of criticisms of his radical thesis, Nietzsche had a point when he argued that mankind has constructed a falsified world in which he was at home, in which he survived and prospered. His critique of previous knowledge based upon "convenient fictions," therefore, was grounded in his philosophical response to modern *scientific* discoveries and theories. In a sense, then, his thinking in this regard anticipated that of some recent and contemporary philosophers of science whose orientations are based upon philosophical responses to facts, discoveries, and theories of the independent sciences. In effect, Nietzsche subverts the pre-scientific standpoint of commonsense realism by appealing to the knowledges of the sciences.

By virtue of a gradual refinement of observation, instruments and thought,

> little by little, the external world is . . . differentiated; but for incalculable periods of time on earth each thing was thought

> of as identical and consubstantial with a single one of its qualities. . . . Only very gradually have the many distinct qualities pertaining to a single thing been granted; even the history of human language betrays a resistance to the multiplication of epithets.[32]

The theories of the natural world Nietzsche became familiar with tended not only to undermine commonsense realism, but erased aesthetic qualities such as color. As early as 1866, Nietzsche was aware of the conception of colorless atoms in constant motion, both in Lucretius's account of Epicurean theory in *De rerum natura* and then-contemporary physics. His later study of Boscovich's theory of nature familiarized him with the reduction of matter to subatomic, non-extended "centers of force." Already in "Schopenhauer as Educator" he lamented the scientific theoretical picture of the grey visage of nature and pointed to the "atomistic chaos" that physical scientists disclosed. He decried the replacement of a full, rich, colorful, aesthetic world of experience by a cold, grey, colorless, senseless dance of atoms. Seeking a place for an aesthetic image of the world, Nietzsche keenly felt the distress generated by de-anthropomorphic scientific world-interpretations. The power of scientific knowledge undermined our inherited commonsense ways of understanding the world, undercut our trust in our aesthetic perceptions, and presented a dehumanized chaos to us. It was physical theory, not classical Greek poets or mythology—as Heidegger insinuated[33]—that led Nietzsche to express his variation on Spinoza's "God or Nature," "*Chaos sive Natura*."[34] His chaos theory, his description of the "indescribable complexity" of the natural world, was derived from physical theory, not the image of a "yawning abyss" in Hesiod's *Theogony*.

In both his notes from the late 1880s and *On the Genealogy of Morals* Nietzsche stresses the negative implications of the domination of a culture of science for our self-image. Put simply, the fragmented depiction of a chaotic cosmic process reinforces the idea of a senseless cosmos, an *objective* nihilism. Out of the growth of scientific practice and the multiplication of theories there emerges a paradoxical antagonism towards science itself, an internal auto-consumption of itself.[35] Placed in the context of his general evolutionary theory, the evolution of science and its conceptions produces a knowledge-framework that subverts mankind's need for illusions and aesthetic embellishments, sacrifices them for pragmatic, utilitarian, and technological values. Now, Nietzsche tells us,

> the *passion for science* is . . . a formidable, new, growing power, the like of which has never yet been seen, with eagle's wings, owl's eyes, and the feet of a dragon. . . . [I]t is already so strong that it grasps itself as a problem and asks:

> "how am I possible among *mankind*? How will mankind be possible *with me*!"[36]

The growth and spread of scientific theories and concepts is not only a source of internal tension for the sciences. It undermines previously extant beliefs in "eternal truths," the quest for permanence, and a useful, functional commonsense conception of the world that has served mankind well for millennia. Paradoxically, the will to truth fueled by a will to power evolves into a mode of thought and inquiry that strips away every appearance and illusion, places mankind in the lineage of animals, and dwarfs the human world in a boundless, chaotic cosmos. Nietzsche wonders where science is going and where it is leading mankind. A powerful culture of science threatens to nullify competing perspectives and erase the life-enhancing value of art.

One phenomenon that the evolved emergence of scientific consciousness has generated, Nietzsche argues, is a metastasizing skepticism. This was especially the case in the neo-Kantian scientific environment of his own time in which agnosticism about the ultimate constituents of the natural world became prevalent. And, of course, the recrudescence of antirealism in recent thought recapitulates, in a more sophisticated way, the scientific atmosphere to which Nietzsche responded. As he sees it, the refinement of observation, the stricter the methods of discovery, the more difficult it becomes to claim that our "knowledge" of entities and facts is equivalent to precise knowledge, to say nothing of "truth." The advance of scientific methodology leads us to a point at which we no longer speak of truths in any "absolute sense." Our faith in objective knowledge gradually wanes.[37]

Nietzsche views the intensification of the "drive for truth" in the exact sciences as having the paradoxical outcome of eroding our belief in objective truth. This evolved inquiring, skeptical way of thinking tends to produce detrimental effects on mankind's life-enhancing impulses, its need for aesthetic illusions. This is what Nietzsche has in mind when he asserts that "There is no pre-established harmony between the promotion of truth and the welfare of mankind."[38] At times he adopts the scientific mode of inquiry and its methodological restraint in his denial that there is any holistic "Truth" precisely *because*, as the sciences show us, there are many truths, or as William James puts it, "truths in the plural."

Nietzsche is keenly aware that few individuals could retain confidence and an affirmation of existence in a cognitive context of fragmentary relative truth, the absence of purpose in the cosmos, the demotion of our status in the universe, and the seemingly indefinite proliferation of replaceable theories in the sciences without significant cultural ideals. The de-anthropomorphic and chaotic picture of actuality he describes is nihilistic and demoralizing. Hence, the need for the edifying aesthetic ideal of the *Übermensch*, a "principle of selection" embodied in the challenge of the thought of eternal return, and the Dionysian affirmation of life and existence. However, this projection of daunting ideas for the few is grounded in the belief that "Science shows the flux, but not the goal; however, it provides the *presuppositions* with which the goal must agree."[39]

Seeking a human meaning for the world, Nietzsche proposes an interpretation of actuality according to the physical sciences that is based upon "human analogy." He relies, as we've said, on Boscovich's dynamic theory of nature[40] and humanizes it in the form of his "reduced formula," the will to power, in an effort to synthesize a scientific interpretation of the natural world and a metaphoric transference of his understanding of the essential psychological propensity of human beings.

Boscovich's theory of non-extended "centers of force" as the ultimate constituents of nature leads Nietzsche to respond enthusiastically to this early hint of the "dematerialization" of the world.[41] On the other hand, he sees that mankind is no exception to this energistic conception of actuality. For we are, abstractly considered, construed as conglomerations of "forces" that wax and wane. His adaptation of the evolved scientific paradigm of knowledge is apparent in the depiction of "the pure concept of 'Nature'" as "the dehumanization of nature and the naturalization of man." This is a stage at which Nietzsche seems to pause for a moment before transferring the human drive towards more and more to actuality *in toto* in his metaphoric interpretation of "reality" as a vast conglomeration of interacting "wills to power."

A great deal of the content of Nietzsche's critical epistemology was a consequence of his philosophical response to various perspectives in the sciences. His own thinking emulates his sense of the progress of scientific inquiry and understanding, the sequence of theory-replacement, the hypothetical, provisional, experimental approach to knowledge. He eschews fundamental truths and proposes provisional, probable, heuristic principles.[42] More specifically, he clearly relies upon the model of scientific thinking when he advocates the critical analysis of all beliefs and convictions, the imaginative construction of "working hypotheses," and the unremitting analysis of and testing of "probabilities" (*Wahrscheinheiten*).[43]

HISTORICITY EVOLVED

Although in "On the Use and Abuse of History for Life" Nietzsche attacked the hypertrophy of historical sense or historical consciousness, he never denied the relevance and importance of history for understanding cultural, valuational, and ideational systems. In fact, he emphasizes the way history and attitudes towards history condition the lives of individuals and entire cultures. A recent claim that after his untimely observations on history this topic "largely disappears" from Nietzsche's writings "except for some residual jibes at German historiography"[44] could not be further from the truth. Rather, he insists that concepts and values can be understood only in a historical-evolutionary context. In *Human, All-Too-Human* he laments the lack of historical sense in philosophers, their failure to see that "everything has become," that "there are no *eternal facts*," "no absolute truths."[45] Unlike those who construe history as characterized by discontinuity, Nietzsche consistently defends his views concerning development, transformation, and evolution in multiple, coeval, continuous processes. What may be characterized as cultural-intellectual paradigm shifts are construed as evolutionary and historical phenomena subject to "*historical* philosophizing." Nietzsche avers that what separates him from previous philosophers is that he believes that there are "no eternal concepts, no eternal values, eternal truths." And philosophy, if it is not science or legislation, "means only the most general extension of the notion of 'history'." On the basis of "etymology and the history of language we take the view that all concepts have *evolved*, many are still evolving. . . ."[46] An implication of this standpoint is that cultural history is a continuation of evolutionary natural history and that it establishes the temporary parameters of the range of knowledge. And, since evolution has no directionality, human understanding is not moving towards some convergence on theoretical unity or holistic "truth."

Heidegger's claim that Nietzsche was engaged in "metaphysical thinking" ignores the provisional, tentative, and experimental approach to philosophy that Nietzsche embraced. The transcendence of narrow, dogmatic perspectives, as well as the increase in the number of viable perspectives, leads to the elevation of mankind, a liberation from uniperspectival claims to "truth." Given Nietzsche's increasing commitment to the evolved historicity of human knowledge, it is clear that he must hold that perspectivalism has evolved out of historical transformations. Hence his own reflections are rooted in the historicity that shapes, but does not dictate, all thought and values.

The affirmation of a suprahistorical transcendence of the "river of becoming," the suggestion of an experimental/conceptual leap beyond one's times, seem to crash against the reef of Nietzsche's strongly stated commitment to historical philosophizing. His own stress upon cultivating a balanced "historical sense," placed in juxtaposition to his evolutionary epistemology, seems to subvert attempts to attain states of being that go beyond one's historical context. The rescue of existence from triviality that fuels much of Nietzsche's suprahistorical tendencies, as well as his dramatization of individual existence, are undercut by their very proposal of attaining transhistorical states of being and thought, primarily because the field of action in general and of cultural action in particular is construed as ineluctably historical. If historicity is transcended, it occurs only momentarily in peak experiences or in what Kierkegaard, Emerson, and Nietzsche called "the Moment"—in the "blink of an eye" (*Augenblick*).

If a philosophical historical sense has evolved, what are we to make of the prescription of ways of thinking and feeling that are considered suprahistorical, as means of escaping the powerful nets of historicity in which we are typically entangled? Are intensified subjective states of thought and *pathos*—the appropriation of the "thought" of eternal recurrence, a Dionysian affirmation of life, for example—means of escape from the labyrinth of history? In regard to such questions, Nietzsche's typical reflexivity is absent. But it need not be.

Perhaps the proposal of esoteric means of striving for and even attaining suprahistorical states of being and thought in ecstatic experience is an aim that is itself a consequence of an evolved historicity. Perhaps it has arisen out of a postreligious, postmetaphysical, scientifically oriented, secularist, politically volatile historical period. Thus, Nietzsche's endeavor to eternalize temporality and, like a "flash of lightning," to cut through the bonds of evolutionary history and throw off the weight of historical consciousness, is itself historically formed. Perhaps the search for a way out of the labyrinth of history and the craving for *ecstasis* are distinctively historical phenomena that surface precisely in a skeptical, perspectivalist, and increasingly relativistic historical epochs. If we grant this possibility, then Nietzsche's prescriptions for attaining transhistorical existential states of being reveal a perspicuous *reflection* of a spiritual striving for a transcendence of time in temporality that has emerged out of the evolved historicity of mankind.

Chapter Eight

Tragic Knowledge and a Will-to-Power Psychology

> [T]he dreadful basic text of *homo natura* must again be understood . . . man put back in nature; becoming master of many vain . . . interpretations . . . that have till now . . . painted over the eternal basic text of *homo natura*.
>
> Nietzsche, *Beyond Good and Evil*

> The philosopher of tragic knowledge . . . controls the unleashed drive for knowledge, not by means of a new metaphysics . . . a new faith. He feels it . . . tragic that the ground of metaphysics has been cut away and can never be satisfied by the colorful kaleidoscope of the sciences.
>
> Nietzsche, *Nachlass*

Nietzsche often appears to contradict himself in his voluminous writings. This is especially the case in regard to formulations of the idea of the will to power. Even the presentation of a theory of the nature of reality seems to contradict a forceful denial of the possibility of attaining metaphysical truth. How can Nietzsche proclaim that there is no ultimate truth and then proceed to develop a reductive, explanatory principle that is presented as the answer to the riddle of existence? A passionate antimetaphysician appears to end his reflections by propounding what has been called his "metaphysics of will to power." Some have charged him with radical inconsistency in this regard while others have held that he regressed to a positive metaphysical standpoint, which he had abandoned even before the appearance of *The Birth of Tragedy*.[1] But the conception of a universal will to power acting through all beings is neither a claim to metaphysical truth nor a claim to positive knowledge about "ultimate reality," nor a novel discovery of a "principle of explanation." The hypothesis of a universal will to power (or, more accurately, the hypothesis of a plurality of "wills to power") is an elaborately crafted, sophisticated myth that is put forward as an experimental, metaphorical, poetic "truth." Nietzsche never abandoned his view that we have no access to "truth-in-itself," to a knowable transcendental "Truth."

The idea of *the* will to power or "wills to power" is a mythical, poetic interpretation of actuality that is intended as an aesthetic vision of the cosmos conceived of as a "self-creating work of art." The aesthetic-philosophic interpretation of the underlying nature of the cosmos is based upon interpretations of the natural world in physical theory that are understood to be provisional, hypothetical constructs. This global interpretation of actuality is supported by a questionable argument buttressed by concepts that Nietzsche characterizes as conceptual fictions. The imaginative positing of a will to power or wills to power does not represent, nor was it intended to represent, any positive metaphysical claim to truth or knowledge of a putative unconditioned reality.

NIETZSCHE'S PROJECT

The philosophical thought of Nietzsche does not *conclude* with a radically critical epistemology that undermines claims to objective knowledge or unvarnished truth. In the earliest stages of his thought, he already expressed negative evaluations of the pretension, in philosophy or science, to grasp truth or to possess objective knowledge. Under Kant's influence, he came to the conclusion that metaphysics in its traditional form was finished. Kant had shown that the only things we can truly know are phenomena constituted by our *a priori* intuitions of space and time, our senses, and our categorical schema. We have no access to the world-in-itself or to "reality-in-itself." Pushing Kant's skepticism one step further, Nietzsche proposed that everything we constitute as known is phenomenal (including the categories by which we constitute any object of knowledge), that both the "internal" and the "external" worlds are interpretative representations constructed by virtue of our psychophysical "organization." His agnosticism prohibited him, for a time, from making any claim to know what the ground of our psychic and physical "organization" is. As has been argued, Nietzsche was profoundly influenced by radical phenomenalism *and* the agnosticism espoused by philosophical scientists. He cherishes the "value of an *inner* and an *outer* phenomenology" and admits that a phenomenology of the non-human, non-subjective domain is relatively more accurate than that of "inner processes." But both psychic "movements," as well as external motions, are "signs" or symptoms of unobserved "inner events."[2] In an early letter to his friend, Carl von Gersdorff, Nietzsche (paraphrasing Lange) remarks that "our organization remains . . . unknown to us."[3] For a long time he hesitated to speculate about the nature of what psychic and physical changes, movements, and events were symptomatic of in an ultimate sense.

Nietzsche was often confronted by conventionalist interpretations of scientific concepts and principles. He shares the general attitude towards the ultimate nature of reality expressed by the nineteenth-century scientist, Emil du Bois-Reymond: "We shall never know." What scientists conveyed to him was that we are ignorant about the ultimate constituents of nature or the ground of actuality. Nietzsche absorbed this agnosticism and refined it in his perspectival approach to knowledge. His youthful enthusiasm for a phenomenalism-cum-agnosticism was not only an early infatuation. It remained a persistent, underlying theme in most of his writings, published and unpublished.

The assumption that will to power underlies and pervades all phenomena and processes is an imaginative, aesthetically conceived answer to the riddle of life and existence. The distinctly anthropomorphic nature of this "hypothesis" is only the most obvious clue to its mythopoetic nature. Because Nietzsche discovered that we cannot escape from the circle of anthropomorphism no matter what "method" of interpretation we may rely upon, all "truths" are, in the final analysis, "anthropomorphic truths" (*anthropomorphische Wahrheiten*). And we know, from our previous discussion of this theme, any "truth" that is shown to be anthropomorphic is necessarily a transformation of actuality, a species of "conditional knowledge," a hypothetical construction.

Nietzsche continually sought to escape from the labyrinth of skepticism, to overcome the negations and uncertainties of skeptical consciousness. But he saw that there was no exit from this labyrinth by way of *knowledge*. He then proceeded to construct escape ladders out of scientific interpretations he considered as provisional and sought to create disguised fables that would serve as the centerpieces of a paradoxical, tragically optimistic, Dionysian "religion" of life.

As early as 1872, Nietzsche questioned the role of the philosopher in a scientific age dominated by "practical interests." *The Birth of Tragedy* revealed intriguing aspects of his thought: an apparent commitment to a Schopenhauerian metaphysics of will and a concern with the relation between "science" in the broadest sense (*Wissenschaft*) and art. Only through the aesthetic transformation of reality and experience by means of the illusory power of art would Germano-European culture be rejuvenated and given a new direction. Richard Wagner, he then believed, would be the spearhead of this cultural renaissance. The programmatic and inspirational tone of *The Birth of Tragedy* may be contrasted with the disquieting questions and doubts that are sprinkled throughout his notations of 1872 and his unpublished essays of 1873. Epistemic skepticism was already eroding the positive assertions of his first work during the year in which it was published and in the following year as well.

Later admitting that in *The Birth of Tragedy* he had not yet had the confidence to speak in his own voice, Nietzsche viewed his reference to a "primal will" as an expression of his admiration of Schopenhauer. It was also the swan song of his metaphysical aspirations. In 1883, he tells us that in his "first period" he practiced a form of "Jesuitism" by "consciously holding fast to illusion and compulsorily interpreting it as a *basis of culture*."[4] From now on his thinking is decidedly postmetaphysical.

In his early notes, Nietzsche struggles with the question of the role of philosophy in the face of value-free "iconic historiography" and the natural sciences. The unrestrained drive for knowledge will tend to undermine the unity of authentic culture. Repeatedly, he implies that with the fusion of the drive to accumulate knowledge in the sciences and the pragmatic application of this knowledge to the world, art and cultural unity will undergo dissolution. In effect, the aesthetic interpretation of existence would eventually be obliterated in a world dominated by a culture of science and a mass consciousness that would level artistic values and seek to efface whatever is different from itself. Later, Nietzsche calls attention to the probable negative consequences of a dominant techno-scientific ideology that places greatest value on practical, utilitarian matters and sees people as tools or helots whose primary purpose is to service the State and the socioeconomic system.

In his incisive phenomenology of nihilism, which is preserved in the *Nachlass* that some Nietzsche commentators would like to delete, Nietzsche delineates the following salient factors: the cultural decline in traditional religious faith will lead some to feel that life in this world is without meaning; there will be a period of spiritual and intellectual exhaustion; the era of "grand politics" will generate conflicts on a national and global scale; the spread of cultural, physical, and psychic decadence[5] is accelerating in late modernity; intellectual despair emerges as a result of the loss of belief in transcendental values and a consequent sense that there is no locus of value at all; finally, the powerful scientific interpretations of life, mankind, and nature demythologizes and dehumanizes the world, reducing man's stature profoundly and reducing the natural world to an odorless, grey, soundless, and senseless chaos. Science is not intentionally nihilistic in its "will to knowledge," but its unpretentious truths more and more disclose a fragmentation of the world and undermine the common sense understanding of actuality. Thinking of the effects of a purely scientific world-interpretation, Nietzsche observes that "the more we de-humanize nature, the emptier and more meaningless it becomes for us."[6]

The nihilism of the twentieth century and beyond would come about, Nietzsche believed, because of the confluence of currents of thought, sentiments, and anxieties that would be overwhelming. The great danger, he accurately saw, was the emergence of *practical nihilism*: a destructive action surcharged with collective energy and technological powers. Needless to say, the marriage of technical, scientific knowledge and practical (=political) interests has already brought havoc to the twentieth century and will, unfortunately, continue to aggravate the condition of man in the twenty-first. Rudiments of this disturbing vision of the future driven by a potentially dangerous mass-supported technology can be found even in Nietzsche's earliest notes. All of his positive and constructive philosophical energies were devoted to the creation of new myths that would, he hoped, prevent the catastrophe he saw on the horizon.

The cultural ideal of a perfectly egalitarian, technocentric, utility-oriented social ideal could only be opposed by dramatic countermyths. In the realm of cultural ideals, there is a conflict of *tables of values* that is invariably experienced and understood as a conflict of passionately embraced "truths." But the question, Nietzsche believed, was no longer associated with "truth," but with the penetration of the long-range consequences or "effects" of a system of values on human civilization and culture, with forging a powerful "counter-ideal" out of a carefully crafted humanized metaphoric image of "reality."

The indiscriminate pursuit of knowledge tends to produce specialized *Gelehrten*—learned individuals who are "rootless"—as well as a growing majority who either despise or are indifferent to knowledge. At the same time, a culture of learning becomes fragmented, relativistic, and skeptical. The philosopher's task in a period in which the *Wissenschaften* or general sciences flourish and seek dominion of a culture is to emphasize "the problem of existence."

Nietzsche acknowledges a trend that has been exacerbated by time: a decline in the quality of education and a decreasing valuation of philosophy and philosophers. The cultural base necessary for an authentic cultural pyramid is eroding and philosophers are more and more isolated from the general society.[7] Science is already beyond its possible self-destruction, but it may yet be guided or controlled. After all, the sciences are themselves rooted in philosophical assumptions that should be elucidated. What it comes down to is a question of which shall guide future Western culture and which shall be predominant: science or philosophy?[8] Although we know only too well the outcome of this competition so far, philosophy still had prestige and influence in the latter part of the nineteenth century, a status bolstered by the thought and writings of a number of decidedly philosophical scientists. Nietzsche, at any rate, believed that it was still possible for a powerful philosophical vision to influence, if not co-opt, the scientific orientation and its applied technical power in the modern world.

In his early speculations, Nietzsche saw the philosopher as not only a "physician of culture," but as a potential creator of a new culture. The scientific *Weltanschauung* was necessary, he believed, in order to transcend the stagnation of the Middle Ages. However, in modern times scientific knowledge must be encompassed or surpassed by art in order to "return to life." The fascinating, imaginative illusions of art are necessary in order to overcome the negative effects of the crepuscular world disclosed by the exact sciences, a world in which nature is reduced to an "atomistic chaos" and humanity is profoundly decentered. Probing, analyzing, and dissecting the world, the "exact sciences" remove veil after veil until only senselessly rushing atoms remain, until every quality that gives splendor to life is reduced to a quantity or a quantitative formula. Nietzsche saw the world of the later nineteenth-century, the world according to science, as an immensely complex process characterized by a chaotic action and reaction of forces. This reductivism is also reflected in a growing social atomism in which each individual seeks his or her egoistic ends.[9] It is possible that a new, stimulating, philosophical myth may yet rescue Western civilization from further dissolution and chaos, from the leveling of values and the effacement of the aesthetic interpretation of life.

A major consequence of the advancement of scientific culture is the demythologizing of myth. In order to forge a new cultural ideal, the philosopher would have to awaken belief in a *mythisches Gebaude*, a "mythical construction." However, in the wake of the agnostic consequence of Kant's *Critique of Pure Reason*, the powerful instinctive need for such a construction is unlikely to arise again. At this point in his reflections from the 1870s Nietzsche envisions a new form of philosophy brought forth by the emergence of a "philosopher-artist" who could fill the empty space left by the demise of myth. What might be created would be a *Kunst-Werk*, an art-work possessing "aesthetic value."[10] This is a truncated, embryonic statement of Nietzsche's long-range philosophical project. He put on the mantle of the "philosopher-artist" who would create a new and strange vision of this world for the sake of a higher form of existence.

While admitting the enormous value of the accumulation of knowledge, Nietzsche also emphasized the balanced value of the stimulating forms and illusions of art. Aesthetic illusions have the same value as knowledge if they are believed. Endurance of life, as well as its enhancement, requires illusions or "untruths" that are accepted as if they were "true." A primordial requirement of life is the spontaneous projection of illusions as "truths." The functional value of logical and empirical "truths" is never denied since they are truths for us in our world, our pragmatic domain. However, aesthetic "truth" (which, from the standpoint of knowledge and science, is "untruth") has had and continues to have powerful, long-range, life-affirming effects.

Our propensity towards truth is construed as a primal striving for subjective conviction, as an expression of *pathos*. This *pathos* results from the struggle between two basic approaches to "truth": logico-scientific "truth" and aesthetic, mythopoetic "truth."[11] This insight goes to the center of one of the basic tensions in Western culture: the conflict between the logical, empirical, and scientific forms of "truth" and the spiritual, mythical, metaphysical, and poetic forms of "truth." Nietzsche's ambitious project, then, is to create new myths that will be relatively consistent with scientific interpretations of the world, to form a Centaurian perspective that combines science, art, and philosophy.

Philosophical theories are elaborate "interpretations" that have visionary form and aesthetic value. Their truth is manifested in a striking, persuasive metaphor. We are imbued with an unconscious artistic power that creates and imposes forms on what we experience. Philosophy is a sophisticated expression of this same artistic, creative *nisus*. It is based upon a kind of "picture-thinking" (*Bilderdenken*) that invents forms and images beyond the domain of experience. That is, it creates a conceptual domain that is stable and secure, but is like a spider's web that traps, retains, and neutralizes whatever enters it. The inventive power of philosophy is a disguised continuation of the "mythical drive."[12] To a large extent Nietzsche never significantly deviates from this earlier position. It is a direct presentation of his overarching view of an epochal sea-change in the value-orientation of Western civilization and one whose ramifications are still very much with us.

Nietzsche's account of his "present age" highlights scientific culture, the decline of religion, the advance of an enormous majority combined with material "egoism." Society and the State employ science in their service in order to exploit it for very practical purposes.[13] Utilitarian research, utilitarian values, and *ad hoc* practical political "values" conglomerate to form a domain that virtually excludes or devalues genuine art, myth, contemplation, and philosophy in its edifying, aesthetic form. Such a cultural landscape, for Nietzsche, is essentially a culturally nihilistic scene.

The overcoming of nihilism involves, in part, the overcoming, *via* philosophical imagination, of the domination of utilitarian, collective, pragmatic, and technocratic world-orientations. Nietzsche's central concern is not the negation of such a fruitful and practically valuable world-orientation, but its indirect mastery and guidance. Philosophy as a holistic, meaning-giving, aesthetically significant life-orientation retains its value by virtue of its "beauty and sublimity." The "aesthetic value" of philosophy is found in its long-range effects, its culturally binding meaning, and, particularly for Nietzsche, the retention of the tragic sense of life in a Dionysian tragic optimism. For him, imagination transcends the rationalist drive for knowledge and restores meaning to the qualitative world of human experience. As he says often enough, man needs to have a purpose, a *telos*, in order to have a sense of meaning. This is the case even when that purpose, as in Nietzsche's understanding of Buddhism, is not to be: *nirvana*.[14] Genuine cultures need a meaningful teleology. But such a cultural teleology must be created, projected in the form of a challenging, aesthetically conceived philosophical myth or fable that would combine art and science.

The revealing fragmentary reflections found in the notes of 1872–73 contain a prolepsis of Nietzsche's later philosophical efforts. That he is not thinking of the creation of a romantic, pessimistic metaphysics along the lines of Schopenhauer's thought (as found in *The Birth of Tragedy*) is clear because he completely accepts "the consequences of the Kantian theory": *Ende der Metaphysik als Wissenschaft*.[15] Moreover, he calls attention to the purely aesthetic and metaphorical nature of metaphysical thinking. What is abundantly clear is that, even before *The Birth of Tragedy* appeared, Nietzsche no longer believed that metaphysics yielded genuine knowledge, and he rejected the Schopenhauerian echo in his first major work. Very early in his thought, then, he held that there is no accessible "absolute truth," no known or knowable ultimate "Truth." It is implausible, then, that the idea of a universal will to power is presented as a "metaphysical" truth or as an empirically rooted "principle of explanation."

TRAGIC KNOWLEDGE

At one point in his notes Nietzsche boasts that he is the first thinker not to claim to possess ultimate truth, the first to renounce the possibility of such truth.[16] In *Human, All-Too-Human*, however, he praises the "exact sciences" for valuing "unpretentious truths . . . discovered by means of rigorous method."[17] This is often said to be an embrace of positivism, though strictly speaking that is not the case, because the "truths" of the exact sciences are only comparatively more valuable than the pretensions to complete knowledge in dogmatic metaphysics. For they are neither absolute facts nor absolute truths.

> The fact that one can *enumerate* phenomena, such as . . . chemical phenomena, and likewise predict them, provides no warrant for the supposition that one has thereby touched on "absolute truths."[18]

Nietzsche was radically opposed to scientism and adopted, as we've seen, a conventionalist and fictionalist interpretation of scientific knowledge under the influence of proto-philosophers of science. As indicated, he agreed with Kant that laws of nature are not discovered in nature, but are projected onto the natural world. For this reason, both the philosophical and the scientific understanding of the natural domain is a "world as representation."[19] And, for Nietzsche, representation does not entail mirroring something. It is a process of *Veranderung*, or *Verwandlung*: transformation, modification, or transubstantiation. And this capacity to create forms, to invent (*erdichten*)—in the sense of fictionalizing or rendering something dense or coherent by means of *poiesis*—is virtually identical to perpectivalism.[20]

A scientific "world-interpretation" involves an effort to represent the natural world by means of translating it into abstract, numerical symbols or formulas expressing knowledge. And, in Nietzsche's own terms, it *is* knowledge—that is, a creative transformation of what is experienced, observed, and interpolated by means of (1) perceptual selectivity and the perspectival "abstractions" of the senses; (2) conceptual categorization via simplification and "dehistoricizing";[21] (3) reducing or abbreviating by means of sedimentations of tropic or metaphoric signs; and (4) explaining by imposing familiar schema on novel or unfamiliar phenomena.[22]

As much as he strove to transcend skepticism, Nietzsche was pulled back into it by virtue of critical, ironic tendencies and the typical parameters of his thought. Despite his different styles, "philosophies," and voices, there are thematic threads that run through his *corpus* even though, in Hegel's phrase, a "skeptical self-consciousness" became the hallmark of his thinking. Sometime in 1873, he tells us that he didn't "believe in a blessed thing." He was "in the throes of moral skepticism and dissolution."[23] He tried to overcome "romantic pessimism" by deliberately forcing himself to face "the problematic elements characteristic of all existence."[24] In this preface (written in 1886), Nietzsche shows us that his novel experimental-skeptical perspective embraces a tragic standpoint, one that had been his position from his early notes of 1872 and is still his basic orientation.[25] Thus, from 1872 to 1886, he had not substantially changed his mind about the underlying tragic nature of existence and had not been able to overcome skepticism in any purely cognitive, theoretical way. The tone of these prefatory remarks is a replication, in different terms, of an earlier description of a "tragic philosophy."

In notes from 1872 Nietzsche refers to the loss of belief in the possibility of absolute truth or metaphysical knowledge as "tragic." It is a condition that has been brought about by many factors. Specifically in philosophy it is linked to the agnostic consequences of Kant's *Critique of Pure Reason*. The death knell of "the Absolute" is the occasion for the emergence of the "tragic philosopher," a philosopher for desperate times.

This new thinker has the task of mastering the uninhibited drive for knowledge that, paradoxically, has led to a questioning of the objective validity of knowledge. The "tragic philosopher" (alias Nietzsche) considers it drastic that the foundation of metaphysics has crumbled. At the same time, he rejects satisfaction with the complex "game" of science and seeks a new mode of existence based upon an aesthetic foundation. The tragedy embraced by this kind of philosopher can be overcome *nicht durch eine neue Metaphysik* ("not through a new metaphysics"). Rather, it may be transcended by guiding and controlling the burgeoning knowledge-drive, putting it in the service of a new, powerful, and demanding cultural ideal.

Tragic knowledge comes about through the realization that there is no way back to metaphysical truth or "truth-in-itself." Such a tragic *pathos* is further aggravated by the insight that "one must even will illusion." One core aspect of tragic knowledge is tantamount to what Nietzsche later calls the "nihilistic belief" that "there is no Truth." The corrosive tendencies of the scientific, logico-empirical drive have begun to wear away the optimism with which it began, despite its impressive technological creations. The unrestrained "will to knowledge" has, unintentionally, led to the erosion of the notion of purely objective knowledge, the negation of absolute truth, and even a caution about certain specific claims to truth. This social, cultural, historical counterfinality is aptly christened *tragische Erkenntnis* (tragic knowledge): the knowledge of the limits of knowledge.

There are three basic features of *tragische Philosophie*: (1) the loss of belief in transcendental metaphysics; (2) the insight (presented in *The Birth of Tragedy*) into the pain and suffering of existence; and (3) the *pathos* entailed by the realization that illusion must be consciously *willed*. The last of these characteristics lies at the heart of Nietzsche's paradoxical project: the self-conscious realization that his positive philosophy is a *consciously* willed "illusion." He fully understands that the maximal expression of affirmative, ascending life requires what is no longer possible for mankind: the *unconscious* projection of fables or illusions that accentuate the vitality and joy of existence.

The ideal conditions for a full existence would be to make "knowledge instinctive," to play upon the aesthetic surface of life, to achieve what is suggested in *Thus Spoke Zarathustra*: the buoyant, carefree openness to experience, the simple joy of existence; freedom from the tyranny of the past, the tyranny of absolute truths; the child-like recovery of "the innocence of becoming." The tension in Nietzsche's positive, aesthetic interpretation of actuality and his prescription for "self overcoming" is generated, in large part, because he encourages the appropriation of "tragic knowledge" and, at the same time, seeks its "self-suppression" in maximal life-affirmation. The "tragic perspective" cannot be transcended by the accumulation of more knowledge or deeper understanding of actuality; it can only be overcome, insofar as it can be, by a transformation in *Existenz*. But in order for a Dionysian affirmation of life to take place, new myths must first be created, fables that should not violate scientific knowledge nor submit to its hegemony. It would be a "joyful science" that would find a space for the aesthetic perspective and propose a cultural *telos*. Science discloses the flux and extraordinary complexity of all events, but discovers no goal. However, Nietzsche insists that "it provides the *presuppositions* to which the new goal must conform."[26]

A WILL-TO-POWER PSYCHOLOGY

The idea of a universally immanent will to power (or an immanent multiplicity of wills to power) acting through all beings is itself derived from what is first and foremost expressed as a critical *psychological* interpretation of the psychodynamics of *homo natura*. Despite the presence in us of numerous desires, drives, impulses, and passions, we are imbued, beneath the threshold of consciousness, with a primal urge for power. Human beings strive for power (or the "feeling of power") because they lack it, because they feel weak, frail, threatened, because they are fearful of others. Our striving for more, for power, is described as if it were a phylogenetic trait we have inherited. In our ontogenic psychic development we seem to recapitulate unconsciously the phylogenetic development of our ancestors and we have acquired highly diverse means, direct and indirect, of expressing our striving for power or for the hypothetical ultimate *Trieb* (drive) from which all our other passions, impulses, and urges radiate.

In *Human, All-Too-Human*, the striving for power is illustrated by the "exploitation" of others (specifically, the "exploitation" of workers that Nietzsche criticizes) by the industrialists and speculators who manipulate economic forces and by the striving for preeminence over others.[27] The psychology of motivation that Nietzsche developed over time was gradually transformed into a metaphorical perspectival interpretation of the nature of actuality. This theory of motivation in terms of a posited will to power is *not*, however, a mythical notion. Rather, it is an independent interpretation of the primordial springs of human behavior. The hypothesis that a striving for power is a basic characteristic of mankind is a viable psychological hypothesis put forward as a conception of the ultimate *nisus* underlying human motivation. Such an interpretation stands apart from the myth of a universal will to power and is postulated in the form of a proto-psychoanalytical hypothesis that presupposes a depth understanding of ourselves and others.[28] We can consider and evaluate this psychodynamic conception of the underlying irrational, predominantly unconscious craving for power in man without considering the imaginative possibility of a universal, impersonal will to power acting through all entities whatsoever.

Nietzsche's earliest attitude towards the power drive was ironic and critical.[29] And in *Zarathustra*, where "self-overcoming" is preached to the "wisest," they are told that their "danger" lies not in the river of becoming, but in "the will to power" itself.[30] Before Freud, but after Hartmann's *Philosophy of the Unconscious* (1868), Nietzsche sought to look beneath or behind the masks of civility, to uncover the primitive drives and impulses of mankind—to expose "the tiger"[31] that is hidden within each of us and threatens to burst forth into overt or covert aggression for the sake of power. The hypothetical reduction of all drives or urges to a will to power as a psychological interpretation of natural mankind is not only not presented as a myth, but is clearly intended as an autopsy of the human psyche that discloses what is considered as a "terrible truth," one central to Nietzsche's stark "natural history of man," his suspicious interpretation of *homo natura*.

Already in an unpublished "preface," "Homer's Contest" (1872), Nietzsche foreshadows his later insights on the "spiritualization" of the instincts and the psychological will to power. Discussing good and bad *Eris* (strife), he refers to the former as expressed "as jealousy, hatred, and envy." These feelings serve as "spurs . . . to activity" which can lead us on to excellence (*arete*). The contest (*agon*) waged by tragedians against one another produces a positive competition that is creative and transforms (or, in later terms, "spiritualizes") emotions that are potentially dangerous. Nietzsche, alluding to the actions of the heroes in Homer's *Iliad*, maintains that "if we take contest [or constructive strife] out of Greek life, we at once see into that [pre-Homeric] abyss of a horrifying savagery of hatred and lust to destroy."[32] Here he anticipates the cruelest, most terrible expression of a primitive will to power. Using the model of the earliest literary representation of the ancient Greeks, Nietzsche already suggests the psychology of a potentially dangerous natural proclivity in mankind to desire to surpass others, to triumph over them, or manifest a naked "will to power."

In *Twilight of the Gods* (1889) Nietzsche reprises this earlier portrait of the ancient Greeks and opposes it to overidealized, aesthetically designed images of an explosive people. Their "strongest instinct" was a fearsome "will to power." The arts and festivals of their city-states served to make them feel above others, superior, "at the top." Here a more civilized expression of a striving for power was manifested in an "agonal instinct."[33]

In *Daybreak* the psychological interpretation of a posited universal will to power in us is predominant. The drive for distinction or "secretly desired domination" has many forms and so many degrees of differentiation that a catalogue of them would virtually amount to "a history of culture." The antipodes in this scale are grotesque barbarians, past and present, and the ascetic personality. Both satisfy their "drive for distinction" in different ways. The striving for superiority over others, though often enough harsh and direct, is also expressed in various indirect forms, even in purely subjective feelings (with no external social basis) or daydreams.[34] Here we find a rare extension of a striving for power into the domain of fantasy, a "striving" that requires no public effort, no overt manifestation, and encompasses internal aggression and points to pathology in an extreme form. Nietzsche thereby emphasizes the profound and extensive nature of the craving for "the liveliest feeling of power," bolsters his reductionist argument, and anticipates the analysis of *ressentiment* in *On the Genealogy of Morals*.

Nietzsche finds in the ascetic Hindu Brahmins an extravagant "lust for power" as well as the ability to control themselves and manage the "feeling of power" they presumably were able to attain.[35] Except for their idealist metaphysics and some specific beliefs—e.g., that a state of deep sleep is a union with the deity—Nietzsche does not attack the Brahmin priests' striving for power, and claims that Christians lack the self-control and "recipes" needed to become comfortable with a "feeling of power."[36]

The ascetic priests described in the *Genealogy*, despite his contempt for their rancor, anti-life affects, resentment, and psychic self-laceration, are, at one point, depicted as desiring "to become master . . . over life itself, over its most profound, powerful, and basic condition." That this desire is characterized as "an insatiable instinct and power-will" obviously links it to an intense "will to power."[37] Since Nietzsche describes life as striving for more, as "nothing other than striving for power,"[38] the posited "anti-life" impulses of the ascetic type paradoxically remain in the service of life despite this negativity. The internalized will to power of the ascetic destabilizes Nietzsche because of his typical prizing of an outer-directed discharge of a will to more, to power. But the force of disciplining the self, the overcoming of one's *natural* inclinations, as well of the *feeling of power* that would plausibly accompany such a feat of self-mastery, are not inconsistent with Nietzsche's general conception of the psychological will to power. Despite the catena of criticisms Nietzsche hurls at the "ascetic priest," this type is depicted as exceedingly cunning, as a repository of negative affects, as fiercely ambitious, iron-willed, etc. In effect, such a type is, according to Nietzsche's criteria, a spiritual (if negative) expression of the will to power he associates with affirmation of life. That he sees the continuation of the ascetic ideal in scholars, scientists, and philosophers, that by means of it man has once again become an "interesting animal," belies his final charge that it generated a "will to nothingness."

There is an internal contradictory tension in Nietzsche's remarkable phenomenology of the ascetic personality that reaches an apogee when he argues that the "hard, severe, abstinent, heroic spirits who constitute the honor of our age"—the "atheists, anti-Christians, immoralists, nihilists . . . skeptics, [and] ephectics" who are possessed of an "intellectual conscience"—are the "most spiritualized product" of the ascetic ideal.[39]

Given that this characterization of Nietzsche's is as close to his own most radical philosophical portraits as one can imagine, we may wonder at the meaning of this self-criticism. The rationale for criticizing such radical, secular "free spirits" and thereby distancing himself from them is that they "*still have faith in truth*," that they still cling to a metaphysical belief in "the absolute value of truth."[40] This apparent distinction between himself and the enigmatic thinkers he alludes to is supported by his claim that the difference between his philosophical standpoint and that of earlier thinkers is "*that we do not possess truth*."[41] But it is questionable that he consistently maintains such a posture since he recognizes a "plurality of truths," the "small, apparent truths" of the exact sciences, and asserts his own truths and insists that "I am the voice of truth . . . my truth is frightful."[42] In *The Antichristian* Nietzsche once again expresses the value of truth in a distinctly self-reflexive way:

> One must wrestle for truth every step of the way; one must give up almost everything to which the heart, to which our love, to which our trust in life attaches itself. . . . The service of truth is the hardest service. . . . *[I]ntegrity* of spirit . . . is harsh against one's heart, despises "beautiful feelings," . . . makes every Yes and No a matter of conscience.[43]

Given the above indications of Nietzsche's belief in the value of truth, as well as many assertions of his truths versus the "lies" of religious believers and other philosophers sprinkled throughout *Ecce Homo,* it is difficult to defend the view that Nietzsche is not referring to his own "contamination" by the ascetic ideal. In his portrait of philosophers[44] there are frequent associations between this type and the ascetic personality with the emphasized absence of "moralic acid." The practices, habits, and preferences of philosophers are described as analogous to those of the ascetics even though they are supposedly *not* "virtues," but "appropriate and natural conditions of their best existence, their *most beautiful* fruitfulness."[45] These contemplative thinkers are adept at control of their drives and masters of sublimation (particularly of sexual feelings) in the manner of the "ascetic priests" he castigates. The chief trait of Nietzsche's philosopher is a quiet, inward, narcissistic pride, an affirmation of "his existence and only his existence."[46] Throughout this phenomenological sketch of "the philosopher" Nietzsche seems to engage in a kind of Hegelian *aufgehoben* in which the negative aspects of ascetic existence are negated, but significant aspects of such a way of life retained in a transmuted way. As much as Nietzsche desired to distance himself from his version of the ascetic personality, he returns to it obsessively, analyzes it from a number of perspectives, caricatures it, admires it, modifies it, condemns it, and is fascinated by it. A dialectical yes and no pervades his descriptions of the ascetic personality and the ascetic ideal to such an extent that one could easily characterize Nietzsche's attitude toward this human type and ideal as one of radical ambivalence.

In the course of his dissonant phenomenology of the ascetic type and the emergence of "bad conscience," Nietzsche imagines those masters, conquerors, and "beasts of prey" (in some unspecified, remote time) who established the pre-form of the "state" through violence and maintained it by means of tyranny. These guiltless warriors creatively imposed forms on their world and subjugated people like "unconscious artists." The "*instinct of freedom*" of the oppressed, forced into latency, pushed back, and turned against itself, gave birth, as Freud will remember in *Civilization and Its Discontents*,[47] to "bad conscience."[48]

What we are told about the creation of negative ideals and "bad conscience" is revealing in more ways than one. After a catena of biting criticisms of the unhealthy class of ascetic priests, Nietzsche nonetheless describes them as "among the greatest conserving and yea-saying forces of life."[49] These presumably "weak" individuals manage, by devious pathways, to express their "will to power." It turns out, then, that the "internalization" of a will to power is not only in the service of preserving life, but is an expression of the "strongest life-affirming drive."[50] And, as Nietzsche says in a number of places, where there is a psychological will to power there is an ascendancy of life, a sign of health.

Nietzsche obviously objects to the ascetic use of a presumably natural drive for power. The problem is that, aside from dramatic rhetorical arguments, nowhere in the *Genealogy* does he justify this implied distinction between an affirmative and negative will to power. Not only that, but his characterization of the ascetic's behavior as "life against life" turns out not to hold in his own terms since he sees such types as seeking the preservation of life, the expression of a will to live. Moreover, the charge against his ascetic targets—that they are "anti-life"—is refuted by his own words, even though it may be conceded that they are, by virtue of their war against basic "animal" instincts, "anti-natural." If we apply what Nietzsche says about what is good in *The Antichristian* to this issue, then his despised ascetics could be described as "good." For they seek "what heightens the feeling of power . . . the will to power, power itself."[51]

Since Nietzsche insists that the will to power is a natural, morally neutral *conatus*, he cannot consistently condemn the use of this primal drive by ascetic personalities, particularly since he does not (in the *Genealogy* at least) distinguish between a positive and negative will to power. For the reasons stated, we cannot say, in terms of Nietzsche's description of the ascetic type, that it manifests a "will to nothingness."[52] This is *a fortiori* the case if he makes an equation between such individuals and "the weak" at the same time as he claims that the unmitigated "will to power" of the weak is practically pandemic.[53]

In his extensive autopsy of the admittedly powerful ascetic ideal and ascetic personality, Nietzsche at one point equates an "instinct for freedom" with "the will to power."[54] As far as I know, it has never been noticed that this equivalence of an "*Instinkt der Freiheit*" and a psychological will to power changes the concept of the fundamental motivational basis for human action. An instinctive drive for freedom may, in some instances, take the form of a striving for more; but it is not logically or psychologically the same as a striving for power. The interpretation of human behavior in terms of a will to power is stronger than an instinctive desire for freedom especially in terms of Nietzsche's sometimes harsh descriptions, but not prescriptions, of a will to power as a striving for domination over others. A will to freedom does not entail an active desire to overwhelm what is weaker or to overpower others.

Although Nietzsche has a tendency, at times, to appear tough-minded in the extreme and to adopt an overcompensating, swashbuckling stance, in calmer moments he makes his basic standpoint clear. Considering the characteristics of those with a "higher nature," he tells us that their quality "lies in difference, in incommunicability, in distance of rank, *not* in any kind of effects."[55] What they value is freedom, independence, self-respect, the ability to overcome resistance, and the retention of instincts that are mastered, checked, and "pressed into service." It is only in liberation from heteronomous goals, "ends," or "purposes," only in "the innocence of becoming," that we attain "the *greatest freedom*."[56] What all of this pertains to is a radical conception of freedom "as positive power, as will to power."[57] Here we see a fusion of a will to power and an affirmative, instinctive expression of what can be called a will to freedom. This positive expression of a will to power, which encompasses a coeval "instinct for freedom," is opposed by Nietzsche to all hedonistic conceptions of what mankind desires. Neither pleasure nor happiness is the primary goal or motivating project of human beings. What is the underlying striving for us is a desire for a "feeling of power" or, for that matter, a feeling of freedom.

As in the case of later psychodynamic theories, Nietzsche packs a great deal into his reductionist conception of the primal basis of human motivation. There is no doubt that, at times, will to power (or more precisely, willing to power) is imbued with a strong erotic component. Feelings of "force," intense desire, and subjective narcissistic feelings of superiority are incorporated into a striving for power.[58] The often-noted comparison to Freud's attempt to uncover our fundamental drives is more than appropriate given the close relation between psychoanalytic theory and Nietzsche's "depth psychology." In one place he remarks that the libido seeks to render the destructive instinct harmless by diverting it outwards. Then it is designated as "the destructive instinct, the instinct for mastery, or the will to power."[59] Just as Nietzsche explored the vicissitudes of will to power, its positive and negative expressions, so, too, did Freud struggle with the relationship (or disrelationship) between the "life instincts" and aggressive drives. Whereas Freud eventually developed a dual-instinct theory, Nietzsche retained his reductionist will-to-power interpretation and described the multiple ramifications of this deeply rooted drive or "instinct."

In his regressive analysis of and interpretation of both the spiritual and bodily aspects of the individual, Nietzsche engages in a kind of archaeology. As early as 1872, as we've seen, he speculates about the unconscious repository of irrational aggression within us. Following this insight in "On Truth and Lies in an Extra-Moral Sense," he makes a number of attempts to probe the core of *homo natura*. In the first part of *Zarathustra* he condemns the "otherworldly" for their flight from this world and elevates the contradictory, confusing, creating, willing, evaluating, and honest "I" as the "measure and value of things." If "healthy," this is the I-body that is opposed to the metaphysical "subject"—the supposed timeless, will-less, pure, knowing entity—that Nietzsche never tires of lambasting. This earth-affirming "I" is a source of pride and has the capacity to create "the meaning of the earth."[60]

In "Of the Body-Despisers" the bodily "self" is praised as the "commander," the intelligence that expresses the "I." It is the ground of our being, a "creative self" deeper than our thoughts and feelings. The spiritual and affective dimensions of the self are tools of this dynamically active bodily core of our being.[61] Nietzsche returns often to this emphasis on the natural, physiological basis of our existence. As an interpretation of the self it anticipates Maurice Merleau-Ponty's conception of the bodily subject or what could be called the I-body.[62]

Some have argued that Nietzsche discusses the body by way of "metaphors" in order to remain within the domain of metaphysics and yet avoid metaphysical hypostasis of the body,[63] but the conclusion is questionable, given Nietzsche's assertions about the body and its physiology. In *Beyond Good and Evil* he considers the body our "securest possession" and asks if there is anything other than one's body that one at present believes in "more firmly."[64] What is proposed is a psychology or "physio-psychology" construed as a morphology—a term, coined by Goethe, meaning a theory of the form and structure of an organism regarded as a whole—and as *a "theory of the development of will to power."*[65] Whereas the previously cited conception of the bodily dimension of the self in *Zarathustra* would seem to be a physiological reductionism, hailing the "wisdom" of the body, Nietzsche shifts gears and introduces a further dimension of "under-wills"—"a social structure composed of many souls" that is "our body."[66]

Before turning to a critique of Nietzsche's psychology that has appeared in recent times, the following unambiguous defenses of the primordial nature of a psychic, affective will to power in his psychological interpretation of the fundamental impulse of human behavior are offered. Like any psychodynamic interpretation of the nature of the individual and the primary springs of human action or agency, including the most recent, Nietzsche's theory inevitably depends upon presuppositions that touch upon or are indirectly derived from various "metaphysical" insights, speculations, conceptions, or theories. But this is also the case whether we are considering a radical behaviorism such as B. F. Skinner's or an elaborate post-Freudian, semiotic-philosophical-literary psychoanalysis such as Jacques Lacan's.

Contrary to the views of some philosophers, Nietzsche's reductionist interpretation of the psychodynamics of human existence is neither anomalous, peculiar, idiosyncratic, nor hyperbolic. Neither the behaviorism favored by analytical philosophers during their long dominance of Anglo-American philosophy nor the Freudianism (or pseudo-Freudianism) embraced by French philosophers in the last quarter of the twentieth century was disengaged from a number of metaphysical beliefs. Nietzsche's psychological interpretation of *homo natura* is as viable as theirs and as relevant today as a possible conception of human nature as it was when he first promulgated it in spite of the prevalence of the postmodern *metaphysics* of the social-historical-ideological "construction" of the "self." With the exception of the undefended behaviorism that dominated linguistic-analytic philosophy, the absorption of Freud in France, and the adoption of Lacan's psychological theories in Europe and, here and there, in England and the United States, philosophers have, in general, been critical of, dismissive of, and condescending towards the rich and profound psychodynamic theories that have flourished for more than a century with the significant advantage of clinical experience or knowledge.

On the *camino real* to the positing of a will to power as the origin of our values and the fundamental "force" operative in us as manifested in manifold forms, Nietzsche speculates about what lies beneath the threshold of consciousness, thoughts, sensations, and feelings (*Affekts*). Just as there are natural influences such as electricity operating at each moment of which we are unaware, so, too, there could be "forces" we never sense continuously influencing and acting on us.[67] Our subjective intentional aims and purposes are understood as expressions and symptoms of something more than a conscious willing. Nietzsche interprets these psychic processes as manifestations of a deeper *conatus*: willing to be stronger, willing growth, willing as a means to these states. At this point he raises the question whether

> all conscious *willing*, *all conscious purposes*, *all valuations* are perhaps merely *means*, with which something essentially *different is to be obtained* than what appears in consciousness.[68]

Pursuing this regressive analysis, Nietzsche speculates about inaccessible changes in our organic functioning that may be expressed in various conscious states of being. Is it not possible that our conscious purposes, intentions, and willing of something are themselves suppositions of the action of a purposive "I"? Is it not also possible that purposes, intentions, willing, etc., are "a semiotics for something essentially different—namely something not willing and unconscious?"[69] Such speculative analyses might seem to suggest a form of materialism, physicalism, or, if the term be permitted, physiologism. Some, in fact, have understandably concluded that, in this instance, Nietzsche is referring to a "bodily unconscious."[70] This is a level of our being for his psychology and is consistent with the occurrence of a vast multiplicity of physiological processes, particularly complex hormonal changes and intricate brain-chemistry events, that we are unaware of even as we are subjected to their effects. But Nietzsche, being strongly anti-materialist, could not cease his reductive analysis at this point.

Invariably, Nietzsche endeavors to seek out the dynamic spiritual dimension of our existence. In *Beyond Good and Evil*, for example, he insists that there is "some granite of spiritual *fatum*," immune to counsel, intact "deep down."[71] Here there seems to be an allusion to something deeper than a bodily unconscious, to what may be called a "spiritual" unconscious that lies at the core of our being.

Against Spinoza's principle that a striving for self-preservation is a fundamental aim of living beings, Nietzsche avers that "all living beings [desire] *not* to preserve themselves, but to *become* more." Schopenhauer's conception of a basic "will to live" is not the primary striving in organic being either because "life is merely a *special case* of will to power." It is completely "arbitrary to maintain that all striving is . . . encompassed in *this* form of will to power."[72] As is often the case, Nietzsche here argues for the priority of what could be called a willing to power over other of its forms, which are often mistaken for it. He does not deny that there is a will to live, but he insists that it is a *Form* of a primordial striving for more. Life is at least on one occasion redefined as *Wille zur Macht* and is said to be a signification of its immanence. That is, "What *all life* shows, as a diminutive formula, in respect of its total propensity: is a new definition of the concept of 'Life,' as 'will to power'."[73] It is more typical for Nietzsche to consider life as not only a "unique case," but as a manifestation of the drive to acquire more power. In a note from the 1880s he reformulates the same relationship again. "Life itself," he writes, "is not a means to something: it is the expression of growth-forms of power."[74] For a thinker who has a deserved reputation for being contradictory, Nietzsche is quite consistent in his psychological interpretation of "natural man."

In *Zarathustra* Nietzsche is internally consistent in his psychology when he asserts that "Only where life is, is there . . . will to power.

Wherever life is found there is also will to power . . . even in the will of servants I found the will to be master." In the segment "On Self-Overcoming" life, will, will to life, and a will to mastery are consistently presented as subservient to a posited will to power, to more.[75] Those who would prescind reference to Nietzsche's extensive notes or *Nachlass*, for whatever reason, would be hard-pressed to claim that his psychology there is not coherent with his published will-to-power psychology and his general psychological observations. He was by no means jocose or bragging when he told the Swedish dramatist, August Strindberg, "I am a psychologist."[76] The neglect of the psychologistic dimension of Nietzsche's philosophical orientation is, essentially, the erasure of the core of his thought.

Repeatedly throughout his notes from the late 1880s Nietzsche posits power as the subjective *telos* of our strivings, the attainment of which entails a positive "consciousness of difference." Dynamic physical and psychic forces [*Kraften*] are reducible to a striving for more, for becoming more. Moreover, "All occurrences due to intention are reducible to the intention to gain more power."[77] In this instance we are not concerned with an unconscious propensity towards something, but with an intentionality consciously directed towards an end. The only intentionality we are aware of (with the exception of metaphorical transference to nonhuman organic beings) is our own. At a minimum, this means that we cannot casually dismiss the view that "the will to power" is "*merely* psychological or anthropological."[78]

The priority given to the sexual drive or libido in Freudian psychoanalysis is sometimes juxtaposed to Nietzsche's psychology of a *nisus* towards power. The analogy is flawed, since Nietzsche sees the "sexual instinct" as linked to procreation or to "the real achievement of the individual . . . his highest interest, his highest expression of power."[79] This is not to say he is unaware of sexual pleasure independent of a desire for procreation. Perceptively, he observes that "sexual love . . . desires to overpower, to take possession" of another even if "it *appears* as self-surrender."[80] Once again, he traces the desire for power from the pole of a manifest effort of overpowering to disguised modalities of seeking the same goal by indirect or even deceptive means. Nietzsche admired the ancient Greeks and celebrated their Dionysian passion (up to a point) as a surplus of force or energy. He attributes to them an affirmation of life, change, and death: life as the will to continuation of life, "through the mysteries of sexuality."[81] His eroticizing of the primal instinct of the ancient Greeks, his stress on "the *sexual* symbol" in their culture seems to indirectly link *eros* and "will to power." It has been observed that Nietzsche sometimes joins pleasurable erotic excitation to a more primordial craving for power. This is specifically the case in his analysis of the artistic personality and temperament. Obviously alluding to the desire for power he asserts that "It is one and the same force [*Kraft*] expended in artistic conception and in the sexual act: there is only one kind of force."[82] By observing that serious artists, motivated by a "will to mastery" in their creative activity, are at least moderate in their sexual life and sometimes chaste, Nietzsche implicitly relates the "sublimation" of a desire for power to the sublimation of libido for the sake of a "dominant instinct" (artistic creativity and mastery). His reference to a single kind of force operative in the creative process and sexual activity could be read either as an implicit fusion of will to power and sexuality *or* as a suggested subordination of sexual drive to a more fundamental striving for power.[83]

Under the rubric "Psychological Will to Power" Nietzsche says that "the will to power is the primitive affect, that all other affects are only elaborations of it."[84] What is apparent here is that this language parallels the description of "the" will to power "as a more primitive form of the world of affects" in *Beyond Good and Evil,*[85] but refers only to a human, psychological "primitive *Affekt-Form.*" But before turning to this crucial published argument for what has come to be called the "cosmological" version of Nietzsche's hypothesis of will to power, we must first consider a critique of the psychological theory of a basic willing towards power.

Some time ago Maudemarie Clark argued that Nietzsche's psychological conception of will to power is a viable empirical hypothesis. Explanations of behavior in terms of power, it has been claimed, depend upon, for example, a contrast between a desire for power and sexual drive. Given the hypothesis that the act of rape is primarily concerned more with "a sense of power" than with sexual gratification, an explanation of such an act in terms of a "will-to-power" psychology loses its "enlightened character." Moreover, it implies a denial of sexual drive or that the actual goal is power.[86]

It is assumed that Nietzsche's "empiricist" psychology can avoid internal problems if power is defined as "the ability to do or get what one wants" and has to do with "one's *effectiveness* in the world." So defined, the "desire for power" can and should be distinguished from "other desires one wants to be able to satisfy."[87]

The initial problem here is that Nietzsche's psychology is construed as empirical. Since it clearly deals with speculations about and interpretations of the psychodynamics of the "mind"—motives, dynamic forces, psychic energy, and instinctive drives—it more closely resembles the metapsychology of Freud, which, in some significant respects, it anticipates.

Second, the proffered redefinition of the concept of will to power actually introduces a new element that deviates from *Nietzsche's* account of the complex modes and ramifications of the expression of a postulated striving for power. Whether or not our effort to attain more, our movement towards power, is "effective in the world" is not relevant to the interpretative description of the underlying, typically unconscious, motive of our actions Nietzsche proposes. Moreover, as we've seen, a "feeling of power," a subjective affect, is presented as a valued goal. Despite the redefinition cited above, a "sense of power" is inconsistently introduced as the satisfaction of the drive for power. Moreover, a sense or feeling of power is held to be "the reflection in consciousness of success in satisfying one's impulses."[88] But as Nietzsche says, this need involve no external manifestation "in the world." This is the case for the "feeling of power" he believes contemplative Brahmins attain. And the same inward sense of power is experienced by some mystics, and by artists who anticipate mentally the art-work they will create. There are a variety of forms in which such constructive, subjective states of being are experienced,

Even more contestable, given the many instances in which Nietzsche insists upon the fundamental nature of the desire for power, is the view that will to power is a "second-order desire for the ability to satisfy one's other, or first-order desires."[89] A will to power is understood as a second-order desire presumably because its object is "another desire." However, in another reversal of field, a willing to power is admitted *not* to qualify as a second-order desire because its object is not another desire, but an ability to satisfy other desires.

Derived from distinctions made in a discussion of freedom of the will[90] that seems to employ the logical distinctions between first- and second-order statements in a contestable way and that seriously distorts Nietzsche's reductive analysis, this argument of Clark's ignores Nietzsche's view that desire *is* striving for power. The entire notion of an "ability" to satisfy other desires is already encompassed in the broadly conceived idea of willing-towards-power. Any reference to an "ability" or a "desire" is a first-order statement as distinguished from second-order statements, which are "statements about first-order statements"[91] All of the assertions in Nietzsche's various formulations of the centerpiece of his psychology are first-order assertions since they refer to posited, usually unconscious, actual psychic processes. It is a distortion of Nietzsche's interpretation of our underlying motivations to aver that "the desire for power" is built upon the "foundation of other desires."[92]

Even granting that a psychological "doctrine" of willing to power is an "empirical hypothesis," it nevertheless lacks "plausibility" in terms of an analysis that does not adhere to Nietzsche's reasonably consistent reduction of human *desire* to one fundamental drive. Moreover, Clark maintains that his psychological theory is not "intended to provide knowledge." Ostensibly, it must be "interpreted" as a specialized version of "the doctrine of the world as will to power" that itself is a "myth."[93] Aside from the already mentioned questionable classification of Nietzsche's metapsychological theory as "empirical" in any unqualified sense, the observation that it is not intended to convey knowledge is misdirected. Nietzsche is quite aware, as previously argued, that all conceptions of human nature or *all* philosophical anthropologies are perspectival interpretations. Nonetheless, he offers insights and observations that (as Freud and Adler recognized) have value for an understanding of the psychodynamics of human development. Naturally, like all theorists, he is persuaded of the validity of his own model of human existence. Furthermore, it is not the case that the interpretation of *homo natura* under consideration is a specialized mode of a conception of the world *in toto* as "will to power." The latter is, indeed, a "myth," but it is not at all an interpretation of the primal basis of *human* motivation.

The psychological analysis of a striving for power, for a "feeling of power," mastery, for more, for control, was a centerpiece of Nietzsche's thought long before he presented a "cosmological" interpretation of all "actuality" (*Wirklichkeit*). The view that the cosmological version is "mythical" is, as I will show, central to my own understanding of Nietzsche's attempt to recuperate a *human* interpretation of the natural world. The psychological interpretation is decidedly not derived from a myth or itself mythical: it is a perspectival interpretation of our fundamental being that is entirely independent of the *transference* of this psychodynamic conception to the nonhuman domain.

Chapter Nine

The Cosmic Will to Power as Fable

> . . . the beauty and grandeur of a world-construction (alias philosophy) is what is now decisive for its value—it is judged as art.
>
> Nietzsche, *Nachlass*

AN EXOTERIC MYTH

Although Nietzsche was vaguely familiar with the distinction between esoteric teachings for the elect and the exoteric representations of popular beliefs or external doctrines taught to the majority in medieval Islamic philosophy,[1] he was quite familiar with its earlier adoption in Hindu thought. His friend Paul Deussen's *Das System des Vedanta* (1883) had been read and praised in a letter to Franz Overbeck (March 6, 1883) as an "excellent" study. In a letter to his mother (August 19, 1887) he alludes to a work edited by Deussen, *Die Sutra's des Vedanta,* and accurately described him as the leading authority in Indian philosophy in Germany.

The references to the esoteric-exoteric disjunction in Nietzsche's published and unpublished writings are sparse, as one would expect in the works of a thinker who intends to adopt this distinction. In *The System of the Vedanta* Nietzsche found extensive material on the use of an "exoteric metaphysics." Deussen devotes chapters to variations on this theme: "Exoteric and Esoteric Vedanta Doctrine," "The Exoteric Picture of Creation," and "Esoteric Theology." Deussen's still-valued study of Vedanta philosophy had a strong effect on Nietzsche's thought. The notion of being "beyond good and evil" is indebted to the same conception discussed by Deussen. That is, one who truly knows Brahman achieves liberation and puts both good and evil deeds behind and beneath him or her. There is little doubt that the ancient principle and practice of writing within the framework of the esoteric-exoteric difference was primarily absorbed by Nietzsche *via* Deussen's detailed examination of Vedantic thought. And I am convinced that he applied this technique to his own corpus and particularly to what Heidegger and others mistakenly consider as his "metaphysics" of the will to power.

The extension, by means of analogical reasoning, of the will to power to *all entities* entailed the supposition, which Nietzsche embraced, that man is a microcosm. The unending striving for "more" that he believed was characteristic of mankind is attributed, by way of anthropomorphic projection and transference, to nonhuman organisms and inorganic entities. This "hypothesis" is a skillfully created amalgam of science and art. It was designed, as Sarah Kofman argued for different reasons and in a different way, as a carefully crafted myth that would serve as one of the bases of a new, unified culture. The need for myth was long considered as essential for a significant, positive, and meaningful culture. Nietzsche had not forgotten that, in *The Birth of Tragedy*, he had said that

> Without myth . . . every culture loses its hearty, creative, natural power, it is only a horizon encompassed with myths that round off to unity a cultural movement. . . . [M]yths free all the powers of the imagination.[2]

Nietzsche's cultural movement or "counter-ideal" entailed a "transvaluation of values" and offered a sea-change in one's conceptions, attitudes, and feelings. It was a blueprint for an "aristocratic radicalism," an aristocracy of spirit, for those who felt a "*pathos* of distance" from social values associated with the emerging culture of scientism (or German *Positivismus*), commercialization, and the leveling process that proclaimed everyone as "the same." The troika of countermyths presented in a philosophic-aesthetic way comprised the image of man "beyond-man," the thought of the eternal recurrence of the same, and the artfully constructed, exoteric notion of a universal will to power (or wills-to-power) immanent in actuality (*Wirklichkeit*). Simply put, Nietzsche desired to construct a conception of actuality for "exceptions," an image of life and existence that called for spiritual courage, discipline, psychic strength, and the ability to accept the loss of eternal meaning and purpose in the cosmos, the capacity to appropriate an *objective* nihilism, while striving to create meaning in one's own existence. Nietzsche reverses the emphases of previous attempts to ground meaning in God, the Absolute Being, the world of ideas, the ideal world, the transcendental domain. A *human* meaning for this life, this realm of becoming, is genuinely possible only if there is no transhuman source of meaning, no objective teleology in which we are construed as puppets fulfilling some grand transcendental plan.

As Sarah Kofman first emphasized (in a Derrida-like framework), the analogical construction of a universal, dynamic will to power was an essential part of Nietzsche's total "mythical construction." In spite of her penetrating insights into Nietzsche's frequent use of metaphor, his creation of a metaphoric philosophy, and his poetic style and "strategies," there are a number of notions in her analysis that are contestable and questionable.

In the first place, *The Birth of Tragedy* is said to be preoccupied with a "generalization of metaphor" that is still entangled in "the closure of metaphysics,"[3] even though Nietzsche had renounced metaphysics at least by 1868 and characterized the "artists' metaphysics" of *The Birth of Tragedy* as a species of "Jesuitism." Kofman, on the other hand, correctly criticizes Heidegger's claim that Nietzsche is the "last metaphysician" and that his "metaphysics" is composed of a "subjective," "anthropomorphic," and "nihilistic" theory of a relentless will to power. However, she equates, on no discernible basis, the "simple metaphorical name" of will to power to the "mythical figure" of Dionysus, Apollo, and Oedipus.[4] Earlier, she treats the will to power as identical to the metaphorical notion that is symbolic of the artistic force of interpretation behind "the proper" (the literal, the non-metaphoric).[5] In the next breath, she realizes that if the distinction between "literal meaning" and metaphor in Nietzsche's writings were retained, he would be tangled in metaphysical implications. Compounding the problem of stressing distinctions and then subjecting them to *rature* is the use of a highly ambiguous, polysemic French term, *le propre*, as well as playing on it and around it in the manner of Derrida, for a conception ("proper") central to much of her argument.[6]

More closely related to my view that the will to power interpretation is entirely metaphorical and a deliberately constructed exoteric myth is the questionable rationale given by Kofman for Nietzsche's use of metaphor. She maintains that he relies on and prizes metaphorical language because it is uncommon, aristocratic, and alien to the language of the majority. But this is not the case since, in Nietzsche's view, metaphors pervade philosophical, scientific, *and* ordinary language. The "metaphoric drive" is universal, not exclusive. Even granting that the metaphors in speech and writing in everyday life may be spontaneous, they are ubiquitous. In his lectures on rhetoric Nietzsche emphasizes the figurative, tropic nature of all language. "All words in themselves, with regard to their meanings, are tropes from the beginning."[7]

The irony of the recurring claim that Nietzsche's image of the totality of actuality is a ("cosmological") metaphysics is that he seems to signal to his readers, by virtue of his profuse use of tropes, anthropomorphisms, and metaphors, that he is not making metaphysical claims to truth. It is more plausible that he is proffering an imaginative, poetic, metaphoric, exoteric fable that is an amalgam of philosophical, artistic, and scientific perspectives. Nietzsche effectively manipulates metaphors that partially conceal and partially reveal his esoteric meaning. That is, that we cannot *know* the ultimate nature of actuality, cannot explain it with any degree of certainty, and cannot discern its primal ground. Nietzsche rejects metaphysics as dualism and as transcendental idealism. The only mode of global metaphysical exploration he admitted since 1868 was that of *Begriffsdichtung*, "conceptual poetry."[8] The positive overcoming of agnosticism or, for that matter, nihilism is expressed in a Dionysian affirmation of existence in face of the suffering, pain, and absurdities of life, a Nietzschean "negation of the negation" that overcomes *objective* nihilism in *Existenz*.

For some time now the nature of the "cosmological" will-to-power hypothesis has seemed to me to be at least problematic. Nietzsche responded to Lange's proposal for a new, aesthetic-poetic, philosophical vision expressed from "the standpoint of the ideal." This enhancing ideal looked beyond the limits of the "fragments of truth" offered in the exact sciences and served as a counterforce against dogmatic materialism. It influenced Nietzsche's passage through "positivism" toward a visionary projection of a universal will to power into the cosmos. The late Sarah Kofman's *Nietzsche and Metaphor* (1972) insightfully called attention, as previously noted, to the metaphorical nature of the "cosmological" depiction of a will to power acting through all beings. Thereby she put in question the then-current view that Nietzsche, the dedicated anti-metaphysician, was presenting a dramatic new "metaphysics."[9] Conspicuously absent from her account, as pointed out earlier, is any sustained analysis concerning why Nietzsche concocted such an elaborate pseudo-metaphysics. Or, put differently, what issue internal to his thought led him to formulate what appears to be the kind of global metaphysics that he had previously criticized and repudiated?

Before turning to a consideration of one of the few arguments that seeks to answer the question posed, we should examine Nietzsche's attitude towards holistic metaphysics and the presence of metaphysical language in his works. In *Human, All-Too-Human* he does not advocate refutation of metaphysical speculations, since he realizes that, in a strict sense, they cannot be refuted. Attempts to do so invariably become entangled in the nets of alternative metaphysical schemata. The appropriate stance is to "put on ice" such ambitious systems. This is not a sentiment held only in what is typically called his "positivistic" stage of development, since he had become quite skeptical about such claims to truth as early as 1868 and often expressed doubts in notes from 1872 onward. In the latter he recognizes any general "world-construction" as "art" and prizes its "aesthetic values."[10] When Nietzsche advised that metaphysics be put on ice he was not suggesting cryogenic preservation for the sake of later revival. For, the difficulty in producing a "scientific demonstration" may engender "a mistrust of metaphysics" that would serve as a form of refutation in advance.[11] Here Nietzsche is not referring to "science" (*Wissenschaft*) in its broad sense nor is he alluding to the logic of a demonstration. In this instance and in the context of his assertions he is making reference to the pressure to present a "metaphysics" consistent with the sciences. His own efforts to search out scientific bases for his exoteric pseudo-metaphysics lends indirect support to such a reading.

Overcoming metaphysics in any complete sense would require the cessation of philosophical discourse. What may be called micrometaphysical terms, expressions, or belief-statements are ineliminable from such discursive practices. Nietzsche himself, despite recognizing and trying to avoid this difficulty (except in his exoteric fable about the vicissitudes of a will to power underlying all cosmic events), frequently expresses such micrometaphysical beliefs or claims to knowledge. This is not peculiar to him, but is endemic in philosophy. Inherited linguistic habits are difficult to shake and the new language-games envisioned by thinkers such as Rorty will not only be long in coming, but will probably never arrive in pristine form.[12]

The ideality of language easily carries us away from actuality and creates a precision and a kind of perfection that continues in what may be characterized as prestige terms: "cognition," "knowledge," and "science." Ineluctably, an anthropomorphic "reality" is mirrored in language. Our vaunted "*rational thinking is interpretation in terms of a [linguistic] schema which we cannot cast aside.*"[13] Granting this, the free creation of a new language is, at least, problematic.

If, as Nietzsche often insists, "humanization" transfigures what is experienced or known and thereby generates a degree of "falsification," then our language will always be anthropomorphically tinted. Perhaps *only a radical change in our being* might produce novel linguistic forms. It is the qualitative, poetic-aesthetic dimension of our experience of ourselves and the world, as Nietzsche saw so clearly, that plants us in an imaginative realm that infiltrates cognitive language and, *a fortiori*, metaphysical creations.

Let us return to the question: Why did Nietzsche extend what was originally a psychological conception of will to power into the entire domain of reality? It has been said that the reason why he projects a mythic "ontological doctrine" of will to power is to offer an "idealized" picture of the world that creates the world in the image of his philosophical ideal. This is related to a type of individual who is life-affirming, able to enrich everything, who would view the world as an "overflowing of energy" that is a purposeless cosmic play. This "ontology," which is a "myth," represents Nietzsche's "values." A cosmic vision that entails an overpowering fluctuating process, a will to power acting through all entities is held to be compatible with a so-called "empirical" psychological conception that treats "will to power . . . as one desire among others." If the psychology of will to power, as defended here, is operative, then the "cosmological" myth of will to power is superfluous. Moreover, the reference to a striving for power as a second-order desire is nullified if the reductive nature of a pervasive will to power is "this desire writ large."[14]

The view that Nietzsche is driven to interpret the cosmos as structured in accordance with his "values" is weak in light of his history of anti-metaphysical sentiments. Moreover, he has *already* made his values—self-overcoming, remaining faithful to the earth, affirming existence in spite of its genuine "terrors," accepting a transitory "becoming" as the realm of our existence, overcoming passive nihilism, embracing the aesthetic dimension of life, etc.—quite plain independent of any supplemental image of the cosmos. That Nietzsche interprets the totality of actuality as a relentless will to power is not an "idealized" depiction of the world because it includes profound negativities, senseless chaos, and inevitable suffering on a large or small scale. The cosmological notion of a ceaseless interaction of "wills to power" is indeed a "myth"; but it is not only a consoling one. Nor is the psychological interpretation of our nature derived from or dependent upon such a metaphorical construction.

If there is any validity to the psychological interpretation of our fundamental drive as a striving for more, for power, then it is nothing we choose and nothing we need represent in metaphysical disguise. Given the rather common expression of this drive in destructive ways, without its transformation by means of "sublimation," it can just as well be a curse or a blessing. However, in spite of the volatile and explosive potential of this posited drive, Nietzsche insists that its absence would lead to the negation of life, action, change, striving, growth, and creativity. Ironically, in this perspectival interpretation of our primal being, our most valuable desire, drive, or impulse is also our most dangerous trait.

Although some who had previously accurately characterized as a myth the conception of the will to power as universally immanent in the cosmos have dropped this designation,[15] there is nonetheless supplemental support for the argument derived from the model for the pluralistic version of Nietzsche's metaphorical creation.

Oddly, many interpreters of Nietzsche have not focused on the fact that his seemingly crucial conception of a plurality of "wills to power" is based upon an imaginative, syncretistic philosophical interpretation of selective scientific notions that he fully realizes are derived from biological analogies and world-interpretations in physics. He insists that science does not provide us with "truth-in-itself," but proffers numerous more-or-less well-founded or functional interpretations of, or perspectives on, a variety of phenomena. That a reflexive thinker who conceives of the sciences in general, and the world-interpretations of physicists in particular, as constructed by means of provisional assumptions, conventions, working hypotheses, and instrumental fictions would then found a "metaphysics" on them in a dogmatic spirit is counterintuitive and highly implausible.

Throughout his writings Nietzsche repeats a refrain: we only *know* what has been filtered through our selective senses, classified by our categorical schema, framed by our language, shaped by our psychology and our instrumental needs. We know phenomena or "effects" as constituted, in numerous aspects, by ourselves. However, the realm of phenomenal appearances is not our creation (as in idealism): "*we* alone are not what causes" such phenomena to appear.[16] The phenomena of the "external world" encountered as "obstacles" or resistances and objects we become conscious of are "the sum of experienced restraints [*Hemmungen*]."[17] Throughout his intellectual life Nietzsche consistently characterizes the process of knowing as involving an imposition of a false identity upon things, simplification, assimilation, organization, and schematization.[18] If knowledge is a consequence of the constitutive, synthetic activities of sensory perception, language-use, conceptualization, and psychistic importation, then it entails "humanization" of something, incorporating it into a familiar schemata, appropriating, and transmuting it.

If knowledge can never escape from the anthropic circle, if common beliefs, as well as metaphysics and scientific theory, are pervaded by metaphoric "anthropormorphisms," then, as Nietzsche said in his early notes, "*the picture of existence*" may be completed, at least in a mythic way. The alien, nonhuman domain of blind forces engaged in constant pulsating interactions, the "atomic chaos" disclosed in dynamic physical theories, can yet be given a human meaning. Knowledge and the knowledge-drive could then be valued for the enhancement of "the best life" possible. The unintended, unforeseen consequences of the will to knowledge (which is an expression of our psychological drive for power) are the diminishment of our image of mankind, the growth of a skeptical self-consciousness about knowledge and a waning of belief in it, and the uncovering in the "hard sciences" of a destructured, depersonalized, seemingly indefinitely reducible,[19] exceedingly complex realm of relentless interactive processes that virtually obliterate the aesthetic world of human meaning and value.

The "tragic philosopher" accepts the inevitability of anthropomorphism and uses it in order to create an exoteric myth that is a conglomeration of biology, psychology, and physical theory in a pseudo- metaphysical form that is so skillfully devised (rarely in published works and extensively in notes) that many able interpreters of Nietzsche have taken it to be a genuine metaphysics. In emulation of the vast multiplicity of cellular structures described in biology (and their cooperative and sometimes antagonistic interactions), with the projection of a will-to-power psychology into organic and inorganic entities (that are no longer differentiated), Nietzsche proposes a reductive depiction of a cosmic field of interacting *wills-to-power* that is designed to appear to "explain" actuality. Thereby he sought to avoid the self-negation of the knowledge-drive in a process of autoconsumption that he saw emerging years before he began to design his fable. Towards what end? For the sake of a *kunstlerishche Kultur*, an "artistic culture."[20]

From early on Nietzsche intended to fashion an image of actuality that would *complete* the anthropomorphic "picture" of it in order to control and master an unrestrained knowledge-drive that sought knowledge as an end in itself rather than for the sake of life and the preservation of an aesthetic perspective he saw threatened by a hegemonic culture of science. The persistent false dichotomy of nature "and" man could be put to rest if all actuality could be reduced to the action and reaction of "wills to power" (modeled after our psychological wills to power) since every entity would be represented in such a metaphoric portrayal as rooted in an ostensible "ontological" ground. Invariably, the notion of interacting, inter-related, underlying "will-points," "power-centers" or "will-quanta" is offered as a hypothesis, an interpretation, a "diminutive formula."[21]

In *Beyond Good and Evil* a rare argument for what amounts to a plurality of wills to power is delineated. After describing life as a striving after power, as a tendency to discharge energy for the sake of augmented power, Nietzsche asserts that willing is an "affect" falsely ascribed to a single "will." The sense of freedom of the will is considered as a "complex state of delight" experienced by an individual in an act of willing. Willing is an affect of command that entails the feeling of the successful activity of "under-souls" (*Unter-Seelen*) or "under-wills" (*Unterwillen*). The body itself is said to be a "social structure composed of many souls."[22] This pan-psychistic posit is presented without irony or proviso. And it is associated with an earlier reference to the value of the "soul-hypothesis." Even though it is contended that the conception of the soul as an eternal, indestructible "monad" or "atom" should be banished from science, in the next breath we are told that the *Seelen-Hypothese* is not only useful, but fruitful if it is presented in a different form with novel refinements. Thus, the soul may be construed as "a social structure of the drives and affects."[23]

Although radically opposed to what he calls "soul atomism," Nietzsche postulates a plurality of "under-wills" (or what he elsewhere calls "wills to power") that are considered as the underlying dynamic "forces" composing "the body." He is sanguine about *his* notion of a plurality of wills to power perhaps because he is quite aware that he is not propounding it as a dogmatic metaphysical theory. Rather, he suggests that it is an "invention" that may lead to "discovery."[24] We recognize this approach to the interpretation of phenomena as the postulation in science of hypotheses as heuristic devices. What is being offered is clearly a "thought-experiment," not an ontological assertion.

Nietzsche's approach to the question of fundamental constituents of actuality represents a philosophic version of thought-experiments put forward by imaginative scientists. The idea of a plurality of "under-wills" represents a purely hypothetical *model* of the *nisus* that is presumed to underlie actuality. From his careful reading of philosophical scientists, he was familiar with the creative, inventive, and imaginative nature of scientific theory-construction. He understands physics, for example, as a "world-interpretation," as an "exegesis of the world" put forward "to suit us." He denies that physical theory provides a "world-explanation."[25] If the "hard" sciences offer an instrumental world-interpretation, then Nietzsche's notion of a plurality of wills to power should, *a fortiori*, be considered as an experimental, imaginative construction that may have heuristic value.[26]

The interpretation of the body as a well-founded phenomenon that is the objectivication of the activity of a vast number of dynamic wills to power seems to echo Leibniz's metaphysics of "spiritual atoms" or "monads." However, Nietzsche insists that his interpretation is analogical only and includes an assumption that is excluded from Leibniz's theory of noninteractive "windowless" monads: a posited dynamic *interaction* between hypothetical "under-wills." The hypothetical assumption of energistic wills to power is put forward as a way of considering what all life manifests in a presumed *nisus* towards power, which appears to be the strongest urge that has directed organic evolution thus far. Even this perspectival notion of evolution is based upon human analogy. Nietzsche first assumes that a striving for power is the central drive in human existence. He then ferrets out apparent instances of this same tendency in nonhuman organic beings. Finally, he posits this *Tendenz* towards power as prevalent in all modalities of life. This, in turn, is taken as a model for *all* actual entities. Thus, from a highly specific perspectival interpretation of the nature of man, an anthropomorphic conception of the underlying nature of all actuality is developed. This is analogical, hypothetical, anthropomorphic, and experimental reasoning of the most extreme kind—precisely the kind of reasoning he discloses and *criticizes* in commonsense beliefs, scientific thinking, and metaphysics. The difference is that such previous thinking was characterized either by an *unconscious* or a naïve anthropomorphism.

The phenomena of life display movement, development, and growth. Organic bodies may plausibly be conceived of as societies made up of interacting cells that are themselves undergoing movement and dynamic processes. A general description of the phenomena of life is unsatisfying, for Nietzsche, because it does not complete our picture of living beings. What he repeatedly, selectively seeks is what imbues living organisms with a tendency towards growth. However, our sensory-cognitive and psychic "organization" cannot entirely penetrate the internal dynamics of actuality because it discovers only "effects" or already constituted phenomena.

Inferences proffered to account for the internal dynamic *nisus* of organisms are unjustified, in Nietzsche's own terms, as a species of *knowledge*. Relying on a biological model of actuality, he assumes that each cell (like each individual) is imbued with a propensity towards augmenting its power.[27] He persistently presupposes that growth, movement, and striving cannot be explained in mechanistic or materialistic terms. Rather, they are typically construed as "symptoms" of underlying processes that appear to be more like "spiritual" than material events.[28]

Nietzsche speculated about the dematerialized "forces" presumed to act through living systems in order to overcome metaphorically the then-scientific agnosticism about the ultimate basis of the "becoming" of actuality, to undermine mechanistic materialism, and to emphasize the *spiritual* dimension of actuality. The smallest particle of "matter" is described as imbued with a diminutive expression of "will to power." Again, this does not represent a regression to a metaphysical standpoint, since the "hypothesis" of the nonmaterial basis of all phenomena was suggested to Nietzsche by his perspectival interpretation of the primordial "urge" or "drive" in us and, ironically, by a dynamic physical theory construed as analogical to the psychodynamic interpretation of *homo natura*.

The self-sustaining, independent psychological theory of will to power is comprised of three basic components: (1) the postulation of an unconscious, primitive craving for power primarily rooted in our evolutionary development; (2) the related notion of an unconscious or sometimes conscious tendency to achieve power over others because of deeply rooted feelings of fear, insecurity, and weakness (a concept such as a drive for power entails a condition of lack); and (3) the idea that we have a capacity to channel this primitive drive into constructive and creative expressions through a process of sublimation by which we satisfy this urge in indirect, "spiritual" ways in order to acquire an intense subjective "feeling of power."[29]

The myth of the will to power is derived from this psychological theory of the springs of human behavior. It is a psychologistic construction that is transferred first to all biological activity and then to the interior dynamism of microphysical quanta. This ascription involves an *aesthetic* interpretation of biophysical phenomena and "material" phenomena that is neither empirical nor metaphysical, even though it emulates the language of both in a persuasive way. As I will argue later, Nietzsche openly presents his hypothetical speculations about this universal underlying "desire" for power in terms of concepts he declares *fictions*.

Nietzsche's study of Boscovich's *Philosophia naturalis*, as we have seen, had a profound and long-lasting impact on his thinking.[30] He fully understood that Boscovich's theory of dynamic centers of force dispensed with traditional concepts of matter. Physical-theoretical conceptions of solid matter or of substantial "materiality" were displaced by Boscovich's theory and by the theories of his nineteenth-century followers. By the 1870s, there was considerable speculation about the ultimate constituents of the physical world, speculation that tended to support Boscovich's mathematical physical theory and strongly suggested the existence of *Unteratomen* (subatoms).[31]

Although profoundly impressed by and influenced by Boscovich's interpretation of the substructure of the physical world, Nietzsche did not adopt this theory uncritically. For as I've tried to show, he saw that this "force-point theory" was a highly abstract, provisional, hypothetical, mathematical model of the elementary structures of the natural world. *In Beyond Good and Evil*, he applauded Boscovich for having presented a theory of nature that transcends sense-experience. However, he believed that even a theory that eliminates "clump-atoms" is nonetheless a "world-interpretation." He discerned the demise of mechanistic materialism in the first wave of the new physics. He seized upon this relatively dematerialized conception of the constituents of nature and closely linked it to his metaphoric projection of wills to power into "the world seen from within."

Although a great deal of circuitous argumentation could be introduced at this point, it is more economical to summarize my main points, which are a synthesis of two basic assumptions: that the psychological individual is a constellation of interactive, competitive "under-wills," that atoms are purely theoretical entities, that phenomena are composed of "under-atoms" (or, today, particles), and that these, in turn, are composed of "force-points," "point-centers," or "will quanta." In effect, the metaphoric extension of a plurality of "wills-to-power" to preorganic entities is a psychologistic interpretation of a dynamic physical interpretation of nature. The hypothesis of a universal *Wille zur Macht* is an imaginative, philosophical interpretation of a dynamic world-interpretation in physics combined with a psychological reductionism of the psychophysical self to a dynamic complex of psychic drives and unconscious physiological functions. Such a construct should make plain that Nietzsche is not "doing" metaphysics and not claiming to have discovered the secret identity of reality. Rather, he is creatively inventing a "world-construction" built out of a number of layered perspectives.

In the *Nachlass* of 1887–88, Nietzsche attempts a reductive analysis of the most elementary ontological constituents of actuality. This attempt lends other than literary support to the argument that Nietzsche is engaged in exoteric myth-making. He argues that in a search for the underlying basis of "becoming," we may refer, in a relative sense, to "atoms and monads." These are, of course, precisely the kind of entities that Nietzsche said he wanted banished from science in *Beyond Good and Evil.* Looking more closely at this intriguing statement, we find the postulation of *Willens Punktationen* or "will-points" that gain and lose power. These supposed immaterial will-points are construed as "wills to power" or "centers of power" (*Machtzentren*). These are obviously Boscovich's "point-centers" conceived of as capable of desire, appetition, or "willing." Even though this form of pan-psychism is not based upon Leibniz's "spiritual atoms" or *Monaden* in a strict sense, it could plausibly be identified as a variation on a monadology. As such, it conflicts with Nietzsche's earlier strong criticism of "soul-atoms" or "monads." Rather than being a blatant inconsistency, the projection of "willing" into hypothetical entities serves Nietzsche's pragmatics: the building of a persuasive mythical interpretation out of the bricks of metaphor. That the conception of wills to power is an inventive construct is shown by the fact that it is formed out of cross-disciplinary analogical theoretical entities and processes that Nietzsche realizes are psychistic anthropomorphic fictions.[32]

Two arguments concerning the will to power overtly reveal Nietzsche's myth-making powers and intentions. In notes that constitute *The Will to Power* we are told that the concept of *Kraft* (force) in dynamic physical theories (such as Boscovich's) is too abstract, too amorphous. The irreducible posit of physics, the idea of force (or energy), must be completed by positing an "inner world" [*eine innere Welt*] ascribed to force: this is designed *Wille zur Macht*. Curiously enough, the definitions of "will to power" presented in this context are not precisely synonymous with previous descriptions of the psychological striving *for* power. The inner world ascribed to "force" is characterized as "an insatiable desire to manifest power" (which suggests *dunamis* or "potentiality," as well as the discharge of energy) and "the employment and exercise of power, as a creative drive" (suggesting the "sublimination" or "spiritualization" of power into creative activity). Again, it is assumed that the appearances, effects, motions, and laws dealt with in science should be understood as "symptoms of an inner event." We are, then, the analogical models for the interpretive understanding of the nature of this putative "inner" event-process.[33]

The observable "effects" manifested by "force" are to be construed as manifestations of a putative inner activity, of a *nisus* toward power or a propensity to express power. As far as knowledge is concerned, we may only be said to apprehend effects that, as constellations of elements, constitute phenomena for us, the world for us. Phenomena and their motions are presented as if they were *caused* by unknown processes interpreted in a purely anthropomorphic manner. This compressed argument for the hypothesis of will to power is riddled with suppositions that Nietzsche has consistently criticized and repudiated elsewhere.

In the first place, "effects" are phenomena that exist, as we've seen, for us, for our selective sensory experience, our "conditions of existence." Given Nietzsche's conventionalistic interpretation of science, any knowledge of theoretical entities presumed to be the causes of experienced "effects" is precluded. Furthermore, he frequently criticizes the objective validity of the concept of causality and denies that there are any genuine "causes" or "effects." These notions are considered as "conventional fictions." The belief in causality is derived from our subjective (but misleading) *belief* that there is a "will" that produces "effects."[34] Nietzsche repeatedly proclaims that there is no will. Finally, the anthropomorphic interpretation of a conception in physics (i.e., force) must be strictly considered by Nietzsche, given his criticisms of anthropomorphic projection in science, as a *falsification* of actuality.

Having spilled a great deal of ink pointing to the humanizing nature of scientific theory,[35] Nietzsche in this defense of the idea of the will to power now oddly relies upon a humanistic understanding of the underlying, unobservable "inner event" that is presumed to be *expressed* in "force." The effort to convince us that there is such a hypothetical cosmic will to power is an elaborate, cleverly devised deception. This reductive analysis leads to the assumption of an inner process that serves, at best, as a metaphorical "principle of explanation," a substitution for what is not yet accessible to genuine knowledge.

If the previous analyses are not persuasive enough to serve as evidence of Nietzsche's inventive creation of a philosophical myth, let us examine critically the strongest argument for the "hypothesis" of a dynamic will to power. In *Beyond Good and Evil*, Nietzsche presents an ingenious argument that is impressive, but cunningly misleading.

> We may suppose that nothing else is "given" except our (subjective) world of desires, passions and drives. May we not experimentally grant that this basic "given" is sufficient for an understanding of the "mechanistic" or "material" world? Let us assume, then, that there is a primitive form of the world of affects that has as much reality as our own affects. Let us grant that this primitive form of the world of affects is contained within a "powerful unity" before it undergoes ramifications in specific organic processes. This primordial form of the world of affects may be considered as "a pre-form of life." In order to make this experiment in thought, we should (for the sake of "the conscience of *method*") reduce our idea of causality to a single kind of causation. Let us assume, then, a basic form of causality: *efficient causality* of the will. Having posited a causality of will hypothetically, as the only modality of causation, we must note that will can only act on will, not on "matter." Let us further assume that wherever there are effects, they result from "will acting on will." All mechanical occurrences are, insofar as there is "force" active in them, "effects of will," *Willenskraft* ("will-force"). Finally, let us suppose that our whole instinctive life is a ramification and development of one basic form of will: will to power. "The world seen from within," the world defined in terms of its "intelligible character," would be entirely *Wille zur Macht*.[36]

This completely suppositional *Gedankenexperient* makes not a single positive claim to knowledge or truth. However, this is not what is peculiar in this conjectural thought-experiment. What is peculiar about virtually all of the assertions in this argument is that they have been strenuously and consistently repudiated by Nietzsche elsewhere in his writings.[37]

In the first place, Nietzsche does not consistently hold that the "world" of our affects (= desires, urges, passions) is immediately "given" to us. Typically, he questions the validity of self-observation and considers the "facts" of consciousness as interpretations that have been schematized and simplified as internal "phenomena." In addition, he denies that there are separate and distinct "faculties" or "mental states" that are isolated events. Although we certainly experience *Affekt* or "feeling," we nonetheless interpret the various ramifications of affect as differentiated desires, urges, drives, or passions.

Nietzsche's philosophical psychology precludes the belief that there are immediate *data* for consciousness that are pure, uninterpreted "givens." In fact, he sometimes says that there are no genuine "immediate certainties" discovered in self-reflection.[38] The subjective affects we experience are considered as *symptoms* or *symbols* of an unknown process. And speculation about this process leads to the perspectival hypothesis that the basic "affects" are reducible to a single *Affekt*: "will to power."

The second supposition—that the experience of affects is sufficient for an understanding of the mechanistic material world—entails the belief that there is an analogy between man's subjective psychic experiences and the materio-mechanistic world. Precisely such a belief led to a disclosure of the anthropomorphic aspects of scientific interpretations of nature that here turns back upon his own supposition and undermines the very analogy he proposed. The same difficulty haunts the third assumption that there is an analogy between the subjective world of affects and a putative primitive form of the world of affects and that both have comparable reality. For here is a lavish use of metaphorical transference and microcosmic analogy.

That there is a primordial realm of affect that is a powerful unity is a purely imaginative notion that violates Nietzsche's repeated claim that there are no pure unities anywhere, that the concept of "unity" is derived from our fallacious belief that we are unified metaphysical "subjects." Finally, the very notion of a primordial *Affekt* that is the affect or *pathos* of no being, no person, seems an attempt to point metaphorically to an ineffable *Urgrund*. At best, it is a poetic notion, an apotheosis of human *pathos* construed as "a pre-form of life."

The aspect of this often-cited argument that results in the reduction of modes of causation to the causality of will is the most revealing supposition in this catena of suppositions. That our belief in causality is derived from our *belief* in the effective causation of the will is one of Nietzsche's central ideas. Unfortunately, the ascription of "effective force" to will is described by him as one of the chief errors in human thought. In addition, that there is a faculty or function called "will" that "causes" specific "effects" is characterized as an absolutely *fallacious* assumption.[39] This deliberate use of a set of related notions that are criticized in other contexts is not the result of inconsistency. Rather, it is part of a consistent strategy to develop a plausible fable about the nature of reality that would compete with the scientific conception of the reduction of everything to mechanistic processes and forces.

As if these questionable suppositions do not point sharply enough to the suspect nature of this argument or ingenious fabrication, even the emphasized claim that "will can only act on will" is one that Nietzsche explicitly rejected. For he maintains that

> the concept "cause and effect" originates, psychologically speaking, only from a way of thinking that believes that always and everywhere will acts upon will—that believes . . . fundamentally only in "souls."[40]

The tone of this passage suggests that those who do believe in effective "souls," who believe in spiritual causality, that "will acts on will," are in error because they rely on a misleading "inner phenomenology." More importantly, the use of a "causality of will" in the argument under analysis not only conflicts with Nietzsche's critiques of causality in general and psychic causation in particular, but clearly shows that the only published argument for the reality of "the will to power" is an *exoteric* presentation that conceals his esoteric philosophy.[41] By extension, this may apply to all of the elements of the pseudo-metaphysical "theory" of a pervasive will to power that are found in the *Nachlass*.

Having called attention to Nietzsche's adoption of theoretical standpoints for dialectical purposes, his use of "Jesuitism," his defense of positions he does not entirely embrace, and his employment of a variety of perspectival interpretations throughout my analysis, I am inclined to agree with the observation of a strong critic of Nietzsche's—"that the distinction between the esoteric and exoteric is found in all periods of Nietzsche's thought."[42]

Returning to the controversy over the appeal to a causality of will in Nietzsche's contestable argument, it is perfectly clear the he *does not* adhere to the belief that "will acts on will," but not on matter. In a compressed note from 1886–87 Nietzsche distinguishes between the *exoterisch* and the *esoterish*, the former being the view that "everything is will against will" and "causalism." The latter, the esoteric view, is: "There is no will." "There is nothing like cause-effect."[43] And, as if anticipating later interpreters (such as

Danto, Schacht, and Conway) who might be sanguine about the notion expressed at the heart of the argument (in *Beyond Good and Evil*) designed to persuade us about the verisimilitude of the "tenet" of the will to power—i.e., "wherever 'effects' are recognized, will acts on will"—Nietzsche emphatically asserts:

> I *deny* that a spiritual or soulish phenomenon is the direct *cause* of another spiritual or soulish phenomenon. [*Ich leugne*, dass ein geistiges oder seelisches Phänomen direkte Ursache ist von einem anderen geistigen oder seelischen Phänomen].[44]

A recent critique of the claim that the argument under analysis conflicts with Nietzsche's attack on the notion of a causality of will grants that he "may reject the 'will-will' mode of causality." However, he need not and should not appeal to his criticism of a "will-matter" form of causality in order to reject the former.[45]

In response to this remark, it should be noted that Nietzsche does indeed admit that a causality of will can be posited "hypothetically" since will can only act on will "and not matter," not, for example, on nerves. Then, he proposes that will affects will *wherever* "effects" are recognized. This is very odd given his earlier grudging admission of the existence of a *mechanistic* (material) world. For, even such "effects" would have to be construed as caused by "will." Furthermore, he later explicitly reduces all "mechanical occurrences" to "a force active in them, will-force, effects of will." Seeming to have forgotten what he said about will acting on will, he avers that "all organic functions could be traced back to . . . will to power and one could also find in it the solution of the problem of *procreation and nourishment*." Since the latter by definition are *physical* processes and the *will* to power is not, a will-matter causality has been surreptitiously reintroduced.

Finally, if "will-force" functions in such processes as "effects," then there is no need to consider "mechanical" or material processes as real since will does not affect or act upon "matter." Here Nietzsche seems to come very close to Berkeley's notion that the only mode of causality, "spiritual causation," actually occurs. If this is the case, then this will-to-power argument, taken seriously as metaphysical, would end in immaterialism or "idealism," a metaphysics that Nietzsche often repudiates. It is obvious that there are many problems with his (apparent) appeal to a causality of will and, therefore, with the "metaphysical" content and nature of the argument as a whole. Perhaps the last word on the contested appeal to a spiritual causality of will is found in Nietzsche's *Nachlass*: "*Alle* sogenannte 'geistige' Ursachlichkeit ist eine Fiktion" (*All* so-called "spiritual" causality is a fiction).[46]

Despite his protestations of submitting to a "conscience of *method*" and embracing "a morality of method," Nietzsche's only published argument in defense of his vision of the world "seen from within," the will to power as an immaterial "effective force," is a catena of fictitious claims composing an artfully executed mythopoetic creation. The concluding sentence in the fabricated "argument" on which an anatomy is being performed is a signal to a reader who has perused Nietzsche's writings as if they were a philosophical Enigma code. The world seen from within is said to be "the world described and defined according to its 'intelligible character'." This Kantian phrase is never used in a *positive* sense by Nietzsche and, when used, it is ridiculed. It introduces the "unconditional" and it is related to "transcendental" moral freedom, the freedom of *homo noumenon*, the mysterious "self-in-itself" or "subject-in-itself"—a host of Kant-inspired beliefs that never fail to agitate Nietzsche.[47]

ESOTERICA

It is odd that the distinction between exoteric and esoteric conceptions or "doctrines" in Nietzsche's writings is usually ignored, even in an interpretation, like Sarah Kofman's, that suggests such a distinction. At one point she calls attention to Nietzsche's claim that some authors may not want to be understood, especially not just by "anybody." Select audiences are earmarked by "noble spirits" who create a certain distance by means of subtle style, seeking to reach those attuned to the same wavelengths. Again, Kofman maintains that metaphorical language serves to distance the "noble" spirit from the ordinary, that metaphorical style is "aristocratic,"[48] despite the fact that Nietzsche insists upon the universal prevalence of metaphor. Metaphors, for Nietzsche, are said to be operative in perception (perceiving similarities or analogical characteristics in different phenomena), in ordinary language and, in disguise, in conceptual terms, in all knowing. Hence, the exoteric-esoteric distinction would have served the interpretation of Nietzsche's "texts" more effectively than the metaphor/conceptual paradigm employed in Kofman's *Nietzsche and Metaphor*.

"Everything that is deep loves the mask." And "Every profound spirit needs a mask." These familiar maxims from *Beyond Good and Evil* can be found in paraphrastic form sprinkled throughout Nietzsche's works, published and unpublished. But the only open reference to the differentiation between secret doctrines and accessible public communications that serve the same function as Plato's "noble lie" is found in the same work, the title of which refers to an esoteric notion in Hindu scriptures—that is, that the adept who has attained insight, gnosis, or "liberation," who has acquired spiritual discipline and knowledge (*vidya*), leaves good and bad deeds behind and is "beyond good and evil."[49] Referring to the tradition in ancient Greek thought and in the Persian, Hindu, and Moslem faiths of distinguishing "the exoteric and the esoteric," Nietzsche links it to the belief in "an order of rank" rather than a leveling "sameness" (*Gleichheit*), to a recognition of a "higher" or "lower" way of being or "spiritual" nature.[50]

Granting that Nietzsche is concerned with the creation of exoteric myths that will complete the humanization of the dehumanized, demythological world of the sciences (which he displays in order to stress the nihilistic consequences of a solely scientific world-picture), the will-to-power idea cannot be conceived of as an ontology. Surreptitiously introduced assumptions and premises that embody *rejected* concepts and principles in his only published defense of his "theory" subvert its validity. Nietzsche fulfilled his earlier project: to construct an anthropic-poetic myth that would synthesize art and science and serve as a plausible and challenging image of a dynamic, energistic cosmos imbued with *pathos*. The will to power was intended to serve as an interpretation that is a quasi-scientific, quasi-metaphysical exoteric mask concealing a disturbing Dionysian chaos. Nietzsche sought to craft a will-to-power "theory" as a resolution of the riddle of existence, as a putative answer to the question: Why is there change and movement, dynamic energy, and a constantly renewed life-*nisus*? Or, more generally, why is there a chaotic process of becoming rather than nothing?

Heidegger confidently claimed that Nietzsche's "metaphysics" is lucidly expressed in a note concluding that "will to power is the ultimate fact at which we arrive."[51] This not-quite-accurate quotation pertains to the *psychological* interpretation of our being, not the metaphoric transference (or, *übertragen* [transfer] or *Übertragung* [transference], literally "to carry over," carrying over) of will to power to all entities, to the ostensible elementary beings: "force-centers," "power-centers," or "will-quanta." What is actually recorded in this entry from 1885 is:

> Our intellect, our will, even our sensations are dependent upon our *valuations*: these correspond to our drives and their conditions of existence. Our drives are reducible to *the will to power*. The will to power is the last fact we find refuge in.[52]

While we may question the use of *Factum* here since Nietzsche elsewhere replaces "facts" with value-interpretations, it is clear that he is applying generalizations from physical theory to the human psychic structure or "naturalizing" mankind. In other places, *Trieben* or "drives," "urges," "impulses" are described as waxing and waning in power or strength, engaged in a continuous *agon*.[53] Thus, the psychic dynamics of human beings is derived from a transfer of what is theoretically held to be the case for physical entities in science to our "psychodynamics." It is for this reason, among others, that stress has been placed upon the selective nature of Nietzsche's perspectival interpretation of *homo natura*. Since the supposed primal source of all of our "drives" is a posited active will to power, then it is a value-interpretation of the reductive center of our inner being, a reference to an inferred multiplex process that is purely hypothetical.[54] Given Nietzsche's general conception of our immanence in nature, it is not surprising that throughout his experimental, exploratory thinking he tends to interpret human beings in terms of nature or, more specifically, in terms of various scientific theories of nature, while interpreting nature in accordance with "human analogy." That is, just as we have an active subjective, inner life that is by no means obvious to others or easy to decipher so, too, do we assume that phenomena we encounter in experience, either organic or "preorganic" (even though Nietzsche eventually denies any significant distinction between the two) also have an analogous "inner" being. In a note from 1886–87 he reminds himself to "note well": "*All movement as signs of an inner event: thus the enormous predominant portion of all inner events is only given to us as signs.*"[55] By *inneren Geschehens* Nietzsche does not only mean what we would call "psychic" events because he often refers to the complexity of physiological processes that we are not normally aware of as inner events. He often suggests, along the lines of Spinoza's thought, that physical and mental events are aspects of each other or "signs" of an unknown "third," a neutral process he designates "will to power."

If we assume that the elaboration of the "theory" of the will to power is a metaphoric humanization of a scientific interpretation of the natural world, then it is an aesthetic creation in part derived from and in part imposed upon nature in order to transfer to it a human meaning. For Nietzsche, the "overcoming of nihilism" is most difficult in relation to the increasing authority of the scientific interpretation of nature, specifically in mechanistic theory. Philosophical mechanists insist that all existence is founded upon the theory and laws of mechanics. "But," Nietzsche insists, "an essentially mechanistic world would be an essentially meaningless world."[56]

It is often overlooked that, behind the scenes, in his notes, Nietzsche himself engages in an erasure of humanity from the natural landscape. All human beings and not only previous "philosophers have . . . projected the human into nature—let us dehumanize *nature*."[57] As a consequence of this experiment, we are left with a chaotic dialectical interaction of "forces" or *Energie* from which the qualities we are familiar with (color, solidity, sound, taste, texture, etc.) have been removed, along with all of the aesthetic qualities that enhance existence, all of the positive or creative values that motivate us, encourage striving, and lend meaning to our lives. Acting out the relentless will to knowledge, scientists have inadvertently disclosed a nihilistic vista that has radically diminished mankind's place in this chaos that the universe, theoretically, has become. Ever since Copernicus, whose cosmology removed the earth from the center of our universe, has not mankind been minimized, diminished or "deconstructed"—pushed "into nothingness? into a "*penetrating sense* of [its] . . . nothingness?" A descriptive value-free "historiography" adds to this devaluation of values, this "*nihilistic*" trend, this growing modern sense of the "in vain," "*nada*."[58]

Nihilism is in part a response to mankind's self-diminishment, the sense that what gave meaning to us has been withdrawn by the *nisus* of an insatiable "will to knowledge" or "will to truth." This, Nietzsche indicates, is the last stage in the evolution of the "ascetic ideal" designated as an "esoteric" mode of complete atheism, which is a counterfinality "of two thousand years of training in truthfulness," of "Christian morality itself."[59] Here, as is often the case, Nietzsche is saying too much in a compressed way. What he seems to be saying is that the continuity of the strongest expression of the self-denying, reactive, and negative "ascetic ideal" is found in unconditional atheism and a lack of belief in any ideal other than a will to truth. This is a crisis because we have in this instance a spiritual activity with no goal, with a negative attitude towards life: one that passionately discloses truths that erode confidence in the value of life, our own value. In sum: the startling denouement of the will to knowledge manifested in the will to truth is that knowledge reveals the insignificance of our being, and the last "truth" is that there is no knowable transcendental truth. At this point, to use Nietzsche's pathos-filled phrase, "the tragedy begins" in earnest.

If the will-to-power conception is an exoteric myth designed to overcome the negativities of the will to scientific knowledge, to humanize an immensely complex cosmic process, then is this esoteric doctrine only another, more comprehensive, "complete" form of nihilism?[60] It has been argued that after Nietzsche praises the methods and anti-metaphysical attitude of science he then brands it as the paradigm of modern nihilism.[61] If it were not for the retrieval of an aesthetic perspective on actuality, the enhancing power of artistic transformation, Nietzsche may have painted himself into a narrow corner. In a retrospective reference to *The Birth of Tragedy* in a note from the late 1880s he admits that there one could discern "nihilism," "a radical negation of life." Except that, embedded in this early work is what he elsewhere calls an "overcoming of nihilism" by means of the "*redemptive*" power of art or the aesthetic interpretation of life and actuality. Having experienced it, perhaps having experienced nothing else, he came to know that "art is *more valuable* than truth."[62] This notation refers not only to his first major work, but to the Dionysian affirmation of life with the aid of a global aesthetic perspective, the tragic optimism of his later reflections. If we interpret the cosmos from the perspective of art, then its value is restored and its affirmative, life-enhancing power negates the de-anthropic mechanistic world-picture and the depreciation of life and the natural world in the "ascetic" will to truth without goal.

Nietzsche accepts the tragic vision of *objective nihilism*: the absence of human meaning in an indifferent chaos of interacting elements; the absence of a divine meaning-giver; the existence of arbitrary and capricious suffering; the lack of any convergence on a holistic "Truth" in science or anywhere else; the apparently endless flux of becoming that consumes everything. But he does *not* end in nihilism even though he passes through it. The often-cited Dionysian "yea-saying" is not only the admonition to affirm and embrace life in spite of its genuine injustices, terrors, sufferings, and absurd contingencies. It entails the overcoming of the negative, debilitating, and demoralizing power of nihilism by confronting it and accepting its actual, though tragic, *objective* actuality.

Reversing his perspective on "the nihilistic possibility" that Kierkegaard had already experienced and "leaped" out of, Nietzsche negated it, or advised others to negate this negation, in *Existenz*. In order to create a human meaning for the "earth," this transitory world, he needed to erase objectively given meaning, to efface the last vestige of an objective teleology that ostensibly gave meaning to our existence. Nietzsche liberates a subjective *nisus* toward meaning, a subjective teleology that is fueled by art *and* thought. Barring a rejected "leap of faith,"[63] there is no access to an overarching meaning disclosed by the sciences (as far as we know or Nietzsche knew) and their immensely complicated theoretical and experimental revelations conceal as much as they reveal. It is his acquaintance with science and not his "poetic reason" that leads Nietzsche to call the universe an eternal "chaos" and to assert that "*The true world of causes is concealed from us*: it is unspeakably complicated."[64] Thus, there is, in Nietzsche's view, neither a transcendental "world of truth" nor an immanent, trans-phenomenal "world of truth." Neither metaphysics nor science lead to any indisputable "Truth."

The "esoteric" aspect of Nietzsche's thought is not found in one single maxim. Rather, it is his existential communication, as well as "the transvaluation of values" that is already embedded in his variegated writings (and, therefore, did not need to be a future project); it is in his perspectival model of knowing; his conception of the bodily self; his strong defense of independence and thinking against public, as well as "professional," opinion, and much more. Nietzsche repeatedly urges us towards personal, experimental, trans-theoretical "truths" that cannot be understood in a cool, detached way. Following the reductivism of the sciences, as well as Nietzsche's emulation of it, we could say that what encompasses his "esoteric" teaching is his entire provisional, hypothetical, and experimental approach to philosophical explorations, his analytic and surgical approach to concepts and values, his capacity for reflexive self-criticism, his psychological observations, his honesty and cunning subtlety, and, finally, his recognition of the limits of intelligibility. Like any serious thinker, he is often tempted to try to break the code of actuality, to decipher its numerous "signs," to see behind the "mask" of our world of phenomena that, to some extent, we have "created" by all that we bring to our experience of its "stimuli," "resistances," and alterity.

All that we are acquainted with in the process of knowing is conditioned, constituted, transubstantiated, anthropomorphically colored. But, like a philosophical internist, Nietzsche sees such phenomena as "symptoms" of something else, an underlying process that can neither be grasped conceptually nor expressed in language. The exclamatory note that offers an abbreviated expression of his "task" is puzzling. If what he proposes were possible, it would, in terms of his own analysis of knowing, not gain access to actuality as he has described it. "Task: *to see* things as *they are*! *Means*: to be able to see them out of a hundred eyes, out of *many* persons!"[65] Positing an immanent will to power is no claim to knowledge or truth. Nietzsche never intended the will-to-power image, as Heidegger held, as "an ontology of the Being of beings" or, more turgidly, as "the truth of beings as such in their totality."[66] Given his scrutiny of the texts of Nietzsche and, in particular of the numerous notes "left after" (*Nachlass*) his death, notes in which he claimed to find Nietzsche's authentic philosophy, it is surprising that Heidegger did not notice the rare references to esotericism there and especially in *Beyond Good and Evil*. But then, wasn't Heidegger's method of interpretation one that involved a detailed deep reading of a text and, subsequently "doing violence to the text"?

Long before the late 1880s Nietzsche saw that "mankind represents the existence of other things by analogy with his own existence, in other words anthropomorphically and, in any case, with illogical transference."[67] Analogical thinking is often used to try to explain something not completely clear and is related to induction as a heuristic process that itself serves as a means of framing hypotheses. It is erroneous, however, to say that since we are "exceptionally complex wills to power ourselves, we are ideally suited to 'mirror' reality"[68] because we have a privileged insight into it. Nietzsche's skepticism about the belief that we can literally "mirror" anything independent of and outside ourselves does not support such an assertion. But it is clear that metaphoric transferences or analogies signal poetic invention or anthropic transformation. In a note from the early 1870s following lamentations about the detrimental effect of Kant's undermining of "belief in metaphysics" and the withdrawal of the ground of metaphysics, Nietzsche distinguishes his "tragic philosopher" from "the philosopher of *desperate knowledge*." The latter anticipates his depiction of the thinker who continues the ascetic propensity in the absence of goals or ideals. For, the "philosopher of *desperate knowledge* will be absorbed in blind science: knowledge at any price." Opposed to this rampant "will to knowledge," the "tragic philosopher" sees the emergence of "metaphysics" as "merely anthropomorphic," a completion of "*the picture of existence*."[69]

Nature, in such a world-picture, is to be construed in terms of human analogy (as actuality *in toto* will be represented), "as erring, experimenting, good and evil—as struggling and overcoming itself."[70] In an esoteric sense, actuality is implicitly an impersonal chaos upon which we necessarily project and impose order, meaning, and value. This idea of chaos is, of course, an interpretation; but it is one that, for Nietzsche, is strongly suggested by scientific data and theories. The very notion that the entire cosmos is an "atomistic chaos"—the objective nihilism seen as tragic, but nonetheless probably an "ugly truth"—is repeatedly impressed upon Nietzsche's mind not by Greek or other myths, but by the natural scientific picture of actuality. The metaphor of constantly interacting "wills to power" is in part designed to reintegrate the human into the natural world, to project "spirituality" into what "mechanists" depicted as matter acting on matter in accordance with "laws of nature," and, in part, a creative incorporation of theories and concepts in physics, biology, and physiology into an artfully constructed philosophical interpretation.

The cosmic will to power is the name for what is unknown and "a reduced formula" that serves, exoterically, to "explain" what underlies the "symptoms" of consciousness and "matter," spirit and nature, reason, the senses, affects, movement, resistance, and the awesome phenomenon of life itself. The construct of the will-to-power metaphor is built out of hypotheses, provisional experimental points of views, and regulative fictions just like scientific views that "may be granted admission and even a certain value in the realm of knowledge."[71] However, in the aesthetic creation of an exoteric "metaphysics"—that has been understood as an ontology, a genuine statement of Nietzsche's conception of reality, by most interpreters of his thought—the "convictions" (*Ueberzeugungen*) that suggest going beyond the evidence—are sought by a powerful, yet subtle, use of rhetoric.

Metaphor is linked to the pragmatics of language or sign-functions, to the endeavor to communicate to others a specific perspective, a mode of interpreting something, to convince them of the "appropriateness" of a particular perspectival interpretation of actuality *in toto* or some aspect of life, nature, and existence. Nietzsche fully realized that by means of metaphors, similes, and anthropomorphisms we can, in a strict sense, prove nothing, but may yet persuade or convince. Science has a natural aversion to such rhetorical devices and it attempts, by means of its form of expression, to promote a cold attitude of mistrust.[72] Hence, the aim of projecting an existential-aesthetic interpretation of life and actuality (*Wirklichkeit*) on a provisional scientific world-interpretation and thereby generating a Centaurian philosophy. Subsequently, Nietzsche dared to construct an elaborate exoteric fable—relying on metaphorical transferences—with the bricks of scientific theory.

It is doubtful that Nietzsche was ever persuaded of the plausibility of his creative world-interpretation of the fluctuating process of "becoming" or "suchness" that expresses itself in the billionfold Protean forms of dynamic energy, unless an artist of language may come to love the artwork he has created. The overwhelming complexity, the incongruities and contradictory tensions of an actuality that eludes representation, conceptualization, and "linguistic means of expression" remains as the field in which the enhancement, rather than the devaluation or negation of life, of "this world," may yet be prized and elevated in the "higher culture" of which Nietzsche dreamed.

After a lengthy, labyrinthine, sometimes vertiginous journey, Nietzsche closes his ring of interpretations by retrieving, by shrewd esoteric methods, a transfigured, more sophisticated anthropomorphism.

Notes

Chapter One

1. Sander Gilman, Carole Blair, and David Parent, ed. and trans., *Friedrich Nietzsche on Rhetoric and Language* (Oxford: Oxford University Press, 1989), 246–51. In 1988 a controversy arose about these writings on rhetoric, language, and the essay "On Truth and Lying." It was claimed in a few places that much of this material was derived from a work by Gustav Gerber, *Die Sprache als Kunst* (1871), which Nietzsche had borrowed from the library at the University of Basel. Lecture notes on rhetoric and language were, in many instances, abridged transcriptions of Gerber's writings. This is uncontestable. Nevertheless, the claim that the emphasis on the metaphorical nature of language in "Truth and Lying" simply appropriates Gerber's conception of metaphors is questionable. Claudia Crawford has shown that Arthur Schopenhauer, F. A. Lange and Eduard von Hartmann had already shaped Nietzsche's thought on the transformation of sensory stimuli into metaphors (and later, concepts) by an unconscious process some time before he read Gerber. See: Claudia Crawford, *The Beginnings of Nietzsche's Theory of Language* (Berlin and New York: de Gruyter, 1988), ch. 14. What is not mentioned is that Nietzsche was an admiring and recurrent reader of Ralph Waldo Emerson. In *Nature* and elsewhere he stressed the prevalence of metaphors and anthropomorphisms in language. Cf. G. J. Stack, *Nietzsche and Emerson* (Athens, OH: Ohio University Press, 1992), 145ff.

2. *Sämtliche Werke*, 15 vols. (Berlin and New York: de Gruyter, 1980), 1:847. (Hereafter cited as *SW*, vol., sections (when appropriate), and page[s].)

3. *SW* 1:39. In a note from 1883 he admits that he expressed an "artists' metaphysics" he did not entirely embrace. "Behind my first period grins the visage of Jesuitism: I mean, the conscious holding fast to illusion and compulsorily incorporating it as the basis of culture" (*SW* 10:507). By "Jesuitism" he presumably means equivocating, dissembling, and cloaking one's actual views.

4. It is an exaggeration to claim that Nietzsche not only denies "transcendent knowledge," but also the very possibility of knowledge in general. See Allan Megill, *Prophets of Extremity* (Berkeley: University of California Press, 1985), 359n. As I will attempt to show, Nietzsche does not deny knowledge as much as redefine it.

5. Nietzsche's primary target was not the French positivists, but the optimistic and materialistic positivism of his contemporary, Eugen Dühring. In his *Natürliche Dialektik* (1865) he argued for a strict realism and held that human knowledge apprehends reality as it is. For Dühring, there are no ambiguities in existence and no room for doubt.

6. *Werke, Grossoktavausgabe*, 2nd ed., 19 vols. (Leipzig: Naumann Verlag, 1901–13), 12:33. (Hereafter cited as *Werke* (*GOA*) vol. and page(s)).

7. Ibid., 13:59. Here Nietzsche seems to rely upon Ernst Mach's psychologistic understanding of cause and effect. Causality is construed as a conceptual "artifice" serving the method of "economy of thought." See Ernst Mach. *The Science of Mechanics*, trans. T. J. McCormack (LaSalle: Open Court, 1942). Originally published in 1883, Nietzsche read this work, according to his sister, in 1884. Since she cites it in its original and correct title, *Die Mechanik in threr Entwicklung*, we have no reason to think that, in this case, there is any deception at work. See Elizabeth Foerster-Nietzsche, *Das Leben Fr. Nietzsches*, 2 vols. (Leipzig: Naumann, 1895–1904).

8. *SW* 2:I, 19.

9. Nietzsche grasped the underlying thrusts and implications of Kant's thought. It is an overstatement to say (especially about perspectivalism) that "Nietzsche . . . is merely rehashing familiar Kantian themes minus the rigor of Kant's exposition." Ken Gemes, "Nietzsche's Critique of Truth," *Philosophy and Phenomenological Research* 52 (1992): 210.

10. *Werke* (*GOA*), 11:180. In *The Gay Science* "phenomenalism and perspectivism" are related to the reduction of the world to a "surface and sign-world." What becomes conscious is tainted by "falsification, reduction to superficialities, and generalization." This is a harsh depiction of our general, commonsense consciousness of phenomena. The joining of phenomenalism and perspectivism in this passage is often cited without comment even though it is at odds with the more typical view that phenomena are that which we know as a *consequence* of perspectival interpretation. *The Gay Science*, trans. W. Kaufmann (New York: Vintage, 1974), sec. 354.

11. Ibid., 10:121.

12. Ibid., 13:5.

13. Rudolf Eisler, *Nietzsches Erkenntnisstheorie und Metaphysik* (Leipzig: Hermann Haacke, 1902), 21.

14. *Werke in Drei Bänden*, ed. Karl Schlechta, 3 vols. (Munich: Carl Hanser Verlag, 1966), 3:428. (Hereafter cited as *WDB*, vol. and page(s).)

15. Martin Heidegger, *Nietzsche* (Pfullingen: Neske, 1961), 2:127.

16. No doubt Nietzsche would have been pleased by the inevitability of including the observer (O) as a central factor in the scientific observational situation in quantum physics. In the conventional quantum theory an individual subjective element is involved in the measurement of microphysical particles. Physicists such as E. P. Wigner have insisted that in quantum mechanical theory there is no reality independent of the observer. Eugene P. Wigner. *Symmetries and Reflections* (Woodbridge, CT: Ox Bow Press, 1979), ch. 14.

17. *WDB* 3:291–99. Cf. "Homer's Contest," trans. Christe D. Acampora, *Nietzscheana* 5 (1996): 1–8.

18. *Gesammelte Werke* (Munich: Musarian Verlag, 1920–29), 6:334ff.

19. For accounts of the influence of Ralph Waldo Emerson on Nietzsche's thought, see: Eduard Baumgarten, *Das Vorbild Emersons im Werk und Leben Nietzsches* (Heidelberg: Karl Winter, 1957); Stanley Hubbard, *Nietzsche und Emerson* (Basel: Verlag für Recht und Gesellschaft, 1958), and George J. Stack, *Nietzsche and Emerson* (Athens: Ohio University Press, 1993).

20. Friedrich Nietzsche, *Sämtliche Briefe* (Berlin and New York: de Gruyter, 1986), 2:184. (Hereafter cited as *SB*, vol. and page(s).)

21. Carl A. Bernoulli, *Franz Overbeck und Friedrich Nietzsche: Eine Freundschaft*, 2 vols. (Jena: Diederichs, 1908), 1:146. Cited in Jörg Salaquarda, "Nietzsche und Lange," *Nietzsche-Studien* 7 (1978): 237.

22. *SW* 1:3, 355–56. Heinrich von Kleist, the nineteenth-century dramatist and novelist, had a romantic philosophy of life that was an optimistic idealism. After he grasped the implication of Kant's critique of reason and the limitations of sense perceptions, his creative work dramatized error and agnosticism. Eventually, he committed suicide. Cf. Oscar Walzel. *German Romanticism* (New York: Unger, 1965), 245–51.

23. *WDB* 3:312–13.

24. Hermann Helmholtz, *Physiologische Optik*, sec. 26. Cited in W. M. Salter, *Nietzsche the Thinker* (New York: Henry Holt, 1917), 483. As early as the mid-1860s Nietzsche made a note to read, "*Helmhol[t]z über die Erhaltung der Kraft Berlin 1847*" and "*ueber die Wechelwirkung der Naturkrafte 1854*." *Historisch Kritische Gesamtausgabe Werke* (Munich: C. H. Beck, 1935), 3:394.

25. F. A. Lange, *The History of Materialism and Criticism of Its Present Importance*, trans. E. C. Thomas (London: Routledge and Kegan Paul, 1925), 2:217. Nietzsche expresses this in notes by asserting that "language does not capture things or events, but stimuli. . . . The complete essences of things is never captured." *Gesammelte Werke* (Munich: Musarion, 1922), 5:298.

26. In a letter to his friend Carl von Gersdorff (August 1866), Nietzsche quotes this statement from Lange's history of materialism and identifies it as one of his main conclusions. Cf. *WDB* 3:970.

27. *SW* 3, *Morgenröte*: 117, 110.

28. *The Will to Power*, trans. Walter Kaufmann and R. J. Hollingdale (New York: Vintage Books, 1968), 270.

29. Ibid., 305.

30. Ibid., 315.

31. *Werke* (*GOA*) 13: 80–85, 130.

32. Cited in F. A. Lange, *History of Materialism*, 2: 205. Cf. Georg Christoph Lichtenberg, *Aphorisms*, trans. R. J. Hollingdale (London: Penguin, 1990). Hollingdale uses "perceive" in lieu of "know" in his translation.

33. *The Will to Power*, 339.

34. *SW* 3:3, 468.

35. Ibid., 473.

36. The most insightful analysis of Nietzsche's use of metaphor is the late Sarah Kofman's *Nietzsche and Metaphor*, trans. Duncan Large (Stanford: Stanford University Press, 1993). Although her orientation in this work (a translation of the second edition of *Nietzsche et la métaphore* [Paris: Galilee, 1983]), is very compelling and persuasive, I find her "strategic" analysis questionable and, despite her recognition of it, her treatment of Nietzsche's relation to scientific theory somewhat understated.

37. Lange, *History of Materialism*, 2:395–96. Gustav Fechner (1801–1887), the German founder of psychophysics, also expressed (in his *Zend-Avesta* [1851]) a psychistic pantheism that held that mind and body are, as in Spinoza, two aspects of all things. He was an anomaly in his time and his profession, an anti-materialist who

defended a visionary philosophy of spiritualism. For a brief and enthusiastic account of his *Zend-Avesta* (named after the scripture of the religion of Zoroaster or Zarathustra), see William James, "Concerning Fechner," in *A Pluralistic Universe* (New York: Longmans, Green and Co., 1909), Lecture 4.

38. *The Will to Power*, 334.

39. Ibid., 335–36.

40. Ibid., 338.

41. Ibid., 350.

42. Ibid., 263–64.

43. Albert Einstein, *Relativity: The Special and General Theory* (New York: Methuen, 1961), 136–39. Einstein also held that physical concepts of space, time, and event have a "psychological origin."

44. Ibid., 47–48.

45. *The Will to Power*, 305.

46. Marshall Spector. *Methodological Foundations of Relativistic Mechanics* (Notre Dame and London: University of Notre Dame Press, 1972), 159–60.

47. Nietzsche borrowed Boscovich's *Theoria Philosophiae Naturalis* from the library at the University of Basel over four semesters between 1873 and 1875. See Luca Cresenzi, "*Verzeichnis der von Nietzsche aus der Universitätbibliothek" in Basel, entleihenen Bücher* (1869–79)," *Nietzsche-Studien* 23 (1994): 388–442.

48. Lange, *History of Materialism*, 2:388.

49. We may compare Einstein's remark that the "real external world" is the "sum total" of all "space-time events." *Relativity*, 140–41.

50. At one point in his notes he reminds himself to "note well." *Die Prozesse als "Wesen"*. In effect, he is alluding to the idea that processes are the "essence" of reality. Cf. *The Will to Power*, 346.

51. *The Will to Power*, 349.

52. Ibid.

53. *SW* 3:5, 373. ". . . eine essentiell mechanische Welt ware eine *sinnlose* Welt!"

54. Wilfrid Sellars, *Science, Perception, and Reality* (London: Routledge and Kegan Paul, 1963), 96.

55. *The Will to Power*, 265–66. This process of transforming something "new" into something familiar is illustrated by the trend earlier in this century—particularly in the physicist Niels Bohr's model of the structure of the atom—to picture subatomic particles in the atom as analogous to a miniature solar system. In more general terms, this process is a consequence of the tendency towards anthropomorphic projection that Nietzsche analyzes from a number of points of view. What is familiar is sought underneath or behind phenomena in the search for scientific explanation in general. Simply put, "*was bekannt ist, ist erkannt*" (what is familiar is known): *SW* 3: 5, 594.

Chapter Two

1. For a translation of Nietzsche's "Zur Teleologie," see Claudia Crawford, *The Beginnings of Nietzsche's Theory of Language* (New York and Berlin: de Gruyter, 1988), 238–52.

2. Although Nietzsche does not embrace a form of pragmatism, his views on the practical and evolutionary value of knowledge are reminiscent of James's belief that "it is impossible to strip the *human element* out from even our most abstract theorizing." As Nietzsche does, James construes our truths as man-made. William James, *Collected Essays and Reviews* (New York: Longmans, Green, 1920), 450–51. F. C. S. Schiller strongly influenced James's emphasis upon a humanistic theory of knowledge. For a detailed argument that Schiller was himself deeply influenced by many of Nietzsche's epistemic views, see George J. Stack, "Nietzsche's Influence on Pragmatic Humanism," *Journal of the History of Philosophy* 20, no. 4 (October 1, 1982): 369–406.

3. *SB* 2:269 (Letter to Paul Deussen, April/May, 1868).

4. Cf. George J. Stack, "Nietzsche and Lange," *The Modern Schoolman* 57, no. 2 (January 1980): 137–48. Cf. also: J. Salaquarda, "Der Standpunkt des Ideals bei Lange und Nietzsche," *Studi Tedeschi* 22, no. 1 (1979): 1–28.

5. Immanuel Kant, *Kritik der reinen Vernunft* [Critique of Pure Reason] (Hamburg: Felix Meiner Verlag, 1956), 28.

6. Immanuel Kant, *Prolegomena zu jeder künftigen Metaphysik* [*Prolegomena to any Future Metaphysics*] (Riga, 1783), 8, 167. Cited in F. A. Lange, *The History of Materialism and Criticism of Its Present Importance*, trans. E. C. Thomas (London: K. Paul, Trench, Trubner, 1925), 2:162–63.

7. Ibid., 204. Having sought to provide philosophical validity for the scientific (Newtonian) concept of nature, Kant would have been surprised to find scientists like Emil du Bois-Reymond insisting in 1872 on the limits of natural scientific knowledge. See Emil du Bois-Reymond, *Ueber die Grenzen des Natureskennens*. 7th ed. (Leipzig, 1916). First published 1872.

8. Lange, *History of Materialism,* 2:192.

9. Ibid., 2:193, n. 2.

10. Ibid., 200–201.

11. Ibid., 2:217.

12. *SB* 2:160. An Carl von Gersdorff (August 1866).

13. Lange, *History of Materialism,* 2: 218. Cf. Immanuel Kant, *Critique of Pure Reason*, trans. Max Müller (London: Macmillan, 1896), 226: "[W]hat according to the pure understanding should be the absolutely internal of matter is a mere phantom, for matter is never an object of the pure understanding."

14. R. J. Hollingdale, *Nietzsche* (London: Routledge, 1973), 138.

15. Immanuel Kant. *Anthropology from a Pragmatic Point of View*, trans. Mary Gregor (The Hague: Nijhoff, 1974), 192: "[I]t . . . belongs to the basic composition of a human creature and to the concept of his species to explore the thoughts of others but to withhold one's own—a . . . quality that does not fail to progress . . . from *dissimulation* to *deception* and finally to lying." Kant also indicated the following as primary inclinations: superiority, a mania for power and possession. Ibid, 138–40.

16. *SW* 1:4, 39.

17. J. T. Wilcox, *Truth and Value in Nietzsche* (Ann Arbor: University of Michigan Press, 1978), 100.

18. Lange, *History of Materialism,* 2:234.

19. Ibid., 2:343.

20. Ibid.

21. *SW* 1:18. Cf. J. T. Wilcox, *Truth and Value in Nietzsche*, 109.

22. *SW* 1:879.

23. Hans Vaihinger, *The Philosophy of "As-If,"* trans. C. K. Ogden (New York: Barnes and Noble, 1955), 313–15.

24. Wilcox, *Truth and Value in Nietzsche*, 110.

25. *SW* 2:1, 3.

26. *WDB* 3:844.

27. Nietzsche, *The Will to Power*, trans. Walter Kaufmann and R. J. Hollingdale (New York: Vintage Books, 1968), 9.

28. Ibid., 15.

29. Ibid., 530.

30. Kant, *Critique of Pure Reason*, 10.

31. Ibid.

32. *The Will to Power*, 239.

33. *SB* 8:144 (Letter to Heinrich Koselitz, 8 September 1887).

34. *SW* 5: 20, 34.

35. In this work Kant characterizes man "as an animal endowed with the *capacity for reason*," a being who "can make of himself a *rational animal*." As such, "he first *preserves* himself and his species." Subsequently, Kant refers to reason as a weapon which substitutes for the "claws and fangs" of other animals. In a footnote he speculates on man's origins and suggests that the "orangutan" acquired a "human form." Kant, *Anthropology from a Pragmatic Point of View*, 183–88. Nietzsche makes only one reference to this work in regard to Kant's comments on the common, but unknown, root of sensibility and understanding, and his admission that the tracing of these functions back through man's natural history eludes understanding. Cf. *SW* 7:149.

36. *The Will to Power*, 307.

37. Kant, *Critique of Pure Reason*, 27–29.

38. *The Will to Power*, 263. If Nietzsche had seen Kant's *Opus Postumum*, he might have accepted the modified version of the "thing-in-itself" found there. Curiously, Kant's posthumous writings include the name "Zoroaster" (Zarathustra) in two planned works. Cf. Vaihinger, *The Philosophy of "As-If"*, 313–14.

39. Ibid., 298.

40. Ibid., 267.

41. Ibid., 301.

42. Ibid., 303.

43. Ibid.

44. Schacht avers that "Nietzsche . . . like Kant . . . stops short of idealism, refusing to equate reality with the world as we experience it but maintaining that our experience is as it is . . . in consequence of the way in which we constitute it." Richard Schacht. *Nietzsche* (Boston: Routledge, 1983), 62. It should be noted that the *constitution* of our world includes much more for Nietzsche than Kant considered. This notion was derived from (among others) Heinrich Czolbe's conception of the exclusion of appeals to a supra-sensible domain and his emphasis on empirical knowledge (which he characterized as "sensualism" or "sensationalism"). Nietzsche, however, completely rejected Czolbe's atomistic materialism. Cf. Heinrich Czolbe. *Neue Darstellung des Sensualismus* (Leipzig: H. Costenoble, 1855).

45. *The Will to Power*, 277–78, 313–14.

46. Ibid., 273.

47. Ibid., 270.

48. Ibid., 330.

49. *Werke* (*GOA*) 2:36.

50. *The Will to Power*, 306.

51. *Werke* (*GOA*) 1:171.

52. Ibid., 12:24. Science, too, yields a "*simplified*, thoroughly artificial, suitably constructed and suitably falsified world."

53. *SW* 2:1, 29.

54. Wilcox, *Truth and Value in Nietzsche*, 124. Clark follows Wilcox, but goes further by claiming that Nietzsche rejects "the existence of metaphysical truth—correspondence to the thing-in-itself." Maudemarie Clark, *Nietzsche on Truth and Philosophy* (Cambridge: Cambridge University Press, 1990), 21. Although Nietzsche does indeed criticize any "correspondence" to things-in-themselves, his critique of metaphysical truth also pertains to any holistic or transcendental metaphysics: Hegel, Plato, Christian metaphysics, *et alia*.

55. *Werke* (*GOA*) 12:30, 42. In order to come to know a "mechanical world-order," we must adopt a specific perspective, "a perspective-apparatus which makes possible (1) a certain stability, (2) simplification, (3) selection and elimination." *SW* 11:99.

56. Ibid., 30.

57. *The Will to Power*, 327.

58. Ibid., 280.

59. Ibid., 281.

60. Ibid., 346.

61. Ibid., 330. *Werke* (*GOA*), 16:33, 55.

62. *Werke* 16: 33, 55. He refers to the "fluid Proteus-nature of actuality" (*Wirklichkeit*). Again relying on scientific theories, he asserts that "the actual world . . . [is] infinitely *richer in movements* than we *surmise*" (die wirkliche Welt . . . [ist] endlich *reicher an Bewegungen* als wir *ahnen*). *SW* 9:513. Cp. *Werke (GOA)*, 13:50.

63. P. F. Strawson, *The Bounds of Sense* (London: Methuon, 1966), 39.

64. Ibid., 251–52.

65. Kant, *Critique of Pure Reason*, 147. Thomas Nagel has succinctly and accurately summarized Kant's position in this regard. "The Kantian view that primary qualities, too, describe the world only as it appears to us depends on taking the entire system of scientific explanation of observable phenomena as itself an appearance. . . . Primary qualities are nothing more . . . than an aspect of our world picture, and if that picture has an explanation, it must be in terms of the effect on us of something outside it, which will be for that reason unimaginable to us—the noumenal world." Thomas Nagel, *The View from Nowhere* (New York: Oxford University Press, 1989), 101.

66. In an earlier work I argued that Nietzsche in his notes experimented with the de-anthropic world-interpretation derived from physical theories in order to disclose a "stark interpretation of a meaningless cosmos . . . that lacks a human meaning." George J. Stack, *Lange and Nietzsche* (Berlin and New York: Walter de

Gruyter, 1983), 243. In effect, Nietzsche wanted to draw out the nihilistic consequences of a strictly scientific interpretation of actuality. This interpretation has not been altered by time. A recent German study that covers similar ground as my own suggests that Nietzsche intended to overcome anthropomorphism in his various "thought-experiments" in later notations and offered a thorough critique of science that entailed not only the erasure of pure objective knowledge, but the interrogation of his own interpretation of actuality. For, "*Nietzsches 'Interpretation' soll selbst ein 'subjektlöser Vorgang' sein*" [Nietzsche's "interpretation" must itself be a "subjectless process"]. This assumes that the negation of the metaphysical subject effaces the *self* and undermines the retrieval of the human perspective in the positive and creative aspect of the metaphoric idea of the "will to power." See Klaus Spiekermann. *Naturwissenschaft als subjektlöse Macht? Nietzsches Kritik physikalischer Grundkonzepte* (Berlin and New York: de Gruyter, 1992).

Chapter Three

1. Cf. William M. Salter, *Nietzsche the Thinker* (New York: Holt, 1917), 183; George A. Morgan, *What Nietzsche Means* (New York: Harper and Row, 1965), 272; Arthur Danto, *Nietzsche as Philosopher* (New York: Macmillan, 1965), 92.

2. Müller-Lauter's clear and thorough account of the link between science and Nietzsche's philosophy approaches but does not affirm the way in which scientific theory is used in the creation of the will-to-power hypothesis. See Wolfgang Müller-Lauter, *Nietzsche: His Philosophy of Contradictions and the Contradictions of His Philosophy*, trans. D. J. Parent (Urbana and Chicago: University of Illinois Press, 1999). Alistair Moles also offers very detailed and informative accounts of Nietzsche's "cosmology" (including links with Boscovich) in *Nietzsche's Philosophy of Nature and Cosmology* (New York: Peter Lang, 1990).

3. It was Boscovich's "theory which later influenced Faraday . . . and led to the notion of force-fields rather than matter as the fundamental physical entities." Mary B. Hesse, "Action at a Distance," in *The Concept of Matter in Modern Philosophy*, ed. Ernan McMullin (Notre Dame: University of Notre Dame Press, 1978), 125.

4. Bernd Magnus, *Nietzsche's Existential Imperative* (Bloomington and London: Indiana University Press, 1978), 22.

5. Walter Kaufmann, *Nietzsche*, 3rd rev. ed. (New York: Viking, 1968), 207.

6. *WDB* 2:576–77.

7 *Werke* (*GOA*) 16:56.

8. Arthur Danto, *Nietzsche as Philosopher* (New York: Macmillan, 1965), 211. Even though Danto denies that the dynamic theory he cites (that of Kant) influenced Nietzsche, the suggestion is there. Such a suggestion is not supported by the facts. Boscovich presented his earliest explorations of a dynamic theory of matter in his work of 1745, *De viribus vivis*. Most of Kant's writings dealing with "the power in corporeal bodies" and related topics date from 1747. Cf. L. L. Whyte, *Essays on Atomism* (Middletown: Wesleyan University Press, 1961), 56: "Immanuel Kant . . . argues that matter does not fill space by absolute impenetrability, but by

repulsive forces between ultimate particles localized at points, reaching this idea soon after Boscovich, and perhaps independently." For a detailed account of the difference between Kant's dynamic theory of nature and that of Boscovich, see: Alistar Moles, *Nietzsche's Philosophy of Nature and Cosmology* (New York: Peter Lang, 1990), 176–80.

9. Freidrich A. Lange, *The History of Materialism and Criticism of Its Present Importance*, trans. E. C. Thomas, 3 vols. in one, 3rd ed. (London: K. Paul, Trench, Trubner, 1925), 2:364.

10. Kaufmann, *Nietzsche*, 263. For a detailed discussion of the similarities and differences between Nietzsche's views on monadic perspectives and Leibniz's monadology, see Moles, *Nietzsche's Philosophy of Nature and Cosmology*.

11. Roger J. Boscovich, *A Theory of Natural Philosophy* (Cambridge, MIT Press, 1966), 67.

12. There is a similarity between Boscovich's theory of matter (and, by implication, Nietzsche's conception of "nature" as a dynamic process of becoming that is comprised of a multiplicity of "power-centers" in reciprocal relations of opposition or "cooperation") and recent physical theory. It has been said that "when we look beyond the electron, we still seem to be left with the alternatives of regarding the ultimate units of matter as unextended centres of force, or of imagining an infinite series of structures, one within another, and each more minute than the last." W. C. D. Dampier-Whetham, *A History of Science* (New York: Macmillan, 1929), 319. In addition, "the results of modern physics suggest that we should give up the idea of a substance or essence. They suggest that there is no self-identical entity persisting during all changes in time . . . that there is no essence that is the persisting carrier or possessor of the properties or qualities of a thing. The universe now appears to be not a collection of things, but an interacting set of events or processes." Karl Popper and J. C. Eccles, *The Self and Its Brain* (New York: Springer International, 1977), 7.

13. Boscovich, *Theory of Natural Philosophy*, 20.

14. Ibid., 24–25.

15. Ibid., 197.

16. Ibid., 201.

17. Ibid., 204.

18. For an analysis of the "scientific" or empirical argument for the eternal recurrence of the same, see Bernd Magnus, *Nietzsche's Existential Imperative* (Bloomington and London: Indiana University Press, 1978), 69–110. One commentator on Nietzsche's philosophy saw that his emphasis upon becoming, Heraclitean flux, and constantly shifting power relationships, as well as his claim that in every instant there is something new, that emergent qualities appear in "the world," conflicts with the theory of the eternal recurrence of the same. "The recurrence is identical, and Nietzsche has otherwise denied identities in nature; but he bases that denial on the improbability of any two things being exactly alike . . . and this he continues to maintain except for eternal recurrence, where of course the histories are identical. In these and other respects eternal recurrence contrasts with the tendency of his other cosmological views." Morgan, *What Nietzsche Means*, 289–90.

19. Harold Alderman, *Nietzsche's Gift* (Athens: Ohio University Press, 1977), 5. In a few articles Magnus has put in question the use of Nietzsche's *Nachlass*. He

claims that the use of these unpublished notes leads to misinterpretations of the ideas of the "beyond-man," eternal recurrence, and will to power. On a few points his argument is weak. Will to power could only be understood as "a first order" description of the world in itself or as a depiction of "the world's intelligible character" by relying on notes (even though a passage in *Beyond Good and Evil,* 36—a passage Magnus cites—is compatible with his notes). Also, even though Nietzsche quotes others in his notes (a reader recognizes this clearly, but may see the origin of some of his basic ideas), there are some passages in the notes that are only remotely related to published writings (this is to be expected). Magnus's underlying purpose in blighting the fascinating notes—which, for example, include a remarkable analysis of nihilism and hundreds of insights that were thankfully not subject to Magnus's prohibitions—is perhaps revealed in his desire to push "Nietzsche's thought in a postmodern direction." Bernd Magnus, "Nietzsche's Philosophy in 1888: *The Will to Power* and the *Übermensch,*" *Journal of the History of Philosophy* 24:1 (January 1988): 79–98.

20. *SW* 5:12, 26. In a note from 1881, Nietzsche says that Boscovich "has destroyed the matter-superstition with his theory of the mathematical character of atoms." *SW* 9:643. Elsewhere, he has a short list of denials which includes "*kein Stoff* (Boscovich)." *SW* 11:231.

21. *WDB* 3:704–5.

22. Ibid., 455.

23. Ibid., 542.

24. Ruediger H. Grimm, *Nietzsche's Theory of Knowledge* (Berlin and New York: de Gruyter, 1977), 182–87. Although the details in Nietzsche's inchoate theory of natural processes are accurately presented in this work, the author mentions neither Boscovich nor Lange as sources for many of the central features of Nietzsche's dynamics.

25. Moritz Schlick, *Philosophy of Nature*, trans. A. von Zeppelin (New York: Philosophical Library, 1949), 102. Although Schlick makes a number of references to Boscovich's theory of nature and matter, he does not mention its possible influence on Nietzsche, even though he refers to Kant and Helmholtz in this context. At one point, he suggests the compatibility of Boscovich's physical theory with twentieth-century "electro-atomism," especially with regard to the "essence" of "electrical and magnetic forces." For, "an electron is not to be conceived as a specific, electrically charged volume. . . . [O]n the contrary, the numerical estimate of the diameter of such a particle is only to be conceived as the average distance representing the limit to which the supposed centres of the particles can approach one another. And—as in the dynamic theory of . . . Boscovich—this fact must be regarded as the expression of definite regularities in events, and not as signs of the existence of an 'impermeable Substance' or something else of the kind. A particle of electricity cannot be separated from the environment . . ." (119).

26. Magnus, *Nietzsche's Existential Imperative,* 23.

27. *WDB* 3:312–14.

28. Ibid., 314.

29. *WDB* 2:576.

30. Ibid., 585.

31. *WDB* 3:726.

32. Ibid., 844. In a similar vein William James preferred "truths in the plural" to any "Absolute" and found "all the little 'lower-case' truths—and errors—which life represents" more interesting than "the Truth in capital letters." William James. *A Pluralistic Universe* (New York: Longmans, 1909), 142.

33. Ibid., 495.

34. *Werke (GOA)* 13:72.

35. *WDB* 3:903. Again, this criticism is primarily directed against the *Positivismus* and realism of his contemporary Dühring. He was an "optimistic positivist" who held that rational consciousness is completely adequate to comprehend the world as it is. He defended what he called a "philosophy of reality" with the advantage of a genuine knowledge of the history of mechanics and science in general. Cf. Eugen Dühring, *Logik und Wissenschaftslehre* (Leipzig, 1878) and *Kritische Geschichte der Principien der Mechanik* (Berlin, 1873).

36. For Nietzsche, the basic concepts employed in science (e.g., "atom," "substance," "cause," "gravity," "action at a distance," "object," etc.) are "interpretations with the aid of psychistic fictions." *Werke (GOA)* 13:313–31. There is no "permanent law of things," no "invariable order," and the sequences of events manifest no "law," "principle," or "order."

Although this general orientation towards scientific conceptions seems reminiscent of Berkeley's analyses of scientific concepts in *De motu*, it has been said that Nietzsche's "conventionalism" in regard to science, as well as his phenomenalistic interpretation of scientific concepts and principles, is primarily derived from his sympathy with that aspect of Kant's metaphysics of experience that emphasizes that "reason does not derive its laws from nature, but prescribes them to nature." In regard to Nietzsche's stress upon the productive, creative, spontaneous, and active character of knowledge, it has been pointed out that "there Is . . . much more of Kant in Nietzsche than is generally imagined." Hans Vaihinger, *The Philosophy of "As-If,"* trans. C. K. Ogden (London: Routledge and Kegan Paul, 1924), 349n.

37. *WDB* 2:959.

38. *WDB* 3:685.

39. Danto, *Nietzsche as Philosopher*, 222.

40. *SW* 3:5, 581.

41. *SW* 2:2, 696.

42. *WDB* 3:291.

43. An interpretation largely indebted to Lange's psychologistic version of Kant's theory of knowledge. See Vaihinger. *The Philosophy of "As-If,"* 330.

44. It has been said that if there is any "absolute" in Nietzsche's thought, it is the idea that he consistently affirmed: that actuality or reality is a dynamic becoming. From the continuous flow of our experiences to the world as a flux of energies described by the sciences, Nietzsche found a "presumably absolute flow of happenings." Morgan, *What Nietzsche Means*, 268.

45. *WDB* 3:371.

46. Lange, *The History of Materialism*, 3:336.

47. *WDB* 3:547–48.

48. Ibid., 502. The "psychological necessity" of believing in causal relations is traced to the inconceivability of events occurring apart from intentions.

49. Ibid., 778.

50. Ibid., 455. Müller-Lauter points out that "inner event" in this note should actually be "*eine innere Welt*" comprised of "a multiplicity of power-wills." *Nietzsche: His Philosophy of Contradictions and the Contradictions of His Philosophy*, 226n. This "inner world" of dynamic power-wills (or "wills to power") not only supports Müller-Lauter's interpretation, but underscores the connection to Boscovich's physics and the anthropomorphic projection at work in the image of "power-wills."

51. Ibid., 778.

52. Morgan, *What Nietzsche Means*, 274n: "Nietzsche uses the terms *Kraft* and *Energie* without apparent distinction." As previously mentioned, there are numerous similarities between many of Nietzsche's speculations on dynamics and contemporary microphysics. When he insists upon the way the "perspective" of each *Machtzentrum* determines the "appearance," the language of physical science is suggested. The notion that each "center of force" has its own "mode of action," its own "mode of resistance," is parallel to the result of Planck's discovery of the elementary quantum of action. "The existence of the elementary quantum of action expresses . . . a new trait of individuality of physical processes . . . the basic assumption of the individuality of processes involved . . . an essential renunciation of the detailed causal connection between physical events. . . ." Niels Bohr, *Atomic Physics and Human Knowledge* (New York: Wiley, 1958), 17–18. In regard to the equation of force and energy, it has been said that, already in the nineteenth century, the term *Kraft* or "force" was being replaced by the term *Energie*. Yehuda Elkana, *The Discovery of the Conservation of Energy* (Cambridge: Harvard University Press, 1974), 129.

53. *WDB* 2:600–601.

54. Ibid., 586. Nietzsche compares scientific interpretations of nature to philological interpretations of a "text." Naturally, he defends his own interpretation: a nature in which there are "relentless" enforcements of "claims to power." His rationale for the transference of a psychological account of our most basic drive for power to the natural world *in toto* lends support to my view that scientific thinking informs his own philosophical interpretation. "So fruitful has been the natural scientific experiment of translating the inanimate (which appears to our senses as lifeless, dead) in terms of movements, etc., that it is also permissible to translate *all* phenomena into the animate in terms of 'our vital functions,' desires, feelings, perceptions, etc." *SW* 12:190.

55. Kaufmann, *Nietzsche*, 267.

56. *WDB* 3:504. It is for this reason that Nietzsche maintains that "*die Mechanistik kann. . .nur Vorgänge beschreiben, nicht erklären*" [mechanics can. . .only describe processes, not explain them].

57. Ibid., 776.

58. Ibid., 391.

59. Morgan, *What Nietzsche Means*, 91.

60. *WDB* 3:685. Walter Kaufmann and R. J. Hollingdale translate *Willens-Punktationen* as "treaty drafts of will." They say that the meaning of this phrase is "unclear" and suggest that "perhaps the point is that the will is not a single entity but more like a constantly shifting federation or alliance of drives." Nietzsche, *The Will to Power*, trans. Walter Kaufmann and R. J. Hollingdale (New York: Vintage Books,

1968), 381n. In my view, "will-points" seems an appropriate translation of this phrase, especially if one places it against the background of Boscovich's conception of "point-centers" or "force-points." Nietzsche tends to equate "power-centers," and "energy-quanta" with "power-will" (*Machtwille*) and "will-quanta" (*Willens-Quanta*). He characterizes mechanics as only "a sign-language for the factical world of combative and conquering will-quanta (*Willens-Quanta*)." *Werke (GOA)* 15:296.

61. *WDB* 2:972–73.

62. Ibid., 959–60. The claim that Nietzsche employs conceptions that he regards as fallacious in the sole argument for the "theory" of the will to power in published works, and that this indicates a fabrication of a mythical/metaphorical idea, was first presented in an article of my own on Boscovich and Nietzsche (circulated in 1980, published in 1981). Later it was included in *Lange and Nietzsche* (1983). To my knowledge, no one had previously called attention to this precise critique of the argument in *Beyond Good and Evil* (Sect. 36) even though Schlechta had expressed surprise at the tentative, hypothetical, and cautious nature of Nietzsche's argument. See Karl Schlechta, *Der Fall Nietzsche* (Munich: Carl Hanser, 1959), 120–22.

63. *WDB* 3:878. All knowledge serves "to 'humanize' the world, i.e., to feel ourselves more and more masters within it—." *WDB* 3:428.

64. *Werke (GOA)* 16:133.

65. *WDB* 3:500.

Chapter Four

1. In his master's thesis, Kierkegaard identified a negative phase in Socrates' thought that he designated "the nihilistic standpoint." It was characterized by a negative use of irony that was directed at the conventional beliefs and values of Athenian society. Even though Kierkegaard regards this negativism as a means to cultivation of a "mastered irony" or the moral transformation of the individual, he was the first to call attention to the presence of an element of nihilism at the center of Socrates' ironic method of critical analysis. See Søren Kierkegaard, *The Concept of Irony*, trans. L. Capel (New York, Harper and Row, 1965). Cf. George J. Stack, *On Kierkegaard: Philosophical Fragments* (Atlantic Highlands, NJ: Humanities Press, 1976), ch. 2, "Kierkegaard and Nihilism."

2. *SW* 3:4, 569–70.

3. It has been shown that Nietzsche read and reread Emerson over a twenty-six year period, underlined numerous passages in his *Essays*, and wrote out excerpts from them prior to composing *Thus Spoke Zarathustra*. Cf. Stanley Hubbard, *Nietzsche und Emerson* (Basel: Verlag für Recht und Gesellschaft, 1958), 195. In his essay "Experience" Emerson emphasized the way temperament conditions our experience of the world and our world-views, the way it "enters fully into the system of illusions and shuts us in a prison of glass which we cannot see." Emerson contended that "we do not see directly, but mediately, and . . . these subject-lenses have a creative power." *The Portable Emerson*, ed. Carl Bode (New York: Viking Press, 1982), 266–90. Emerson was the first to suggest to Nietzsche that an

"optical illusion" influences our experience, our perceptions and our thought. Not only did he stress the power of subjectivity to color our experience and thought, but he practiced, via his various perspectives on nature, experience, and man in his *Essays*, a presentation of different points of view. Cf. George J. Stack, "Nietzsche and Emerson: The Return of the Represssed," *ESQ: A Journal of the American Renaissance* 43: 1–4 (1998): 37–38.

4. *Werke* (*GOA*) 13:81.

5. Ibid., 257.

6. Ibid., 11:139.

7. C. S. Peirce held that in the long run scientific knowledge would converge on truth in the sense of agreement by scientific practitioners. This view was based upon the premise that "Truth is that concordance of an abstract statement with the ideal limit towards which endless investigation would tend to bring scientific belief." *Collected Papers of Charles Sanders Peirce*, ed. C. Hartshorne, P. Weiss, and A. Barks, 8 vols. (Cambridge, MA: Harvard University Press, 1931–58), 5:565. The physicist David Bohm denies such a convergence of consensus in regard to the natural world as a whole. "Disclosing theoretical errors will not lead us through a series . . . of successive approximations that converge on some fixed . . . goal, which constitutes an absolute truth." David Bohm, *Causality and Chance in Modern Physics* (Philadelphia: University of Pennsylvania, 1957), 167.

8. Sarah Kofman, *Nietzsche et la métaphore* (Paris: Payot, 1972), 150.

9. Du Bois-Reymond averred that in regard to the ultimate constituents of the natural world, namely, the nature of matter and force, physical science reaches its limits: "*Ignorabimus*." Emil du Bois-Reymond, *Ueber die Grenzen des Naturerkennens*, 7th ed. (Leipzig: Veit Verlag, 1884).

10. *Werke* (*GOA*) 12:28. Robert Mayer was also the scientist who cemented the idea of the conservation of energy in Nietzsche's mind and led him to apply it to life. In addition, Nietzsche appropriated Mayer's conceptions of the "release" or "discharge" of heat as energy, applying it to his view that all "living beings want to discharge their energy." *Beyond Good and Evil*, sect. 13. Nietzsche had read Mayer's *Mechanik der Wärme* (Mechanics of Heat) and praised the section "*Ueber Auslösung*" as its most valuable part. Letter to Peter Gast, April 16, 1881, *SB* 6:84–85. Elsewhere in his notes Nietzsche asserts that "we are not *fine* enough to see the presumable absolute flow of *events*; the *permanent* is there only by virtue of our course *organs*, which summarize and deposit on surfaces *what* does not exist in that way." *SW* 9:554.

11. Ibid., 14:31.

12. Alexander Nehamas, *Nietzsche: Life as Literature* (Cambridge, MA: Harvard University Press, 1985), 62.

13. *SW* 3:5, 627.

14. F. A. Lange, *The History of Materialism and Criticism of Its Present Importance*, trans. E. C. Thomas, 3 vols. in one, 3rd ed. (London: K. Paul, Trench, Trubner, 1925), 1: 217.

15. Nehamas, *Nietzsche*, 65.

16. *SW* 5:3, 365. Nietzsche turns to this visual metaphor on the question of truth in a note under the heading "the experimenter," *SW* 11:498. Aside from

Emerson's stress upon the optical or subjective factors that influence our perceptions, as well as the "principles of selection" that operate on our interests, on what we accept or reject, Gustav Teichmüller's form of "perspectivism" in his study of the history of metaphysics shaped Nietzsche's thinking. For Teichmuller, each metaphysical system is a perspective on a complex reality and contains partial truths. Nietzsche was quite familiar with two of Teichmüller's works: *Studien zur Geschichte der Begriffe* (Berlin, 1874) and *Die wirkliche und scheinbar Welt* (Berlin, 1882).

17. *Werke (GOA)* 12:38.

18. Lange advises that "exact research must be every philosopher's daily bread." And he avers that the philosopher's task, beside projecting new cultural forms "from the standpoint of the ideal," should be "the ideal colligation of the results" of the independent sciences. Without at least some acquaintance with the results of the sciences, Lange remarks, philosophers tend to produce "all kinds of metaphysical hocus pocus." Lange, *History of Materialism*, 2:347–48.

19. Perhaps Nietzsche may have been familiar with the early expression of this often cited notion in Goethe's writings. "*Das Höchste ware zu begreifen, dass alles Faktische schon Theorie ist*" (The most important point to grasp is that everything factical is already theory). *Goethes Werke*, 10th ed. (Munich, 1982), 12:432.

20. Richard Rorty, "Pragmatism, Relativism, and Irrationalism," in *Consequences of Pragmatism* (Minneapolis: University of Minnesota Press, 1982), 160–75.

21. Anthony Quinton, *The Nature of Things* (London: Routledge, 1973), 119. Nicholas Rescher has argued that the criterion for epistemic justification must be pragmatic in form. See *Methodological Pragmatism* (New York: NYU Press, 1977), 23f. Rescher adopts this view for reasons relevant not only to the "cognitive practice" of a scientifically oriented and technologically advanced civilization, but to an appreciation of Nietzsche's perspectival proposal. That is, any epistemic criterion ultimately has to be based upon practical values because the logico-theoretical requirements for epistemic justifications are so general and minimal as to need pragmatic supplementation. Ultimately, Rescher argues, we justify basic beliefs or "theses" because they receive validation from "the scientific method," a "cognitive method" which "we justify" in reference to "*practical* criteria" (230). For Nietzsche, of course, this would be *one* valuable, fruitful, and impressive perspective, the privileging of which he strenuously opposes.

22. Arthur Danto, *Nietzsche as Philosopher* (New York: Macmillan, 1965), 80.

23. In his preface to *Daybreak* (sect. 3) Nietzsche expresses agreement with Hegel's view that "contradiction moves the world, all things are themselves contradictions." Cf. *Werke* (*GOA*) 9:198. "If contradiction is true being. . . then . . . to understand the world in its deepest meaning is to understand contradiction."

24. Ernst Mach, *Knowledge and Error*, trans. C. M. Williams (Dordrecht: Reidel, 1976), 136–37.

25. For a thorough and subtle analysis of the concept of *Gedenkenexperimenten*, see Roy Sorensen, *Thought Experiments* (New York: Oxford University Press, 1993).

26. *SW* 5:3, 12:364. This crucial passage, which is so often cited in any discussion of perspectival knowing, is not by any means crystal clear. In fact, it is, as I'll attempt to show, characterized by internal tensions.

27. *SW* 12:114.

28. A recent lucid defense of Nietzsche's theory of value as based upon a maximal affirmative attitude towards life that serves as a criterion by which to measure competing values argues that Nietzsche's valuations are cognitively justified and persuasive. However, by accepting the metaphysics of will to power as fundamental, this otherwise insightful set of arguments founders on the reef of a deindividualized *origin* of valuation and plays into the hands of the very human school of "antihumanists." See E. E. Sleinis, *Nietzsche's Revaluation of Values* (Urbana: University of Illinois Press, 1994).

29. *SW* 5:3, 12:364.

30. Ibid.

31. *SW* 5:36, 55.

32. *SW* 5:12, 364–65.

33. In *The Gay Science* Nietzsche lectures "sober realists" on the absence of the "reality" (*Wirklichkeit*) they love. "That mountain there! That cloud there! What is "real" in them? Withdraw the phantasms and the entire human *addition* from them, my prosaic ones!. . . There is no "reality" for us—and none for you either, sober ones . . ." *SW* 3:2, 57:421–22.

34. Alan D. Schrift, *Nietzsche and the Question of Interpretation* (New York and London: Routledge, 1990), 158. Otherwise, Schrift's analyses of interpretation in Nietzsche's thought are lucid and insightful. Johann Hofmann's *Wahrheit, Perspektive, Interpretation: Nietzsche und die philosophische Hermeneutik* (Berlin and New York: de Gruyter, 1994) covers pretty much the same ground Schrift did in an admittedly more expansive way.

35. *SW* 2:20.

36. Schrift, *Nietzsche and the Question of Interpretation*, 158–59.

37. *SW* 2:20. Here Nietzsche's advice for the "free spirit" coincides with what he writes in the *Genealogy* in regard to managing one's positive and negative attitudes and values.

38. Ibid.

39. *SW* 6:352–53.

40. *SW* 3:5, 581–82. The "demand for certainty" is ultimately "the demand for a prop, a support" which reveals an "instinct for weakness."

41. In "Spiritual Laws" Emerson describes mankind as "a method, a progressive arrangement, a selecting principle." We select out of the multiplicity that "sweeps and circles around" us what interests us, what we prize, what charms or intrigues us. *The Portable Emerson*, ed. Carl Bode (New York: Viking Penguin, 1946; repr. 1981), 195.

42. *Werke (GOA)* 13:81.

43. Hofmann, *Wahrheit*, 45.

44. John Richardson, *Nietzsche's System* (Oxford: Oxford University Press, 1996), 268.

45. *Werke (GOA)* 9:201–2.

46. Ibid.

47. Henry Staten, *Nietzsche's Voice* (Ithaca and London: Cornell University Press, 1990), 6.

48. Ibid.

49. *SW* 5:2, 326. In the context of seeking the origins of "bad conscience" Nietzsche refers to the active force of an "instinct for freedom" operative in the early violent creators of organized societies as the same drive that, over time, forged negative ideals and bad conscience. That is, the "*Instinkt der Freiheit* (*in meiner Sprache geredet: der Wille zur Macht*)." Ibid.

50. *SW* 5:42–43, 60.

51. The notion that "Nietzsche's perspectivalism is not just a new truth account . . . but a new truth form . . . because truths are achievable" is questionable on many levels. Certainly, the truth-claims derived from informed perspectives lead to the growth of knowledge Nietzsche desired. At best, a perspective on an event or phenomenon could be considered as a putative truth, but certainly not an unambiguous truth. Perspectivalism is more a means to *knowledge* than a "new truth form." See Richardson, *Nietzsche's System*, 263. Nietzsche makes himself quite clear on this point in a note from 1887. He asserts that "die *Werthschätzung* 'ich glaube, dass das und das so ist' als Wesen der '*Wahrheit*' . . . das etwas fur wahr gehalten werden *muss* ist nothwendig, *nicht*, dass etwas wahr ist." (The *valuation* "I believe that this and that is so" is the essence of "*truth*" . . . that something *must* be taken to be true is necessary, *not* that something is *true*). *SW* 12:352.

52. Peter Pütz, *Friedrich Nietzsche* (Stuttgart, 1967), 22. What Pütz means by this is the extension of perspective to *all* entities. This is a position that developed over a fairly long period of time and no doubt emerged in Nietzsche's thought in response to a spate of works in German thought (appearing between the 1860s and late 1870s) that put forward various panpsychistic interpretations of actuality. The original source of such speculative metaphysical theories was the monadology of Leibniz, which postulated spiritual substances or monads as the essential reality underlying what we perceive as "well-founded phenomena." Monads were said to "express" the world from their individual perspectives. There are echoes of this metaphysics in the works of Herbart, Fechner, Lotze, Ueberweg, and in the experimental notes of Nietzsche in the late 1880s included in the non-book, *The Will to Power*.

53. See George J. Stack, "Nietzsche's Earliest Essays," *Philosophy Today* 37:2 (Summer 1993): 153–69.

54. Letter to Erwin Rohde, end of January and February 15, 1870, *SB* 3:95. By interrelating scientific, aesthetic/artistic, and philosophical perspectives Nietzsche illustrates the fruitful, as well as the dissonant, effects that can be generated by relating different knowledge-perspectives.

55. D. F. Krell, "Analysis," in Martin Heidegger, *Nietzsche*, trans. Frank A. Capuzzi (San Francisco: Harper & Row, 1982), 4:269.

56. Lange, *History of Materialism*, 1:217. Nietzsche reprises Lange's observation when he says "I think that today at least we are far from the laughable arrogance of decreeing from our corner that it is only from this corner that perspectives are *permitted*. The world has become '*infinite*' for us once again: insofar as we cannot reject the possibility that *it may include infinite interpretations*." Even the speculation in the same passage concerning the possibility of beings with radically different ways of experiencing time is analogous to Lange's suggestion that there may be beings capable of spatial intuitions of more or less than three dimensions. *SW* 3:374, 626–27.

57. *SW* 9:563.

58. *Werke (GOA)* 13:69.

59. *SW* 12:209. "Das Gleichmachen ist dasselbe, was die Einverleibung der angeeigneten Materie in die Amoebe ist."

60. *SW* 11:687–88. In later notes the neglect of the pre-organic domain is lamented and it is suggested, in an atypical aside, that from a certain point of view it might be valued higher than life itself. *Werke* (*GOA*) 12:229.

61. *SB* 2:121–22.

62. *SW* 11:536.

63. Heidegger, *Nietzsche*, 1:197.

64. *Werke* (*GOA*) 13:227–28.

65. *SW* 11:503. "Die Fähigkeit zum Schaffen (Gestalten Erfinden Erdicten) ist ihre Grundfähigkeit."

66. *SW* 11:503.

67. *Werke* (*GOA*) 13:88.

68. *Gesammelte Werke*, 23 vols. (Munich: MusarionVerlag, 1920), 4:300. It is odd that Nietzsche refers to "actual time" since his phenomenology of time-experience stresses variations in tempo and his speculation about differing modes of experience of time in other forms of life seem to commit him to the idea of the subjectivity of temporality. At one point, he refers to the alteration of the sense of time under the influence of hashish or at the moment of a life-threatening situation. He claims that under such conditions "in a second on our watch, thousands of thoughts can be thought, thousands of experiences can be had." *SW* 11:653.

69. *SW* 11:506.

70. Although defending a modified or pragmatic realism, Rescher, a lucid proponent of scientific rationality, is sensitive to the fact that the gap between what we conceive the world to be and what it actually is like "is absolute and insuperable. . . . We have no way of coming to grips with reality apart from the . . . inherently error-prone, empirical and inductive process of constructing our 'picture of the world.' The *character* of the world is no doubt independent of our cognitive devising, but its *characterization* emphatically is not." Nicholas Rescher. *Empirical Inquiry* (London: Athlone, 1982), 259. Since Rescher discusses scientific truth and scientific knowledge, what he proclaims would, *a fortiori*, apply to all other truth-claims and knowledge-claims.

71. Cf. Maudemarie Clark, *Nietzsche on Truth and Philosophy* (Cambridge: Cambridge University Press, 1990), ch. 2. Clark offers fine discussions of a number of theories of truth, as well as running dialogues with Nietzsche commentators, but Nietzsche's criticisms of truth and his form of perspectival knowing are presented in the terms and formulations of others so often that *his* accounts are sometimes obscured or misrepresented.

72. Alois Riehl, *Friedrich Nietzsche: Der Kunstler und der Denker* (Stuttgart, 1898), 16.

73. *SW* 11:688. The process of "making-the-same" is presumably an instinctive or unconscious process that has been genetically perpetuated by those forms of life capable of such constructively erroneous activities. The critique of languages as conceptual schemata separated from the world by the dualism of scheme and "uninterpreted reality" presented by Davidson does not consider a possibility such as Nietzsche puts forward. That is, that there is a preconceptual, prelinguistic scheme

immanent in perspectival perception. See Donald Davidson. "On the Very Idea of a Conceptual Schema," in *Post-Analytic Philosophy*, ed. J. Rajchman and C. West (New York: Columbia University Press, 1985), 129–43. Relying on Alfred Tarski's Convention T (as Clark at one point does in her Nietzsche-book), Davidson actually winds up in a position virtually as skeptical as Nietzsche's. "Nothing," he writes, "no thing, makes sentences and theories true: not experience, not surface irritations, nor the world, can make a sentence true. . . . The sentence 'My skin is warm' is true if and only if my skin is warm. Here there is no reference to a fact, a world, an experience, or a piece of evidence" (139). Tarski's Convention T is a test of a theory of truth: a satisfactory theory of truth for a given language entails that a sentence (s) in that language (L) must conform to the theorem: "s" is true if and only if S. Thus, "Iron is hard" is true if and only if iron is hard. Tarski presented a formal definition of truth for *formal* languages. He provided no description of nor informal definition of natural languages. This semantic theory of truth yields at best an analysis of a formal higher-order metalanguage that preserves the term "true" by imprisoning it in a labyrinth of a formal theory cut off from the everyday concept of and use of *true*. It becomes a form of semantic antirealism because it excludes the possibility of uttering or writing a sentence that even professes or claims to describe any independent reality-in-itself. Clark misses this point when she argues that the relations of correspondence between beliefs and the world "amount to no more than the equivalence principle" (derived from Tarski's analysis). That is, "Given the world's independent existence, 'snow is white' corresponds to the world [*sic*] if snow is white." Clark, *Nietzsche on Truth and Philosophy*, 39–40. For interesting and subtle treatments of the above issues, see Laurence Bonjour, *The Structure of Empirical Knowledge* (Cambridge, MA: Harvard University Press), 1985, ch. 8, Garth Hallet, *Language and Truth* (New Haven and London: Yale University Press), 1988, ch. 13, and Michael Dummett. *Truth and Other Enigmas* (Cambridge, MA: Harvard University Press, 1978).

74. Daniel Conway. "The Eyes Have It: Perspectives and Affective Investment," *ISP* 23/2 (1991): 104–5.

75. Nietzsche records in his notes his "Deep aversion against finally resting in any total view of the world; magic charm of the opposite way of thinking; refusal to allow oneself to be deprived of the enigmatic character of the world." *SW* 12:142.

76. Conway, "The Eyes Have It," 105–6.

77. Norwood R. Hanson. *Observation and Explanation* (New York: Harper and Row, 1971), 5.

78. *SW* 12:294. "*Methodisch*: der Werth der *inneren* und der *auBeren Phanomenonologie*." Outer or external phenomenology is considered more valuable than internal phenomenology because "the phenomena of the *sensory* world [are] a hundred times more complex, finer, and more accurately observed. External phenomenology gives us by far the richest material and provides the greatest strength of observation, while internal phenomena are difficult to grasp and more transmuted by errors (inner processes are essentially *error-generating*) since life is only possible under the direction of such constricting perspective-creating powers."

79. *SW* 9:625.

80. *SW* 12:396.

81. Daniel Beazeale, ed. and trans., *Philosophy and Truth: Selections from Nietzsche's Notebooks of the Early 1870's* (Atlantic Highlands: Humanities Press, 1979), 32.

82. Thomas Kuhn, "Reflection on My Critics," in I. Lakatos and A. Musgrave, eds., *Criticism and the Growth of Knowledge* (Cambridge: Cambridge University Press, 1970), 266–67. Paul Feyerabend's formulations of his version of the incommensurability thesis are found in "Explanation, Reduction, and Empiricism," in H. Feigl and G. Maxwell, eds., *Scientific Explanation, Space, and Time,* vol. 3 of Minnesota Studies in the Philosophy of Science (Minneapolis: University of Minnesota Press, 1962) and in "Problems of Empiricism," in R. G. Colodny, ed., *Beyond the Edge of Certainty* (Englewood Cliffs, NJ: Prentice-Hall, 1965).

83. *SW* 11:608. This passage in notes from 1885 is revealing because it is one of the rare instances in which Nietzsche refers to *Reiz* or a "stimulus" or "irritation" we receive or accept. Of course, he quickly points out that we are active in the creative construction of *what* the stimulus is and means in "our world." Thus, there is an actuality which acts upon us—a "becoming," a "chaos," or an "indescribably complex" interaction of forces—but one which we continually convert into forms, structures, patterns, and "arranged schemata."

84. Richardson, *Nietzsche's System*, 35.

85. See *Werke und Briefe. Historische-kritische Gesamtausgabe* (Munich: Beck Verlag, 1933–42), 3:387. The first line of *Morphologie* is quoted in an entry from 1867–68 (3:376): "Every living being is not a single entity, but a plurality, even insofar as it appears to us as an individual, it still remains a collection of living beings."

86. Although Clark's *Nietzsche on Truth and Philosophy* contains an interesting discussion of perspectivalism, it focuses on a dialogue with a few select commentators rather than examining Nietzsche's numerous notes on his method. Moreover, at one point she refers to value-judgments as if they were the same as epistemic perspectives (139–41) whereas Nietzsche's critique of "tables of values" is based on *criteria* for his value-ranking that are sprinkled throughout his published and unpublished writings. Finally, Clark seems to adopt Magnus's prohibition about the use of *Nachlass* materials and thereby bypasses Nietzsche's own terms.

87. *SW* 11:181. Such perspectives serve the *Erhaltung* or "conservation" of individuals or groups. Beyond the vast multiplicity of perspectives of individuals, Nietzsche seems to suggest that there is a relative *congruence* within a state, society, culture, ethnic-group, church, or system of belief at certain periods of history even though there is no universal consistency or agreement within macrosocial organizations. If this is plausible, then Nietzsche, in this respect and others as well, anticipates Foucault's conception of dominant knowledge-frameworks (*episteme*) prevailing at particular stages of history. This relationship between Nietzsche and Foucault is touched upon in chapter 6, "The Structuralist Perspective."

88. *SW* 9:500.

89. Richard Schacht, *Making Sense of Nietzsche* (Urbana: University of Illinois Press, 1995), 246.

90. *SW* 11:506.

91. *SW* 9:570. The implication being that if our cognition accurately depicted actuality, it would encounter a chaos, a chaotic process. A genuine chaos would be

worldless and every attempt to elucidate a world-structure would be a perspective. Nietzsche's paradoxical problem is to indicate manifestations of chaos without claiming positive (perspectival/contextual) knowledge of what they disclose. The most typical way he does this is to rely on scientific depictions of nature that disclose the "indescribable complexity" of the natural process. Nietzsche's chaos theory may be considered a global perspectival interpretation suggested by a number of perspectives in biology, physics, chemistry, physiology, etc., and serving as a metaphoric image of a cosmic totality.

92. Although Rorty introduces Nietzsche as an "edifying" thinker, there are many aspects of his extensive analysis of epistemological issues that touch upon Nietzsche's analyses of truth and knowledge and he arrives at an anti-foundationalism anticipated by Nietzsche. See Richard Rorty, *Philosophy and the Mirror of Nature* (Princeton: Princeton University Press, 1979), chs. 3–6. And the critique of the "mirroring" of the world, nature, or reality recalls Nietzsche's remarks on the evolution of knowledge towards completeness. Our "image of the world . . . is only a *reflection*." The "effort to make the mirror ever more adequate" is found in the sciences that seek a "gradual liberation from what is all-too-anthropomorphic." Despite this effort, we cannot transcend our humanization of the world: "*the entire world is* . . . for us . . . a human being." *SW* 7:468–69. Clark acknowledges Nietzsche's anti-foundationalism, but eschews his "falsification thesis" and segregates elements in his epistemic remarks that are linked by him. She argues that if "knowledge is interpretation," then it "amounts to anti-foundationalism." But then it is said that designating "knowledge interpretative differs from calling it perspectival. . . ." Clark, *Nietzsche on Truth and Philosophy*, 131. For Nietzsche, there is no privileged foundation for knowledge *because* of alternative "value-interpretations" expressed in a multiplicity of viable, plausible, or ostensibly valid perspectives. Clark frequently criticizes Nietzsche's "falsification thesis" (which is fundamental to his analysis of knowledge) and tries to separate it from *his* version of anti-foundationalism. The sciences, as well as philosophy, are confronted by the absence of a discernible point at which subjectivity (as Nietzsche understands it) fades and objectivity begins. "Science takes away foundations without providing a replacement . . . science has put us in the position of having to live without foundations. It was shocking when Nietzsche said this, but today it is commonplace [in] . . . *our* historical position . . ." Hilary Putnam. *The Many Faces of Realism* (La Salle: Open Court, 1987), 28–29.

93. *SW* 7:494. The process of simplification in common perceptual judgments inevitably renders them "anthropomorphically colored" (ibid.). Moreover, as a note from 1872–73 declares, "All natural science is nothing but an attempt to understand mankind, the anthropological: more precisely, an attempt to return always to the human by way of the most monstrous detours." *SW* 7:449.

94. *SW* 12:315.

95. *Werke* (*GOA*) 13:169. After asserting that "*the true world of causes* [origins or grounds] *is hidden from us*" and is "indescribably complicated," Nietzsche accurately points out that physiology "yields a concept of indescribable complication." *SW* 11:434.

96. *SW* 11:157. In this note "*Seh-Winkel*" [angle of vision] is tantamount to what is more typically called perspective. That a deindividualized preorganic

entity is said to be imbued with "spirituality" coincides with Nietzsche's critique of materialism and the positivist "philosophy of actuality" that was beginning to dominate German universities in the 1880s. The coordinated movements of organisms express a spiritual activity, a "spiritual occurrence." Ibid. The mechanistic explanation of organic development and behavior is construed as a "sign-language for the internal factical world of combative and conquering will-quanta." *Werke* (*GOA*) 15:296. This hypothetical reductive analysis lends support to my view that Nietzsche sought to relate (analogically) Boscovich's physical-mathematically theory of "point-centers" to the metaphoric notion of wills to power or "will-points."

97. *Werke* 16:60. Cf. *The Will to Power,* trans. Walter Kaufmann and R. J. Hollingdale (New York: Vintage Books, 1968), 556.

98. *Werke* (*GOA*) 14:34.

99. Ibid., 13:21.

100. Ibid.

101. Ibid.

102. Ibid., 13:48.

103. *SW* 12:353. Cf. *The Will to Power*, 560.

104. *SW* 5:3, 12. As we've seen, this is more complicated than it may appear, especially since our "pros and cons" are subject to change based upon life-experiences, stages of life, conditions of existence, etc.

105. Danto, *Nietzsche as Philosopher*, 80.

106. Ibid. Heidegger claims that Nietzsche is "the last metaphysician" who presents us with a metaphysics to end all metaphysics, which is variously described as "complete nihilism," anthropocentric subjectivism, a value-thinking construction of a theory of "subjective" will to power. Even though Nietzsche refers to his "philosophies" and practices "Jesuitism" in his dialectical presentation of different perspectives, Heidegger finds his true philosophy in his notes and insists that Nietzsche proposed a philosophy of Being. In this respect, Heidegger often does violence to Nietzsche's texts and subtleties.

107. *Werke* (*GOA*) 15:434. Although Nietzsche does manage to carry out "the naturalization of man," the "dehumanization of nature" was a phase of his experimental thought that disclosed a nihilistic landscape that violated his own conception of knowledge as humanization and was negated in its original form and presented in an altered form in his metaphorical image of wills to power, one that interprets nature in terms of human analogy.

108. Benjamin Whorf, *Language, Thought, and Reality,* ed. J. B. Carol (New York: MIT Press, 1956).

109. *SW* 13:373–74.

110. What are called "bodies" in the notes from the late 1880s are more or less what Leibniz had already described as "well-founded phenomena." Unlike Leibniz, Nietzsche denies that the monad-like centers of force are substances. In a letter to Koselitz (March 20, 1882) he says that "If anything is well-refuted it is the prejudice of matter: and not . . . by an idealist, but by a mathematician—by Boscovich. He and Copernicus are the greatest opponents of visual appearance: since him *there is no longer matter*. . . . He has thought the atomistic theory to its end. . . . there is nothing other than force!" *SB* 6:183.

111. *Werke (GOA)* 15:56. Cp. *SW* 12:343. "Absolute *exclusion* of *mechanism* and *matter*, both only expressions of lower stages, the least spiritual form of affect ('the will to power')."

112. George Morgan, *What Nietzsche Means* (New York: Harper and Row, 1965), 260.

113. Richard Schacht, "Nietzsche and Nihilism," in *Nietzsche*, ed. R. Solomon (New York: Doubleday Anchor, 1973), 68. Schacht replicates this understanding of Nietzsche in a recent work even though he now refers to his "unorthodox world-interpretation" rather than to his "unorthodox metaphysical world-view." Richard Schacht, *Making Sense of Nietzsche* (Chicago and Urbana: University of Illinois Press, 1995), 43.

114. *Werke (GOA)* 12:240. Cf. *SW* 10:495. The attribution of a will to power to the underlying process that guides the "inorganic world" (and thereby indicates that there is no nonorganic or "inorganic" realm) reveals a close relation between anthropomorphic projection and the hypothetical posit of "will to power." Cp. *SW* 11:504.

115. Ibid., 13:228.

116. Ibid., 16:154. It has been said in this regard that the "renunciation of metaphor does not prevent Nietzsche himself from outlining a metaphoric-anthropomorphic world-picture." Klaus Spiekermann, *Naturwissenschaft als subjeklöse Macht?* (Berlin and New York: de Gruyter, 1992), 71n37. First of all, Nietzsche does not renounce metaphor; he merely disguises it. That Nietzsche presents an anthropomorphic and metaphoric picture of actuality was identified by Sarah Kofman in a literary context and by me in a scientific context some time before this observation.

117. *SW* 11:543.

118. Cf. George J. Stack. *Nietzsche and Emerson* (Athens, Ohio: Ohio University Press, 1993).

119. Of the growing number of studies of Nietzsche's psychology, the following are informative and insightful: Jacob Golumb, *Nietzsche's Enticing Psychology of Power* (Ames: Iowa State University Press, 1987); Graham Parkes, *Composing the Soul: Reaches of Nietzsche's Psychology* (Chicago: University of Chicago Press, 1994); Ronald Lehrer, *Nietzsche's Presence in Freud's Life and Thought* (Albany: SUNY Press, 1995); Paul-Laurent Assoun's *Freud et Nietzsche* (Paris: Universitaires de France, 1980). Cf. Paul-Laurent Assoun, *Freud and Nietzsche*, trans. Richard L. Collier (London: Athlone Press: 2000).

120. *SW* 1:760.

121. The underlying evolved and sustained characteristic of humanity is a *psychological* will to power. "Our intellect, our will, even our sensation are dependent upon our *valuations*, these correspond to our drives and their conditions of existence. Our drives are reducible to the *will to power*. The will to power is the last fact we find refuge in." *SW* 11:661. The conclusion refers to the psychological conception of human beings, not all actuality.

122. Heidegger, *Nietzsche*, 1:620f. Others have argued for the "aptness" of Nietzsche's claims about actuality and that knowledge for him pertains to doing "justice" to something in one's interpretation of it (even though Nietzsche tells us that all strong perspectives are "unjust" by virtue of exclusion). What is "apt" (*aptus* = "fitted") depends upon historical, cultural, and conceptual frameworks. In

Nietzsche's case, the discourse of the sciences influences what he considers apt. Descriptively, the aptness of a judgment is a contextual issue.

123. *Werke* (*GOA*) 13:72. Among many instances of probable, syndromic reasoning, the following instantiates Nietzsche's typical *modus operandi*. "Everything material is a kind of movement-symptom for an unknown event: everything conscious and felt is, again, a symptom of something unknown—The world gives itself to our understanding this way in terms of these two aspects and can still have many other symptoms. Movements and thoughts are symptoms, cravings are proof to us of something behind both, and the fundamental craving is the will to power—'Spirit in itself' is nothing, just as movement in itself 'is nothing'." *SW* 12:25.

Chapter Five

1. R. E. Ornstein, *The Psychology of Consciousness* (San Francisco: Viking, 1972), 17. See *WDB* 3:309–32; Nietzsche, *The Will to Power,* trans. Walter Kaufmann and R. J. Hollingdale (New York: Vintage Books, 1968), 278–80. See also: William F. Salter, *Nietzsche the Thinker* (New York: Holt, 1917), 50–51.

2. The physicist Louis de Broglie remarks that "our coarse senses and our imperfect experimental methods only allow us to establish general phenomena through cooperation of an immense number of elementary phenomena, the inextricable complexity of which we are not capable of following." *Physics and Microphysics*, trans. M. Davidson (New York: Harper, 1960), 196.

3. Louis de Broglie, though sensitive to the evolutionary account of our cognitive adaptation to our environment over a long period of time, states that our capacity to adapt to our world suggests an "analogy of structure" between the world and our mind such that we have survived. Perhaps we have survived because we are "capable of understanding certain of the rules which govern the succession of natural phenomena" to the point of utilizing them to our advantage. *Physics and Microphysics*, 209. A sympathetic account of the "falsification" of our world could emphasize this as a creative, constructive process that does yield genuine knowledge (as redefined) that is adequate for survival, but nonetheless not an authentic depiction of actuality. Such a defense is embedded in prior arguments.

4. *The Will to Power,* 282–83. In Rudolf Carnap's systemic elucidation of the structure of the world he defends a detailed account of the logical "construction" of a world that is a conceptual domain of "objects and quasi-objects," not a theory of actuality (*Wirklichkeit*) or of the "external world." Neither "logical" nor "mathematical objects" are actually objects in the sense of real objects (objects of the empirical sciences). Logic itself "*consists solely of conventions* concerning the use of symbols, and of tautologies. . . . [T]he symbols of logic . . . do not designate objects." Rudolf Carnap, *The Logical Structure of the World*, trans. Rolf George (Berkeley: University of California Press, 1967), 178. Later Carnap points out that the "concept of reality" (independent of any cognitive consciousness) is a metaphysical question that falls outside rational science (282–83).

5. Ibid., 279. Nietzsche implies that a transfer of logical structure to the phenomenal world supports a metaphysics of essentialism, precisely the interpretation he opposes in so many ways.

6. Ibid., 280.

7. Cp. W. V. O. Quine's view that "Physical objects are postulated entities which round out and simplify our account of the flux of experience." "On What There Is," in *From a Logical Point of View* (New York: Harper & Row, 1963), 18. What Quine calls "cultural posits" or "myths" in "Two Dogmas of Empiricism" (ibid., 44) correspond to some of the concepts Nietzsche classifies as "fictions."

8. *The Will to Power*, 288.

9. Ibid., 282.

10. *SW* 3:3, 111.

11. Hans Vaihinger, *The Philosophy of "As-If,"* trans. C. K. Ogden (London: Routledge and Kegan Paul, 1924), viii.

12. *The Will to Power*, 277.

13. Ibid., 302–3. *SW* 12:353.

14. *The Will to Power*, 296.

15. Ibid., 273. Ernst Mach offered a similar psychologistic account of causality and accepted it only as a working assumption. Thus, it is held that "all forms of the law of causality spring from subjective impulses which nature is by no means compelled to satisfy." Ernst Mach, *The Science of Mechanics*, trans. T. J. McCormack (La Salle, IL: Open Court, 1942), 607. The first German edition of this influential work, *Die Mechanik in Ihre Entwicklung Historisch – Kritisch Darstellt*, was published in 1883. Nietzsche received a copy of one of Mach's works (probably *The Science of Mechanics*) that had the inscription "for Herrn Prof. Dr. Nietzsche respectfully yours Ernst Mach." Alwin Mittasch, *Friedrich Nietzsche als Naturphilosoph* (Stuttgart: A Kröner, 1952), 367.

16. *The Will to Power*, 306.

17. Ibid., 338. The emphasis upon the multiplicity within apparent unities was conveyed to Nietzsche, as previously noted, by a passage from Goethe's *Morphology*: "Every living being," Goethe says, "is not a single thing, but a plurality." Cited in Freidrich A. Lange, *The History of Materialism and Criticism of Its Present Importance*, trans. E. C. Thomas, 3 vols. in one, 3rd ed. (London: K. Paul, Trench, Trubner, 1925), 3:38.

18. *The Will to Power*, 270. For an extensive analysis of the self as multiplicity see: Graham Parks, *Composing the Soul: Reaches of Nietzsche's Psychology* (Chicago: University of Chicago Press, 1994).

19. *The Will to Power*, 268.

20. Ibid., 303.

21. Ibid., 280.

22. Ibid., 312. This reference to a change of "tempo of becoming" is linked to the possibility that the "*objective* character of things may be a consequence of our subjective response to" what changes slowly. "That is, we experience such gradual changes as relatively 'objectively' enduring." If so, perhaps what we call (or experience as) "objective is only a false kind-concept and opposition *within* the subjective." *SW* 12: 353.

23. *WDB* 3:769.

24. Arthur Danto, *Nietzsche as Philosopher* (New York: Macmillan, 1965), 78.

25. *SW* 2:1, 30–31.

26. I. Scheffler, "The Fictionalist View of Scientific Theories," in *Readings in the Philosophy of Science*, ed. B. A. Brody (Englewood Cliffs, NJ: Prentice-Hall, 1970), 214.

27. *SW* 3:112, 473.

28. *SW* 5:14, 28.

29. *The Will to Power*, 270. Here Nietzsche seems to follow Ernst Mach's refusal to admit the existence of atoms. Mach characterized atoms as "mental artifices" or "things of thought" which serve at best as "provisional" postulates until "a satisfactory substitute" is found. *The Science of Mechanics*, 588–89.

30. Despite this critique of atomistic theory, Nietzsche, for a time, entertained the concept of human beings as atomic systems. "Man is an assemblage of atoms, completely dependent, in his movements, on all the forces of the universe, their distributions and modifications, and at the same time, like each atom, unpredictable." *Werke (GOA)* 12:202.

31. *Werke* (*GOA*) 12:33.

32. *SW* 2:19, 41. Kant's point is valid, Nietzsche avers, in regard to our "*concept of nature*" which, in effect, is "(nature = world as representation, that is as error) . . . the summation of a great many errors of the understanding" (ibid.). In 1874 Emile Boutroux offered an interesting argument for the contingent character of the laws of nature. He argued that the necessity embodied in the laws of nature is questionable "if the given world were to manifest a certain degree of genuinely irreducible contingency, there would be grounds for thinking that the laws of nature are not self-sufficient [necessary]." Boutroux alludes to the ontological contingency of events in opposition to the assumption of universal laws. *The Contingency of the Laws of Nature*, trans. Fred Rothwell (Chicago and London: Open Court, 1920), 6.

33. Mach, *Science of Mechanics*, 589.

34. For an interesting account of the relation among Berkeley, Mach, and Einstein, see Karl Popper, "A Note on Berkeley as Precursor of Mach and Einstein," in *Berkeley's Principles of Human Knowledge: Critical Studies*, ed. G. Engle and G. Taylor (Belmont, CA: Wadsworth, 1968), 90–100.

35. *The Will to Power*, 276.

36. Mach, *Science of Mechanics*, 589.

37. Ibid.

38. W. V. O. Quine, "On Simple Theories of a Complex World," in *Probability, Confirmation and Simplicity*, ed. M. Forster and M. Martin (New York: Odyssey Press, 1966), 250–51.

39. Ibid. Aside from the perceptual basis of our tendency to select out what is simple, the application of the principle of simplicity to theory selection has often been questioned by philosophers of science. It has been pointed out that even though this principle "is of central importance for the epistemology of the natural sciences" it is not accessible to "objective formulation." Hermann Weyl, *Philosophy of Natural Science* (Princeton: Princeton University Press, 1959), 155. Cp. Karl Popper, *Conjectures and Refutations* (New York: Harper and Row, 1965), 61, 241.

40. M. Bunge, "The Weight of Simplicity in Scientific Theories," in Forster and Martin (eds.), *Probability, Confirmation and Simplicity*, 289–99. Pierre Duhem

maintained that physical theories do not teach us anything about the nature of reality. Rather, they provide a system of mathematical propositions that seek to represent as simply and as completely as possible a domain of experimental laws. Every law of physics is relative and provisional because it is an approximate law that cannot, in a strict sense, be true or false. Pierre Duhem, *The Aim and Structure of Physical Theory*, trans. P. P. Wiener (Princeton: Princeton University Press, 1954), 165–79.

41. Mary Hesse, *Models and Analogies in Science* (Notre Dame: University of Notre Dame Press, 1966), 171.

42. Ibid., 167. Richard Rorty has extended the metaphorical aspect of scientific and philosophic thought (via discourses, various vocabularies and metaphor-sets) to the point at which it approaches Nietzsche's insights in regard to this issue. See *Philosophy and the Mirror of Nature* (Princeton: Princeton University Press, 1979). Nietzsche naturally expresses this view more forcefully. "[T]here is no 'real' *and no genuine knowledge without metaphor . . . . Knowledge* is nothing but working with the most favored metaphors" (*SW* 7:491).

43. Hesse, *Models and Analogies in Science*, 165.

44. S. Toulmin, *Foresight and Understanding* (New York: Harper and Row, 1961), 101. Such world-orientations, whether based on commonsense beliefs or scientific preconceptions, include a strong conventionalist component. Aside from various framing presuppositions which support world-orientations, the constructs used in world-orientations vary. The invention of a given *construct* (e.g., physical object, meson, geometric forms, numbers, etc.) does not provide any assurance that it is scientifically acceptable or part of reality. Henry Margenau. *The Nature of Physical Reality* (New York: McGraw-Hill, 1950), 72–73.

45. Mach, *Science of Mechanics*, 578–79.

46. Nicholas Rescher, *Methodological Pragmatism* (New York: Oxford University Press, 1977), 303–4. In later works, Rescher (though defending a form of critical-pragmatic-realism) emphasizes "our truth," "our reality" and "our science" in recognition that "we cannot even lay claim to a definitively correct and final picture of reality." Nicholas Rescher, *Empirical Inquiry* (London: Athlone, 1982), 258. See also *A Useful Inheritance: Evolutionary Aspects of the Theory of Knowledge* (Savage, MD: Rowan and Littlefield, 1990). There are a growing number of Nietzschean echoes related to our comprehension of "the world" in recent American philosophy.

47. C. I. Lewis, "Alternative Systems of Logic," *The Monist* 42 (1932): 484. Again, for Nietzsche, our logical structuring of experience is a consequence of previously unconscious processes of abstraction and simplification that begin in sensory experience, continue in the further abstraction of cognition, and are expressed in language for the sake of rapid communication. The entire knowing process is pervaded with psychic needs and practical (perspectival) interests.

48. *The Will to Power*, 346.

49. *SW* 5:36, 54. This priority of the bodily self as a dynamic system of interacting "drives" or functions is stressed in *Thus Spoke Zarathustra*. "The body is a great reason, a plurality with one sense. . . . Behind your thoughts and feelings. . .there stands a mighty ruler . . . whose name is self. . . . He is your body." *SW* 4:1, 39–40. Eric Blondel argues that Nietzsche's description of the body is

metaphoric in order to avoid metaphysical claims and to include what many earlier thinkers bracketed—the importance of the bodily subject. Eric Blondel, *Nietzsche: the Body and Culture*, trans. S. Hand (Stanford: Stanford University Press, 1991).

50. *The Will to Power*, 271.

51. Ibid., 366. This formulation is *not* an advance on scientific accounts of change in terms of causality in macrophysical alteration (which it resembles). And it seems to undermine Nietzsche's preference for the *interaction* of "forces" or "powers." The metaphor of "encroachment" (i.e., intruding, usurping the territory of another, making inroads on something else) may be appropriate to one mode of change, but cannot cover many instances of qualitative or quantitative change. It does not fit easily with microphysical theory or the "cooperation" of chemical elements in the formation of compounds. In regard to the latter, as Norwood Hanson said, "The basic concept of microphysics is *interaction*." Norwood R. Hanson, *Patterns of Discovery* (London: Cambridge University Press, 1969), 122.

52. *The Will to Power*, 344.

53. Ibid., 342.

54. Ibid., 339. Specifically referring to atomistic theories, Nietzsche cites perception and psychic projections, as well as the "extended senses" of measuring instruments as subjective fictions. What "mechanists" forget is the perspective of the theorist and the interaction of the "perspective-setting force" of the observer and the observed—something stressed by many recent microphysical theorists.

55. Ibid., 336.

56. As early as 1872–73 Nietzsche remarked that "*Man* as the measure of all things is. . .the basic thought of science. Every law of nature is ultimately a sum of anthropomorphic relations [and]. . .their expression in numerical formulas is a *metaphora*. . ." *SW* 7:494.

57. *The Will to Power*, 335.

58. Ibid., 334.

59. Walter Kaufmann, *Nietzsche*, 3rd rev. ed. (New York: Viking, 1968), 262–63. Danto speculated about the possible scientific confirmation of the theory of relations of dynamic quanta. Danto, *Nietzsche as Philosopher*, 22. In the same context, however, he correctly sees that Nietzsche cannot be making truth-claims about "reality" because he has said that the sciences really tell us nothing about reality.

60. *SW* 5:13, 28.

61. Ibid., 36, 54.

62. R. J. Hollingdale, *Nietzsche* (London: Routledge and Kegan Paul, 1973), 122.

63. *SW* 12:384. Occasional claims that Nietzsche was a materialist profoundly misunderstand his thought. Although Boscovich's influence was delayed, he influenced major physicists in the nineteenth century and anticipated some central conceptions in twentieth-century physics, "advancing far beyond Newton towards the twentieth-century." See "Boscovich's Atomism," in *Roger Joseph Boscovich*, ed. L. L. Whyte (New York: Fordham University Press, 1961), 102–26.

64. *Werke* (*GOA*), 21:33.

65. *SW* 12:385. In his careful and faithful interpretation of Nietzsche's thought (especially in his later notes), Müller-Lauter accurately sees the reduction of actuality

to "wills to power" and touches upon the relation of this notion to science (e.g., the biological theories of Wilhelm Roux). What he did not see is the strong derivation of Nietzsche's nonmetaphysical, metaphorical image of wills to power from Boscovich's theory of "force-centers" and "point-centers." See George J. Stack, *Lange and Nietzsche* (Berlin and New York: deGruyter, 1983), ch. 9, "A Force-Point World." See also Wolfgang Müller-Lauter, *Nietzsche: His Philosophy of Contradictions and the Contradictions of His Philosophy*, trans. David J. Parent (Urbana and Chicago: University of Illinois Press, 1999), chs. 8 and 9.

66. *SW* 12:305. This is the phase of de-anthropomorphism or the "*Entmenschung der Natur.*" It is an image of a "dehumanized" nature that is displayed for consideration and then subjected to a Hegelian dialectical process of "self-suppression" in the metaphorical theory of wills to power. The physicist and philosopher of science C. F. Weizsacker has said that the "position of natural philosophers has not been better described or understood than as Nietzsche has described it." *Wahrnehmung der Neuzeit* (Munich and Vienna, 1983), 103. He refers with approval to Nietzsche's claim that "after the dehumanization of nature and then the naturalization of men have we attained the pure concept of nature." *SW* 9:525.

67. Instrumental fictionalism is often associated with conventionalism or antirealism. Nietzsche's position in regard to scientific knowledge is at times conventionalist at others antirealist. He would probably agree that there is no higher (ontological) truth and no extra-theoretic "truth" uncovered in science. He is not a realist according to the following definition. Marx Wartofsky, "How to Be a Good Realist," in *Beyond Reason*, ed. G. Munevar (Amsterdam: Kluwer, 1991), 30. That is, "realism demands. . .an objective world ontologically independent of cognition or of consciousness" whereas antirealism claims that the world is "totally dependent on the cognitive choice of one or another ontology, one or another linguistic or logical-theoretical framework with its particular ontological commitments."

68. *The Will to Power*, 271.

69. I. Kant, *Critique of Pure Reason*, 115. Cf. *Kritik der reinen Vernunft*, 120.

70. It has been pointed out that "Nietzsche wanted to be a phenomenalist, and you fail to appreciate a whole dimension of his greatness unless you see that his philosophy is at heart a phenomenalism. . . . An account of Nietzsche as a phenomenalist . . . would contain the hard core of his philosophy." Hollingdale, *Nietzsche*, 134. However, it is very questionable that Nietzsche's "metaphysical" speculations were a case of "backslidings" (139) that mar his philosophy. For, it is precisely his assumptions about a "world of becoming," the infinitely complex flux of "reality," that shape his phenomenalism. The "theory" of the "will to power" is a hypothetical interpretation put forward in order to offer a possible explanation of change and becoming. It is, as Nietzsche says in the *Nachlass*, postulated as an anthropomorphic (hence, metaphorical) model by which we may understand, in human terms, the meaning of a dynamic physical theory of the world. *The Will to Power*, 619.

71. Traditional scientific realism is linked to essentialism (whether monoessentialist or polymorphic essentialism). Again, Nietzsche's understanding of scientific theory is certainly nonrealist and nonessentialist. Marx Wartofsky, though defending realism, presents the elements of a "constructivist" (or, for him, antirealist) position

that *includes* practically all of Nietzsche's critical analyses of realism. Nonetheless, there is a residual, reductive realism of sorts in Nietzsche's references to "processes," "becoming," and "chaos." But this is far removed from what Wartofsky calls "a robust realism." Marx Wartofsky, "How to Be a Good Realist," in *Beyond Reason*, ed. G. Munevar (Amsterdam: Kluwer, 1991), 33.

Chapter Six

1. See Jörg Salaquarda, "Nietzsche und Lange," *Nietzsche-Studien* (1978): 236–60. See G. J. Stack, "Nietzsche and Lange," *The Modern Schoolman* 57 (January 1980): 137–49.

2. Freidrich A. Lange, *The History of Materialism and Criticism of Its Present Importance*, trans. E. C. Thomas, 3 vols. in one, 3rd ed. (London: K. Paul, Trench, Trubner, 1925), 3:182n.

3. Ibid., 832.

4. Ibid., 45, 84–85.

5. Ibid., 184–85.

6. Ibid., 186.

7. Ibid., 283–84.

8. *SW* 7:878–79. This understanding of language is already found in the study of the rhetorical nature of language and its reliance on tropes (particularly metonymy, metaphor, and synecdoche). See Sander Gilman, Carole Blair, and David Parent, ed. and trans., *Friedrich Nietzsche on Rhetoric and Language* (Oxford: Oxford University Press, 1989), 23–25. This, of course, is indebted to Gustav Gerber's *Sprache als Kunst* (see chapter 1, note 1 in this volume).

9. *SW* 7:883.

10. Ibid. The indirect influence of Nietzsche by way of F. C. S. Schiller's humanistic pragmatism and his consequent relation to American pragmatism is defended in G. J. Stack, "Nietzsche's Influence on Pragmatic Humanism," *Journal of the History of Philosophy* 20 (1982): 369–406.

11. J. L. Austin, "A Plea for Excuses," in *Classics of Analytic Philosophy*, ed. R. R. Ammermann (New York: McGraw, 1965), 383–84. At one point, Austin seems almost to agree partially with Nietzsche's understanding of ordinary language and, at the same time, to be inadvertently responding to his views. "Certainly ordinary language has no claim to be the last word . . . . It embodies . . . something better than the metaphysics of the Stone Age, namely . . . the inherited experience and acumen of many generations of men . . . that acumen has been concentrated primarily upon the practical business of life . . . . [I]t must be added, too, that superstition and error and fantasy of all kinds do become incorporated in ordinary language [and] . . . in principle it can everywhere be supplemented and improved upon and superseded" (386).

12. Arthur Danto, *Nietzsche as Philosopher* (New York: Macmillan, 1965), 120–21. Danto refers to the similarity between Nietzsche's notion of ordinary language and the views of Austin, Strawson, and Wittgenstein. However, he tends to minimize Nietzsche's assumption that ordinary language (and, subsequently, philosophical language) retains ancient, prehistorical, psychological beliefs and *does* reflect something

very much like the "metaphysics of the Stone Age." Nietzsche's belief in the extensive continuity of the structure of ordinary natural languages is a piece of imaginative speculation for which there is no evidence for or against. The notion of "prehistoric language" sounds like a contradiction in terms. In this regard, de Saussure has said that "language . . . is a historical document." Ferdinand de Saussure, *Course in General Linguistics*, trans. W. Baskin (New York: Philosophical Library, 1959), 223.

13. Danto, *Nietzsche as Philosopher*, 131. "It is, then, not the ordinary beliefs of ordinary men which are under attack, but the philosophical justification of these beliefs by philosophers . . . ." Earlier in his discussion, Danto had discerned that Nietzsche *was* criticizing "ordinary language" and, by implication, the "ordinary beliefs" preserved in it. "Philosophy, Nietzsche has told us, has been . . . a projection of the grammatical structure of ordinary language onto the neutral screen of reality" (122). Insofar as the "structure" of ordinary language retains and reflects (in Nietzsche's opinion) the supposedly crude and primitive beliefs of early men, philosophers who rely upon it, or unconsciously adopt it, perpetuate "the ordinary beliefs of ordinary men" who existed in the remote past.

14. Ludwig Wittgenstein, *Philosophical Investigations*, trans. G. E. M Anscombe (New York: Macmillan, 1953), 4.

15. *SW* 2:2, 55. "*Danger of language for spiritual freedom.* —Every word is a judgment."

16. Ibid., 1:2, 24–25.

17. *SW* 6:5, 77. Jacques Derrida virtually paraphrases Nietzsche's remarks on ordinary language in *Positions*, trans. Alan Bass (Chicago: University of Chicago Press, 1982), 19: "[E]veryday language is not innocent or neutral. It is the language of Western metaphysics, and it carries with it not only a considerable number of presuppositions of all types, but also presuppositions inseparable from metaphysics, which, although little attended to, are knotted into a system."

18. *SW* 6:5, 77.

19. Ibid., 78.

20. Martin Heidegger, *Sein und Zeit* (Tubingen: Niemeyer Verlag, 1963), 100.

21. de Saussure, *Course in General Linguistics*, 6.

22. *SW* 5:20, 34.

23. Ibid., 35. Lévi-Strauss sometimes suggests that physiochemical conditions of life underlie language-use and history. Thus, he traces historical actions to "psychic movements" and these to "the translation of unconscious development." This, in turn, is traced to physiochemical processes. Claude Lévi-Strauss, *The Savage Mind* (Chicago: University of Chicago Press, 1966), 257. This kind of a psychobiological reductionism raises questions about the structuralist belief in universal forms of thought. If, as Nietzsche holds, a culture and a conceptual-linguistic orientation *are* related to "physiological" functions, any significant change in these would presumably, in some way, change a cultural system. This would then no longer be a form of Kantian transcendentalism (that would have to be necessary, universal and *a priori*) without a "subject" insofar as it suggests a "material" basis for psychic states, behavior, culture, and history. In the final analysis, Nietzsche does not adopt a form of psychobiology because of his postulation of a "will to power" or energy *nisus* that is immanent in us.

24. Claude Lévi-Strauss, *Structural Anthropology* (Garden City: Anchor Books, 1963), 33.

25. Cf. Claude Lévi-Strauss, *Les structures elémentaires de la parenté* (Paris: Presses Universitaires de France, 1949).

26. *SW* 3:110, 469–71.

27. *SW* 2:16, 36–38.

28. *SW* 12:193–94.

29. Lévi-Strauss, *The Savage Mind*, 252.

30. Nietzsche, *The Will to Power*, trans. Walter Kaufmann and R. J. Hollingdale (New York: Vintage Books, 1968), 767.

31. Michel Foucault, *The Archaeology of Knowledge and The Discourse on Language*, trans. A. M. S. Smith (New York: Harper and Row, 1976), 191.

32. C. Hartshome and P. Weiss, eds., *Collected Papers of Charles Sanders Peirce*. (Cambridge, MA: Harvard University Press, 1931–35), 8:211–12.

33. *SW* 3:5, 354, 590–93.

34. Ibid.

35. H. W. Schfeller, "Structuralism in Anthropology," in *Structuralism*, ed. J. Ehrmann (Garden City: Doubleday Anchor, 1970), 58–60.

36. *SW* 3:593.

37. *SW* 5:73.

38. Nietzsche, *The Will to Power*, 409.

39. *SW* 1: *Die Philosophie im tragischen Zeitalter der Griechen*, 2, 846.

40. *SW* 13:36. "-the means of expression of language is useless for expressing becoming: it accords with our ineluctable need of preservation to postulate a crude world of stability, of 'things' and so forth."

41. *SW* 6:6, 76.

42. *SW* 13:302.

43. R. H. Grimm, *Nietzsche's Theory of Knowledge* (Berlin and New York: de Gruyter, 1977), 85n, 101n, 133n. Kuhn, unlike Nietzsche, is concerned with prevailing paradigms in scientific domains and the paradigm shifts from "normal science" to revolutions in science that generate new displacing paradigms. For Nietzsche, there are global paradigms that pervade a cultural system (e.g., the emergence of a culture of science or, for that matter, a computer technology or information technology culture).

44. *SW* 13:296–97.

45. Lévi-Strauss, *The Savage Mind*, 268.

46. Wittgenstein, *Philosophical Investigations*, 49e. Cf. *The Will to Power*, 18n. (Translation modified.)

47. *Werke (GOA)* 12:410.

48. W. V. O. Quine, "Two Dogmas of Empiricism," in *From a Logical Point of View* (New York: Harper and Row, 1963), 44.

49. *Werke (GOA)* 15:434. "When power is won over nature [through science], then one can use this power in order to develop oneself further freely . . . [through] self-enhancement and strengthening."

50. See Lévi-Strauss, *Les structures elémentaires de la parenté*.

51. *SW* 3:112, 473.

52. Claude Lévi-Strauss, *The Raw and the Cooked*, trans. J. and D. Weightman (New York: Harper and Row, 1969), 1:11.

53. Lévi-Strauss, *The Savage Mind*, 269.

54. In *On the Genealogy of Morals* Nietzsche asserts that "*All* sciences now have to do the preliminary work for the future task of philosophers: this task is to resolve the *problem of value*, that is, to determine the *rank-order of values*." *SW* 5:1, 17.

55. *SW* 1: "*Versuch einer Selbstkritik*," 12–13.

Chapter Seven

1. Nietzsche read and re-read Emerson over a twenty-six year period, copying out excerpts from his essays in preparation for writing *Thus Spoke Zarathustra*. See Stanley Hubbard, *Nietzsche und Emerson* (Basel: Verlag für Recht und Gesellschaft, 1958), and George J. Stack, *Nietzsche and Emerson* (Athens: Ohio University Press, 1992). Emerson presents his impressionistic evolutionary theory in "Fate," as well as in a number of places in other essays.

2. There are insightful discussions of Schopenhauer's evolutionary ideas in A. O. Lovejoy, "Schopenhauer as an Evolutionist," in *Forerunners of Darwin: 1745–1859*, ed. B. Glass, O. Temkin, and W. L. Straus (Baltimore: Johns Hopkin Press, 1968), ch. 14. Cf. M. Mandelbaum, "The Physiological Orientation of Schopenhauer's Epistemology," in *Schopenhauer: His Philosophical Achievement*, ed. M. Fox (Brighton, England: Harvester Press, 1980), 50–57.

3. Referring to Empedocles' conception of the fortuitous creation of a variety of organic beings, in notes from the mid-1860s, Nietzsche remarks that "This insight anticipates the Darwinian theory." *Werke. Historische-Kritische Gesamtausgabe* (Munich: C. H. Beck, 1937), 4:54.

4. *Werke* (*GOA*) 13:276.

5. Nietzsche, *Daybreak*, trans. R. J. Hollingdale (Cambridge: Cambridge University Press, 1982), 63.

6. Cf. G. C. Simpson, *Tempo and Mode in Evolution* (New York: Columbia University Press, 1984).

7. *More Letters of Charles Darwin*, ed. Francis Darwin (London, 1903), 2:76.

8. Nietzsche, *The Will to Power*, trans. Walter Kaufmann and R. J. Hollingdale (New York: Vintage Books, 1968), 278. Cp. *SW* 5:17. "Behind all logic and its apparent sovereignty of movement there also stands valuations . . . physiological demands for the preservation of a determinate kind of life."

9. *SW* 3:3, 471. A recent account of this phenomenon virtually recapitulates Nietzsche's original observation. A wary, "cautious risk-aversive inferential strategy—one that leaps to the conclusion that danger is present on very slight evidence—will typically lead to false beliefs more often, and true ones less often, than a less hair-trigger one that waits for more evidence before rendering a judgment. Nonetheless, the unreliable, error-prone, risk-aversive strategy may well be favored by natural selection. For natural selection, does not care about truth; it cares only about reproductive success." Stephen Stich, *The Fragmention of Reason* (Cambridge, MA: MIT Press, 1990), 62.

10. *SW* 3:3, 469.

11. Cf. C. J. Lumsden and E. O. Wilson, *Genes, Mind and Culture* (Cambridge, MA: Harvard University Press, 1981).

12. *Werke (GOA)* 16:37. Elsewhere (*Werke* [*GOA*] 16:33) Nietzsche reveals the impact that the scientific world-picture had on his thinking. He says that if our perceptions were different, less coarse, if they were more rapid and acute, we would perceive a cliff as a mobile, dancing chaos.

13. *Werke (GOA)* 13:81. ". . . for a very small part (our perspectival valuations reflect) the conditions necessary to the existence of the individual, for a much greater part those necessary to the human species, for the greater part of all those that make life possible."

14. Simpson, *Tempo and Mode in Evolution*, 53.

15. *Werke. Musarionausgabe* (Munich: Musarion Verlag, 1920–29), 17:117. Synthesizing many of Nietzsche's random comments on mimicry, it is clear that he transposes this phenomenon to mankind and points to its subtle function in the social world. It is linked with social conformity for the sake of adaptation, cultural assimilation, submersion in a group, and basic survival. The group mentality Nietzsche attacks so often is perpetuated, solidified, and transmitted presumably by a kind of cognitive and psychic mimicry.

16. *SW* 3:26, 36–7.

17. *Werke (GOA)* 16:177.

18. *SW* 3:111, 472.

19. *SW* 1:2, 13–4. This is a central theme of Babette Babich's *Nietzsche's Philosophy of Science* (Albany: SUNY Press, 1994).

20. *SW* 3:3, 471–72.

21. W. V. O. Quine, "On Simple Theories of a Complex World," in *Probability, Confirmation, and Simplicity*, ed. Marguerite Foster and Michael Martin (New York: Odyssey Press, 1966), 250.

22. *SW* 3:3, 472.

23. William James, *Pragmatism: A New Name for Some Old Ways of Thinking* (New York: Longmans, Green and Co., 1907), 170.

24. *SW* 3:3, 472.

25. *SB* 2:269.

26. *SW* 3:117, 110.

27. SW 3:107, 464. The inhibiting "counterforce" against such an inclination is "art as the good will to appearance" or the sense that, "as an aesthetic phenomenon existence is still *endurable*."

28. *Werke (GOA)* 13:21.

29. Ibid., 12:28.

30. W. V. O. Quine, "Natural Kinds," in *Ontological Relativity* (New York: Columbia University Press, 1969), 127.

31. Ibid., 116.

32. *Werke (GOA)* 13:21.

33. Martin Heidegger, *Nietzsche*, trans. D. F. Krell (New York: Harper Collins, 1984), 2:94–95. The conception of nature as "chaos" was not based upon Nietzsche's reversion to Greek mythology because he knew that the Chaos of the *Theogony* was a "yawning abyss," not a dynamic multiplicity of interacting forces. Heidegger's suggestion that the idea that, for Nietzsche, the cosmos as a whole was "ineffable" in the sense in which classical Greek poets spoke of it is misleading, as is the additional claim that the construal of the cosmos as chaos was a kind of "negative theology."

Certainly, in the context of *The Gay Science*—in which there are frequent references to science, physics, and mechanistic theory—the depiction of the cosmos as a chaos alludes to the picture of nature that Nietzsche derived from his familiarity with a number of dynamic physical theories.

34. *SW* 9:519.

35. *The Will to Power*, 8. In *On the Genealogy of Morals*, he expands on the point of this note. "Has not man's determination to belittle himself developed apace precisely since Copernicus? Alas, his belief that he was unique and irreplaceable in the hierarchy of being has been shattered for good. . . . Ever since Copernicus man has been rolling down an incline, faster and faster, away from the center—whither? Into the void? Into the 'piercing sense of his emptiness'. . . . All science . . . is now determined to talk man out of his former respect for himself." *The Birth of Tragedy* and *The Genealogy of Morals*, trans. F. Golffing (Garden City: Doubleday Anchor, 1956), 3, 291–92.

36. *Werke* (*GOA*) 12:6.

37. Ibid., 13:21. Rorty's analysis of knowledge and truth in *Philosophy and the Mirror of Nature* reaches conclusions, in a slightly different way, reminiscent of Nietzsche's. This is almost acknowledged in "Solidarity or Objectivity?" in *Post-Analytic Philosophy*, ed. J. Rajchman and Cornel West (New York: Columbia University Press, 1985), 14–15. There is more of Nietzsche (especially in his analyses of knowledge and truth) in Rorty's thought than has been seen or acknowledged.

38. *SW* 2:1, 323.

39. *Werke* (*GOA*) 12:357. This is a crucial orientation in Nietzsche's thought since he seeks to present a human meaning of the scientific world-picture, one that is nevertheless relatively consistent with its fundamental presuppositions. His philosophical interpretation of dynamic theories of nature in terms of his "human analogy," the will to power, is an endeavor to relate his thought to scientific theories of nature such as that of Boscovich—that is, a construal of the natural world as composed of force-centers, "force-points," or centers of energy. In this respect, Nietzsche was one of the earliest philosophers to respond to the apparent *dematerialization* of nature in the physical sciences. See G. J. Stack, *Lange and Nietzsche* (Berlin and New York: Walter de Gruyter, 1983), ch. 9.

40. Cf. G. J. Stack, "Nietzsche and Boscovich's Theory of Nature," *Pacific Philosophic Quarterly* 62 (January 1981): 69–87.

41. *Werke* (*GOA*) 16:56.

42. Ibid., 13:56.

43. Ibid., 16:31.

44. Robert J. Ackermann, *Nietzsche: A Frenzied Look* (Amherst: University of Massachusetts Press, 1990), 72.

45. *SW* 2:1, 2.

46. *SW* 11:613. For an interesting account of evolutionary epistemology, see Nicholas Rescher, *A Useful Inheritance: Evolutionary Aspects of Theory of Knowledge* (Savage, MD: Rowman and Littlefield, 1990). Although optimistic about the growth of scientific knowledge, Rescher indirectly opens a logical space for Nietzsche's views by emphasizing "our science," "reality for us," and the notion that scientific inquiry discloses a "*relational* reality." Granting that "different cognitive perspectives

are possible for interpreting reality," he approaches, but does not embrace, Nietzsche's perspectivalism (78ff).

Chapter Eight

1. As mentioned previously, as early as 1868 Nietzsche held that metaphysics is edifying, "is art, namely the art of conceptual poetry." Natural scientists have shown us that "Whoever wants to know something today contents himself with a conscious relativity of knowledge" (letter to Paul Deussen, May 1868). *SB* 2:269.

2. *SW* 12:294.

3. *SB* 2:160. Lange's original statement was: "the transcendental basis of our organization remains . . . unknown to us."

4. *SW* 10:507. This reference to Jesuitism, as defined by critics of the Jesuit order, suggests craftiness, dissembling, and deception. The use of this term to describe the "artists' metaphysics" presented in *The Birth of Tragedy* raises the question whether Nietzsche practiced "Jesuitism" in other aspects of his published thought.

5. For a perceptive account of Nietzsche's representation of decadence, as well as an argument that seeks to illustrate his complicity in the atmospheric spread of decadence that he analyses, see Daniel W. Conway, *Nietzsche's Dangerous Game* (Cambridge and New York: Cambridge University Press, 1997).

6. *SW* 8:458. Opposed to the depersonalization and decomposition of actuality in scientific theory is the aesthetic perspective. "Art is entirely based upon humanized nature, on a nature encompassed in and interwoven with errors and illusions." Ibid. For Nietzsche, art "is the great rendering-possible of life, the great guide to life, the great stimulus to life." *SW* 13:194.

7. *SW* 7:718–19.

8. Ibid., 423–24.

9. *SW* 1:4, 367. "Wir leben die Periode der Atome, des atomistischen Chaos." Elsewhere, "atoms of force" are related to egoistic organic beings and their subjective "perspectives." This individual perspectivalism is "why a living being is through and through 'egoistic'." *SW* 11:560.

10. *SW* 7:431. Such a philosophy could overcome the "*pessimism*" of the natural sciences and provide an edifying culture [*Bildung*] by drawing "*knowledge* into an artistic world-conception" (436).

11. Ibid., 433.

12. Ibid., 439.

13. Ibid., 444.

14. For a carefully wrought, scholarly critique of Nietzsche's understanding of Buddhism, see Robert G. Morrison, *Nietzsche and Buddhism* (Oxford and New York: Oxford University Press, 1999).

15. *SW* 7:436. "[The] end of metaphysics as science."

16. *SW* 9:52.

17. *SW* 2:3, 25.

18. *Werke* (*GOA*) 14:34.

19. *SW* 2:1, 19.

20. Holger Schmid, *Nietzsche Gedanke der tragischen Erkenninis* (Wurtzburg: Könighauser und Neumann, 1984), 44.

21. "Philosophers . . . believe that they are doing something an honor when they dehistorize [*enthistorisiren*] it, *sub-specie aeterni*—when they make a mummy of it." *SW* 6:74.

22. "Explanation: that is the explanation of a new thing by means of the signs of things known already." *SW* 11:505.

23. *SW* 2:1.

24. Ibid., 13–22.

25. *SW* 7:428. Here he says that the "tragic philosopher" is *not* a skeptic. However, he means that such a thinker is radically skeptical about traditional metaphysical "knowledge" and scientific knowledge, is engaged in a "critique of knowledge." But is *not* skeptical about his or her hard-earned, thought-out *values*.

26. *SW* 10:154. This concession to scientific interpretations of actuality is probably a consequence of the belief that "the *presuppositions* for all previous goals are destroyed." Ibid.

27. *SW* 2:2, 681–82. Cf. p. 656. The psychoanalyst Alfred Adler, who was strongly influenced by Nietzsche's psychological observations, saw the will to superiority as a compensatory effort to overcome feelings of inferiority and inadequacy that in social life expresses itself as a will to power or "prestige-seeking." Franz Alexander and Sheldon Selesnick, *The History of Psychiatry* (New York: Harper and Row, 1966), 226–34.

28. The influence of Nietzsche's psychology on Freud has been thoroughly explored in recent years. Carl Jung was profoundly responsive to Nietzsche's thought, especially in *Thus Spoke Zarathustra*. However, Alfred Adler's individual psychology follows Nietzsche's psychological insights very closely. Cf. F. G. Crookshank, *Individual Psychology and Nietzsche* (London: C. W. Daniel Co., 1933). Cf. also P-L. Assoun, *Freud and Nietzsche*, trans. Richard L. Collier, Jr. (New Brunswick, NJ: Athlone Press, 2000) and Ronald Lehrer, *Nietzsche's Presence in Freud's Life and Though* (Albany: State University of New York Press, 1995).

29. Walter Kaufmann, *Nietzsche*, 3rd rev. ed. (New York: Viking, 1968), 180.

30. *SW* 4:2, 147.

31. The image of the tiger as representing the wild, irrational proneness to violence in man is used in "Homer's Struggle" (in regard to the ancient Greeks), in "On Truth and Lying in an Extra-Moral Sense," to refer to what would be discovered if we penetrated our surface consciousness and could encounter our unconscious, deeply irrational nature. SW 1:775, 783, 873.

32. *Homer's Wettkampf*, *SW* 1:791. Although Nietzsche does not use the term *agon*, *Wettkampf* (struggle or contest) clearly refers to the Greek idea of "contest" (*agon*) in this context.

33. *SW* 6:157. Nietzsche's impression of the "Hellenes" in this context is primarily derived from Thucydides' *History of the Peloponnesian War*. However, Thucydides—in spite of the absence of moralizing about the deeds of the participants in this long war—does not share Nietzsche's fascination with the violent impulses and actions of heroic figures in Hellas and more often laments the suffering and destruction wrought by this "civil war" (*stasis*) and portrays the ruthless "democrat" Cleon in decidedly dark hues.

34. Nietzsche, *Daybreak*, trans. R. J. Hollingdale (New York: Cambridge University Press, 1982), 68.

35. Ibid., 38–39.

36. Ibid.

37. *SW* 5:3, 361. It has been previously noticed that Nietzsche seems struck by the strength of the ostensibly "weak" ascetic priest and, in subsequent sections of the *Genealogy*, launches a rhetorical barrage against sickliness, weakness, and physiological debilitation only to reverse his field again. Although there is psychophysical pathology in the ascetic priest, "he must also be strong, master of himself . . . with his will to power intact" (3, 372). Cf. Henry Staten, *Nietzsche's Voice* (Ithaca and London: Cornell University Press, 1990), 48–57.

38. Nietzsche, *The Will to Power*, trans. Walter Kaufmann and R. J. Hollingdale (New York: Vintage Books, 1968), 689.

39. *SW* 5:3, 398–99. Kaufmann considered the possibility that Nietzsche may be referring to himself here, but then claimed that the "tone" of this passage, as well as the use of plurals, suggest that he is speaking of individuals "very close to him." *On the Genealogy of Morals*, trans. Walter Kaufmann (New York: Vintage Books, 1969), 149n. Again seeing a resemblance to Nietzsche himself in those described as having faith in truth in a later passage (section 24). Kaufmann admits this possibility, but then diverts attention to Nietzsche's friend, Franz Overbeck (151n). These two rejections of a quite plausible self-reference are not overly convincing.

40. *SW* 5:3, 398–99.

41. *SW* 9:52.

42. *SW* 6:365.

43. *SW* 6:230.

44. *SW* 5:3, 349–61.

45. *SW* 5:3, 352.

46. *SW* 5:3, 349–51. If we take Nietzsche at his word here, he believes that the ascetic ideal is useful to the philosopher as a mask, a disguise—"the philosopher sees in it an optimum condition for the highest and boldest spirituality and smiles." This is a spirituality analogous to that ascribed to the Brahmin priests who are alluded to in this discussion: a profound feeling of power. Nietzsche suggests that the philosopher might wish "*pereat mundus, fiat philosophia, fiat philosophus, fiam*!" (Let the world perish, but let there be philosophy, let there be the philosopher, me!). Taken seriously, this is not merely a paradigm of *hubris*, but a suitable motto for a nihilistic egoist.

47. Sigmund Freud, *Civilization and Its Discontents*, trans. James Strachey, vol. 21 of *The Standard Edition of the Complete Works of Sigmund Freud* (London: Hogarth Press, 1961), 21:127–28. Conscience "comes from renunciation of instinct owing to fear of aggression by the *external* authority. . . . [A]fter that comes the erection of an *internal* authority, and renunciation of instinct . . . owing to fear of conscience. . . . The aggressiveness of conscience keeps up the aggressiveness of the [external] authority." The renunciation of outward aggression, leads to an aggression turned against the ego [*Ich*], in Freud's terms, by the severe "super-ego." Cf. Ronald Lehrer's citation of a comparison between Nietzsche's account of the origin of "bad conscience" in the *Genealogy* and Freud's account of the internalization or introjection of aggression (inhibited from external expression) and its

consequent redirection against the "ego." Lehrer, *Nietzsche's Presence in Freud's Life and Thought*, 178–79.

48. *SW* 5:2, 324–25.

49. Ibid., 3, 336.

50. Ibid., 383.

51. *SW* 6:2, 170. In the same context Nietzsche exclaims that "bad" designates "everything that is born of weakness." Applied to his paradoxical analysis of the ascetic type in the *Genealogy*, this would mean that they are bad despite the fact that they are possessed of something elevated as "good": a tenacious will to power.

52. *SW* 5:3, 412. In spite of the rhetorical force of this assertion, it does not cohere with what has been said earlier about the ascetic personality's "form-giving" force. For this capacity is turned upon man's "animal self" and is an emulation, on a smaller scale, of the force of the amoral (or pre-moral) creators who built the earliest primitive "states" by means of violent domination. In this instance and in a number of others, Nietzsche comes close to saying something that undercuts his arguments against the various forms of ascetic types: the "weak" are strong!

53. Ibid., 373. The ascetic type conducts a "war of cunning" with "animal ferocity."

54. Ibid., 2, 326.

55. *SW* 13:498.

56. *The Will to Power*, 787, 789.

57. Ibid., 770.

58. Staten, *Nietzsche's Voice*, 100–101.

59. Sigmund Freud, "The Economic Problem of Masochism," *The Standard Edition of the Complete Works of Sigmund Freud*, 19:163.

60. Nietzsche, *Thus Spoke Zarathustra*, trans. R. J. Hollingdale (Hamondsworth: Penguin Books, 1969), 60–61.

61. *SW* 4:39–40.

62. Maurice Merleau-Ponty, *Philosophy of Perception* (New York: Humanities Press, 1962), 67–174.

63. Eric Blondel, *Nietzsche: The Body and Culture*, trans. Sean Hand (Stanford: Stanford University Press, 1991), 208–38.

64. *SW* 5:10, 23. Curiously, in this same section he criticizes realist philosophers of actuality for a leveling "positivism" despite his affirmation of the reality of the body. This indicates that his naturalistic placement of bodily existence is not, as Blondel claims, "metaphorical." As Daniel Conway contends, there is a mode of vitalism in Nietzsche's account of "human agency" that cannot be displaced as metaphor. Conway, *Nietzsche's Dangerous Game*, 59n. This provocative work, a strong critique of Nietzsche's thought, is an internal analysis that turns Nietzsche against Nietzsche and highlights every instance in which he expresses "metaphysical" *beliefs*. Rather than seeing these expressions as perspectives Nietzsche adopts heuristically in his psychology, Conway combines a number of them into a "vitalism" that requires a universal metaphysics of will to power, a global interpretation that I will attempt to show *is* a metaphorical fable.

65. Ibid., 23, 58.

66. Ibid., 19, 33. This formulation seems analogous to a psychology conceived of as a morphology. The use of this term is rare and reprises a notational reference

from J. W. von Goethe's *Morphologie* (1822) that Nietzsche logged in 1868. Quoting Goethe, he writes that "Every being is not a single thing, but a plurality . . . a collection of living, independent things." This analogy does not preclude a dual analogy, previously mentioned, between Boscovich's conception of "sub-atoms" or *Unteratomen* and Nietzsche's reference to *Unterwillen* (underwills).

67. *SW* 10:654. Here we see, once more, how Nietzsche relies upon scientific conceptions (in physics and physiology) as analogical models for his interpretation of the psychophysical processes occurring in us. Conversely, he employs human analogy in order to interpret natural processes and phenomena.

68. Ibid.

69. Ibid., 655.

70. Michel Harr, *Nietzsche and Metaphysics*, trans. Michael Gendre (Albany: SUNY Press, 1996), 94. Harr does not trace the trajectory of Nietzsche's thought *through* a bodily unconscious to the positing of "underwills" despite the fact that he is aware that he postulates a "plurality" of such "undersouls" (7).

71. *SW* 5:231, 170.

72. *SW* 13:301. Cp. *The Will to Power*, 692.

73. *SW* 12:313.

74. *SW* 12:345. My translation here differs from that of Kaufmann and Hollingdale in *The Will to Power*, 706. Theirs departs from the German text that reads: "das Leben selbst ist kein Mittel zu etwas: es est der *Ausdruck* von Wachsthumsformen der Macht." This is mistranslated as "Life is only a means to something: it is the expression of forms of the growth of power."

75. *SW* 4:2, 147–49.

76. *SB*, 8:509.

77. *SW* 12:105.

78. Harr, *Nietzsche and Metaphysics*, 5. While Harr recognizes that Nietzsche proposes a "philosophy of immanence," he insists, as others do, that the "metaphysics" of will to power aims to overcome an anthropomorphic orientation and serves his so-called anti-humanism (x, 2).

79. *The Will to Power*, 680.

80. Ibid., 776.

81. "What I Owe the Ancients," *SW* 6:4, 158–59.

82. *SW* 13:600. Cf. Staten, *Nietzsche's Voice*, 100.

83. After presenting a convincing case for Nietzsche's tendency to refer to "sexual desire and love in terms that suggest [their] . . . extremely close relation to will to power," Staten softens his argument by saying that he's more concerned "to show that these terms [libido, will to power] are unstable." Staten, *Nietzsche's Voice*, 100. In *On the Genealogy of Morals* philosophers are said to be subject to a "domesticating instinct" during creative periods that inclines them to suppress sexual needs in order to devote greater energy to "the developing work." *SW* 5:3, 8, 355.

84. *SW* 13:300.

85. Nietzsche, *Beyond Good and Evil*, trans. Walter Kaufmann (New York: Vintage, 1966), 36.

86. Maudemarie Clark, "Nietzsche's Doctrines of the Will to Power," *Nietzsche-Studien* 12 (1983): 460. Originally presented at a meeting of the North American

Nietzsche Society on December 2, 1980, Boston, MA.

87. Maudemarie Clark, *Nietzsche on Truth and Philosophy* (New York: Cambridge University Press, 1990), 210–11.

88. Ibid., 23n.

89. Ibid., 211.

90. Harry Frankfort, "Freedom of Will and the Concept of a Person," *The Journal of Philosophy* 62 (January 1971): 5–20.

91. P. F. Strawson, *Introduction to Logical Theory* (New York: Wiley, 1952), 15.

92. Clark, "Nietzsche's Doctrines of the Will to Power," 461. Recently, Clark compounds what appears to me as a serious misinterpretation of Nietzsche's psychology. She admits "that Nietzsche sees [will to power] . . . as the most important second-order drive . . . one that is essential to our constitution and experience of ourselves as agents." How something "second-order" is nonetheless "essential" to us is puzzling. But not as puzzling as the countertextual claim that Nietzsche does not hold that "life is will to power." Maudemarie Clark, "Nietzsche's Doctrine of the Will to Power: Neither Ontological nor Biological." *International Studies in Philosophy* 32/13 (2000): 119. Originally presented at a meeting of NANS on April 2, 1999, Berkeley, Cal.

93. Clark, "Nietzsche's Doctrines," 461.

Chapter Nine

1. *SW* 5:30, 48.

2. *SW* 1:23, 145. In a note from 1872 he advocates "Overcoming [scientific] knowledge by means of myth-forming powers." *SW* 7:439.

3. Sarah Kofman, *Nietzsche and Metaphor*, trans. Duncan Large (Stanford: Stanford University Press, 1993), 16.

4. Ibid., 95.

5. Ibid., 17.

6. Ibid., 149–50n.

7. S. Gilman, Carole Blair, David Parent, eds. and trans., *Friedrich Nietzsche on Rhetoric and Language* (New York: Oxford University Press, 1989), 22. "Alle Worter aber sind an sich und von Anfange an, in Bezug auf ihre Bedeutung, Tropen." (Translation my own.)

8. Jörg Salaquarda correctly linked this idea of metaphysics to suggestions originally found in F.A. Lange's *History of Materialism*. "Nietzsche's Metaphysikritik und ihre Vorbereitung durch Schopenhauer, "in *Krisis der Metaphysik*, ed. G. Abel and J. Salaquarda (Berlin and New York: de Gruyter, 1989), 267.

9. For discussions of this theme see G.J. Stack, "Nietzsche's Myth of the Will to Power," *Dialogos* 17, no. 40 (November 1982): 27–49 and *Lange and Nietzsche* (Berlin and New York: Walter de Gruyter,1983). See also Maudemarie Clark, "Nietzsche's Doctrines of the Will to Power," *Nietzsche-Studien* 12 (1983): 458–68.

10. *SW* 7:434, 444.

11. *SW* 2:42. It has correctly been pointed out that Nietzsche avoids a genetic fallacy even though he sometimes argues that metaphysical views are embraced for

psychological reasons that put them in question. See Jacob Golomb, *Nietzsche's Enticing Psychology of Power* (Ames: Iowa State University Press, 1989), ch. 4. In the *Genealogy* he asks: "Has man perhaps grown *less in need* of a transcendental solution to the riddle of existence now that it has become more casual, impoverished, and dispensable in the *visible* order of things?" *SW* 5:3, 403. The implied answer is "no."

12. Nietzsche believed that no matter how careful we are, we cannot get free of a "philosophical mythology" embedded in language. *SW* 2:247. Since virtually all languages can be said to retain such mythological aspects, they seem essential to language. The possibility of a "new language" is rarely mentioned by Nietzsche and not pursued. Cf. *SW* 5:4, 18.

13. Nietzsche, *The Will to Power*, trans. Walter Kaufmann and R. J. Hollingdale (New York: Vintage Books, 1968), 322.

14. Clark, "Nietzsche's Doctrines of the Will to Power," 461–68.

15. The classification of the will to power as pervasive in actuality as a myth is missing in Maudemarie Clark's later approaches to Nietzsche. See her *Nietzsche on Truth and Philosophy* (Cambridge: Cambridge University Press, 1990), ch. 7 and "Nietzsche's Doctrine of the Will to Power: Neither Ontological nor Biological," *International Studies in Philosophy* 32/3 (2000): 119–35. However, she retains her view that the image of the cosmos as will to power is "a projection of its author's values onto a text provided by science." "Nietzsche's Doctrine . . . Neither Ontological nor Biological," 125. In addition, she admits that she had previously interpreted the drive for power by "making power benign" (135n).

16. *SW* 7:495.

17. *SW* 12:98. The term *Hemmungen* seems to serve in this context as an expression of resistance.

18. *SW* 7:493. "Knowledge, in the strict sense, only has the form of tautology and is *empty*. Each piece of knowledge which advances us is an *identification of unlike things*, the similar, that is, is essentially illogical." This judgment is curiously related to Quine's analysis of kind and similarity as crucial to learning induction and science itself even though rooted in "unreason." Cf. W.V.O. Quine, "Natural Kinds," in *Naturalizing Epistemology*, ed. Hilary Kornblinth (Cambridge, MA: MIT Press, 1994), ch. 3.

19. In an early treatment of Heraclitus's philosophy Nietzsche relates his conception of universal flux to the emerging depiction of nature in the sciences. "Nature is just as unending inwardly as outwardly; now we reach down to the cell and its parts: but there is no absolute limit where anyone would say, here is the final point inward; becoming never ends down to the infinitely small." *Werke* (*GOA*) 19:176.

20. *SW* 7:427–28. This puts in question Clark's belief that Nietzsche's "doctrine of the will to power is a construction of the world from the viewpoint of his moral values." *Nietzsche on Truth and Philosophy*, 227. In later remarks she claims that Nietzsche reads his "values" into his world-picture and even creates this picture after "the image of himself and his values." "Nietzsche's Doctrine of the Will to Power," 126. This raises a number of new questions and is quite contestable.

21. *The Will to Power*, 617. *SW* 12:313. Although the monistic phrase "the will to power" is used here, it is, at this point, shorthand for "wills to power"—a more

accurate description of the centerpiece of the fable. Again, this reference to a "*verkleinerte Formel*" suggests a distancing from a truth-claim. In addition, the assertion that "*all life* manifests, as a diminutive formula for the total tendency observed, [offers] . . . a new definition of the concept of 'life,' as will to power," mitigates the claim that will to power, psychologically considered, is a "second-order" drive.

22. *SW* 5:19, 33.

23. Ibid., 12, 27. This surprisingly positive treatment of the concept of the "soul," as well as the emergence of the unusual term "under-wills," should in themselves signal a change in Nietzsche's "rhetorical strategies." We may compare this published proposal to a notation from 1885–86. "*Man as a multiplicity of 'wills to power': each with a multiplicity of means of expression and forms.*" *SW* 12:25.

24. Ibid.

25. Ibid., 14, 28.

26. Sarah Kofman maintains "that for Nietzsche the will to power is . . . a necessary heuristic hypothesis." *Nietzsche and Metaphor*, 142. Since I'm convinced that the notion of interacting wills to power that wax and wane in pulsating rhythmic processes is an ingenious exoteric myth, my language is more cautious. That is, it *may* have heuristic value as an opening to philosophical interpretations of power and power-relations (as has already been done by Foucault) or it may serve as a dramaturgical version of the ultimate nature of actuality that *discourages* further macrometaphysical speculation. Perhaps Nietzsche's esoteric teaching is one he has iterated a number of times: that everything is ensconced in chaos, an ineffable complexity. "A specific name for this reality would be 'the will to power'." *Werke* (*GOA*) 13:121. Kofman considers the possibility that the idea of the will to power is unique in the history of philosophy as a "mythico-transcendental reflection." *Nietzsche and Metaphor*, 190. Minus the questionable supplement "transcendental," this remark would be compatible with my position, except that my argument includes internal, philosophical reasons why the will-to-power metaphor is a mythic creation.

27. *Werke* (*GOA*) 16:16f. This idea was found in the physiologist Wilhelm Roux's work, *Der Kampf der Teile im Organismus* (1881), which Nietzsche had in his library and refers to in the *Nachlass* of 1883. Cf. *SW* 10:274ff. Roux postulated a struggle of parts within the organism extending from molecules and cells to tissues and organs. This was a Darwinian notion of competitive struggle projected into the internal (physiological) environment.

28. *SW* 12:25. "Everything material is a kind of movement symptom for an unknown event: everything conscious and felt is . . . a symptom of something unknown. . . . Movements are symptoms, thoughts are likewise symptoms: cravings are evidence to us of something behind both, and the fundamental craving is will to power." Although Conway presents a sharp critique of Nietzsche's "symptomatological" analysis of the culture of modernity, he does not contend with Nietzsche's use of symptomatic analysis in regard to the postulation of a "will to power." See Daniel Conway, *Nietzsche's Dangerous Game* (Cambridge: Cambridge University Press, 1997), 82, 87–8, 198–99, 233–36.

29. This transformation was anticipated, as previously shown, in Nietzsche's account of the substitution of social (artistic and political) contests for a direct and violent expression of a will to power in the ancient Greeks. In *Twilight of the Idols* he returns to this theme, attributing to the ancient Greeks "their strongest instinct,

the will to power," which was "discharged . . . in fearful and ruthless external hostility." Institutional festivals, artistic contests, and the politics of the *polis* served "mutual security" against an explosive lust for power. *Twilight of the Idols*, trans. R. J. Hollingdale (Middlesex: Penguin, 1979), 10, 3, 107–8. Despite Nietzsche's emphatic stress on the attribution of an unvarnished and ruthless will to power to the ancient Greeks, it has been said that, for him, "the will to power was one among other drives"! Furthermore, the sublimated expression of this forceful drive in "institutions" is interpreted as directed "against the will to power." Clark, *Nietzsche on Truth and Philosophy*, 224. This observation is erroneous because the socially useful institutions referred to are not established "against" the primal drive ascribed to the ancient Greeks: they are an expression of it, a transformed manifestation of it, a ramification of it. There *is*, ironically, something problematic in this passage that is not noticed. Nietzsche strongly suggests that the traits of the Hellenes he speaks of were not *natural* qualities (e.g., physical strength, "reckless realism," and "immoralism"), but "produced." *Twilight of the Idols*, 108. Such a claim runs counter to Nietzsche's general naturalistic orientation and contradicts the notion of an *instinctive* deeply rooted drive, as well as numerous claims about "physiological" weakness or strength. He often proclaims that differences of ability, intelligence, strength, etc., are fundamentally *natural*, not products of culture alone. Commenting on the ancient Hindu *Laws of Manu*, he remarks that it is "Nature, not *Manu* [that] separates from one another the predominantly spiritual type, the predominantly muscular and tempermentally strong, and the third type distinguished neither in the one nor the other." *SW* 6:57, 242.

30. Letter to Peter Gast, August 1883, *Selected Letters of Friedrich Nietzsche*, ed. and trans. C. Middleton (Chicago: University of Chicago Press, 1969), 217. Nietzsche recalls in this letter his studies of atomistic theory and Boscovich. He calls him the first "to demonstrate mathematically that, for the strict science of mechanics, the premise of the solid corporeal point-atoms is an unusable hypothesis: a proposition which today has canonical validity for mathematically trained natural scientists." *SB* 6:442. (Translation my own.)

31. F. A. Lange, *The History of Materialism and Criticism of Its Present Importance*, trans. E.C. Thomas, 3rd ed. (London: K. Paul, Trench, Trubner, 1925), 2:376.

32. Müller-Lauter's scrupulous analysis of the pluralistic conception of wills to power accurately represents Nietzsche's textual expressions of his thought and shows, against Magnus's prohibition on the use of voluminous notations (*Nachlass*), the fruitfulness of probing Nietzsche's incisive experimental thinking. Unfortunately, he does not link notions such as "will-quanta" (= "power-quanta") to Boscovitch's conception of "centers of force" and thereby does not discern this support for his concerns about the question as to whether Nietzsche has, in fact, presented a metaphysics. At first, he avers that Nietzsche opposes metaphysics "as a two-worlds theory." Wolfgang Müller-Lauter, *Nietzsche: His Philosophy of Contradictions and the Contradictions of His Philosophy*, trans. David J. Parent (Urbana and Chicago: University of Illinois Press, 1999), 122. Elsewhere, he says that if metaphysics means "the question of being as a whole . . . then one must . . . characterize Nietzsche as a metaphysician" (218n). Finally, under the sway of Heidegger's *Nietzsche*, he agrees that "*the* will to power as *essence*" is an accurate interpretation of Nietzsche's

thought (219n). This is another instance in which Heidegger distorts Nietzsche in order to indict him as "the last metaphysician." No one previously had thoroughly attacked the notion of "essence" than he. The only "essences" he allows are "processes." Müller-Lauter would have been wiser to have held to his accurate insight that "One cannot do Nietzsche justice if one imputes to him that he himself falls back into the form of metaphysics that he . . . criticized [as] . . . Heidegger does" (218n). The late Gilles Deleuze's reaction to Heidegger's treatment of Nietzsche, which is a paradigm of French finesse, is on target. "Heidegger gives an interpretation of Nietzschean philosophy closer to his own thought than to Nietzsche's. . . . [For he] is opposed to every conception of affirmation which would find its foundation in Being." Gilles Deleuze, *Nietzsche and Philosophy*, trans. Hugh Tomlinson (New York: Columbia University Press, 1983), 220.

33. *SW* 11:563. Nietzsche's argument here depends upon the validity of the analogy between human "inner" drives, striving for power, cravings, etc., and our externalized actions. These are presumably symptoms of complex inner events just as manifestations of force or energy are said to be. All the "Funktionem des organischen Lebens aus diese Einer Quelle." Ibid. This one source of all functions of organic life is "designated as 'will to power'." The question remains whether he can meaningfully claim to *know* what this primal source is.

34. *The Will to Power*, 350. Cf. *SW* 3:482.

35. *SW* 3:112, 473. "Es ist genug, die Wissenschaft als möglichst getrue Abmenschlichung der Dinge zu bretrachten . . ." (It is sufficient to regard science as the most precise humanization of things possible). Kaufmann renders this, for some reason, as: "It will do to consider science as an attempt (?) to humanize [sic] things as faithfully as possible." Nietzsche, *The Gay Science*, trans. Walter Kaufmann (New York: Vintage, 1974), 172–73.

36. *SW* 5:36, 54–55. My version of this argument seeks to follow its crucial steps.

37. It is gratifying to see that what has come to be epitomized as "BGE 36" is still a center of interest (as indicated by a recent North American Nietzsche Society colloquium on this theme in March 1999). See *International Studies in Philosophy* [32/3] (2000): 83–135. Karl Schlechta's insight that the tentative, cautious nature of Nietzsche's only published argument for the universal conception of a pervasive will to power, the use of the subjunctive mood (suggesting supposition and hypothetical speculation), implied that Nietzsche presented the ostensible centerpiece of his thought with little confidence or assurance. (See Karl Schlechta, *Der Fall Nietzsche* [Munich: Hanser Verlag, 1959], 120–22.) Previously, I held that the argument was questionable because it relied on conceptions (such as "causality of will") "that Nietzsche repudiates." Circulated in 1980, but published in January 1981, my article raised questions about Nietzsche's "dramatic new metaphysics" (which was then left intact for dialectical purposes) and strongly questioned the integrity of this "argument" for the universal extension of "the will to power." G.J. Stack, "Nietzsche and Boscovich's Natural Philosophy," *Pacific Philosophical Quarterly* 62, no. 1 (January 1981): 64–87. A short time later, in *Lange and Nietzsche*, an anticipation of the more detailed argument presented here was made explicit.

38. *Werke* (*GOA*) 16:5. Cp. *SW* 12:295. ". . . inner phenomena are difficult to grasp and are transformed by error (inner processes are essentially *error-generating* . . .)." Since all knowing entails "falsification," Nietzsche is probably referring

to a difference of degree of distortion or error between observation of external phenomena and self-observation. Cf. *SW* 5:16, 29–30. Absent from Clark's earlier analysis of "BGE 36," though present in her Nietzsche book (*Nietzsche on Truth and Philosophy*, 213–14), is a critique of the first premise of Nietzsche's contestable argument. Prior to this, attention was called to the "internal phenomenology" Nietzsche relies on as one in which there are no "pure facts," but only simplifications and interpretations. Cf. Stack, "Nietzsche and Boscovich's Natural Philosophy," 84.

39. *SW* 6:3, 90–1. Cp. *SW* 3:127, 482. The belief in the will as the cause of effects is a belief in the will as "a magical effective force."

40. *SW* 12:135. In a later notation in which a critique of the concept "cause" is presented, we are told that, psychologically, "the concept of 'cause' is our feeling of power from so-called willing—our concept 'effect' the superstitution that this feeling of power is itself the power which moves . . ." *SW* 13:260.

41. This point was reported by Georgio Colli (one of the editors of the most recent edition of Nietzsche's "complete works," *Kritische Gesamtausgabe*, 1967ff.) in his commentary on Nietzsche's notes from the fall of 1885 to the fall of 1887. His perceptive observations lend support to the concept of "will to power" as exoteric and to Nietzsche's critique of epistemology and metaphysics (while he engages in the former and pretends to engage in the latter) as masks disguising his intentions. Colli makes one point in this otherwise insightful commentary that is questionable: "The entire first exposition of the system of the will to power . . . is nothing other than a camouflaging of Schoperhauerian thought." *SW* 13:653.

42. Stanley Rosen, "Poetic Reason in Nietzsche," in *The Ancients and the Moderns* (New Haven and London: Yale University Press, 1989), 223. Rosen argues that the chaos Nietzsche posits is unintelligible and the schemata by which theory is constructed interprets, creates, and distorts what is "known" and encourages artistic metaphysics. The celebration of a free use of "poetic reason" leads to an erasure of the difference between the esoteric and the exoteric in Rosen's view, one I do not share.

43. *SW* 12:187. Elsewhere one finds a pithy entry: "Mythology of the concept of causality." *SW* 12:99.

44. *SW* 11:434.

45. Conway, *Nietzsche's Dangerous Game*, 63. Only Clark's observations on this question are cited in the context of Conway's tangential remarks on the single published argument in defense of the "theory" of will to power.

46. *SW* 13:591.

47. The *locus classicus*, if such it may be called, for the expression of this agitation is the previously cited third essay (Section 12) in *On the Genealogy of Morals*. "(Incidentally, even in the Kantian concept of the 'intelligible character of things' something remains of the prurient ascetic schism that loves to turn reason against reason: for 'intelligible character' signifies . . . that things are such that the intellect understands just enough of them to know that they are—completely incomprehensible.)"

48. Kofman, *Nietzsche and Metaphor*, 112–15. An unusual feature of her insightful study (which seems to have been inherited by deconstructionist thinkers) is the appreciation of the metaphoric and mythical nature of the "will to power" image and the repeated reference to it as if it were a genuine ontological force.

Thus, Kofman refers "artistic force," "essence," the source of the unity of diverse forms of life, the power of interpretation, and much more to "the will to power."

49. It is a phrase and religious concept found in various segments of the *Upanishads* and familiar to Nietzsche in the writings of his friend Paul Deussen, particularly *Das System des Vedanta* (1883). In the *Genealogy* Nietzsche refers to the maxim "beyond good and evil" as a "dangerous slogan," which it certainly is. He also specifically links it to Buddhist and Vedantist scriptures and alludes to Deussen's works (in which Deussen discusses "esoteric" teachings in Vedantism). In a note from 1884, Nietzsche writes: "Therein, that the world is a divine play and beyond good and evil—have I Heraclitus and Vedanta philosophy as predecessors." *SW* 11:201.

50. *SW* 5:30, 48. There is a strong suggestion of a relation between esoteric thinking and the recurring theme of a "pathos of distance." Moreover, *Beyond Good and Evil* has so many direct and indirect references to the esoteric/exoteric distinction that it could be seen as self-referential, particularly in regard to the argument for a universal will to power.

51. Martin Heidegger, *Nietzsche*, 2 vols. (Pfullingen: Verlag Gunther Neske, 1961), 2:155–56.

52. *SW* 11:661.

53. *SW* 12:315. "Every drive is a kind of thirst for power: each has its perspective which it wants to force on the other drives as a norm."

54. The reductive analysis of human psychic processes to a single source the nature of which is inferred from its effects parallels the reductive analyses in physical theory to "force," "energy," or *dynamis* (as Nietzsche sometimes refers to the "inner quality" of phenomena). *SW* 11:565. This is reminiscent of the Eleatic Stranger's remark in Plato's *Sophist* (247e) that "anything has genuine being if it has the power to affect something else or be affected." The "distinguishing sign of real beings is that they are nothing but power (*dynamis*)." As in the case of Nietzsche's hypothetical source of energy and power, *dynamis* (potentiality or power) is known by its effects. Francis Cornford, *Plato's Theory of Knowledge* (New York: Liberal Arts Press, 1957), 234–35.

55. *SW* 13:498.

56. *SW* 3:373, 626.

57. *SW* 9:532.

58. *SW* 5:3, 25–6.

59. Ibid., 127.

60. Stanley Rosen has argued for the contestable notion that the Dionysian affirmation of the world and life as it is (including accepting the thought of the eternal recurrence of all events) is a transition point between Nietzsche's ostensible esoteric doctrine (ostensibly "complete" nihilism) and his exoteric doctrine—that is, the affirmation of a life-enhancing creation of new values. Stanley Rosen, "Remarks on Nietzsche's 'Platonism'," in *The Quarrel between Philosophy and Poetry* (New York and London: Routledge, 1988), 198–99.

61. Jean Granier, *La problème de la verité dans la philosophie de Nietzsche* (Paris: Seuil, 1969), 75. ". . . après célèbre les vertus antimetaphysique de la science, il a été amène a reconaitre dans la science l'expression ultime du Nihilisme modern." Granier and many after him mistakenly argue that science *is* nihilistic. What

Nietzsche avers is that the unintended *consequence* of the scientific form of the will to knowledge is a mode of nihilism that no one intends. The one-sided emphasis on scientific reductionism has profound negative effects on our concept of ourselves and our qualitative, aesthetic orientation toward our world and experience.

62. *Nietzsche's Werke*, 11 vols. (Leipzig: Naumann Verlag, 1906), 10:101.

63. In *Thus Spoke Zarathustra* it is said that suffering, powerlessness, and weariness created "afterworlds" or the "other world." A "Weariness, which wants to attain the ultimate in a single leap, with a death-leap . . . which no longer desires even to want . . ." *SW* 4:13. Kaufmann called attention to this unintended criticism of Kierkegaard's leap of faith and Hollingdale suggests that Nietzsche may be directly criticizing him, even though he told the Danish literary critic, Brandes, he had never read him.

64. *SW* 11:434. "Die wahre Welt der Ursachen ist uns verborgen: sie ist unsäglich complicirter." This does not prevent him from employing the "simplification" apparatuses of our sense and intellect in order to produce "Our *false*, reduced, logicized world of causes . . . in which we can live" (ibid.).

65. *SW* 9:466.

66. Martin Heidegger, *Holzwege* (Frankfurt-am-Main: Klostermann, 1950), 193. In fact, a list of all of Heidegger's assertions about will to power and its meaning would create a small pamphlet.

67. *SW* 1:847.

68. John Richardson, *Nietzsche's System* (New York and Oxford: Oxford University Press, 1996), 263. This assumes the validity of one of Nietzsche's formulations of our psychological nature and then assumes an analogical relation of human beings to an objective reality on the basis of the hypothetical interpretation of the fundamental nature of reality. Furthermore, there is the assumption that human beings do or could "mirror" the reality-in-itself that is here assumed, but denied by Nietzsche.

69. *SW* 7:428.

70. *SW* 10:495.

71. *SW* 3:344, 574.

72. This cold mistrust fueled Nietzsche's recurrent skepticism while his deep aesthetic values clashed with the scientific perspective. This is not a feature of any single period of his reflective life since it runs through all of his thought. It is a polarity that infuses his thinking and writings with a kind of electromagnetic intensity. What he could not cease to admire about "the spirit of science" was that it "cools down the fiery passion of belief in final, conclusive truths." *SW* 2:1, 204.

Selected Bibliography

Ackermann, Robert J. *Nietzsche: A Frenzied Look.* Amherst: University of Massachusetts Press, 1990.

Alderman, Harold. *Nietzsche's Gift.* Athens: Ohio University Press, 1977.

Assoun, Paul-Laurent. *Freud and Nietzsche.* Translated by Richard L. Collier, Jr. New Brunswick, NJ: Athlone Press, 2000.

Austin, John L. "A Plea for Excuses." In *Classics of Analytic Philosophy*, ed. R. R. Ammermann. New York: McGraw-Hill, 1965.

Babich, Babette. *Nietzsche's Philosophy of Science.* Albany: SUNY Press, 1994.

Baumgarten, Eduard. *Das Vorbild Emersons im Werk und Leben Nietzsches.* Heidelberg: Karl Winter, 1957.

Bernoulli, Carl A. *Franz Overbeck und Friedrich Nietzsche: Eine Freundschaft.* 2 vols. Jena: Diederichs, 1908.

Blondel, Eric. *Nietzsche: the Body and Culture.* Translated by Sean Hand. Stanford: Stanford University Press, 1991.

Bode, Carl, ed. *The Portable Emerson.* New York: Viking, 1982.

Bohm, David. *Causality and Chance in Modern Physics.* Philadelphia: University of Pennsylvania Press, 1957.

Bohr, Niels. *Atomic Physics and Human Knowledge.* New York: John Wiley and Sons, 1958.

Bonjour, Lawrence. *The Structure of Empirical Knowledge.* Cambridge, MA: Harvard University Press, 1985.

Boscovich, Roger J. *A Theory of Natural Philosophy.* Cambridge: MIT Press, 1966.

Breazeale, Daniel, trans. and ed. *Philosophy and Truth: Nietzsche's Notebooks of the Early 1870's.* Atlantic Highlands, NJ: Humanities Press, 1979.

Carnap, Rudolf. *The Logical Structure of the World.* Translated by Rolf George. Berkeley: University of California Press, 1967.

Clark, Maudemarie. *Nietzsche on Truth and Philosophy.* Cambridge: Cambridge University Press, 1990.

———. "Nietzsche's Doctrine of the Will to Power: Neither Ontological Nor Biological," *International Studies in Philosophy* 32/3 (2000): 119–35.

———. "Nietzsche's Doctrines of the Will to Power." *Nietzsche-Studien* 12 (1983): 458–68.

Conway, Daniel. "The Eyes Have It: Perspectives and Affective Investment," *International Studies in Philosophy* 23/2 (1991): 103–13.

———. *Nietzsche's Dangerous Game.* Cambridge: Cambridge University Press, 1997.

Cornford, Francis. *Plato's Theory of Knowledge*. New York: Liberal Arts Press, 1957.
Crawford, Claudia. *The Beginnings of Nietzsche's Theory of Language*. Berlin and New York: Walter de Gruyter, 1988.
Cresenzi, Luca, "Verzeichnis der von Nietzsche aus der Universitätsbibliothek in Basel, entleihenen Bücher (1869–79)," *Nietzsche-Studien* 23 (1994): 388–442.
Danto, Arthur. *Nietzsche as Philosopher*. New York: Macmillan, 1965.
Davidson, Donald, "On the Very Idea of a Conceptual Schema," in *Post-Analytic Philosophy*. Eds. J. Rajchman and C. West. New York: Columbia University Press, 1985.
De Broglie, Louis. *Physics and Microphysics*. Translated by Martin Davidson. New York: Harper and Brothers, 1955.
Deleuze, Gilles. *Nietzsche and Philosophy*. Translated by H. Tomlinson. New York: Columbia University Press, 1983.
de Man, Paul. *Allegories of Reading*. New Haven: Yale University Press, 1979.
———. *The Rhetoric of Romanticism*. New York: Columbia University Press, 1984.
Derrida, Jacques. *Positions*. Translated by Alan Bass. Chicago: University of Chicago Press, 1982.
De Saussure, Ferdinand. *Course in General Linguistics*. Translated by Wade Baskin. New York: Philosophical Library, 1959.
Deussen, Paul. *The System of the Vedanta*. Translated by Charles Johnston. New York: Dover, 1973.
Du Bois-Reymond, Emil. *Ueber die Grenzen des Naturkennens*. 7th ed. Leipzig: Veit Verlag, 1884.
Dummett, Michael. *Truth and Other Enigmas*. Cambridge, MA: Harvard University Press, 1978.
Ehrmann, Jacques, ed. *Structuralism*. Garden City: Anchor Books, 1970.
Einstein, Albert. *Relativity: The Special and General Theory*. New York: Methuen, 1961.
Eisler, Rudolf. *Nietzsches Erkenntnishtheorie und Metaphysik*. Leipzig: Hermann Haacke, 1902.
Elkana, Yehuda. *The Discovery of the Conservation of Energy*. Cambridge, MA: Harvard University Press, 1974.
Foerster-Nietzsche, Elizabeth. *Das Leben Fr. Nietzsches*. 2 vols. Leipzig: Naumann, 1895–1904.
Foster, Marguerite H., and Michael L. Martin, eds. *Probability, Confirmation, and Simplicity*. New York: The Odyssey Press, 1966.
Foucault, Michel. *The Archaeology of Knowledge and The Discourse on Language*. Translated by A. M. S. Smith. New York: Harper and Row, 1976.
Frenzel, Ivo. *Friedrich Nietzsche: An Illustrated Biography*. Translated by J. Neugroschel. New York: Pegasus Press, 1967.
Gilman, Sander, C. Blair, and D. Parent, eds. and trans. *Friedrich Nietzsche on Rhetoric and Language*. New York: Oxford University Press, 1989.
Golomb, Jacob. *Nietzsche's Enticing Psychology of Power*. Ames: Iowa State University Press, 1989.

Granier, Jean. *La Problème de la verité dans la philosophie de Nietzsche*. Paris: Seuil, 1969.

Grimm, Ruediger. *Nietzsche's Theory of Knowledge*. Berlin and New York: Walter de Gruyter, 1977.

Hallett, Garth. *Language and Truth*. New Haven and London: Yale University Press, 1988.

Hanson, Norwood. *Observation and Explanation*. New York: Harper & Row, 1971.

———. *Patterns of Discovery*. London: Cambridge University Press, 1969.

Harr, Michel. *Nietzsche and Metaphysics*. Translated by Michael Gendre. Albany: SUNY Press, 1996.

Harris, Errol. *Cosmos and Anthropos*. Atlantic Highlands, NJ: Humanities Press, 1991.

Hartshorne, Charles and Paul Weiss, eds. *Collected Papers of Charles Sanders Peirce*. 8 vols. Cambridge: Harvard University Press, 1931–35. Vols. 7 and 8 edited by A. W. Burks. Cambridge: University Press, 1958.

Heidegger, Martin. *Holzwege*. Frankfurt-am-Main: Klostermann, 1950.

———. *Nietzsche*. 2 vols. Pfullingen: Verlag Gunther Neske, 1961. [*Nietzsche*. Translated by D. F. Krell, J. Stambaugh, and F. A. Capuzzi. 4 vols. San Francisco: Harper & Row, 1979–1987].

———. *Sein und Zeit*. Tubingen: Neomarius Verlag, 1957. [*Being and Time*. Translated by J. Macquarrie and Edward Robinson. New York and Evanston: Harper & Row, 1962].

Hesse, Mary. *Models and Analogies in Science*. Notre Dame: Notre Dame University Press, 1970.

Hofmann, Johann N. *Wahrheit. Perspektive, Interpretation: Nietzsche und die philosophische Hermeneutik*. Berlin and New York: Walter de Gruyter, 1994.

Hollingdale, R. J. *Nietzsche*. London: Routledge and Kegan Paul, 1973.

Hubbard, Stanley. *Nietzsche und Emerson*. Basel: Verlag für Recht und Gesellschaft, 1958.

James, William. *Collected Essays and Reviews*. New York: Longmans, Green, 1920.

———. *A Pluralistic Universe*. New York: Longmans, Green, 1909.

———. *Pragmatism: A New Name for Some Old Ways of Thinking*. New York: Longmans, Green, 1907.

Kant, Immanuel. *Anthropology from a Pragmatic Point of View*. Translated by Mary J. Gregor. The Hague: Martinus Nijhoff, 1974.

———. *Kritik der reinen Vernunft*. Hamburg: Felix Meiner Verlag, 1956. [*Critique of Pure Reason*. Translated by Norman Kemp Smith. New York: St. Martin's Press, 1965.]

Kaufmann, Walter. *Nietzsche*. 3rd rev. ed. New York: Viking, 1968.

———, ed. and trans. *The Portable Nietzsche*. New York, 1954.

Kaufmann, Walter, and R. J. Holingdale, trans. *The Will to Power*, New York: Vintage Books, 1968.

Kline, Morris. *Mathematics: the Loss of Certainty*. New York: Oxford University Press, 1980.

Kofman, Sarah. *Nietzsche et métaphore*. Paris: Payot, 1972. [*Nietzsche and Metaphor*. Translated by Duncan Large. Stanford: Stanford University Press, 1993 (Translation based upon the 2nd edition of *Nietzsche et métaphore*, 1983)].

Korblinth, Hilary, ed. *Naturalizing Epistemology*. Cambridge: MIT Press, 1994.

Kuhn, Thomas S. "Reflections on My Critics." In I. Lakatos and A. Musgrave, eds. *Criticism and the Growth of Knowledge*. New York: Cambridge University Press, 1970.

———. *The Structure of Scientific Revolutions*. 2nd ed. Chicago: University of Chicago Press, 1970.

Lange, Friedrich A. *Geschichte des Materialismus*. 2nd ed. 2 vols. Frankfurt-am-Main: Suhrkamp Verlag, 1974.

———. *The History of Materialism and Criticism of Its Present Importance*. Translated by E. C. Thomas. London: Routledge and Kegan Paul, 1925.

Lehrer, Ronald. *Nietzsche's Presence in Freud's Life and Thought*. Albany: SUNY Press, 1995.

Lepin, Jarrett, ed. *Scientific Realism*. Berkeley: University of California Press, 1984.

Levine, Peter. *Nietzsche and the Modern Crisis of the Humanities*. Albany: SUNY Press, 1995.

Lévi-Strauss, Claude. *The Raw and the Cooked*. 2 vols. Translated by John Weightman and Doreen Weightman. New York: Harper and Row, 1969.

———. *The Savage Mind*. Chicago: University of Chicago Press, 1966.

———. *Structural Anthropology*. Translated by C. Jackobson and B. G. Schoepf. New York: Basic Books, 1963.

———. *Les Structures elémentaires de la parenté*. Paris: Presses Universitaires de France, 1949.

Lewis, Clarence I. "Alternative Systems of Logic." *The Monist* 42, no. 4 (October 1932): 481–507.

Lichtenberg, Georg C. *Aphorisms*. Translated by R. J. Hollingdale. London: Penguin, 1990.

Lovejoy, A. O. "Schopenhauer as an Evolutionist." In *Forerunners of Darwin: 1745–1859*, edited by B. Glass, O. Temkin, and W. L. Straus. Baltimore: Johns Hopkins Press, 1968. Chapter 14.

Lumsden, C. J. and E. O. Wilson. *Genes, Mind and Culture*. Cambridge, MA: Harvard University Press 1981.

Mach, Ernst. *Knowledge and Error*. Translated by C. M. Williams. Dordrecht: Reidel, 1976.

———. *The Science of Mechanics*. Translated by T. J. McCormack. La Salle: Open Court, 1942.

Magnus, Bernd. *Nietzsche's Existential Imperative*. Bloomington and London: Indiana University Press, 1978.

———. "Nietzsche's Philosophy in 1888." *Journal of the History of Philosophy* 24:1 (January 1986): 79–98.

Mandelbaum, M. "The Physiological Orientation of Schopenhauer's Epistemology," in *Schopenhauer: His Philosophical Achievement*, edited by M. Fox. Brighton, England: Harvester Press, 1980.

McMullin, Ernan, ed. *The Concept of Matter in Modern Philosophy*. Notre Dame: Notre Dame Press, 1978.

Megill, Alan. *Prophets of Extremity: Nietzsche, Heidegger, Foucault, Derrida*. Berkeley: University of California Press, 1985.

Middleton, Christopher, ed. and trans. *Selected Letters of Friedrich Nietzsche*. Chicago and London: University of Chicago Press, 1969.

Mittasch, Alwin. *Friedrich Nietzsche als Naturphilosoph*. Stuttgart: A. Kröner, 1952.

Moles, Alistar. *Nietzsche's Philosophy of Nature and Cosmology*. New York: Peter Lang, 1990.

Morgan, George. *What Nietzsche Means*. New York: Harper & Row, 1965.

Morrison, Robert G. *Nietzsche and Buddhism*. Oxford and New York: Oxford University Press, 1999.

Müller-Lauter, Wolfgang. *Nietzsche*. Berlin and New York: Walter de Gruyter, 1971.

———. *Nietzsche: His Philosophy of Contradictions and the Contradictions of His Philosophy*. Translated by David J. Parent. Urbana and Chicago: University of Illinois Press, 1999.

———. "Nietzsches Lehre vom Willen zur Macht," *Nietzsche-Studien* 3 (1974): 1–60.

Nagel, Thomas. *The View From Nowhere*. New York: Oxford University Press, 1989.

Nehamas, Alexander. "The Eternal Recurrence." *Philosophical Review* 84 (July 1980): 331–56.

———. *Nietzsche: Life as Literature*. Cambridge, MA: Harvard University Press, 1985.

Nietzsche, Friedrich. *Kritische Gesamtausgabe Werke*. Edited by G. Colli and M. Montinari. Berlin and New York: Walter de Gruyter, 1967ff.

———. *Sämtliche Briefe. Kritische Studienausgabe*. Edited by G. Colli and M. Montinari. 8 vols. Berlin and New York: Walter de Gruyter, 1986.

———. *Sämtliche Werke. Kritische Studienausgabe*. Edited by G. Colli and M. Montinari. 15 vols. Berlin and New York: Walter de Gruyter, 1980.

———. *Thus Spoke Zarathustra*. Translated by R. J. Hollingdale. Harmondsworth: Penguin Books, 1969.

———. *Werke*. 19 vols. Leipzig: Naumann, 1901–13.

———. *Werke in Drei Bänden*. Edited by Karl Schlechta. 3 vols. Munich: Carl Hanser Verlag, 1966.

———. *Werke. Musarionausgabe*. 23 vols. Munich: Musarion Verlag, 1920–26.

———. *Werke und Briefe. Historische-Kritische Gesamtausgabe*. 5 vols. Munich: Beck Verlag, 1933–42.

———. *The Will to Power*. Translated by Walter Kaufmann and R. J. Hollingdale. New York: Vintage Books, 1968.

Ornstein, Robert E. *The Psychology of Consciousness*. San Francisco: Viking, 1972.

Popper, Karl. *Conjectures and Refutations*. New York: Harper and Row, 1965.

Popper, Karl, and J. C. Eccles. *The Self and Its Brain*. New York: Springer International, 1977.

Putnam, Hilary. *The Many Faces of Realism*. La Salle: Open Court, 1987.

Pütz, Peter. *Friedrich Nietzsche.* Stuttgart, 1967.
Quine, W. V. O. *From a Logical Point of View.* New York: Harper & Row, 1961.
———. "On Simple Theories of a Complex World." In *Probability, Confirmation, and Simplicity,* ed. Marguerite Foster and Michael Martin. New York: Odyssey Press, 1966.
———. *Ontological Relativity and Other Essays.* New York: Columbia University Press, 1969.
Quinton, Anthony. *The Nature of Things.* London: Routledge and Kegan Paul, 1973.
Rescher, Nicholas. *Empirical Inquiry.* London: Athlone, 1982.
———. *Methodological Pragmatism.* New York and London: Oxford University Press, 1977.
———. *A Useful Inheritance: Evolutionary Aspects of Theory of Knowledge.* Savage, MD: Rowan and Littlefield, 1990.
Richardson, John. *Nietzsche's System.* New York and Oxford: Oxford University Press, 1996.
Riehl, Alois. *Friedrich Nietzsche: Der Künstler und der Denker.* Stuttgart: Fromenans Verlag, 1898.
Rorty, Richard. *Consequences of Pragmatism: Essays 1972–1980.* Minneapolis: University of Minnesota Press, 1982.
———. *Contingency, Irony, and Solidarity.* Cambridge: Cambridge University Press, 1989.
———. *Philosophy and the Mirror of Nature.* Princeton: Princeton University Press, 1979.
Rosen, Stanley. *The Ancients and the Moderns.* New Haven and London: Yale University Press, 1989.
———. *The Quarrel between Philosophy and Poetry.* New York and London: Routledge and Kegan Paul, 1988.
Salaquarda, Jörg. "Nietzsche und Lange." *Nietzsche-Studien* 7 (1978): 236–60.
———. "Der Standpunkt des Ideals bei Lange und Nietzsche." *Studi Tedeschi* 22, no. 1 (1979): 1–28.
Salter, William M. *Nietzsche the Thinker.* New York: Holt, 1917.
Schacht, Richard. *Making Sense of Nietzsche.* Urbana and Chicago: University of Illinois Press, 1995.
———. *Nietzsche.* London and Boston: Routledge and Kegan Paul, 1983.
Scheffler, Israel. "The Fictionalist View of Scientific Theories." In *Readings in the Philosophy of Science,* ed. B. A. Brody. Englewood Cliffs, NJ: Prentice-Hall, 1970.
Schlechta, Karl. *Der Fall Nietzsche.* Munich: Hanser Verlag, 1959.
———, ed. *Friedrich Nietzsche: Werke in Drei Bänden.* Munich: Carl Hanser Verlag, 1966.
Schlick, Moritz. *Philosophy of Nature.* Translated by A. von Zeppelin. New York: Philosophical Library, 1949.
Schmid, Holger. *Nietzsche Gedanke der tragischen Erkenntnis.* Wurtzburg: Konigshausen & Neumann, 1984.
Schrift, Alan. *Nietzsche and the Question of Interpretation.* New York and London: Routledge and Kegan Paul, 1990.

Sedgwick, Peter R., ed. *Nietzsche: A Critical Reader*. New York: Blackwell, 1995.

Sellers, Wilfrid. *Science, Perception, and Reality*. London: Routledge and Kegan Paul, 1963.

Simpson, George G. *Tempo and Mode in Evolution*. New York: Columbia University Press, 1984.

Sleinis, E. E. *Nietzsche's Revaluation of Values*. Urbana: University of Illinois Press, 1994.

Sorensen, Roy. *Thought Experiments*. New York and London: Oxford, 1992.

Spector, Marshall. *Methodological Foundations of Relativistic Mechanics*. Notre Dame and London: University of Notre Dame Press, 1972.

Spiekermann, Klaus. *Naturwissenschaft als subjektlose Macht? Nietzsches Kritik physikalischer Grundkonzepte*. Berlin and New York: Walter de Gruyter, 1983.

Stack, George J. *Lange and Nietzsche*. Berlin and New York: Walter de Gruyter: 1983.

———. "Nietzsche and Boscovitch's Natural Philosophy," *Pacific Philosophical Quarterly* 62 (1981): 69–87.

———. *Nietzsche and Emerson*. Athens: Ohio University Press, 1992.

———. "Nietzsche and Emerson: The Return of the Repressed," *ESQ: A Journal of the American Renaissance* 43, no. 4 (1998): 37–68.

———. "Nietzsche and Lange." *The Modern Schoolman* 57, no. 2 (January 1980): 137–48.

———. "Nietzsche's Influence on Pragmatic Humanism," *Journal of the History of Philosophy* 20, no. 4 (October 1982): 269–406.

———. *On Kierkegaard: Philosophical Fragments*. Atlantic Highlands, NJ: Humanities Press, 1976.

Staten, Henry. *Nietzsche's Voice*. Ithaca and London: Cornell University Press, 1990.

Stich, Stephen. *The Fragmentation of Reason*. Cambridge: MIT Press, 1990.

Strawson, Peter F. *The Bounds of Sense*. London: Methuen, 1966.

Toulmin, Stephen. *Foresight and Understanding*. New York: Harper & Row, 1961.

Vaihinger, Hans. *The Philosophy of "As-If."* Translated by C. K. Ogden. London: Routledge and Kegan Paul, 1924.

Walzel, Oskar. *German Romanticism*. New York: Unger, 1965.

Wartofsky, Marx. "How to Be a Good Realist." In *Beyond Reason*, edited by G. Munevar. Amsterdam: Kluwer, 1991: 25–40.

Weizsacker, C. F. von. *Aufbau der Physik*. Munich, 1985.

———. *Wahrnehmung der Neuzeit*. Munich and Vienna, 1983.

Whorf, Benjamin. *Language, Thought and Reality*. Edited by J. B. Carroll. New York: MIT Press, 1956.

Whyte, Lancelot L. *Essays on Atomism*. Middleton, CT: Wesleyan University Press, 1961.

———. ed. *Roger Joseph Boscovich*. New York: Fordham University Press, 1961.

Wigner, Eugene P. *Symmetries and Reflections*. Woodbridge, CT: Ox Bow Press, 1979.

Wilcox, John T. *Truth and Value in Nietzsche*. Ann Arbor: The University of Michigan Press, 1974.

Wittgenstein, Ludwig. *Philosophical Investigations*. Translated by G. E. M. Anscombe. New York: Macmillian, 1953.

———. *Tractatus Logico-Philosophicus*. Translated by D. F. Pears and B. F. McGuinness. New York: Humanities Press, 1961.

Index